1954–1975

VIETNAM

THE UNWINNABLE WAR

GERRY & JANET SOUTER
EDITOR D.M. GIANGRECO

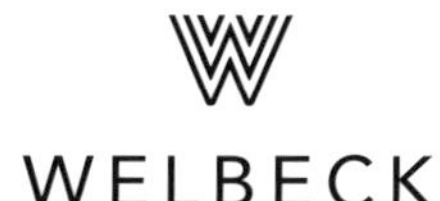

WELBECK

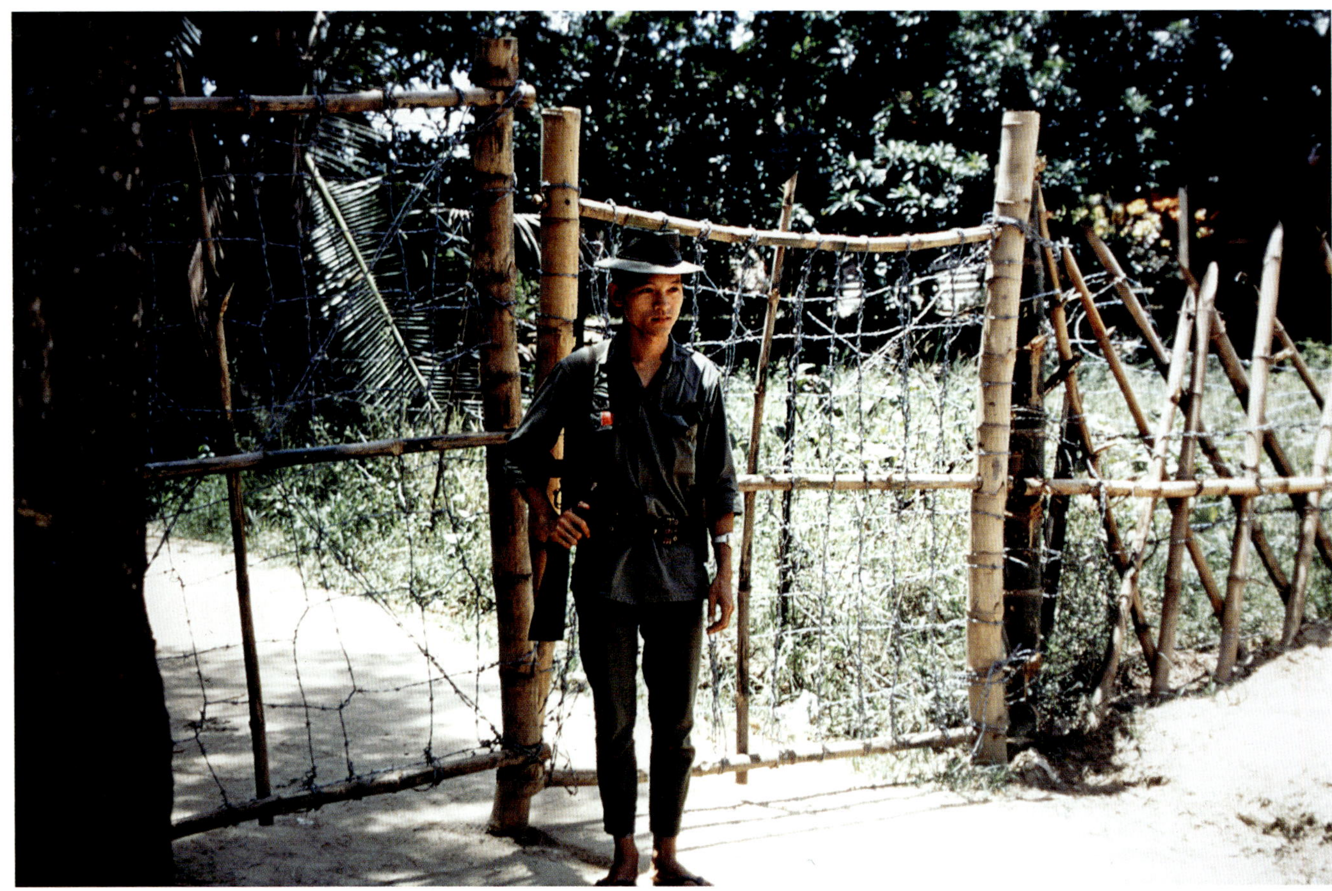

This book is dedicated to the Vietnam combat photographer. Armed with only a camera and film, they risked their lives in the heat of action to concentrate on a viewfinder, shutting out the noise, terror and death around them to capture a moment of truth, and often courage.

Above: South Vietnamese village guard, part of rural defense forces recruited locally to discourage Viet Cong raids. He carries an American M1 carbine.

First published in 2007 by André Deutsch Limited

This edition published by Welbeck
An Imprint of HEADLINE PUBLISHING GROUP LIMITED

1

Cataloguing in Publication Data is available from the British Library

ISBN 978 1 035 42552 5

Printed and bound in Dubai by Oriental

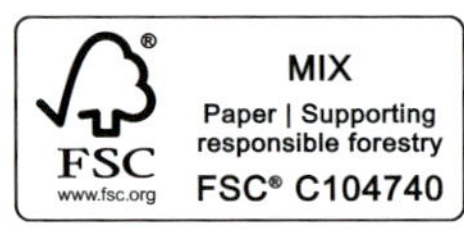

Headline's policy is to use papers that are natural, renewable and recyclable products and made from wood grown in well-managed forests and other controlled sources. The logging and manufacturing processes are expected to conform to the environmental regulations of the country of origin.

HEADLINE PUBLISHING GROUP LIMITED
An Hachette UK Company
Carmelite House
50 Victoria Embankment
London EC4Y 0DZ

The authorised representative in the EEA is Hachette Ireland, 8 Castlecourt Centre, Dublin 15, D15 XTP3, Ireland (email: info@hbgi.ie)

www.headline.co.uk
www.hachette.co.uk

CONTENTS

INTRODUCTION

THE VIETNAM WAR FOR INDEPENDENCE LASTED 30 YEARS, BEGINNING IN 1945 WITH THE END OF THE JAPANESE OCCUPATION IN WORLD WAR II. IN 1954, WITH THE DEFEAT OF THE FRENCH BY COMMUNIST FORCES, THE U.S. BECAME INVOLVED DEFENDING THE NEW SOUTH VIETNAMESE GOVERNMENT. COMBAT OPERATIONS FINALLY ENDED IN 1975. ITS BASIS WAS A CONFLICT IN IDEOLOGIES AND ITS ULTIMATE GOAL WAS THE INDEPENDENCE OF A PEOPLE FROM COLONIAL RULE. THE GOAL WAS ACCOMPLISHED AT THE COST OF HUNDREDS OF THOUSANDS OF BRAVE MEN AND WOMEN EXPENDED IN BLOODY BATTLES THAT, IN HINDSIGHT, MIGHT HAVE BEEN AVOIDED WITH THE STROKE OF A PEN, COMPASSION, AND DIPLOMATIC COMPROMISE. TODAY, THE SOCIALIST REPUBLIC OF VIETNAM LIVES IN PEACE WITH THE UNITED STATES, FRANCE, AND THE OTHER WESTERN ALLIES. AMBASSADORS HAVE BEEN EXCHANGED, TRADE AGREEMENTS SIGNED, AND TOURISTS NOW WALK THE STREETS THAT, DECADES AGO, WERE PITTED WITH BOMB CRATERS AND STREWN WITH THE DETRITUS OF COMBAT.

Vietnam: The Unwinnable War has been created for the children of those who fought and died there. With the help of veterans from both sides of that conflict, historic documents, hand-scribbled orders, after-action reports, and strike maps, the authors present personal reflections along with combat strategies and tactics. This war taught hard lessons about fighting battles where there were no front lines, where mobility was key to success, and flexibility and adaptation were necessary. We'll meet the generals who created the strategies, and the infantry, airmen, and sailors tasked with gaining victories whether they wore G.I. boots or Uncle Ho sandals. The weapons used by both sides are described, from *punji* sticks coated with cow dung to M-16 and AK-47 assault rifles. Phantom and Crusader jets duel Mig 17s and 21s as S.A.M.s cut trails through the skies and high above the green landscape, flights of B-52s lose tons of iron bombs into the fiery march of "Rolling Thunder." The Riverine War pitted a gunboat navy against an invisible enemy ashore and Huey and Sikorsky helicopters added a new fighting chapter to the U.S. Cavalry and Marine Corps while saving battlefield lives. Meanwhile, the N.V.A./V.C. trained themselves to live in deep tunnels, enabling them to strike at their enemy and vanish.

In the United States, the conflict rumbled through the administrations of five presidents and created an unprecedented backlash among its citizens. Riots erupted, Civil Rights leaders added their protests, and citizens' interpretations of patriotism were challenged in the streets. Brave men armed only with a Nikon or a Leica camera, with cine cameras and microphones, brought the savage war home to people's living rooms. Photojournalists delivered images and sounds of war as it was, all the dirt, pain, suffering, and often heroic human spirit.

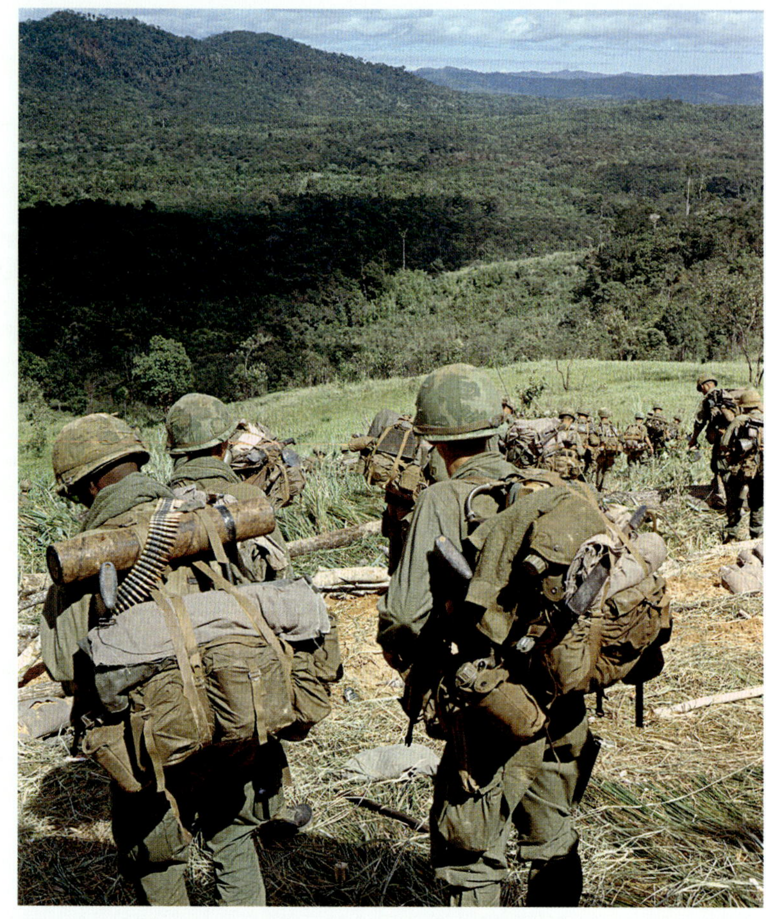

Above: A platoon of heavy laden infantry moves forward during one of the "Border Battles" where the N.V.A. sought to draw U.S. and A.R.V.N. troops away from population centers before the Viet Cong launched the Tet Offensive in 1967–68.

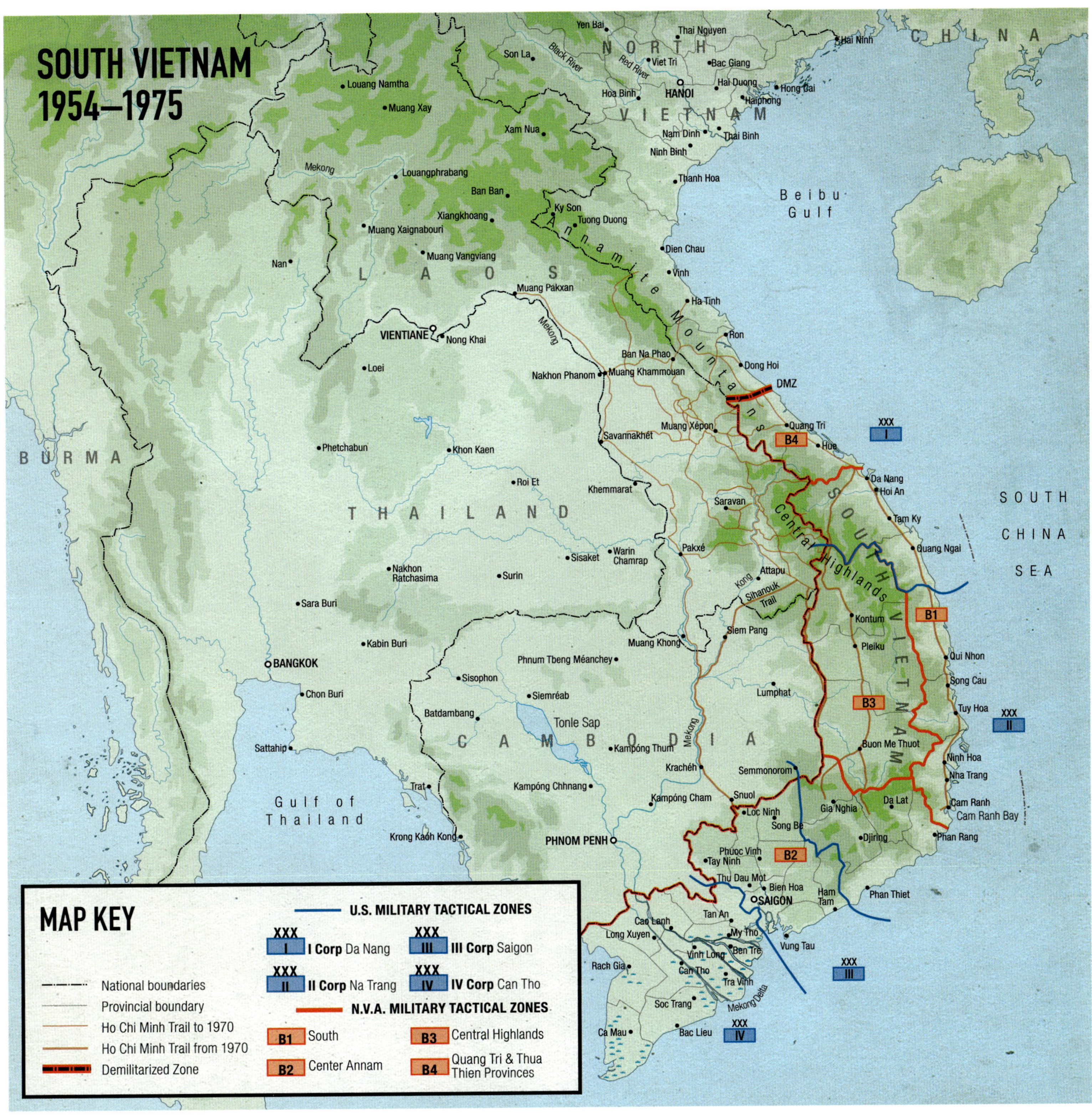

From the escalation to its abrupt end, *Vietnam: The Unwinnable War* will explore the conflict, the soldiers' lives in the field, the decisions, the strategies, tactics, and weapons that evolved into an international tragedy. Whether they are scarred on the outside or carry deeper, unseen scars, the Vietnam War remains an experience no survivor will ever forget and in *Vietnam: The Unwinnable War*, words, photographs, maps, and actual memorabilia are available to help explain what it was like for so many brave men and women who fought for their country.

Gerry and Janet Souter
Arlington Heights, Illinois

SETTING THE STAGE

THE VIETNAMESE EMPIRE'S FIRST MAJOR CLASH WITH A EUROPEAN POWER CAME IN 1847, WHEN FRENCH GUNBOATS ATTACKED THE PORT OF DA NANG, SINKING SEVERAL VESSELS AND DESTROYING A COUPLE OF FORTS. THE FRENCH WERE RESPONDING TO THE ARREST OF A CATHOLIC MISSIONARY, ALTHOUGH BY THE TIME THEY ARRIVED HE HAD BEEN RELEASED AND SENT TO SINGAPORE. THE FRENCH SAILED AWAY, BUT THE ATTACK WAS A PORTENT OF THINGS TO COME.

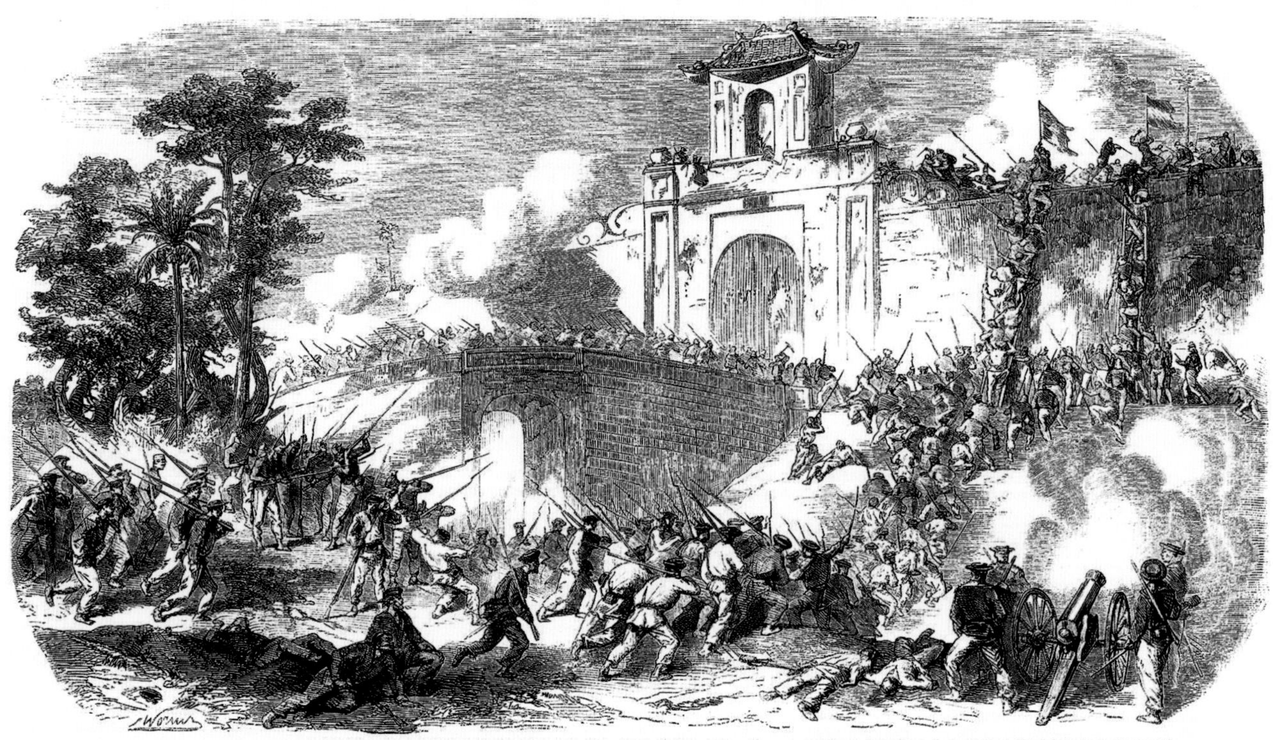

The hostility of successive Vietnamese emperors to Catholicism throughout the first half of the nineteenth century, the success of Catholic missionaries in Indochina, and the key part played by Frenchmen in this Christianizing of the country all contributed to a subsequent French invasion in 1858, when Da Nang was occupied. In 1861, a renewed French intervention seized the area around Saigon and the Mekong river delta in the south of Indochina, which the French named Cochinchina. The French gradually extended their control over other parts of Indochina until, in 1893, the French Indochinese Union incorporated Cochinchina, Cambodia, and Laos, together with areas of Vietnam the French annexed under the names of Tonkin (the far north) and Annam (the center). By exploiting cultural and ethnic prejudices in the region, where both India and China had wielded influence, the French made it difficult for any nationalist sentiment to emerge.

Various individuals did work toward an independent Vietnam, among them a Marxist who called himself Nguyen Ai Quoc. In 1930 he organized the Indochinese Communist Party. In 1933 he went to the Soviet Union and received treatment for tuberculosis and effectively disappeared, to the relief of the French authorities. In 1938 he began working with the Chinese

Above: On February 17, 1859, a joint Franco-Spanish naval expedition under the command of Vice Admiral Charles Rigault de Genouilly, an action initiated by Napoleon III, attacked Saigon to aid colonial expansion on the pretext of the anti-Christian policies of Tu-Duc, Emperor of Vietnam.

Opposite: General Vo Nguyen Giap (right) and Ho Chi Minh (center) confer with Chinese advisors during the French-Indochina War (1949–1954). Portraits of Chairman Mao ZeDong and Ho Chi Minh hang behind them.

HO CHI MINH—PRESIDENT OF NORTH VIETNAM (BELOW CENTER)

Born Nguyen Tat Thanh on May 19, 1890, in the village of Kimlien, Annam (central Vietnam), after schooling in Hue he wandered through odd jobs until after World War I when, under the pseudonym Nguyen Ai Quoc (Nguyen the Patriot), he helped found the French Communist Party. After training in Moscow he was sent to China to organize Communist Vietnamese. Eventually, he founded the Indochinese Communist Party, spent two years in a British prison and suffered tuberculosis. Nguyen made his way back to Vietnam, founded the Viet Minh, and fought against the Japanese. With his new name, Ho Chi Minh ("the Enlightener"), he created the Democratic Republic of Vietnam to unify the country. He died on September 3, 1969, before realizing his dream of one Vietnam.

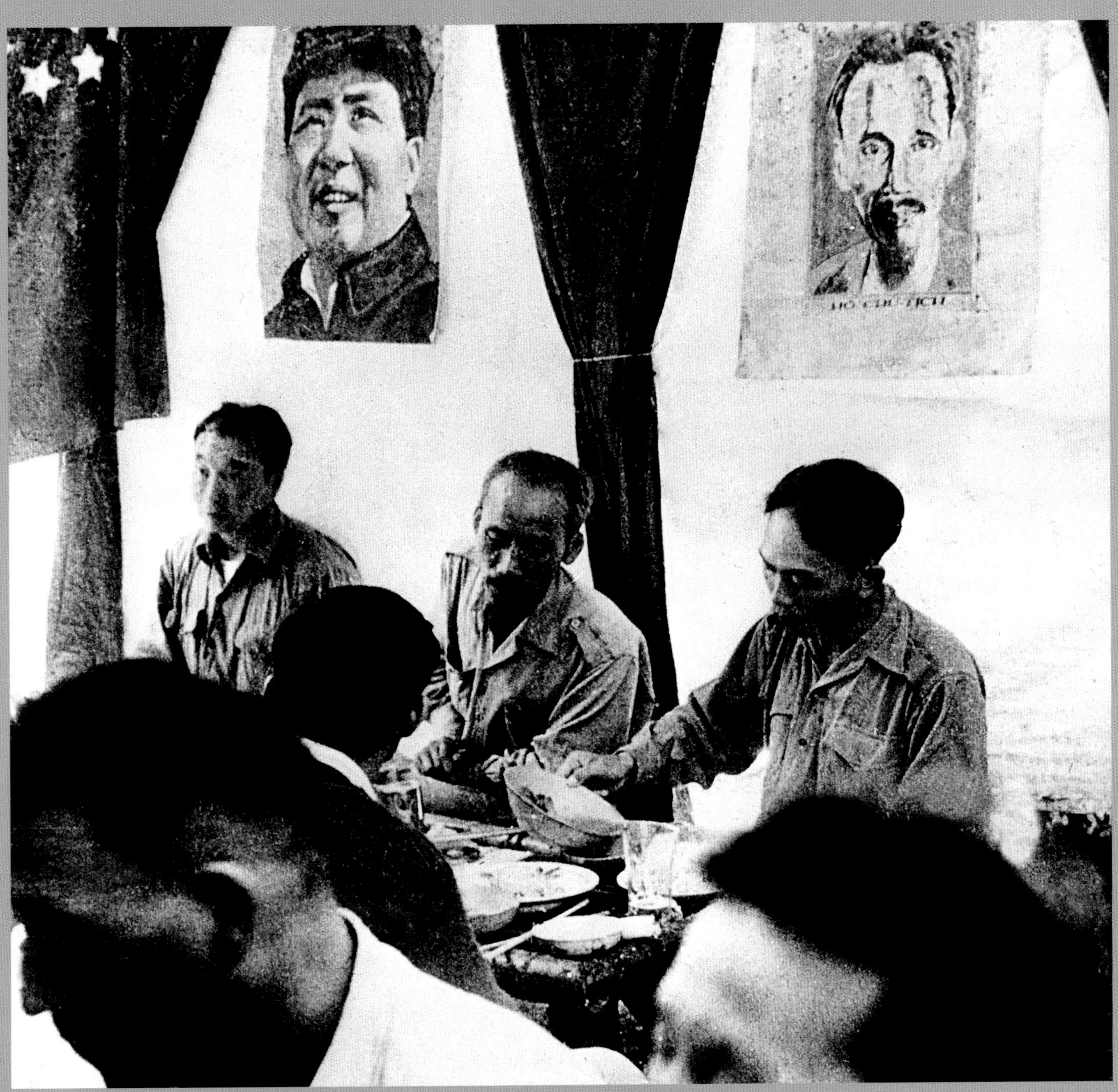

DEAN ACHESON, SECRETARY OF STATE

Dean Acheson (1893-1971) was President Harry S. Truman's Secretary of State from 1949-53. The acerbic Acheson was always a controversial figure, but his advice to three presidents was often very valuable. President Ho Chi Minh had sent Truman a number of telegrams asking for the support of the U.S. against French Colonial rule throughout the late 1940s and 50s. Acheson supported this position and advised Truman to aid the Vietnamese leader. Truman instead half-heartedly gave aid to the French in Indochina, leaving Ho Chi Minh to continue accepting weapons, training, and political advice from China and the Soviet Union.

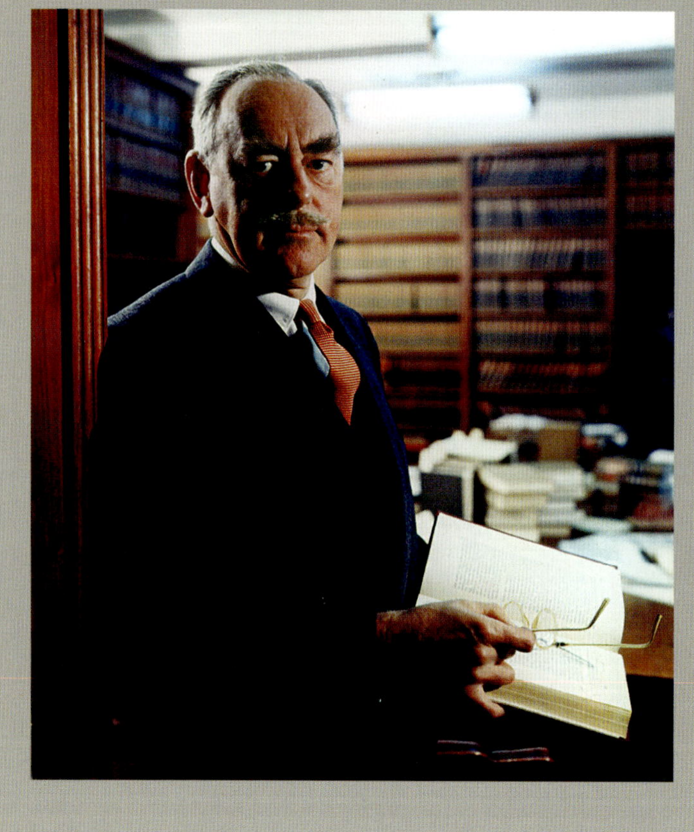

INDOCHINA 1954

Map of Indochina in 1954.Showing Vietnam's relationship to Cambodia, Thailand, Laos, and China before its division into North and South Vietnam. At this time, France's control of Indochina was coming to an end. The Communist takeover of China had occurred in 1949.

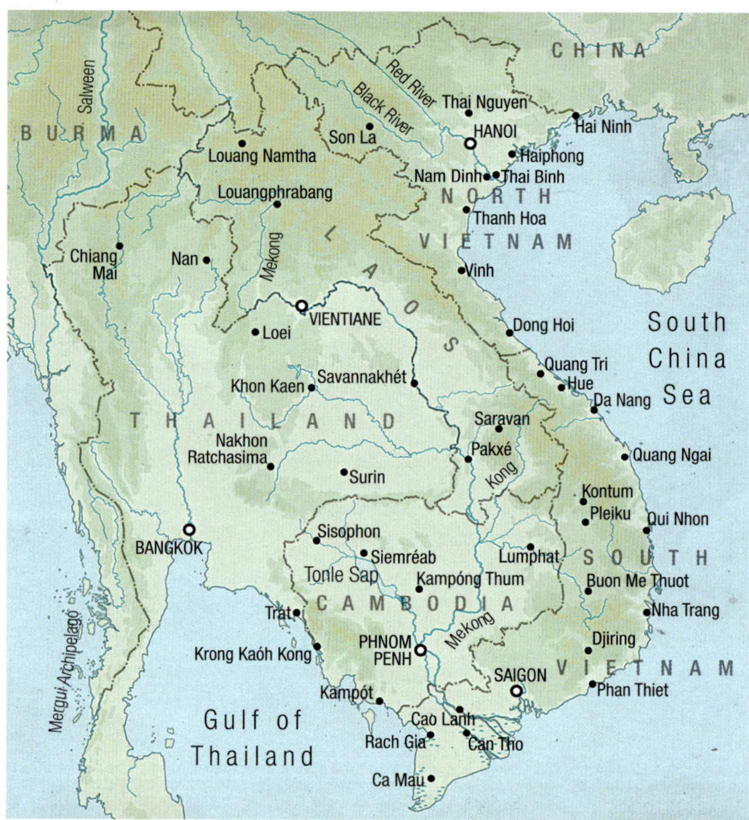

Communists then engaged in fighting both the nationalist government of China and Japanese invaders.

The defeat of France by Germany in 1940 was followed by the occupation of Indochina in July 1941 by the Japanese. Nguyen Ai Quoc had already arrived two months earlier with a new name, Ho Chi Minh, and a new revolutionary idea, a League for the Independence of Vietnam, or the Viet Minh.

Until 1944, the Viet Minh lacked weapons, but carefully built up networks of informers and supplies. The United States, having grudgingly accepted Communists as allies against Germany, Italy, and Japan, sent military aid to Ho Chi Minh. A small shipment arrived in March and a hit-and-run war with the Japanese began in December, commanded by Ho's trusted colleague, Vo Nguyen Giap.

On September 2, 1945, as the Japanese formally surrendered to the Americans in Tokyo Bay, the Japanese in northern Vietnam surrendered to Ho Chi Minh. On that same day, Ho declared the Democratic Republic of Vietnam to be independent. The document proclaiming this new nation began with the words: "All men are created equal. They are endowed by their Creator with certain inalienable rights, among these are Life, Liberty, and the pursuit of Happiness." This immortal statement was made in the Declaration of Independence of the United States of America in 1776. In a broader sense, this means: "All the peoples on the earth are equal from birth, all the peoples have a right to live, to be happy and free...."

Three weeks after this document had been read to a festive crowd of Vietnamese in Hanoi, French soldiers, supported by British troops who had been the first Allied forces to reach Indochina, reclaimed Saigon from a ramshackle Viet Minh administration. And so the stage was set for the Vietnam War.

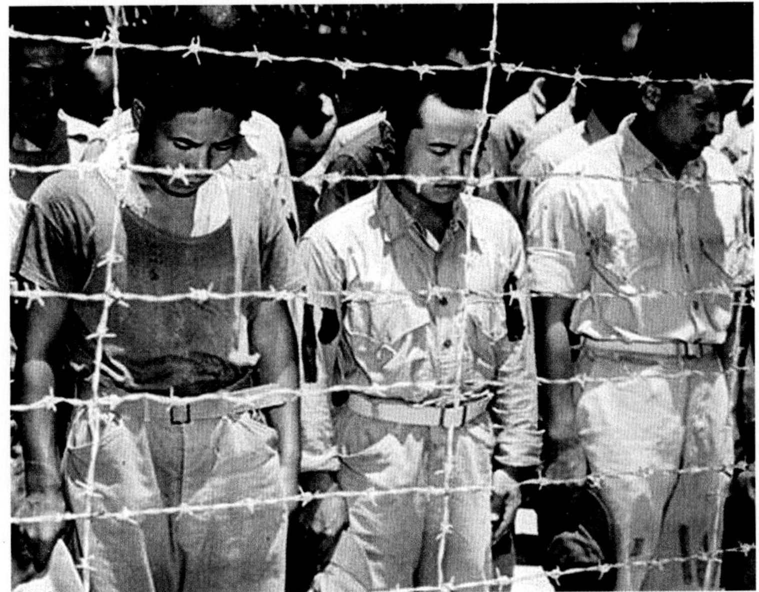

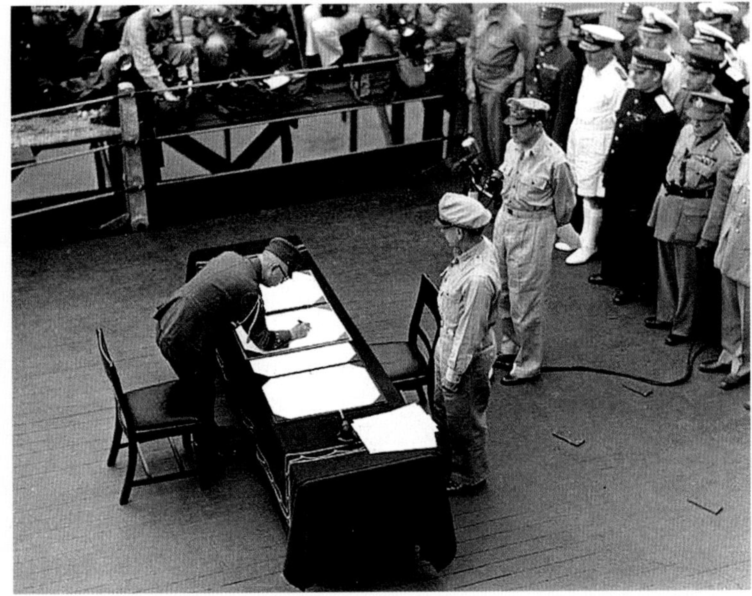

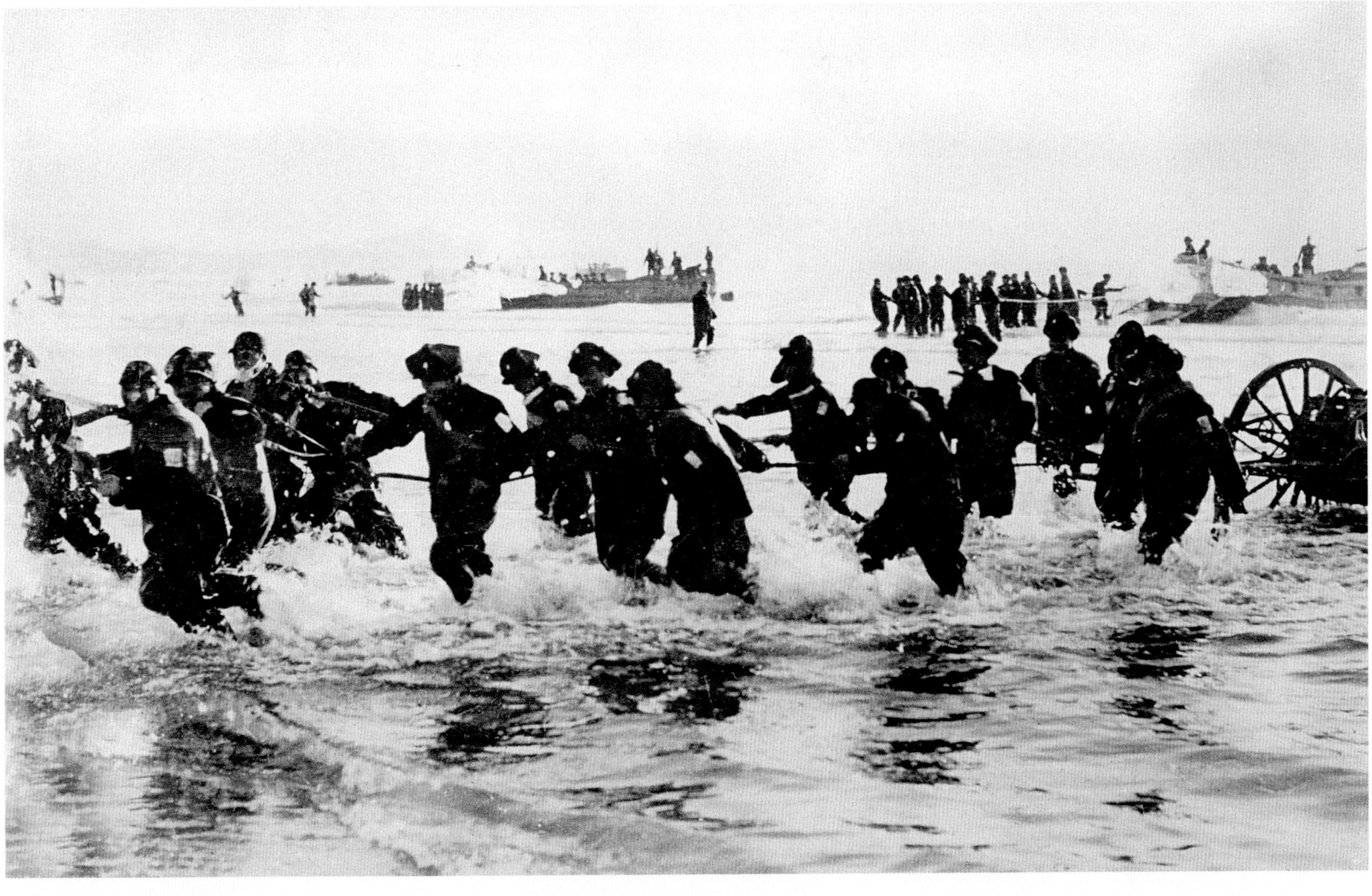

Top left: Japanese prisoners of war in barbed wire stockade are informed that Japan has accepted surrender terms on August 15, 1945. The Japanese Bushido code of warfare did not permit surrender in combat. These men face an uncertain future since they did not give their lives for their emperor.

Top right: Japanese General Yoshijiro Umezu signs the surrender documents aboard the battleship U.S.S. *Missouri* (BB-63) in Tokyo Bay on September 2, 1945. Some of the members of the Japanese who signed the surrender later committed ritual suicide back in Tokyo.

Above: Japanese land on south-east Asia beaches in 1942 to begin their occupation of French colonies. France had been defeated by Germany in 1940 and Japan was part of the fascist Axis together with Germany and Italy. French officials remained in Vietnam as a Japanese puppet regime until 1945.

FRENCH SOLDIER—VIET MINH GUERRILLA

THE EIGHT-YEAR WAR BETWEEN THE FRENCH AND HO CHI MINH'S VIET MINH ARMY WAS A CATALYST, BOTH MILITARILY AND DIPLOMATICALLY. KNOWING MORE ABOUT THE COMBATANTS GIVES CLUES ABOUT WHAT FOLLOWED IN THE NEXT 20 YEARS. THAT FRANCO-VIETNAMESE CONFRONTATION PROVED ANY WAR IN VIETNAM WOULD BE A LAND WAR WHERE BOOTS ON THE GROUND WON BATTLES AND THE RESOLVE OF THE SOLDIER IN THE TEETH OF ENEMY FIRE DECIDED EACH DAY'S OUTCOME. NO WARRIORS WERE PERCEIVED TO BE MORE DIFFERENT THAN THE FRENCH PARATROOPERS AND THE VIET MINH GUERRILLAS AT DIEN BIEN PHU.

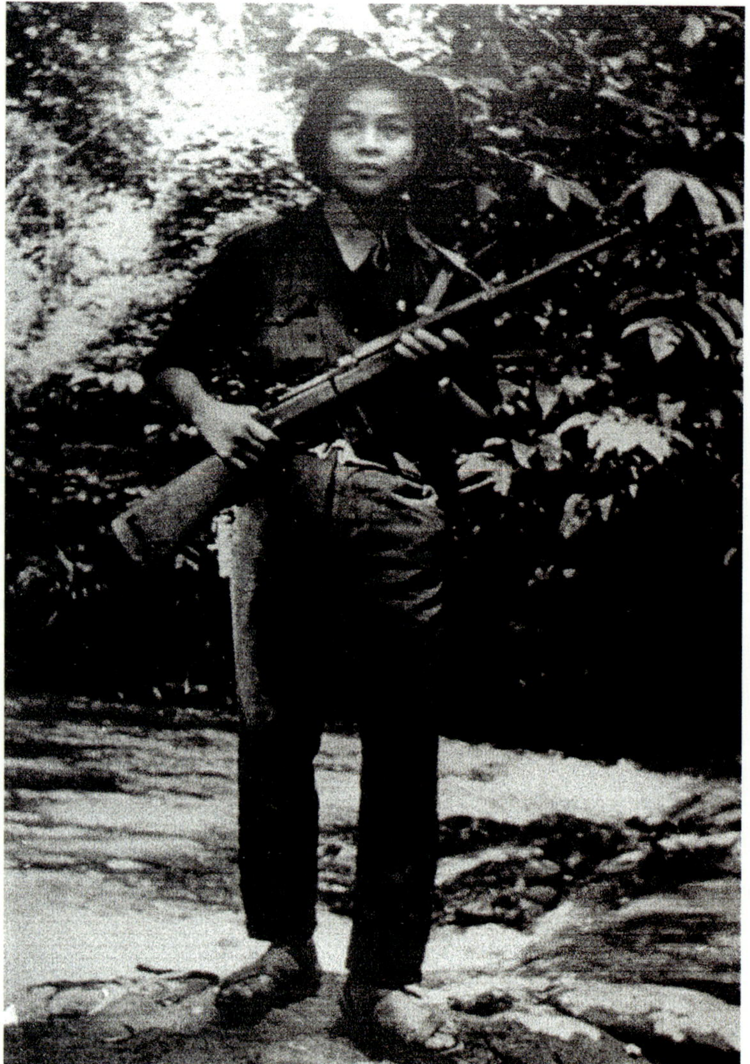

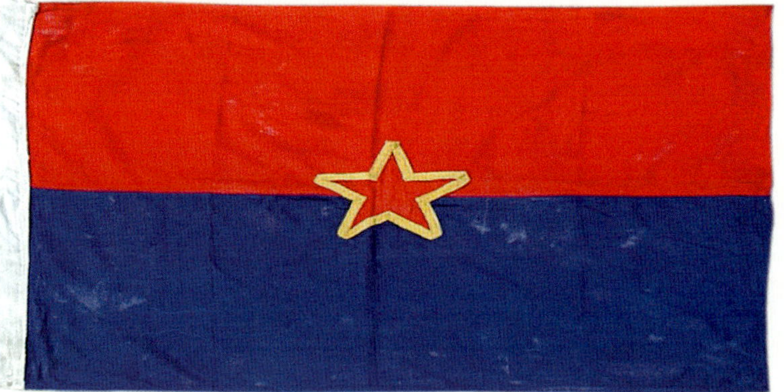

The firebase's defenders represented a microcosm of the French military in Indochina. They included Moroccans, Algerians, Africans, and even Vietnamese who sided with the French. The famous Foreign Legion garnered the most publicity and it was a polyglot force. But the 6th Colonial Parachute Battalion and the 2nd battalion of the 1st Parachute Chasseurs were the spearhead. On these rawhide-tough veterans, blooded in many campaigns, fell the heaviest responsibility. The uniforms worn by the legions were a jumble, as were the weapons.

Besides artillery and tanks, their weapons were a mix of American and other types, although the standard infantry weapons were French: the 7.5mm MAS 36 rifle and the 9mm MAT 49 submachine gun. American .30 caliber M1A1 folding stock carbines were popular with the paras. German-style potato masher grenades hung from canvas-looped belts. The paras wore American-style helmets and camouflage over British pattern wind-proof jump pants.

The opposite number for the paras were the *bo doi* of the Viet Minh, rugged, dedicated, and moderately trained wearing black "pajamas", a round palm leaf hat, and sandals. He (or she) was between 18 and 20 years of age and carried French and Chinese small arms including the French MAT 49 and Chinese copies of Soviet drum-fed submachine guns. They were also trained in firing Soviet 37mm anti-aircraft guns, DKZ-57 recoilless rifles, 105mm and 75mm American-made howitzers and Soviet Katyusha rockets. They carried their field ration of rice with

Opposite left: A member of the Viet Cong (a South Vietnamese term for Communist infiltrators and guerrilla fighters from the North) wears standard black pants and shirt with floppy brim "boonie" hat with chin strap. He carries a captured U.S.-made .30 caliber M1 carbine with a 15-round magazine.

Opposite right: National Liberation Front flag. From the Viet Minh to the People's Army of Vietnam, the North Vietnamese used a variety of battle flags and commemoration flags to spur morale.

Right: The PPSh 41 submachine gun, shown with a 71-round drum magazine, was designed by Georgi Shpagin and copied by the Chinese as the Model 50. It fired 90–100 rounds per minute and was the mainstay of the Viet Minh Army.

Below: The U.S. Navy SB-2C ("The Beast") Helldiver dive bomber prototype delivered in December 1940. It entered combat in 1943 raiding the Japanese base at Rabaul. Never an outstanding performer, it replaced the superior SBD Dauntless Avenger. After the war, France purchased the Helldiver for its French Aeronavale for troop support flying from an aircraft carrier in the Gulf of Tonkin.

WEAPONS OF THE VIET MINH

The Viet Minh was a front organization of the Indochinese Communist Party, and sought popular support for national independence from French colonial rule. Called the *bo doi* by Vietnamese, their weapons ranged from Chinese copies of Soviet Type 56 7.62mm rifles, early model AK-47 assault rifles, and World War II KAR-98 model Mauser rifles to the PPSh 41 submachine gun, either drum or stick magazine-fed. Antique Maxim water-cooled and Soviet Goryunov heavy machine guns were popular. General Giap also had Katyusha rockets and 24 105mm howitzers plus 37mm Soviet anti-aircraft guns, which shot down much of the French air cover.

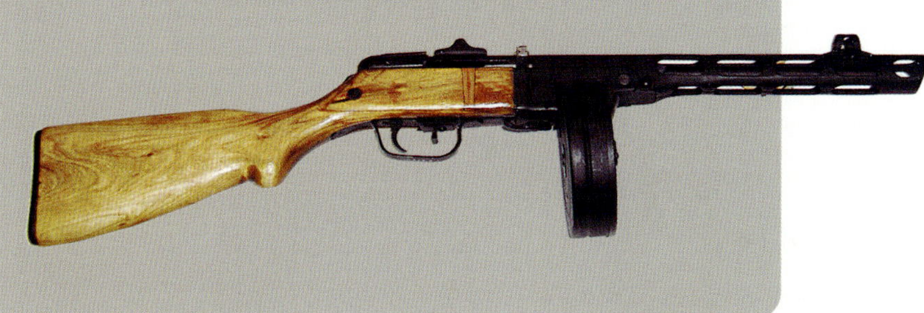

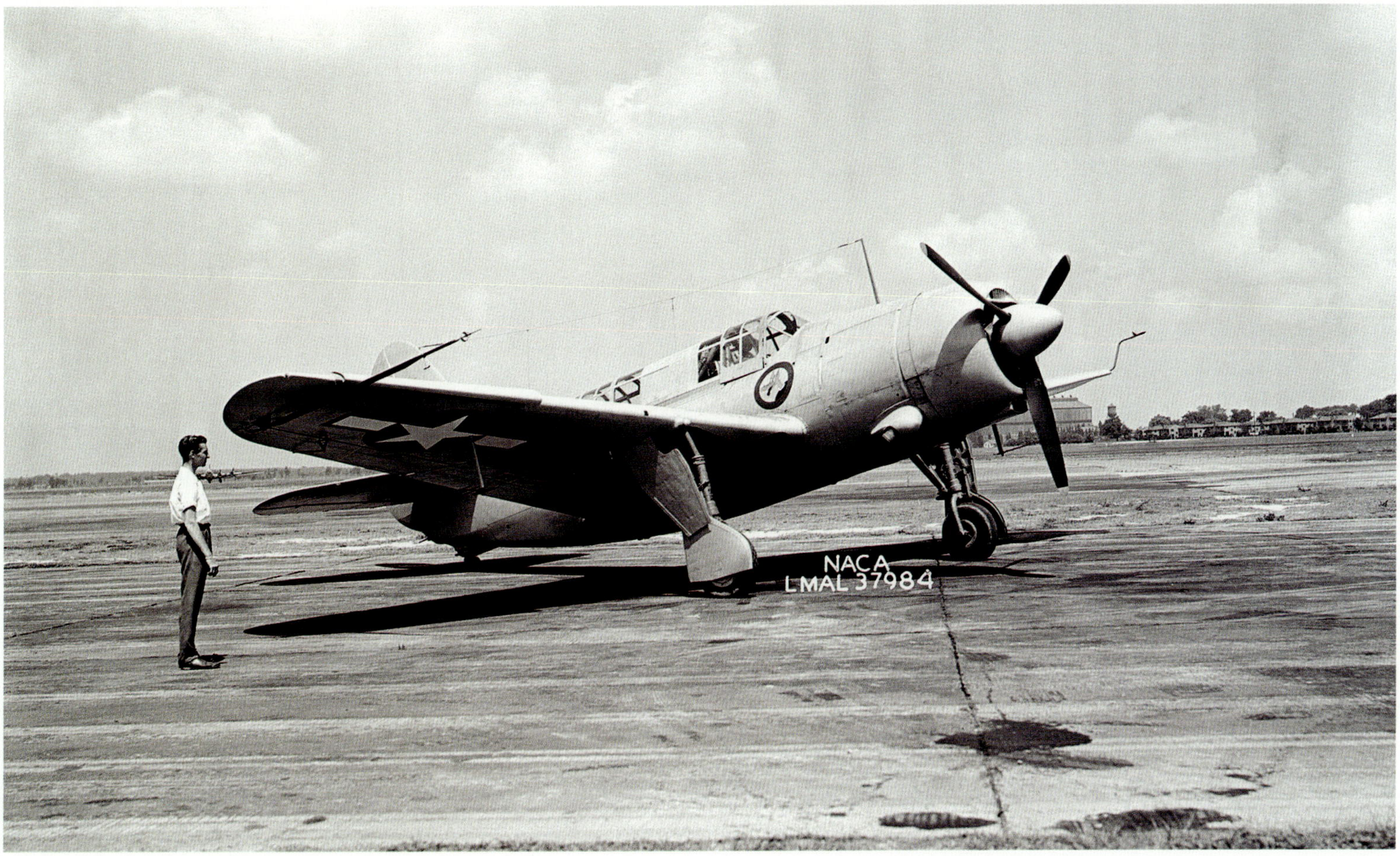

GENERAL VO NGUYEN GIAP

At Dien Bien Phu in 1954, General Giap out-soldiered French General Henri-Eugene Navarre as Giap had also outwitted previous French commanders since 1950. From a group of 34 men in 1944, Giap had created six infantry divisions, 20 independent regiments, and the same number of independent battalions. Before and during the battle Giap pressed 33,500 Patriotic Workers using specially redesigned bicycles, 17,400 horses, and 2,673 junks to snake through trails and rivers with supplies, ammunition, and disassembled weapons. When the time came, the former history professor was ready for the over-confident French general.

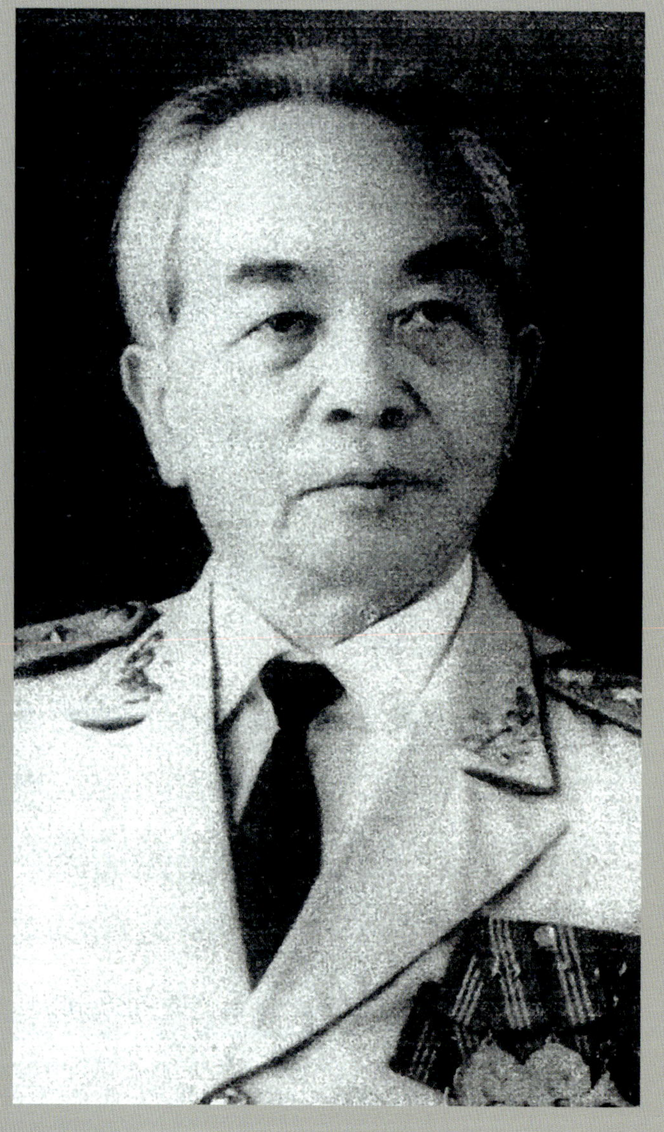

FFL AND COLONIAL WEAPONS

French weapons were a mix of Word War II and post-war small arms. The paratroopers preferred the MAT 49 collapsible stock 9mm submachine gun supported by the 7.5mm Chatellerault M29 light machine gun firing 125 rounds per minute. Crew-served weapons included the DKZ-57mm recoilless rifle and 120mm mortar. A squadron of 10 M24 Chaffee tanks was assembled plus 105mm howitzers and 155mm howitzers. Air cover was provided by World War II propeller aircraft: the F-6F Hellcat fighter and SB-2C Helldiver fighter-bombers from the aircraft carrier *Arromanches* in the Tonkin Gulf. B-26 Marauder twin-engine bombers and four-engine "Privateer" bombers also flew support missions. Supplies were brought in by C-47 and C-119 Flying Boxcar cargo planes.

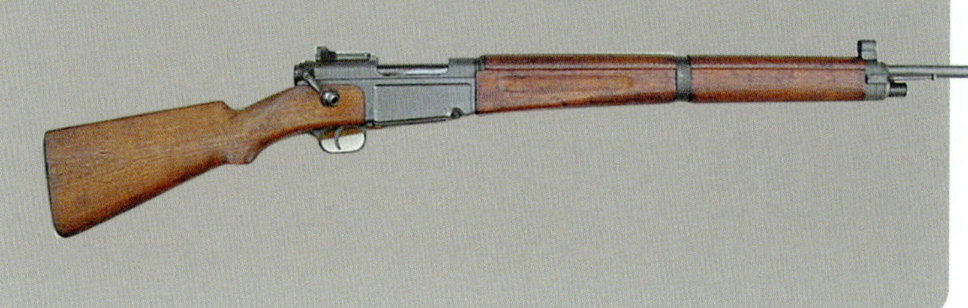

them in a cloth sausage roll as General Giap was fanatical about good hygiene and regular hot meals while on the trail.

This Chu Luc (regular army) of about 125,000 was officered by young men in tan uniforms and canvas shoes, which was the standard N.V.A.—North Vietnamese Army—uniform in 1954 and throughout succeeding years. Viet Minh fire and route discipline surprised the French paras and Legionnaires, as did their numbers and the variety of their weapons and artillery.

The French had all the firepower, air superiority, armor, tactical training, and an aerial supply line. But the Viet Minh had the dedication to hack a 600-mile road to Dien Bien Phu over which they hauled weapons and marched soldiers to tie a noose around the French troops who had been placed in a vulnerable position by over-optimistic generals.

Above: A standard French 7.5mm MAS 36-bolt action rifle dating back to World War II. It weighs eight pounds and fires five rounds loaded from the top of the receiver with reloadable stripper clips. The tube beneath the barrel contains the rifle's slide-out bayonet.

Opposite: A French Foreign Legionnaire walks down a road in Vietnam followed by a French M24 Chaffee light tank with a 75mm gun purchased from the U.S. A Browning .50 caliber machine gun is on the turret pintel mount and a .30 machine gun is hull-mounted. The legionnaire carries a 7.5mm MAS 36 rifle across his shoulder, wears a floppy brim boonie hat and paratrooper pants with side pockets and strap-sealed cuffs.

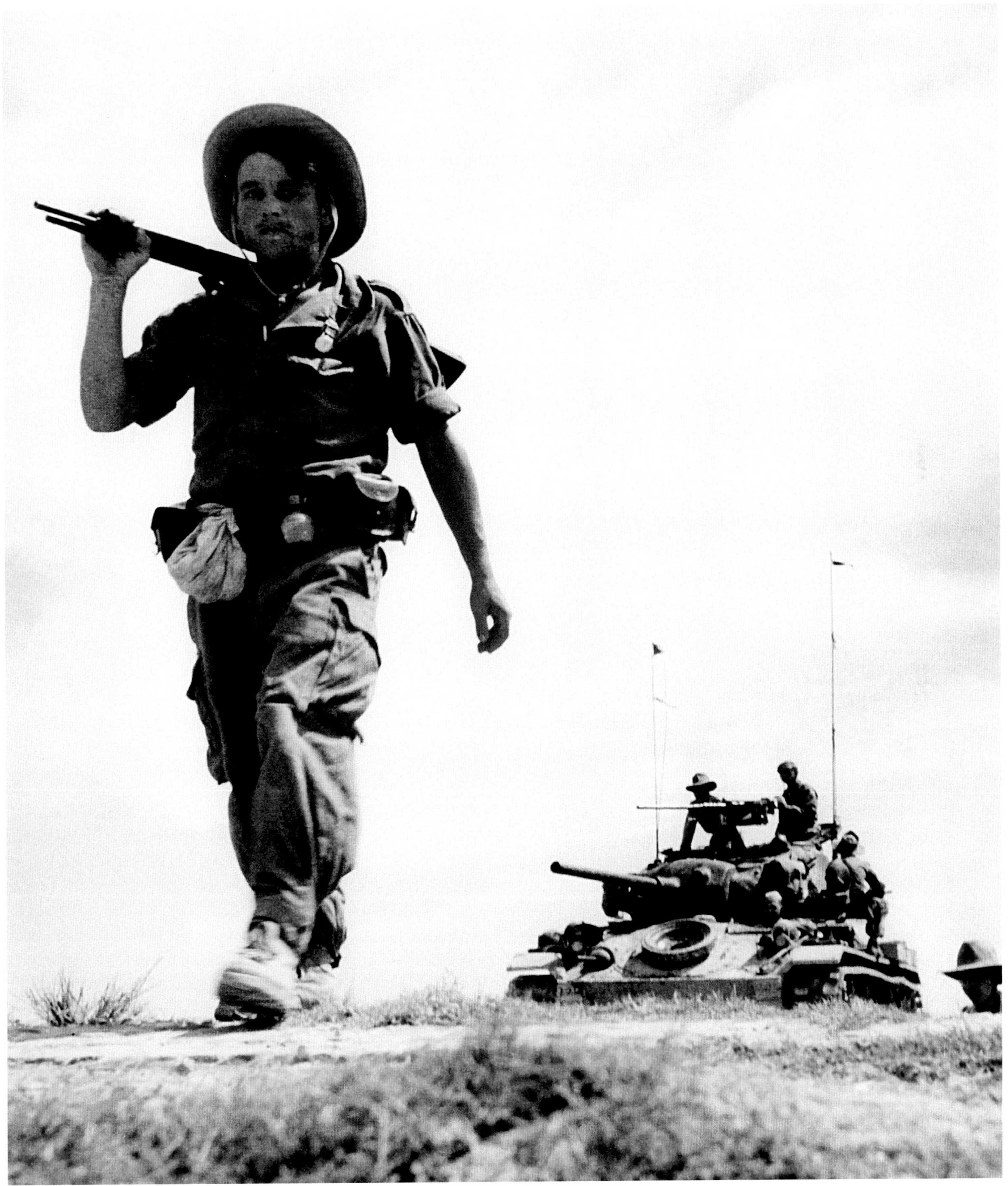

DIEN BIEN PHU

FROM HIS HEADQUARTERS IN NORTH VIETNAM, HO CHI MINH WROTE EIGHT LETTERS TO PRESIDENT HARRY S. TRUMAN, ARGUING THAT THE FRENCH MUST LEAVE VIETNAM. HISTORY WAS NOT ON HO'S SIDE. THE POSTWAR UNITED STATES WAS DETERMINED TO STOP THE SPREAD OF COMMUNISM. IN EARLY 1946, AMERICAN WARSHIPS LANDED FRENCH TROOPS IN VIETNAM. DURING THE LAST WEEKS OF 1946 AND EARLY 1947, USING AMERICAN WEAPONS, THE FRENCH QUICKLY TOOK OVER THE MAJOR CITIES, INCLUDING HANOI, HAIPHONG, DA NANG, AND HUE. IN 1949, THE FRENCH ESTABLISHED A PUPPET STATE WITH ITS CAPITAL AT SAIGON UNDER THE RULE OF EMPEROR BAO DAI.

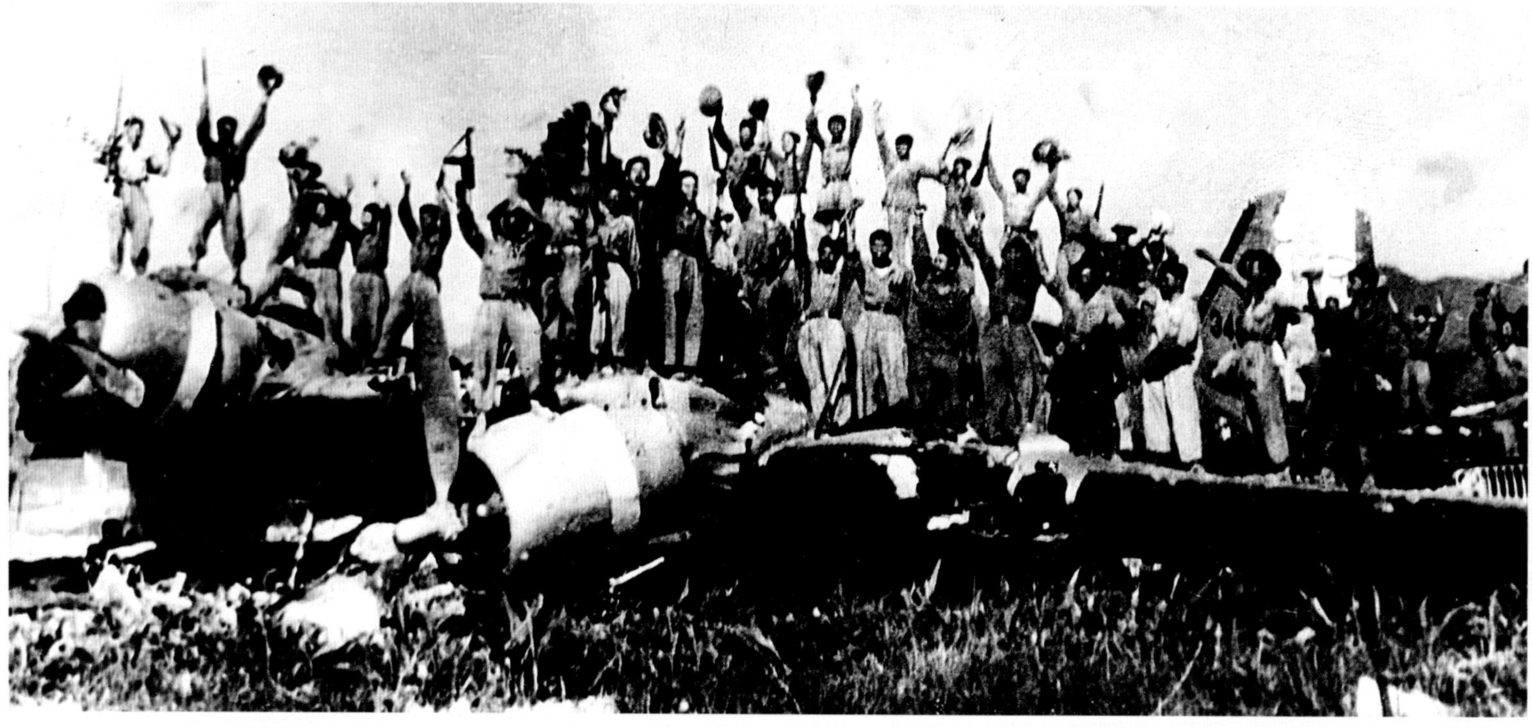

The Viet Minh guerrillas resumed their hit and run campaign but, as casualties rose, both sides faced a loss of popular support. The French attempted to break the stalemate with a daring gamble conceived by General Henri Navarre. He suggested creating a firebase with an elite force of Foreign Legion and other selected units in a bowl-shaped valley surrounded by hills to threaten Viet Minh supply lines. The base would be supplied by air, with aircraft flying into a landing field, or drops by parachute. General Navarre planned to lure the guerrillas into attacks on the firebase. French superior tactics and firepower would accomplish the rest.

Navarre built his trap near the village of Dien Bien Phu, unaware of the numerical strength of General Giap's force, or its firepower. The layout consisted of a main garrison and strongpoints named, it was rumored, after the mistresses of base commander, Colonel Christian de Castries. The 11,000

Above: Viet Minh soldiers celebrate atop a downed French airplane following their victory at the Battle of Dien Bien Phu during the French Indochina War in 1954.

Opposite: A captured Viet Minh soldier is interrogated by French paratroopers during the siege of Dien Bien Phu. Capture by the French was usually fatal due to lack of troops to guard prisoners and in response to atrocities committed by Viet Minh against French who surrendered early in the conflict.

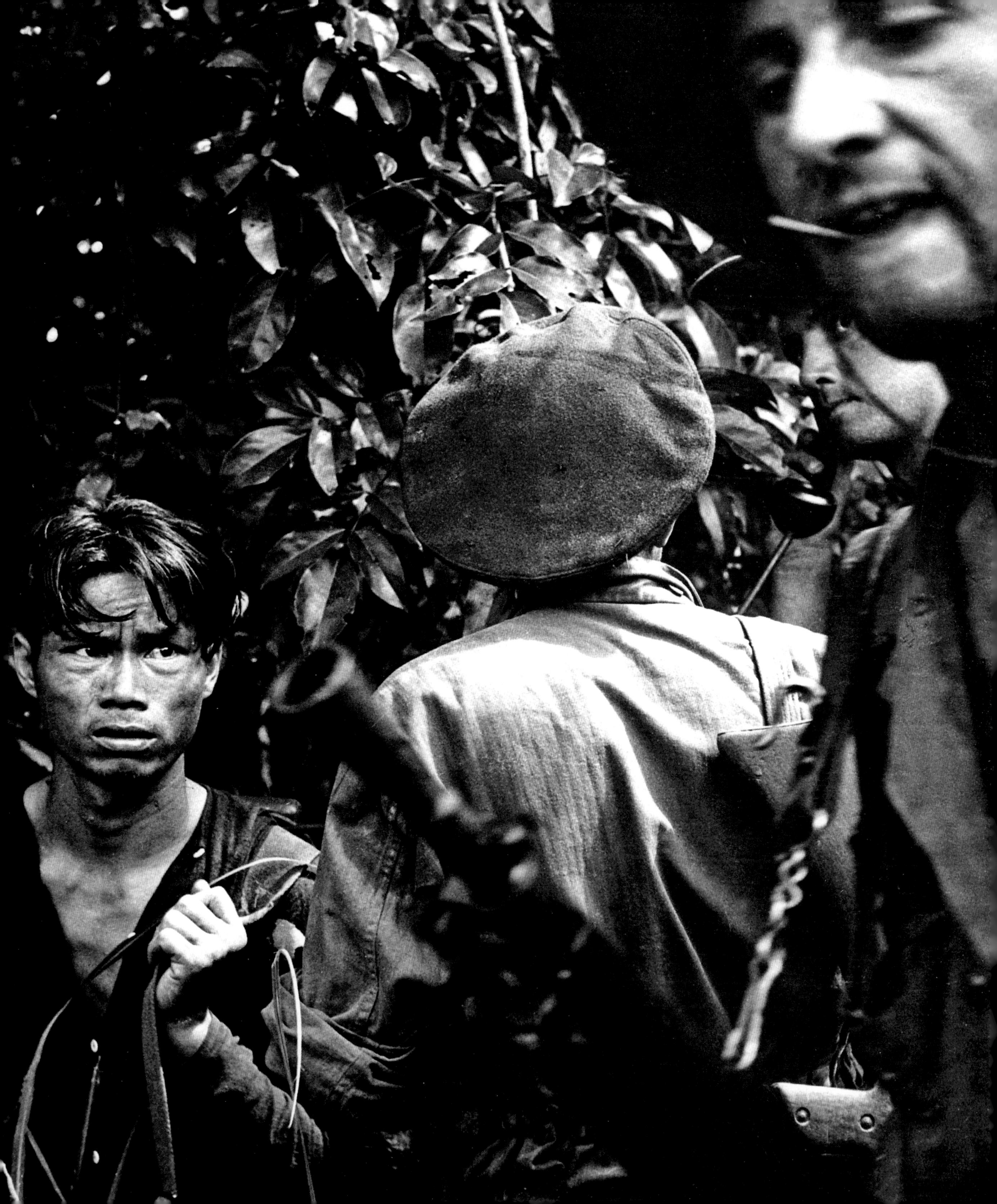

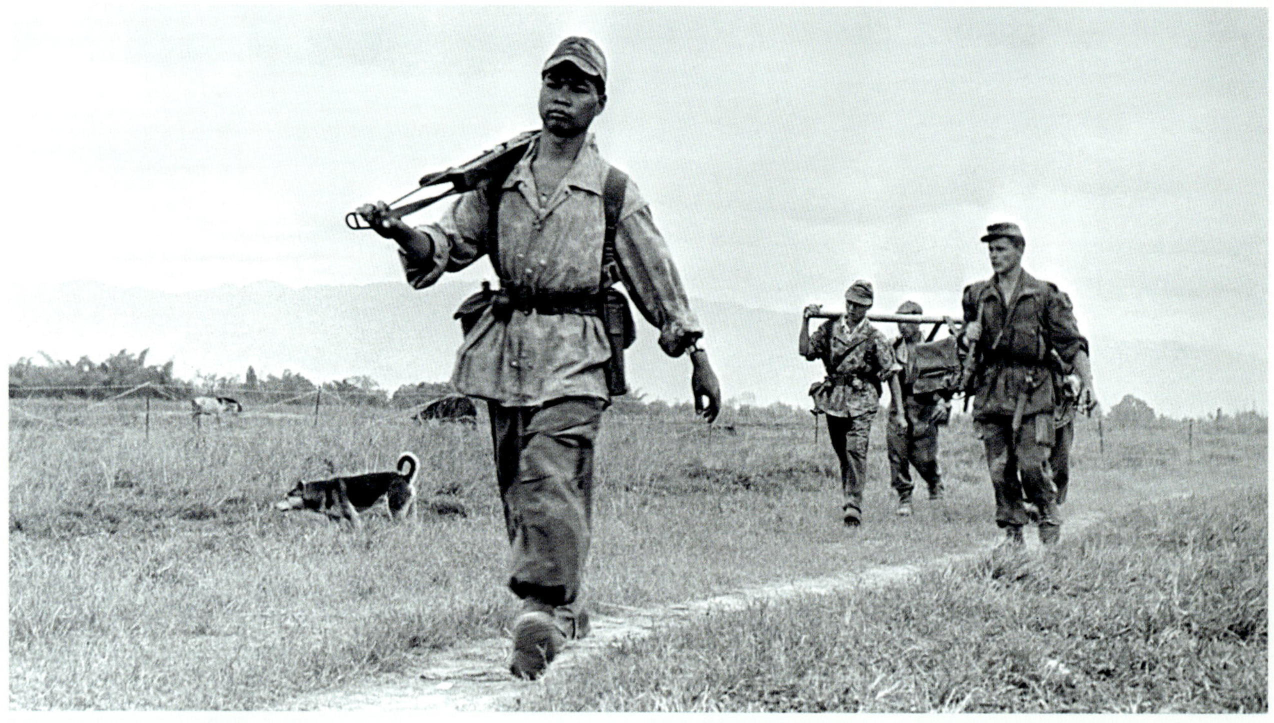

Left: A Viet Cong soldier strides along carrying a French 7.62 MAT 49 submachine gun on his shoulder and an officer's four-button shirt cinched at the waist with a combat harness and sidearm holster. He wears a Chinese field cap similar to the Japanese pattern of World War II.

COL. CHRISTIAN DE CASTRIES (1902–91)

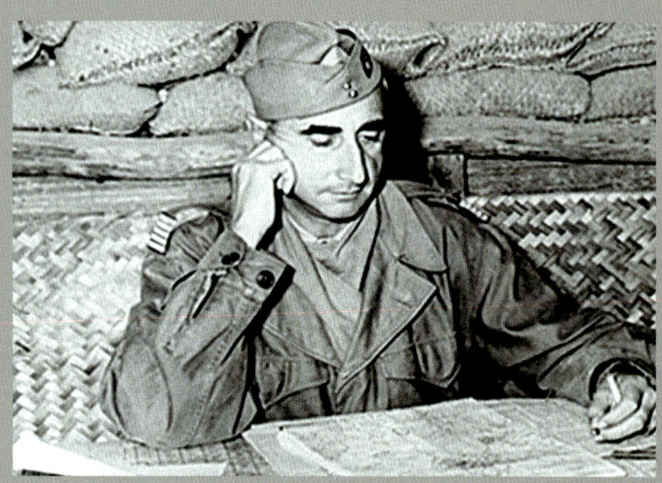

Colonel Christian Marie Ferdinand de la Croix de Castries commanded Dien Bien Phu throughout the battle though tactical situations were delegated to the Parachute Battalion commanders because of their combat experience. Born an aristocrat, his presence still emboldened the men as the Viet Minh's encirclement tightened. Late in the conflict the French command in Hanoi made numerous promises of reinforcements and supplies that never materialized. He was promoted to Brigadier General and was prepared to lead an almost suicidal breakout just before his command was overwhelmed.

DIEN BIEN PHU 1954

Showing location and a close-up of the firebases designed to lure the Viet Minh into a major firefight and destroy them. The separate bases were destroyed in detail and the main base overwhelmed by thousands of Viet Minh and artillery unreachable by French guns.

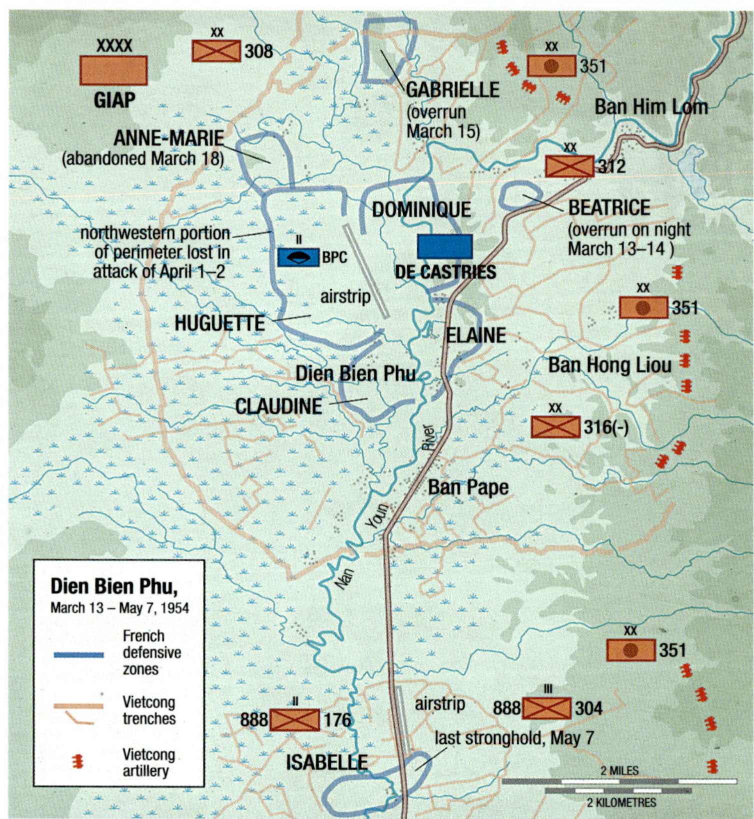

VIỆT-NAM DÂN CHỦ CỘNG HÒA
CHÍNH PHỦ LÂM THỜI
BO NGOAI GIAO

YKB-3739-1

HANOI FEBRUARY 28 1946

MAR 11 RECD

TELEGRAM

PRESIDENT HOCHIMINH VIETNAM DEMOCRATIC REPUBLIC HANOI
TO THE PRESIDENT OF THE UNITED STATES OF AMERICA WASHINGTON D.C.

ON BEHALF OF VIETNAM GOVERNMENT AND PEOPLE I BEG TO INFORM YOU THAT IN COURSE OF CONVERSATIONS BETWEEN VIETNAM GOVERNMENT AND FRENCH REPRESENTATIVES THE LATTER REQUIRE THE SECESSION OF COCHINCHINA AND THE RETURN OF FRENCH TROOPS IN HANOI STOP MEANWHILE FRENCH POPULATION AND TROOPS ARE MAKING ACTIVE PREPARATIONS FOR A COUP DE MAIN IN HANOI AND FOR MILITARY AGGRESSION STOP I THEREFORE MOST EARNESTLY APPEAL TO YOU PERSONALLY AND TO THE AMERICAN PEOPLE TO INTERFERE URGENTLY IN SUPPORT OF OUR INDEPENDENCE AND HELP MAKING THE NEGOTIATIONS MORE IN KEEPING WITH THE PRINCIPLES OF THE ATLANTIC AND SAN FRANCISCO CHARTERS

RESPECTFULLY

HOCHIMINH

Hochiminh

LETTER FROM HO CHI MINH TO TRUMAN 1946

One of eight letters Ho Chi Minh wrote to Truman after World War II beseeching the U.S. to back independence. The letters, although discussed by Truman and Acheson, were never answered.

43 NLT 784
ma

~~TOP SECRET~~

February 2, 1950

MEMORANDUM OF CONVERSATION WITH THE PRESIDENT

Item 2. Recognition of Vietnam, Laos and Cambodia

I discussed this matter with the President, leaving with him the memorandum of February 2 recommending recognition. I also discussed the CIA paper of February 1 "Implications of Soviet Recognition of the Ho Regime in Indochina", pointing out to the President that, although there was no difference of opinion as to the facts before the CIA and the State Department, the CIA took a gloomier view of the situation than we did. The President received the memorandum; expressed himself in a preliminary way as in favor of recognition, and told me that he would give us his definitive reply tomorrow morning.

Dean Acheson

DECLASSIFIED
E.O. 12065, Sec. 3-402
State Dept. Guideline, June 12, 1979
PROJECT NLT 78-36
By NLT-HC NARS, Date 8-24-81

S:DAcheson:mlm

~~TOP SECRET~~

"VIETNAM RECOGNITION LETTER" FROM ACHESON TO TRUMAN 1950

On February 2, 1950, Acheson wrote this memo recommending diplomatically recognizing Vietnam, Laos, and Cambodia and blunting the "gloomy" C.I.A. assessment of the Soviet recognition of Ho Chi Minh's regime.

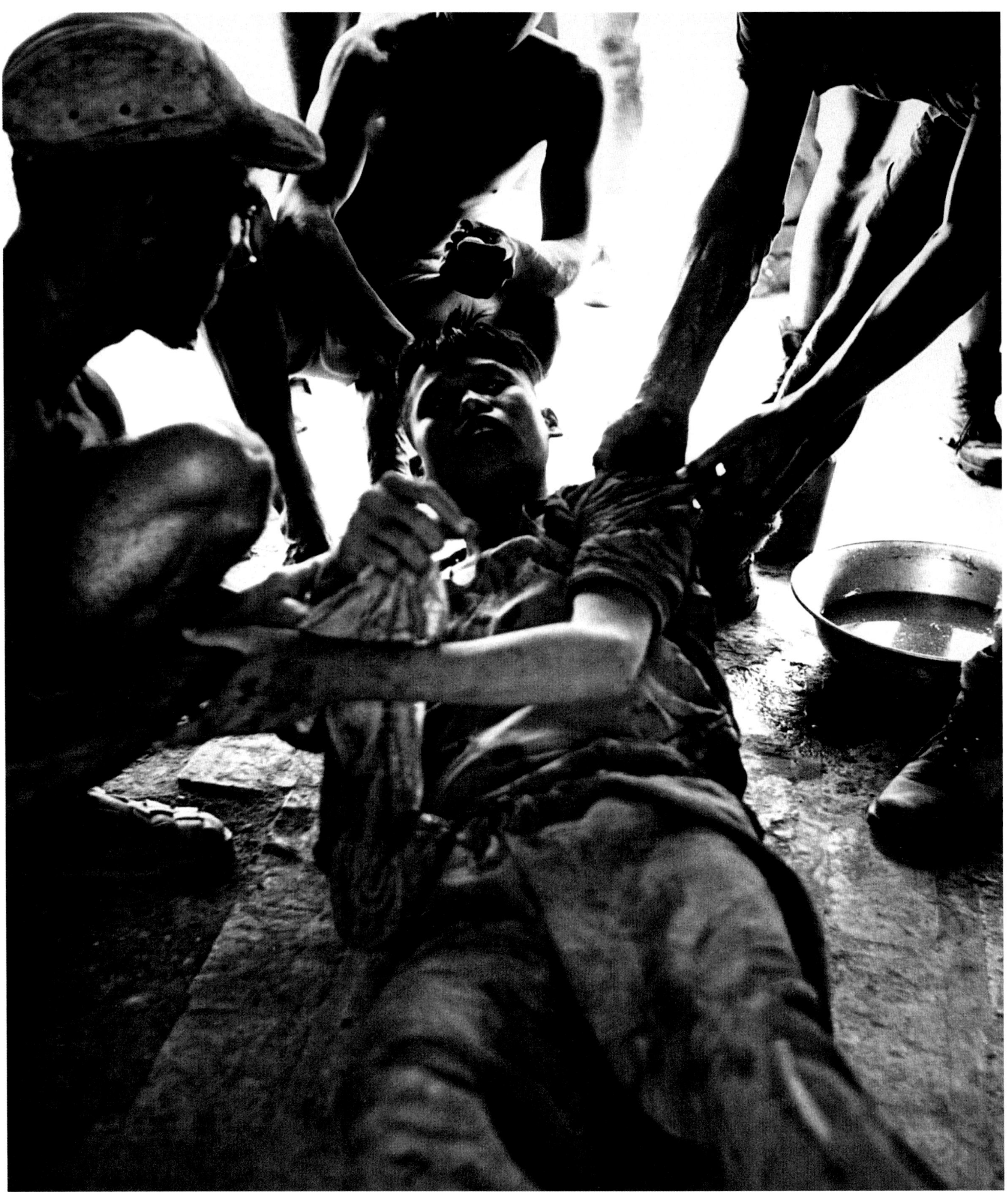

troops felt secure "knowing" Giap only had some bazookas and light weapons.

On March 13, a plunging barrage of artillery suddenly hammered Dien Bien Phu. The Viet Minh had brought 48 American-made 105mm howitzers captured by Communist forces during the civil war in China in 1949, taken them to pieces and hauled them up the far slopes of those hills, where they had been reassembled. The barrage cratered the airfield and closed it. Each strongpoint was enfiladed, and the field-telephone lines connecting them were torn up. Interlocking trenches collapsed. Navarre's miscalculations and faulty intelligence doomed de Castries's command.

C-47 Dakota transports tried landing on the airfield, but Viet Minh mortars and howitzers destroyed many of those that touched down. Civilian pilots James McGovern and Wallace Buford became the first American airmen killed in Vietnam combat when their twin-engine Dakota went up in a fireball. Supply planes dropping parachutes were forced to higher altitudes by Soviet-supplied 37mm anti-aircraft guns. Much of the cargo delivered in this way landed in Viet Minh hands. And then came the "human wave" charges: thousands of screaming, firing Viet Minh crashed over and through French barbed wire, dropped into trenches, and lobbed grenades. Giap had 50,000 troops in the hills, outnumbering the French 5 to 1.

One by one, the strongpoints fell: Anne-Marie, Gabrielle, Dominique, Françoise, Isabelle. On May 7, 1954, the French surrendered with 2,200 killed and thousands more taken prisoner. Giap's Viet Minh suffered 23,000 casualties with 8,000 killed. The military victory brought French rule in Vietnam to an end.

HARRY S. TRUMAN (1884-1972)

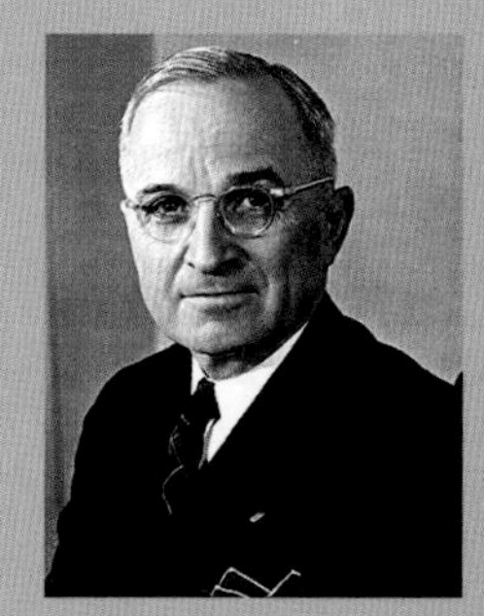

Harry S. Truman was the 33rd President of the United States from 1945 to 1953. Following the French re-occupation of their former colony of Vietnam from the Japanese, Ho Chi Minh, who had led an insurgency against the French and then against the Japanese to win independence for his country, sent Truman eight letters, each requesting support against the French. Truman's U.S. and U.N. commitments were to the French and he feared Ho Chi Minh's ties to Communist China and the Soviet Union.

"THE ANGEL OF DIEN BIEN PHU"

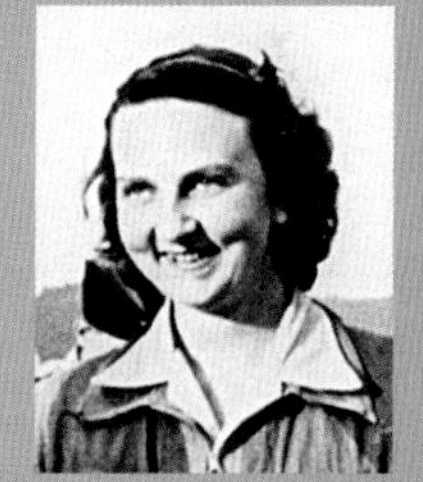

French Air Force Nurse Lt. Geneviève de Galard-Terraube escaped from the last C-47 Dakota aircraft to land at Dien Bien Phu on March 28, 1954, before it was destroyed by artillery fire. She became known at the main base hospital as "Geneviève" as she tended to huge numbers of wounded with a diminishing supply of medicines and bandages. Under shell fire, she visited outlying fortifications and stayed with her many patients until the capitulation and beyond, becoming "The Angel of Dien Bien Phu."

Opposite: A wounded Viet Minh soldier is treated by Franco-Vietnamese in a medical bunker. He was wounded near Hung Yen and feared torture and execution as drilled into him by his Viet Minh officers.

Below: Viet Minh charge from their trenches that encircled each French firebase in the Dien Bien Phu complex. Heavy 105mm howitzers, hand-carried over 600 miles of trails and reassembled on the reverse slopes of surrounding hills, overwhelmed French positions, which could be supplied only by air.against French who surrendered early in the conflict.

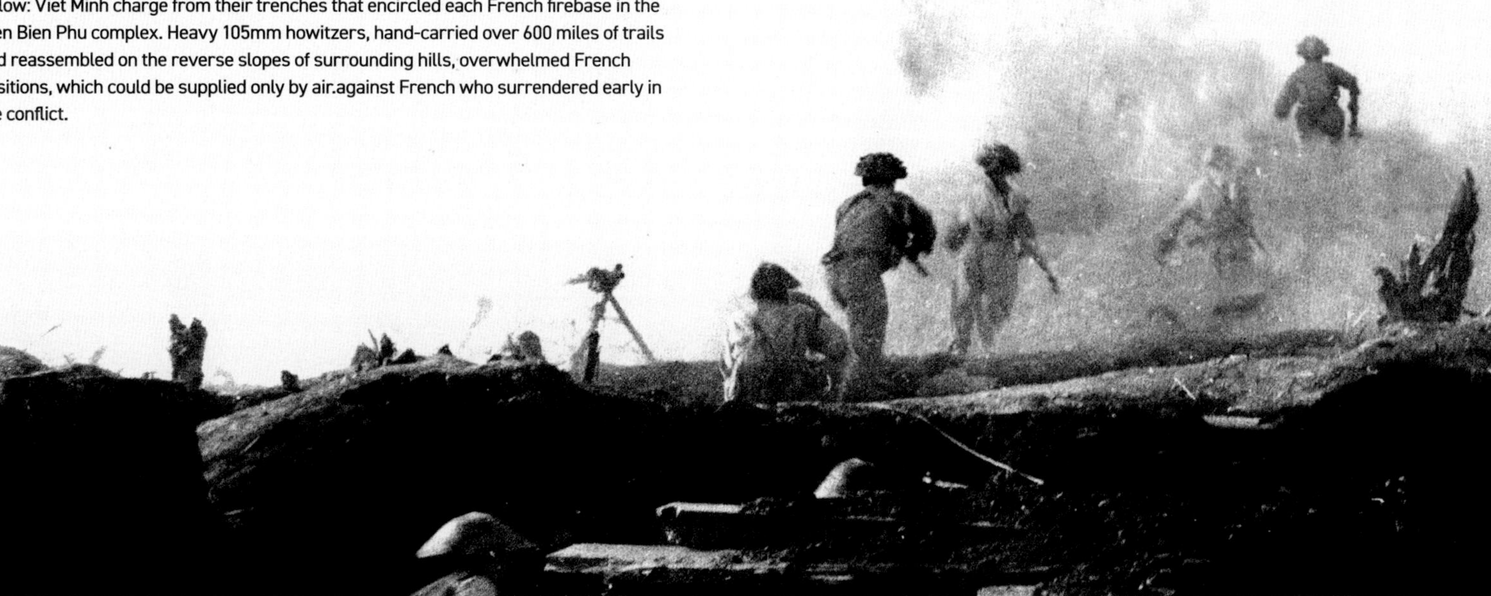

A DIVIDED VIETNAM

THE FALL OF DIEN BIEN PHU SET INTO MOTION THE PARTITION OF VIETNAM INTO THE RELATIVELY INDUSTRIALIZED NORTH, GOVERNED BY HO CHI MINH'S COMMUNISTS, AND THE PREDOMINANTLY AGRICULTURAL SOUTH, UNDER THE FRENCH-DOMINATED ADMINISTRATION OF THE EMPEROR BAO DAI, UNTIL ELECTIONS DUE IN 1956 WOULD ALLOW THE ENTIRE COUNTRY TO VOTE FOR A NATIONAL GOVERNMENT. THIS AGREEMENT WAS SIGNED IN GENEVA, SWITZERLAND, ON JULY 20, 1954. BY 1956, HOWEVER, THE FRENCH HAD GONE, LEAVING SOUTH VIETNAM'S RULERS FREE TO IGNORE THE GENEVA ACCORD. BAO DAI HAD APPOINTED THE CATHOLIC NATIONALIST NGO DINH DIEM AS PRIME MINISTER IN 1954. IN 1955, DIEM HELD A REFERENDUM ON WHETHER SOUTH VIETNAM SHOULD BECOME A REPUBLIC. THROUGH HEAVY-HANDED FRAUD, HE ENSURED THAT BAO DAI WAS DOOMED TO EXILE. WITH AMERICAN BACKING, DIEM BECAME PRESIDENT OF THE NEW REPUBLIC OF VIETNAM.

The Geneva accord, in addition to dividing Vietnam, also created Cambodia under Prince Norodom Sihanouk and Laos headed by Prince Souvanna Phouma. Laos had a large Communist organization, the Pathet Lao, led by Phouma's half brother, Prince Souphanouvong. While Cambodia tried to stay neutral and out of trouble, Laos was torn between rival royalist and Communist factions. Finally—with a push from the United States—Laos swung to the West with its Royal Laotian Army largely equipped and funded by the United States.

The Soviet Union took an interest in the situation as American military aid—advisors, air bases, training, and weapons—poured into Laos. The Soviets countered by backing the Pathet Lao. North Vietnam also sent considerable support to the Pathet Lao. Eventually, in May 1962, the Pathet Lao soundly whipped the Royal Laotian Army on the Plain of Jars and Laos was left badly fractured.

President John F. Kennedy's foreign policy was still recovering from the legacy of the disastrous Bay of Pigs invasion of Cuba in April 1961. Neither Kennedy nor the Soviet Union's Premier Nikita Khrushchev wanted a war in land-locked Laos. Kennedy preferred to make the Diem regime the keystone of U.S. policy in south-east Asia, and an unstable coalition regime was created in Laos. Unfortunately, the South Vietnamese government was

SOUTH VIETNAM DEFENSE FORCE—1961

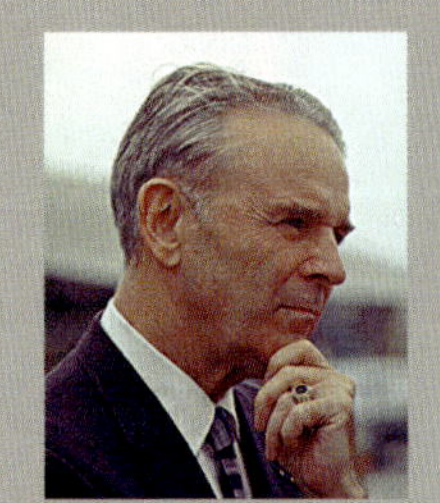

On November 3, 1961, General Maxwell D. Taylor gave a report on the status of Vietnam and the M.A.A.G. (Military Assistance Advisory Group) to President Kennedy. At the time, M.A.A.G. consisted of 342 officers and men. Taylor advised expansion of counter-insurgency, Ranger, Naval, and combat training for the South Vietnamese Civil Guard and Self-Defense Corps. He recommended additional covert operations into the North, into Laos, and in South Vietnam. A radical increase in trainers was needed at every level as were more U.S. Naval, Coast Guard, and Air Force assets and trainers – M.A.A.G. Vietnam was increased by some 2,500 personnel so that at the end of 1961 there were over 3,000 American military personnel in South Vietnam.

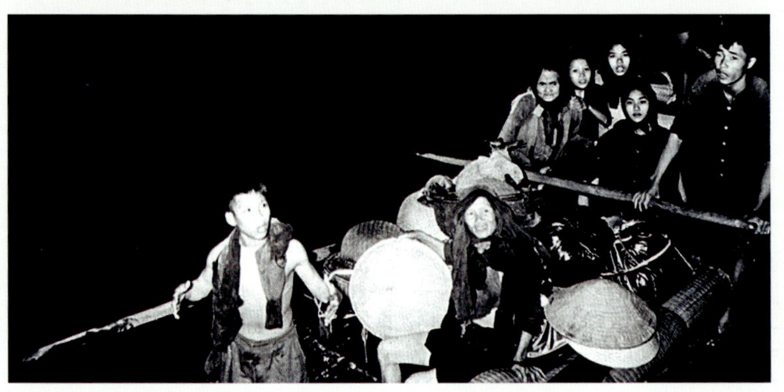

Right: As the First Indochina War winds down in 1954, Catholics escaping Communist territory in the dead of night pull alongside a French landing craft that will take them to safety.

Opposite: A heavily armed Viet Cong cadre stops to chat with a South Vietnamese elder and representatives of a village in 1964. The Viet Cong attempted to coerce outlying villages to provide men, supplies, hiding places, and intelligence about South Vietnamese Army movements. The young Viet Cong wearing the checkered scarf carries a Soviet-designed Rocket Propelled Grenade (R.P.G.) and launcher.

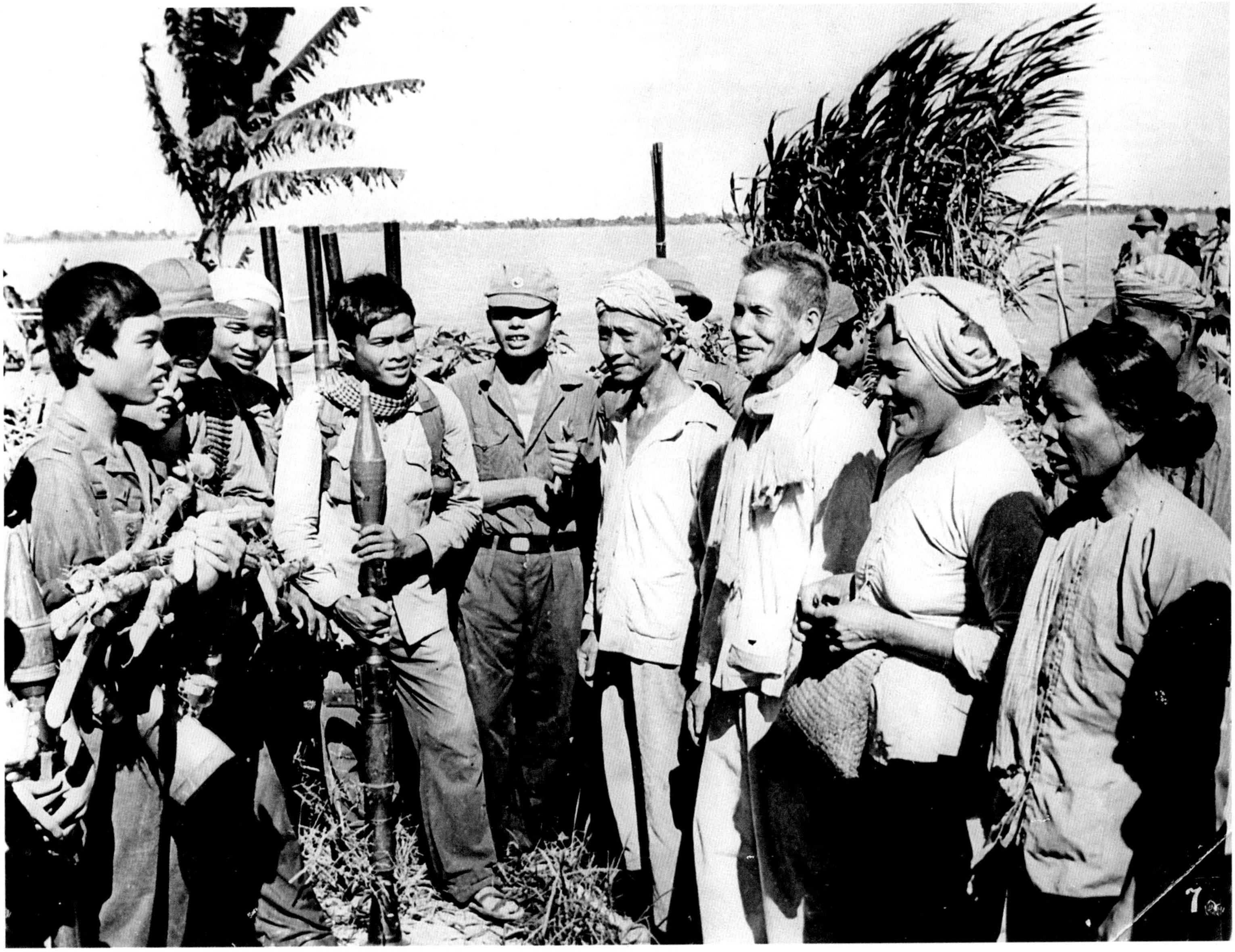

SOVIET–AMERICAN CONFRONTATION IN LAOS

In a letter from Chairman Nikita Khrushchev to President Kennedy delivered on September 29, 1961, among the topics of this "pen pal correspondence" was a finger-wagging caution over U.S. interference with the Laotian government elections. At the same time, the Soviet government saw opportunities to embarrass further the U.S. following the Cuban Bay of Pigs fiasco. Kennedy inherited the fractured Laotian government with the Communist Pathet Lao holding the stronger position. Since the U.S. had "deserted" the Cubans, if they backed away from commitment to Laos, President Diem in Vietnam feared U.S. promises to his country were in jeopardy.

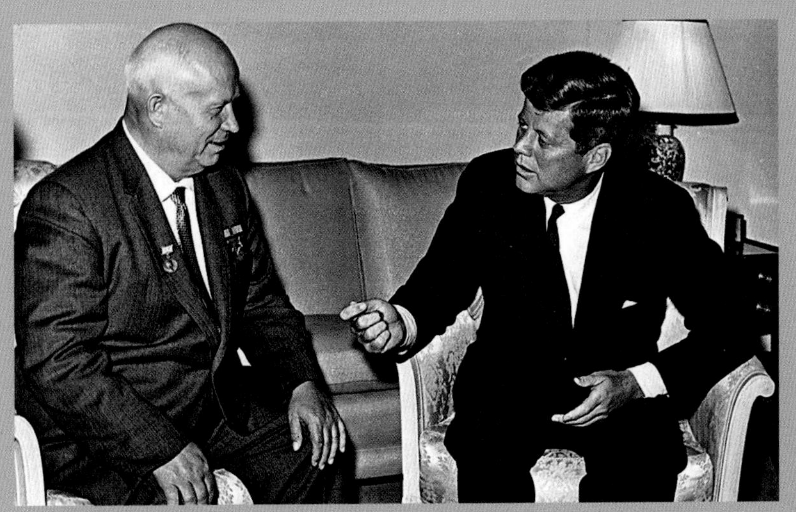

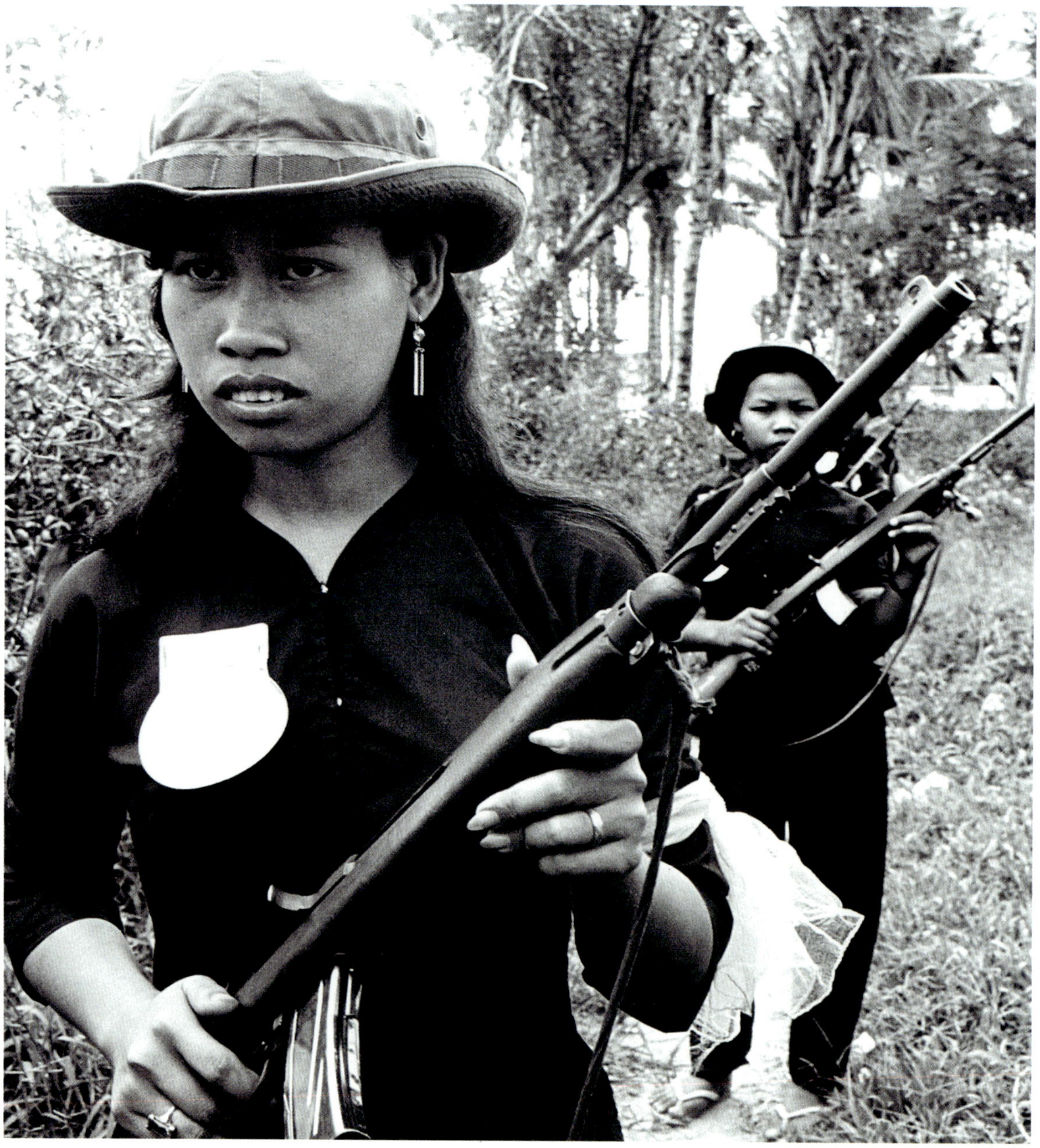

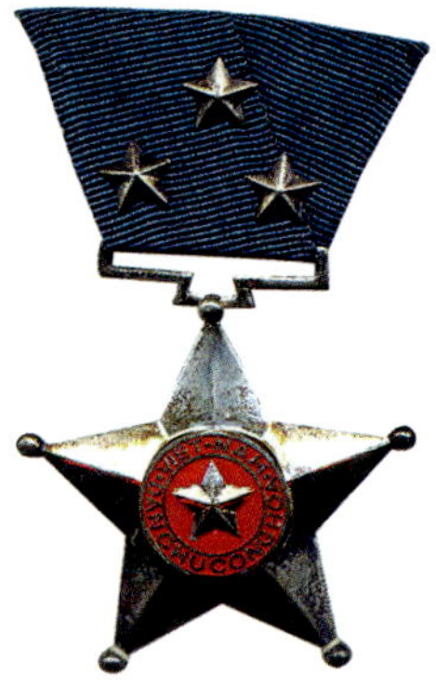

Above: North Vietnam Medal of valor awarded for unit combat bravery.

Left: Girl volunteers of the People's Self-defense Force of Kien Dien, a hamlet in the Ben Cat district 31 miles north of Saigon, patrol the hamlet's perimeter to discourage Viet Cong infiltration in 1960. They carry semi-automatic U.S. Army M1 carbines with 15-round magazines.

Below: (From left) President Dwight Eisenhower, Secretary of State John Foster Dulles, and Clark Clifford meet South Vietnam President Ngo Dinh Diem to discuss U.S. support for Diem's regime.

Opposite: Vietnam refugees jam the Haiphong docks as the U.S.S. *Montague* lowers a ladder over the side to take them on board on August 1, 1954. The U.S. was committed, through N.A.T.O., to support France during the French Indochina conflict that ended with a divided North and South Vietnam.

under extreme pressure from guerrillas supported by Ho Chi Minh's regime in the north and Diem's own ineptitude. Diem demanded more and more aid, and feared Kennedy would desert Vietnam as he had seemingly abandoned Laos.

Kennedy's Vice President Lyndon Johnson had visited Vietnam in May 1961, and was followed by General Maxwell Taylor who was sent in October to determine what had to be done to stabilize the chaotic situation. The Kennedy administration chose to send the U.S. Army Special Forces as advisors to reorganize, equip, and train the Army of the Republic of Vietnam (A.R.V.N.). The highly skilled "Green Berets" went to work in 1962, training Diem's ineffective army. Eventually some 5,000 of these advisors were placed under the Military Assistance Command, Vietnam (M.A.C.V.)—the American military mission to the south.

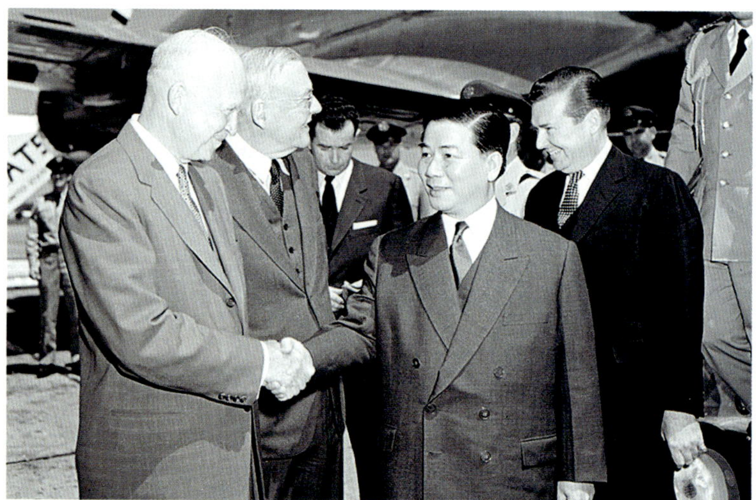

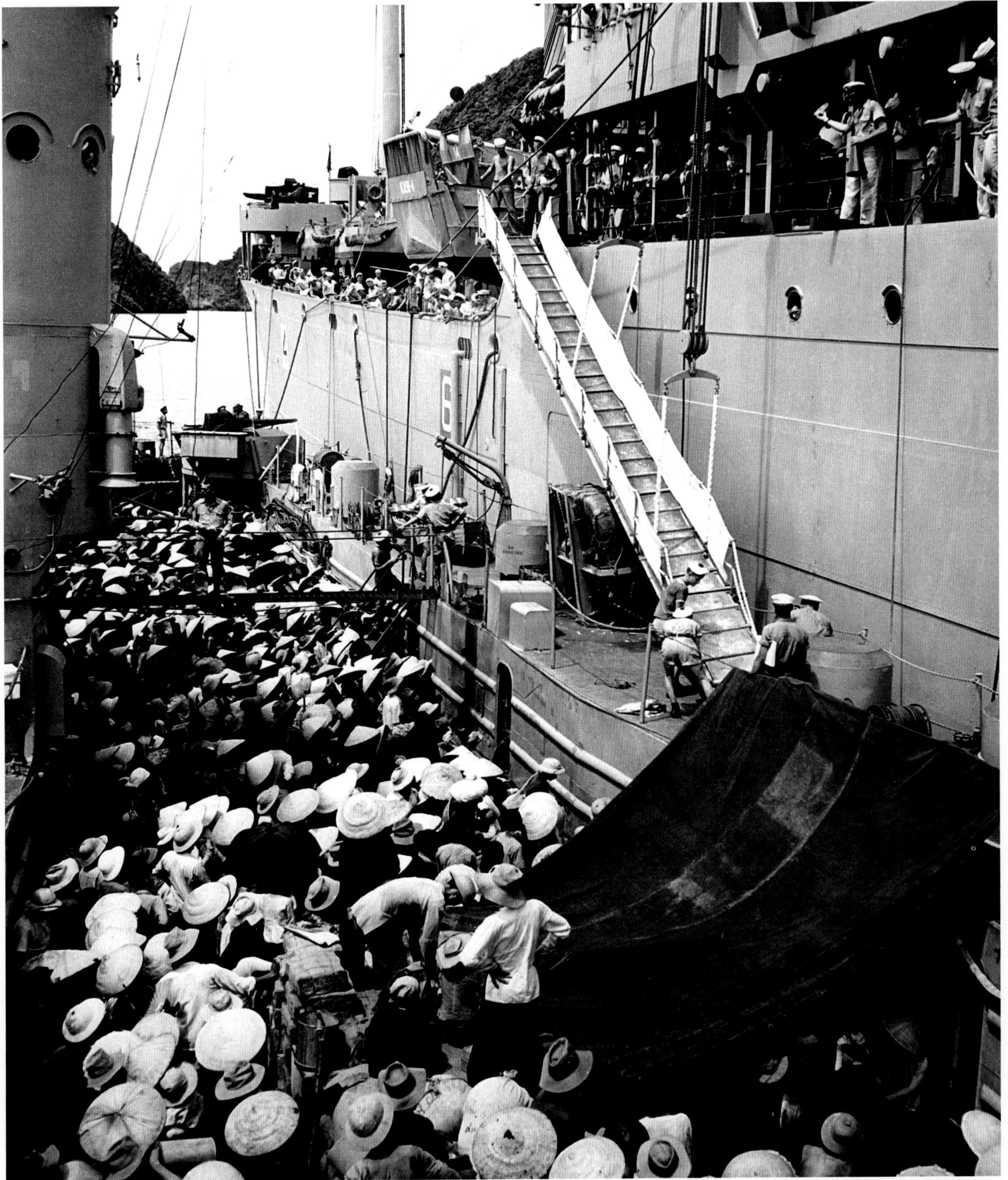

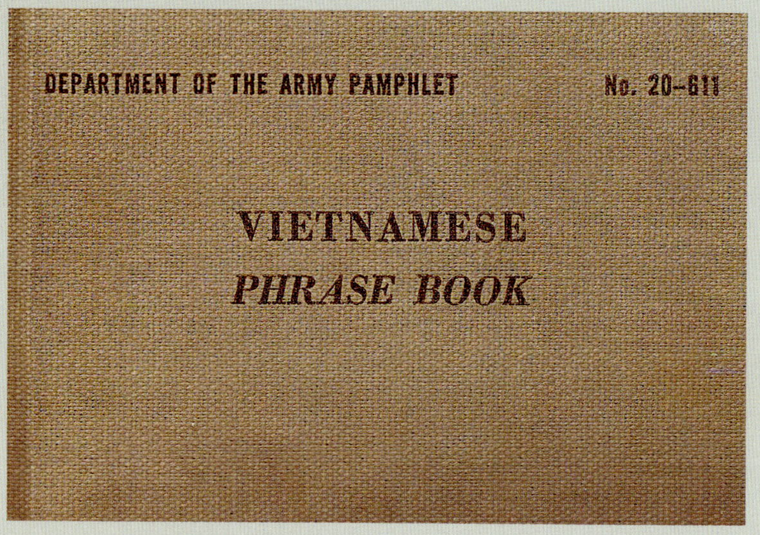

U.S. ARMY PHRASE BOOK 1962

Early U.S. advisors entering Vietnam in 1962–4 needed a book of basic Vietnamese language phrases as most of their work would be with non-English speakers. The Army provided this phonetic phrase book to get soldiers started.

VIETNAMESE PHRASE BOOK

Guide to Pronunciation

Vietnamese (pronounced Viak-nah-mese) is the principal language of Viet-Nam, and is spoken by some thirty million inhabitants of Viet-Nam and by a considerable number of people located in the larger cities of Cambodia and Laos.

This Phrase Book contains the Vietnamese words and expressions you are most likely to need. ALL THE WORDS AND PHRASES ARE WRITTEN IN A SPELLING WHICH YOU READ LIKE ENGLISH, except for those sounds which are non-existent in English, e.g. /kh/ /g/ /w/ /wk/ /wng/. Each letter or combination of letters is used for the sound it normally represents in English and it always stands for that sound.

Vietnamese and English pronunciation are very different because the former is of a tonal language and the latter is not. However, in so far as the vocal formation of tones is concerned, it does not make the two so utterly different. Just ask yourself "Can I hear the difference between He is there. and He is there? in English? You, as an English speaker, can tell a question from a statement just by the tone. And, phonetically speaking, the tone of English is no different in its general nature than the tone

vii

I

INITIAL ENCOUNTER WITH LOCALS

a. Accidental

1. Hello (to a man)	Chàaw âwng	Chào ông
(to a madam)	Chàaw bàa	Chào bà
(to a miss)	Chàaw kee	Chào cô
I am (1) an American soldier (2) an American officer who seeks friends to assist in fighting the enemy.	Toy làa (1) lînn Mẽe (2) (2) shẽe-kwan Mẽe muẫng tìm bạan yúp viậk cháwng kwận dịk.	Tôi là (1) lính Mỹ (2) sĩ-quan Mỹ muốn tìm bạn giúp việc chống quân địch.
2. Who speaks English?	Aay nóy tiẫng Aann?	Ai nói tiếng Anh?
3. Come forward (1) closer (2) alone (3) one of you only.	Dén dây (1) gẫn hơng (2) mọk mînn (3) chẻe mọk ngiòy thoy.	Đến đây (1) gần hơn (2) một mình (3) chỉ một người thôi.
4. (to a man) What is your name?	Ten âwng làa yì?	Tên ông là gì?

1

655769 O - 62 - 2

5. Are you alone? Where are your friends?	Âwng kố mọk mînn fảai khâwng? Bạan kwủa âwng dâw?	Ông có một mình phải không? Bạn của ông đâu?
6. What are you doing here?	Âwng làam yì dây?	Ông làm gì đây?
7. Where are you from?	Âwng từ dâw dén dây?	Ông từ đâu đến đây?
8. How far is your home from here?	Nyà âwng kaaik dây baaw saa?	Nhà ông cách đây bao xa?
(1) in kilometers?	(1) baaw nyiw kây shố?	(1) bao nhiêu cây số?
(2) in hours?	(2) baaw nyiw yờ dâwng hồ?	(2) bao nhiêu giờ đồng hồ?
9. Who is the (one)	Aay làa ngiòy	Ai là người
(1) best known	(1) kố tiẫng nyâk	(1) có tiếng nhất
(2) most trustworthy	(2) dáang tín nyiệm nyâk	(2) đáng tín-nhiệm nhất
(3) most reliable	(3) dáang tin kậy nyâk	(3) đáng tin cậy nhất
in	trawng	trong
(1) this area	(1) vùwng nàay	(1) vùng này
(2) this village	(2) làang nàay	(2) làng này
(3) the nearest hamlet	(3) sóm gẫn dây nyâk	(3) xóm gần đây nhất

2

(4) the nearest town?	(4) thànn-fố gẫn dây nyâk?	(4) thành-phố gần đây nhất?
10. We wish to talk with him.	Chúwng toy muẫng nóy chwiậng vóy âwng ây.	Chúng tôi muốn nói chuyện với ông ấy.
11. We are American soldiers. There are a lot of American troops in this area.	Chúwng toy là lînn Mẽe. Kố nyiw binn-shẽe trawng vùwng nàay.	Chúng tôi là lính Mỹ. Có nhiều binh-sĩ Mỹ trong vùng này.
12. Are there any (1) resistance forces (2) individuals (3) groups (4) fighters (5) patriots (6) guerrillas (7) rebels (8) outlaws (9) escapees (10) deserters in the (1) woods (2) plains (3) hills (4) mountains (5) villages?	Kố (1) kwân kháang chiẫn (2) nyiw ngiòy (3) tuáan kwân (4) chiẫn-shĩ (5) nhà áay-kwâk (6) kwân yu-kík (7) khân fiẫng luạan (8) kẻ shẫwng ngwàay-vàwng fáap-luậk (9) tùe vuậk ngụk (10) lînn dàaw ngũ trawng (1) rừng (2) ruậng (3) dòy (4) núi (5) làang/ khâwng?	Có (1) quân kháng chiến (2) nhiều người (3) toán quân (4) chiến-sĩ (5) nhà ái-quốc (6) quân du-kích (7) quân phiến loạn (8) kẻ sống ngoài vòng pháp-luật (9) tù vượt ngục (10) lính đào ngũ trong (1) rừng (2) ruộng (3) đồi (4) núi (5) làng/ không?

3

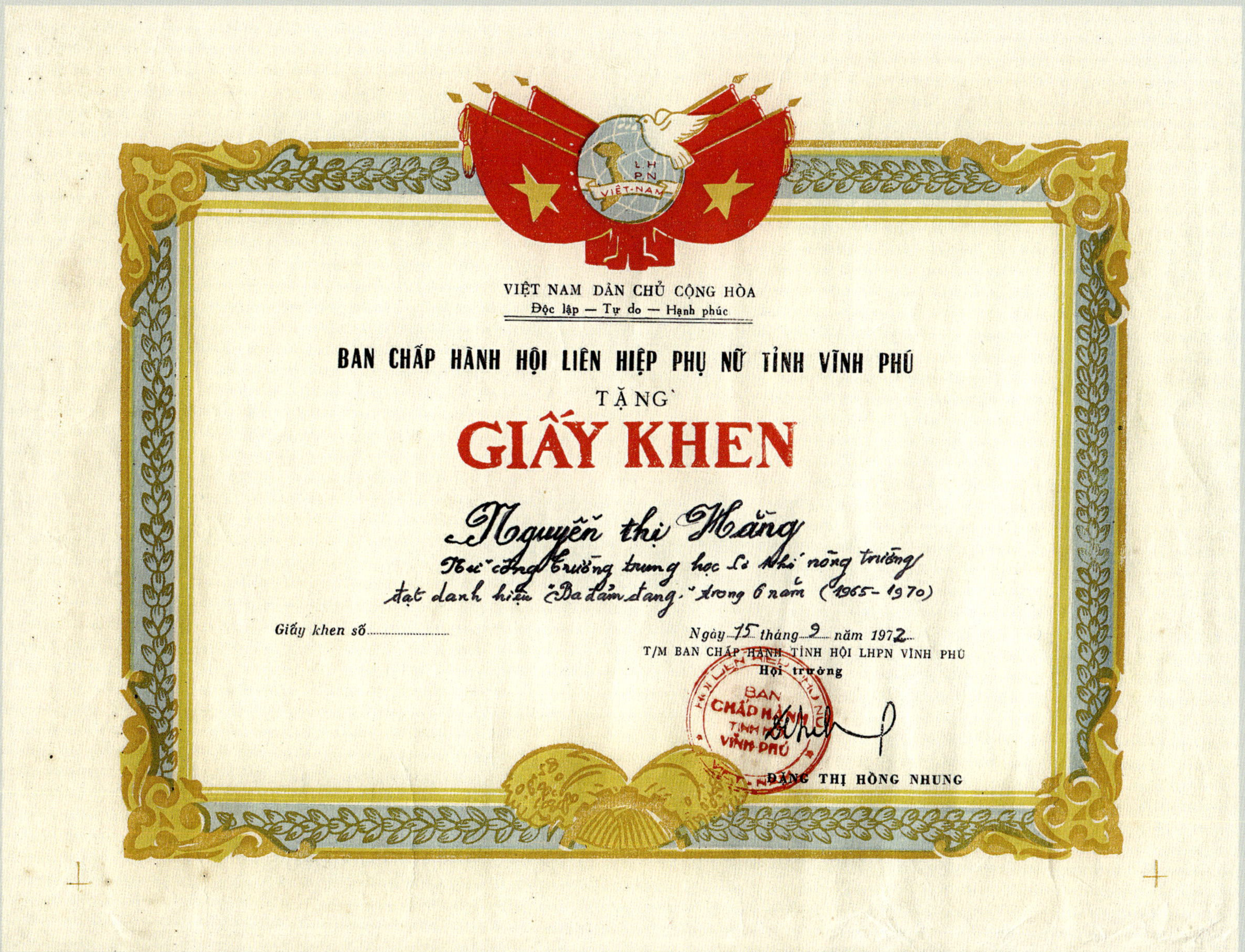

VIỆT NAM DÂN CHỦ CỘNG HÒA
Độc lập — Tự do — Hạnh phúc

BAN CHẤP HÀNH HỘI LIÊN HIỆP PHỤ NỮ TỈNH VĨNH PHÚ

TẶNG

GIẤY KHEN

Nguyễn thị Măng

Nữ công trường trung học cơ khí nông trường
đạt danh hiệu "Ba đảm đang" trong 6 năm (1965-1970)

Giấy khen số.........................

Ngày 15 tháng 9 năm 1972
T/M BAN CHẤP HÀNH TỈNH HỘI LHPN VĨNH PHÚ
Hội trưởng

ĐẶNG THỊ HỒNG NHUNG

P.A.V.N. LETTER OF APPRECIATION

These letters serve as a lower class of award, ranking below a Certificate of Commendation and a Verbal Appraisal (usually delivered in front of an assembled unit). They vary in quality of paper and intricacy of design (the more ornate, the greater the "appreciation"). For translation, see page 156.

CHAPTER 5

A.R.V.N.

BY COMMITTING THE SPECIAL FORCES' COMBAT ADVISORS TO TRAINING AND UPGRADING THE ARMY OF THE REPUBLIC OF VIETNAM (A.R.V.N.), PRESIDENT KENNEDY ALSO TIED THE U.S. TIGHTLY TO THE DIEM REGIME. UNFORTUNATELY, DIEM'S ARMY WAS MORE OF A POLITICAL TOOL THAN AN EFFECTIVE FIGHTING FORCE AND THE GREEN BERET INSTRUCTORS WERE NOT HAPPY TO BE SENT TO VIETNAM TO TEACH BASIC TRAINING WITH WEAPONS AND TACTICS TO A RECRUIT ARMY.

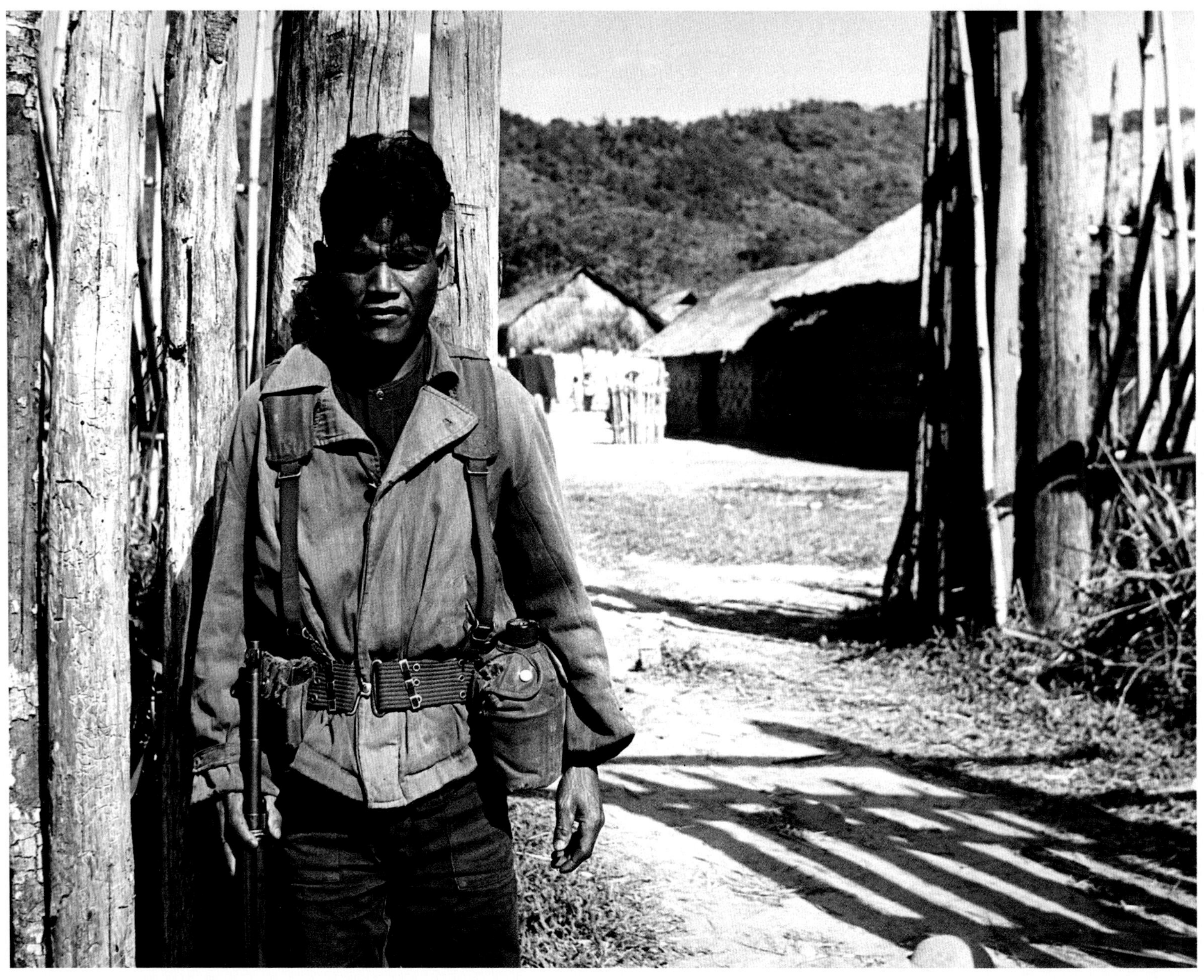

Early trainees were mostly issued World War II weapons. The small, slender A.R.V.N. lugged M1 Garand rifles and the lighter, more popular M1 carbine. Thompson M1 submachine guns, M3 .45 caliber "grease guns," and other old gear were shipped in from musty warehouses. As the Green Berets worked with these new soldiers they came to admire their willingness to learn and their individual fighting spirit. However, a cumbersome chain of command, systemic corruption, and political interference all crippled the force.

It was reported that one A.R.V.N. officer had led an effective raid, defeated the Viet Cong (V.C.) and returned with very few casualties. Instead of a reward, he was dressed down by Diem and warned against having any more casualties. Broken, the officer faded back into the growing ranks of gun-shy commanders.

In January, 1963, Diem was informed of a V.C. radio station established in the village of Ap Bac in the Plain of Reeds, which was guarded by only a company-size force. Anticipating a great

"GREEN BERET" SPECIAL FORCES

Once President Kennedy committed support to the government of South Vietnam, the Military Assistance Command Vietnam (M.A.C.V.) already in place ballooned from 342 to over 3,000. These Special Forces advisors were originally tasked as an elite commando unit for operating behind enemy lines and now, the highly trained paratroopers had to create an army from the South Vietnamese Civil Guard and Self-Defense Force cadres brought in from the provinces. Although these American "Green Beret" troops accepted the job reluctantly, before long the A.R.V.N. were reorganized, retrained, rearmed, and in the field.

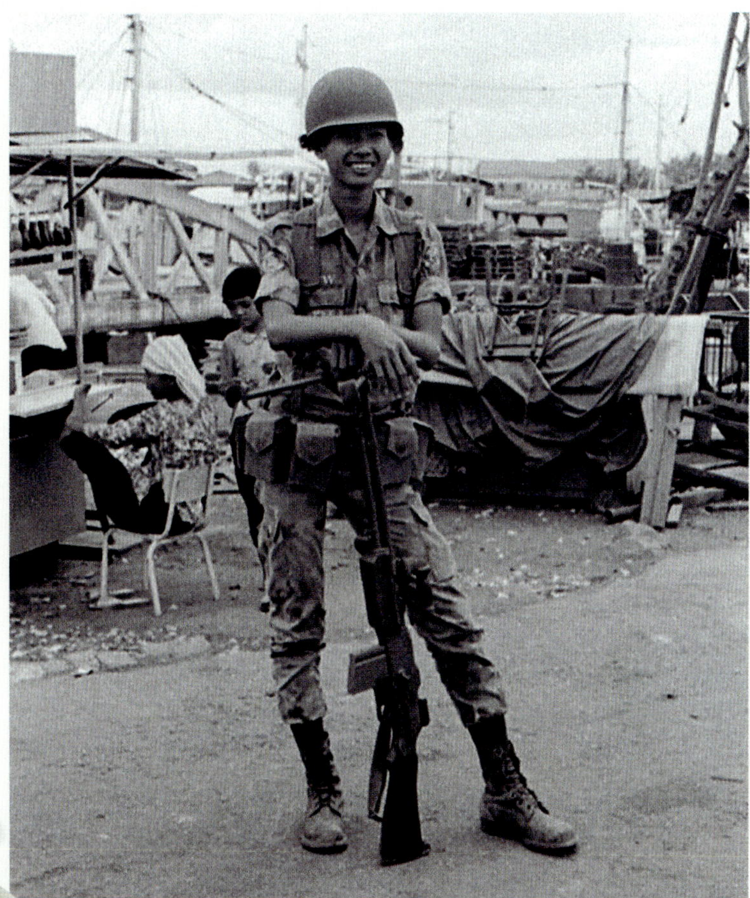

11th Inf Reg
AP TEN THOI
V.C. Positions
4–2nd Cavalry
AP BAC
AP TAN HIEP
Retreating V.C.
Task Force B
Task Force A

MAP KEY
V.C.
A.R.V.N. marched in
A.R.V.N. flown in
4–2nd M113 APCs
Landing Zone
"Hot" Landing Zone

Opposite: A young A.R.V.N. soldier guards the gate to a remote village. He wears a standard issue GI tropical jacket with side pockets, a model 1956 utility web belt, model 1943 equipment suspenders, and a 1910 aluminum one quart canteen with a 1943 canvas cover. The rifle at his side appears to be a Garand M1 rifle, .30 caliber, clip-fed, air-cooled, gas operated, semi-automatic weapon that holds eight rounds and weighs 9.6 pounds.

Above: An A.R.V.N. soldier in full combat uniform. A.R.V.N. troops were smaller in stature than the American soldiers so uniforms had to be considerably altered. He wears a standard M1 steel helmet, 1943 equipment suspenders and web utility belt supporting many ammo pouches for his Browning Automatic Rifle. This 11-pound rifle with bi-pod fired a .3006 caliber round from a 20-round box magazine. On his feet are full lace-up jungle boots.

Left: The Battle of Ap Bac showed the weaknesses of the A.R.V.N. forces. The map shows forces converging on the supposedly weak V.C. position, but bad timing, poor intelligence, and lack of fighting spirit among their officers doomed the A.R.V.N. operation.

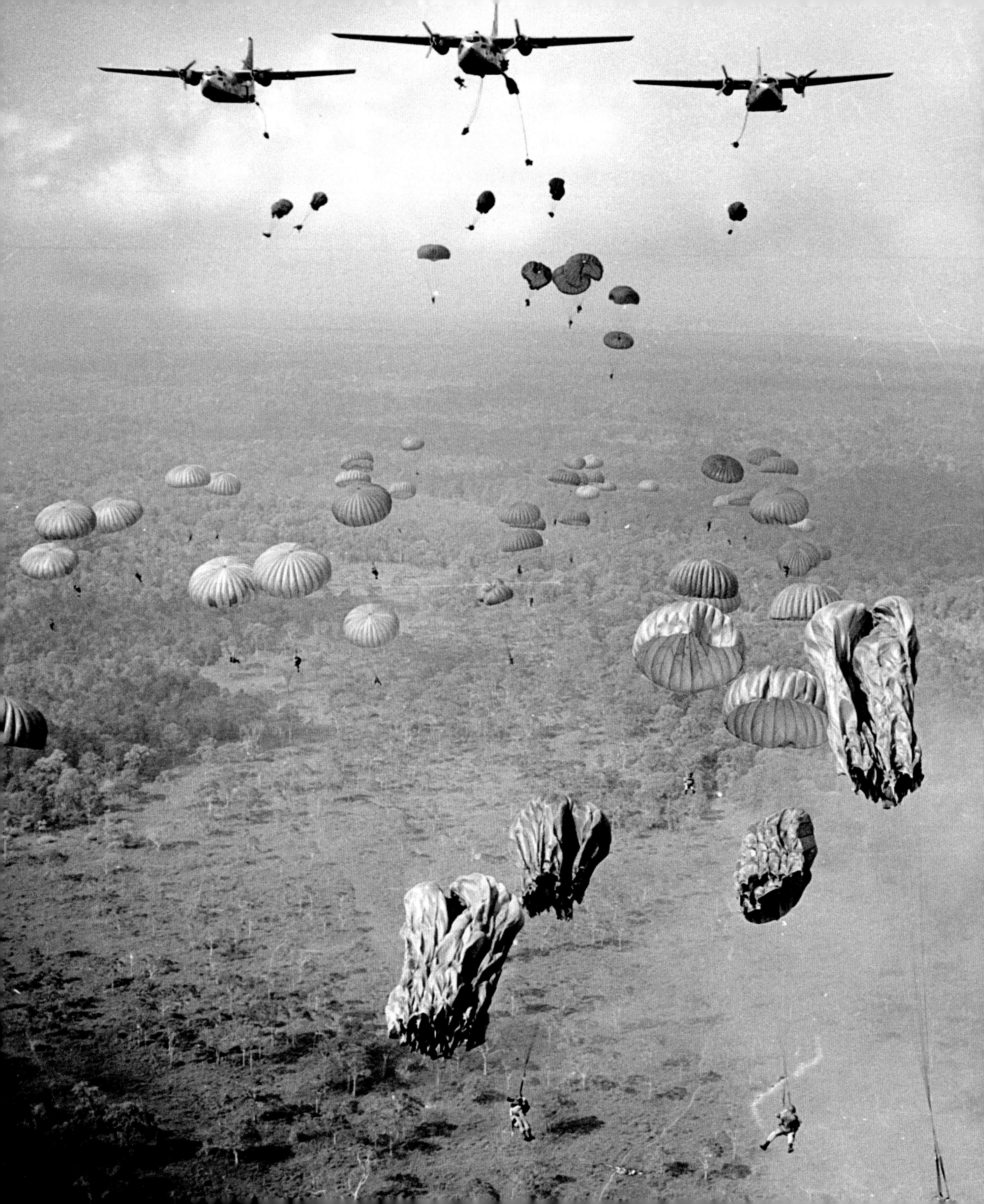

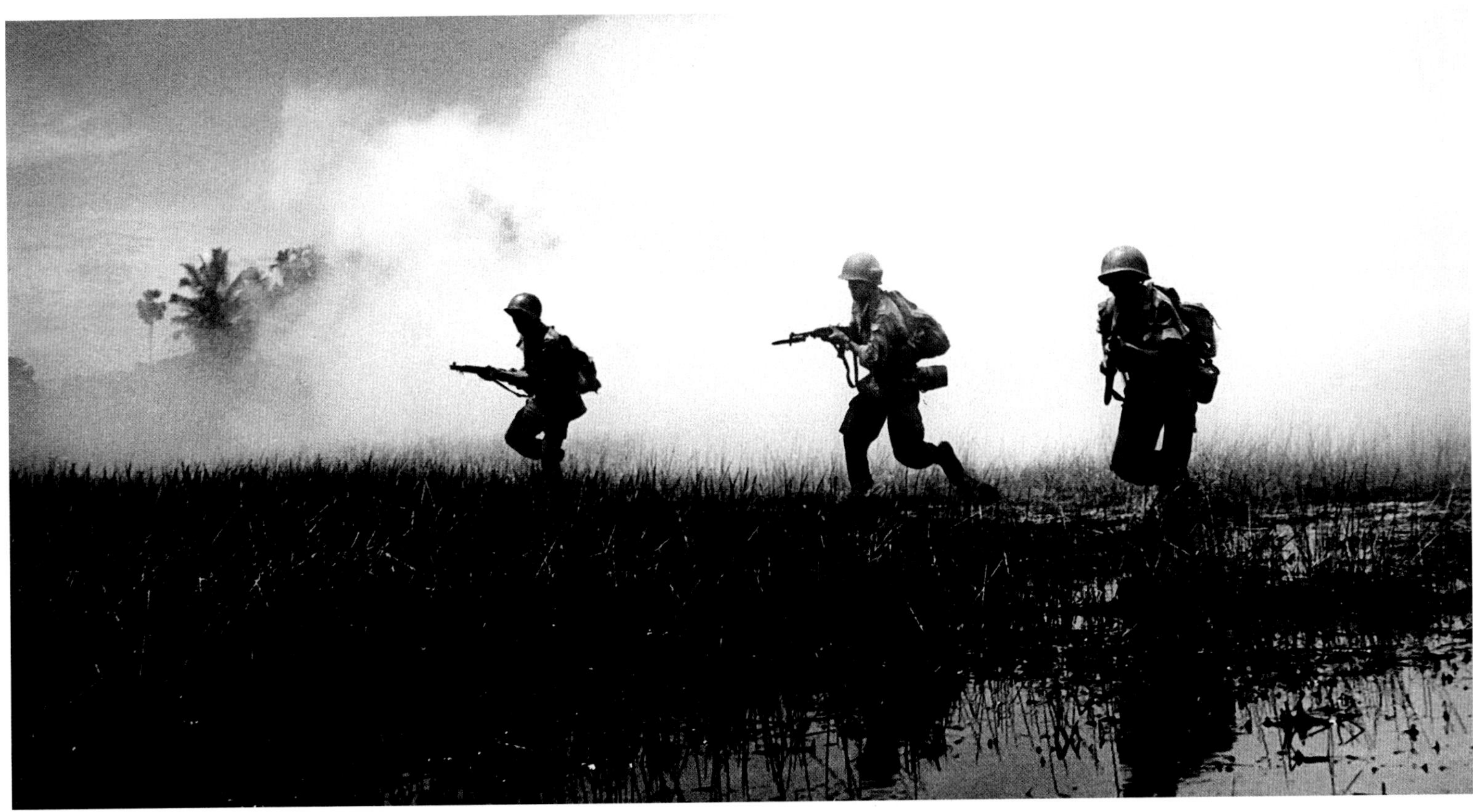

public relations coup for himself and his army, he ordered the station to be destroyed.

American advisors helped assemble a crushing superiority of A.R.V.N. infantry, Rangers, armor, helicopters, and artillery support. Fifty-one advisors went along to direct the assault. Faulty A.R.V.N. intelligence doomed the attack before the first chopper took off. The radio station was protected, not by a company of scruffy guerrillas, but the 514th Viet Cong Regular Battalion of 400 hardened veterans.

As the assault roared in, five helicopters were shot down. A.R.V.N. troops hit the ground running—in all directions—and their officers retreated to cover. American advisors argued to press the attack. Not obliged to follow those suggestions, the A.R.V.N. officers preferred zero casualties. They adopted a similar tactic concerning their armor—no dents and no scratches. Transports zoomed over the battlefield bringing a paratrooper drop that landed somewhere in the distance; then came a leisurely artillery barrage of about four shells every hour.

The V.C. finally went away after causing 65 dead A.R.V.N. and over 100 wounded. Three Americans died, six were wounded, and extensive matériel was lost, including the five destroyed helicopters and 11 more damaged. The V.C. carried away their dead and wounded, but blood trails were few. Diem raged—mostly at the media who reported the debacle. It would take a change of regime to enable A.R.V.N. officers to shoulder their share of the war, and more.

WEAPONS USED BY A.R.V.N.

With the A.R.V.N. growing in number and carrying out missions, they needed additional weapons. To meet this need, surplus arms were shipped from the U.S. including the venerable M1 Garand, a huge load for the smaller-stature Vietnamese. The rifle also fired a powerful .3006 cartridge. More suitable were the .30 caliber M1 carbine and the M1A1 folding stock carbine for airborne troops. Besides crew-served Browning machine guns, the rugged Thompson submachine gun was a favorite together with the .45 caliber "grease gun," howitzers and medium tanks provided artillery, and armed T-28 propeller-driven aircraft added close air support to the infantry and armor.

Opposite: C-119 Flying Boxcars drop sticks of A.R.V.N. paratroopers in an attack on Tay Ninh in 1963. Paratroopers were used in the A.R.V.N.'s first major stand-up battle at Ap Bac that same year. They were dropped too far from the combat area to be useful. Other A.R.V.N. units in the attack were routed by the N.V.A. and V.C. because of bad intelligence and poor leadership.

Above: A.R.V.N. troops attacking with Garand M1 rifles and M1 carbines with bayonets during a training exercise in 1966. The individual A.R.V.N. trooper was tough, brave, and effective under good leadership. But the officer corps was riddled with corruption and self-importance. Under Diem's regime officers were punished for taking casualties and preferred to run away rather than risk losing their jobs.

U.S. ENTANGLEMENT INCREASES

THE DIEM REGIME IN SAIGON HAD RECEIVED OVER $400 MILLION IN AID AND THE AP BAC DEBACLE FUELED THE AMERICAN PRESS WITH QUESTIONS. WHY STAY IN VIETNAM BACKING AN ARMY THAT WON'T FIGHT? WHY CONTINUE TO SUPPORT AN OPPRESSIVE GOVERNMENT AND A COUNTRY IN CHAOS? WHY DON'T WE EITHER GET OUT NOW, OR TAKE OVER THE WHOLE WAR AND END IT?

In May, 1963, conflict between the Buddhist majority and the South's Catholic minority escalated into very public clashes. Diem, a Catholic, had maintained the French laws that favored Catholics and ensured most government vacancies were filled with his coreligionists. Buddhist monks focused international attention on their crisis by soaking themselves with gasoline and setting themselves alight. The government tried to prevent films or stories about these suicides from leaving the country.

In the United States, the Diem government's religious policies, general corruption and mismanagement of the A.R.V.N. became unsupportable. Stuck with the "domino theory" that Communists would take over the world if Vietnam fell, wheels and words were set in motion. A group of disgruntled generals, led by General Duong Van Minh ("Big Minh"), ordered the surrounding of the Saigon Presidential Palace. Diem and his brother Nhu fled and hid. With the promise of safe conduct both men finally surrendered and were immediately shot. "Big Minh" became president until he was bloodlessly deposed by General Nguyen Khanh. The new President of South Vietnam ramped up his demands for greater U.S. participation.

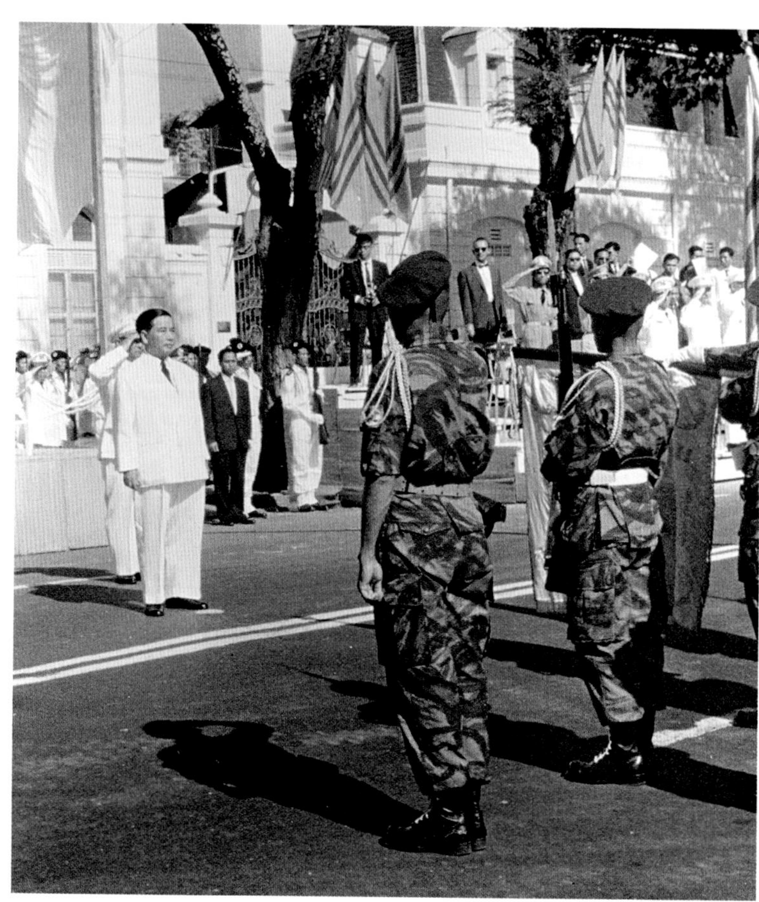

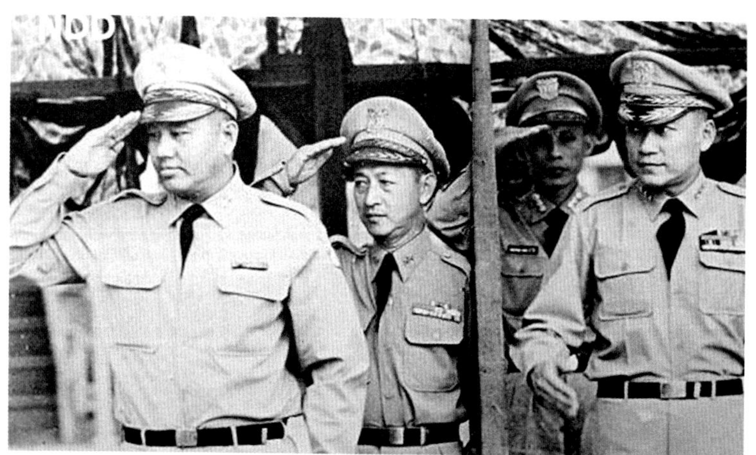

Above: President Diem accepts the salute of the Air Force Color Guard symbolizing a pledge of loyalty to the government following the military unrest among the general staff.

Left: In the confusion that followed President Diem's assassination, General Duong Van "Big" Minh took power, but was only the first in a succession of A.R.V.N. generals to assume the presidency of South Vietnam before President Thieu was sworn in as the U.S.-chosen successor.

Opposite: A Viet Cong is flushed from his hiding place in a field by a U.S. soldier. The number of U.S. "advisors" stationed in Vietnam to ovesee creation and training of the A.R.V.N. grew from hundreds to thousands before actual combat troops were committed to combat in 1965.

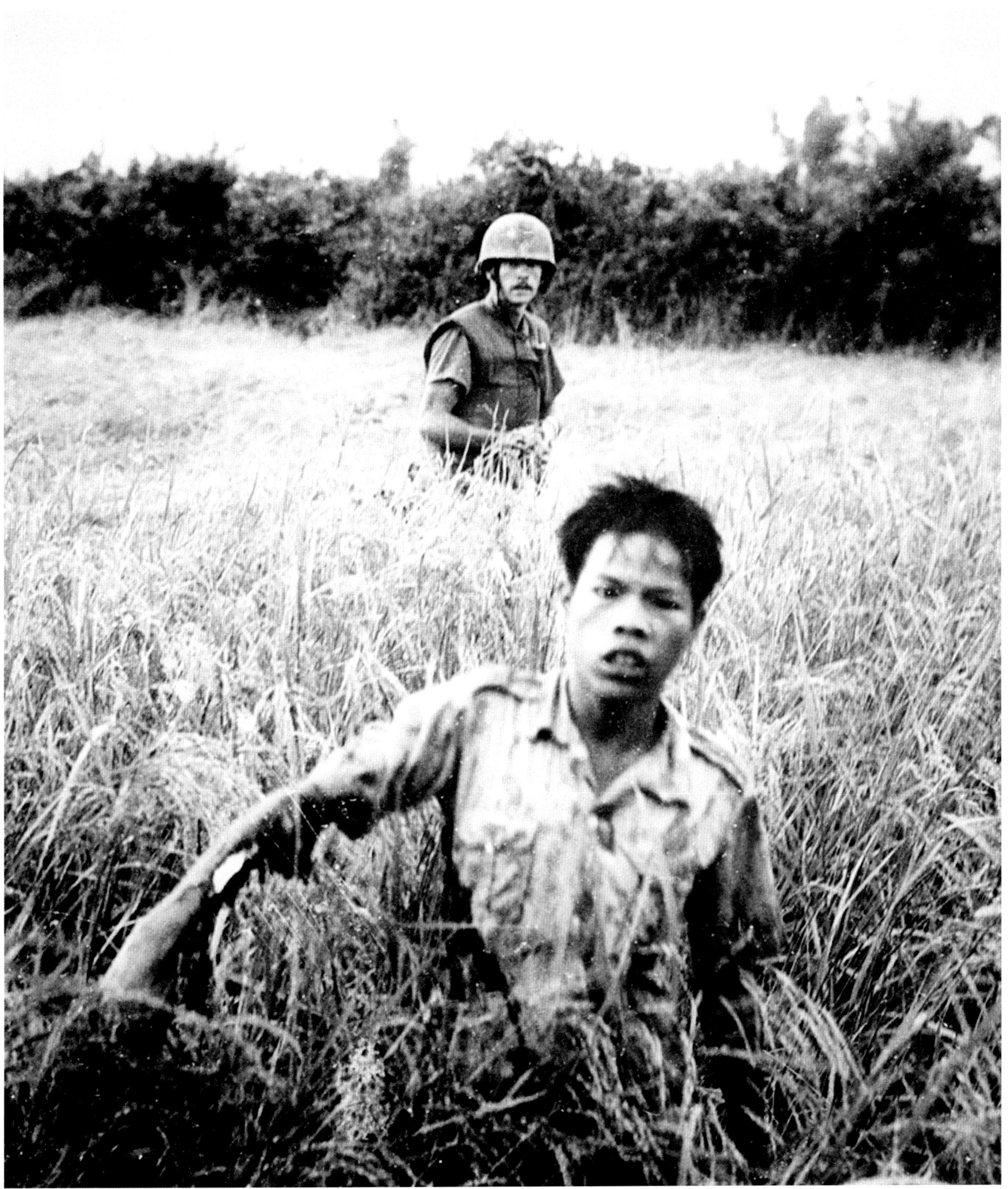

The assassination of President John F. Kennedy on November 22, 1963—three weeks after Diem's death—handed the situation in Vietnam to Vice President Lyndon Johnson. He promised, "American boys will not be sent to Asia to do what Asian boys ought to be doing for themselves."

Secretary of Defense Robert McNamara, and General Maxwell Taylor (now Chairman of the Joint Chiefs of Staff) had visited Vietnam and reported to President Kennedy on October 7, 1963. They had suggested a phased withdrawal of U.S. troops by 1965. Ultimately, that report was considered unworkable by the C.I.A. and pessimistic military authorities, eventually resulting in Johnson's full commitment of U.S. financial and logistical aid to Saigon. While Johnson ran for reelection in 1964, U.S.-sponsored escalation of the war against the North continued.

That escalation included OPLAN-34A, a covert operation of commando raids into the North to kidnap key officials, destroy specific bridges, port facilities, and warehouses as the Viet Cong had done in the South. Another phase of OPLAN had American U-2 spy planes pinpoint targets in North Vietnam for Laotian T-28 aircraft armed with 500 pound bombs flown by Thai and American mercenary pilots in August, 1964. The third part of OPLAN sent American destroyers U.S.S. *Maddox* and U.S.S. *Turner Joy* into the Beibu Gulf (Gulf of Tonkin) to gather information about North Vietnamese ports and docks for possible raids.

LYNDON B. JOHNSON ASSUMES COMMAND

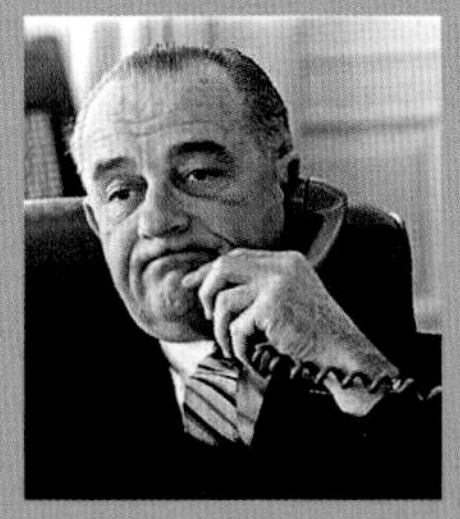

With Kennedy's death, President Lyndon Johnson took over the Vietnam build-up and political situation. The overall picture had deteriorated by the time he took control. Religious oppression of the Buddhist Monks and President Diem's assassination demonstrated the internal strife, while repeated N.V.A. and V.C. attacks caused the President to authorize Operation Rolling Thunder bombing raids. He reacted to the lack of A.R.V.N. success and Ho Chi Minh's rejection of his personal communications with additional troops, raising numbers from 180,000 at the end of 1965 to 550,000 in 1968. The N.V.A.'s failed Tet Offensive that year raised the level of anti-war sentiment at home causing him to retire from the presidency at the end of his term.

Below: Robert McNamara (center) visits Vietnam on a fact-finding tour. McNamara was Secretary of Defense during the Kennedy and Johnson administration. A key architect of early U.S. policy in Vietnam, he supported the U.S. military involvement. When escalation failed to bring results, and as resistance to the war mounted at home, McNamara began to push for a negotiated solution.

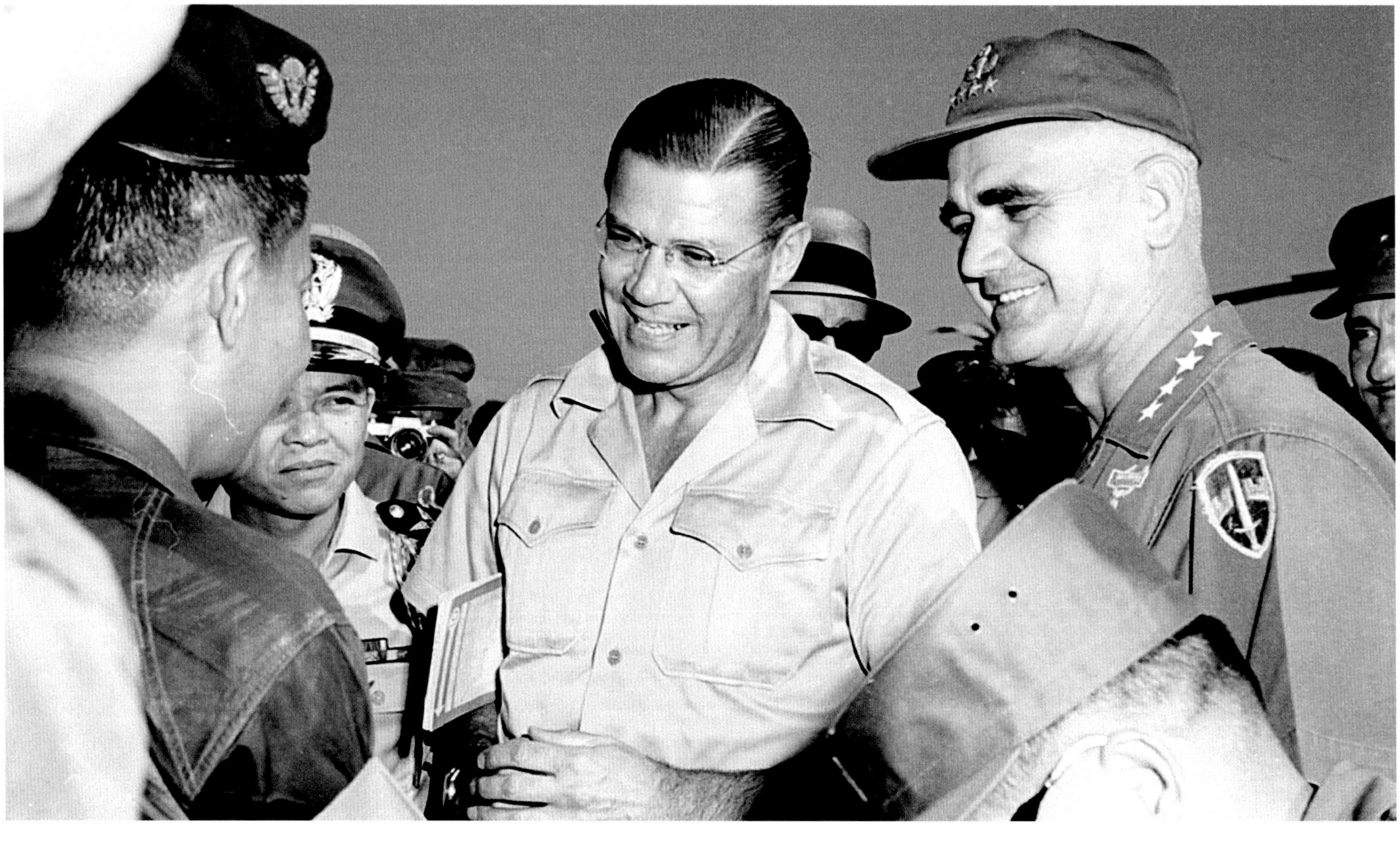

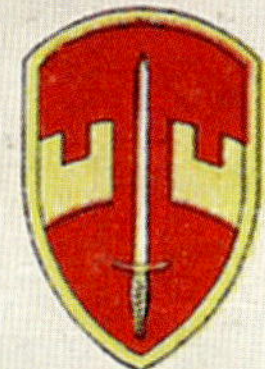

NINE RULES

FOR PERSONNEL OF US MILITARY ASSISTANCE COMMAND, VIETNAM

The Vietnamese have paid a heavy price in suffering for their long fight against the communists. We military men are in Vietnam now because their government has asked us to help its soldiers and people in winning their struggle. The Viet Cong will attempt to turn the Vietnamese people against you. You can defeat them at every turn by the strength, understanding, and generosity you display with the people. Here are nine simple rules:

DISTRIBUTION — 1 to each member of the United States Armed Forces in Vietnam

NINE RULES

1. Remember we are guests here: We make no demands and seek no special treatment.
2. Join with the people! Understand their life, use phrases from their language and honor their customs and laws.
3. Treat women with politeness and respect.
4. Make personal friends among the soldiers and common people.
5. Always give the Vietnamese the right of way.
6. Be alert to security and ready to react with your military skill.
7. Don't attract attention by loud, rude or unusual behavior.
8. Avoid separating yourself from the people by a display of wealth or privilege.
9. Above all else you are members of the U S Military Forces on a difficult mission, responsible for all your official and personal actions. Reflect honor upon yourself and the United States of America.

THE COMMON STRUGGLE

NATIONS OF THE FAR EAST HELP SOUTH VIETNAM REPEL COMMUNIST AGGRESSION

Asian Military Assistance Comes From...

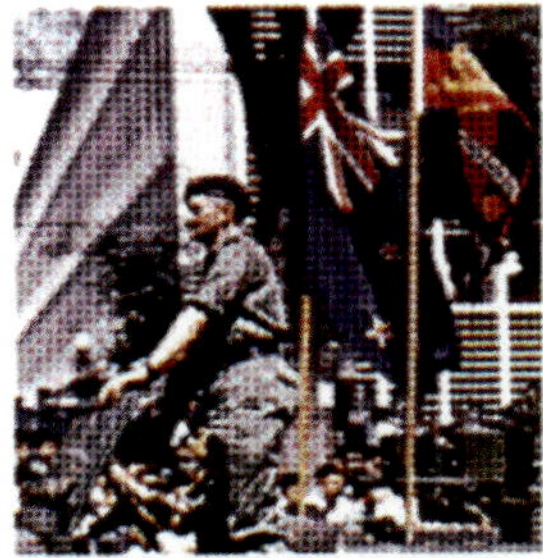

NEW ZEALAND

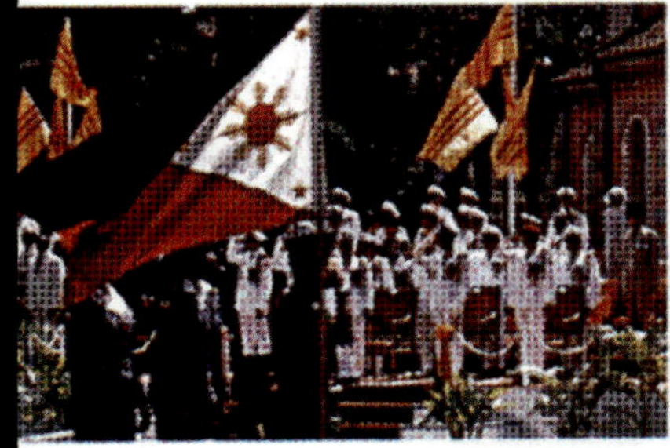

PHILIPPINES

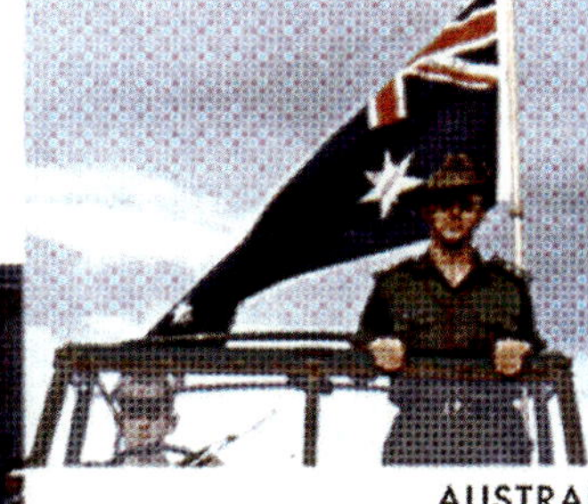

AUSTRALIA

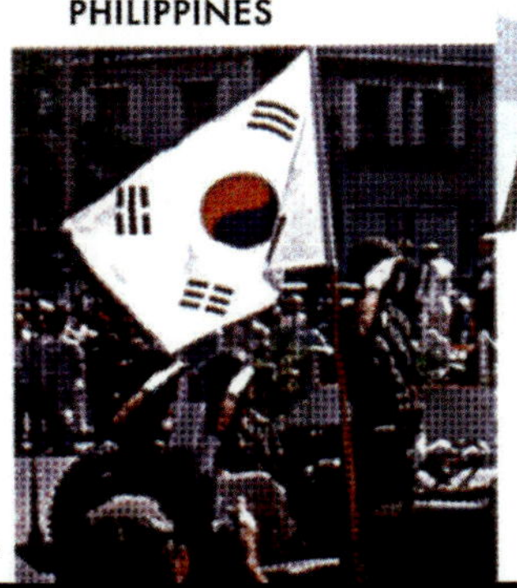

SOUTH KOREA

G.I. 9-RULES CARD

Every soldier leaving for Vietnam from 1965 on received this pocket-size card called the "Nine Rules." It lists the behavior steps needed to be taken by U.S. soldiers to make a good impression on Vietnamese in their country.

COMMON STRUGGLE POSTER

A South Vietnam propaganda poster demonstrating the Australian, New Zealand, South Korean, and Philippines contributions to the war against North Vietnam Communism.

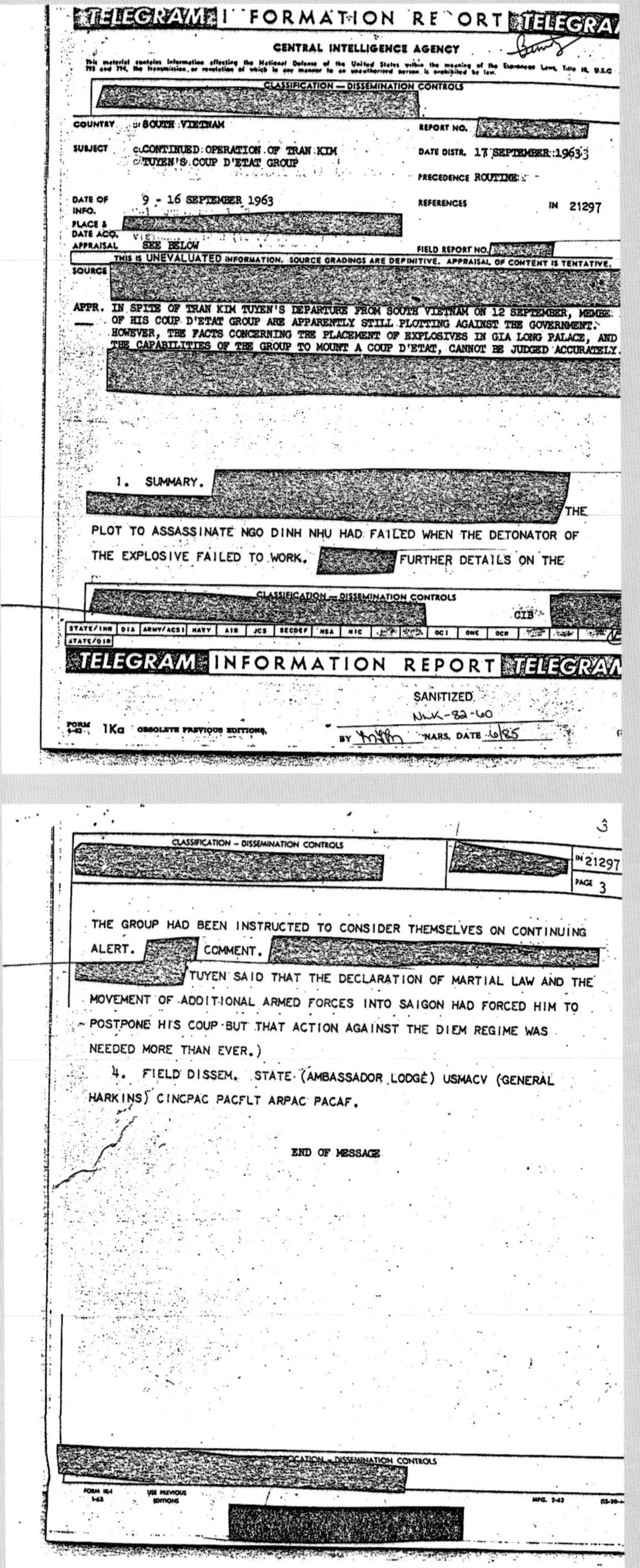

TELEGRAM I FORMATION RE ORT TELEGRA

CENTRAL INTELLIGENCE AGENCY

This material contains information affecting the National Defense of the United States within the meaning of the Espionage Laws, Title 18, U.S.C. 793 and 794, the transmission or revelation of which in any manner to an unauthorized person is prohibited by law.

CLASSIFICATION — DISSEMINATION CONTROLS

COUNTRY SOUTH VIETNAM

REPORT NO.

SUBJECT CONTINUED OPERATION OF TRAN KIM TUYEN'S COUP D'ETAT GROUP

DATE DISTR. 17 SEPTEMBER 1963

PRECEDENCE ROUTINE

DATE OF INFO. 9 - 16 SEPTEMBER 1963

REFERENCES IN 21297

PLACE & DATE ACQ.

APPRAISAL SEE BELOW

FIELD REPORT NO.

THIS IS UNEVALUATED INFORMATION. SOURCE GRADINGS ARE DEFINITIVE. APPRAISAL OF CONTENT IS TENTATIVE.

SOURCE

APPR. IN SPITE OF TRAN KIM TUYEN'S DEPARTURE FROM SOUTH VIETNAM ON 12 SEPTEMBER, MEMBE OF HIS COUP D'ETAT GROUP ARE APPARENTLY STILL PLOTTING AGAINST THE GOVERNMENT. HOWEVER, THE FACTS CONCERNING THE PLACEMENT OF EXPLOSIVES IN GIA LONG PALACE, AND THE CAPABILITIES OF THE GROUP TO MOUNT A COUP D'ETAT, CANNOT BE JUDGED ACCURATELY.

1. SUMMARY. THE PLOT TO ASSASSINATE NGO DINH NHU HAD FAILED WHEN THE DETONATOR OF THE EXPLOSIVE FAILED TO WORK. FURTHER DETAILS ON THE

CLASSIFICATION — DISSEMINATION CONTROLS

CIB

STATE/INR DIA ARMY/ACSI NAVY AIR JCS SECDEF NSA NIC OCI ONE OCR

STATE/DIR

TELEGRAM INFORMATION REPORT TELEGRAM

SANITIZED NLK-82-60

BY NARS, DATE 6/85

FORM 1-63 1Ka OBSOLETE PREVIOUS EDITIONS.

3

CLASSIFICATION – DISSEMINATION CONTROLS

IN 21297

PAGE 3

THE GROUP HAD BEEN INSTRUCTED TO CONSIDER THEMSELVES ON CONTINUING ALERT. COMMENT. TUYEN SAID THAT THE DECLARATION OF MARTIAL LAW AND THE MOVEMENT OF ADDITIONAL ARMED FORCES INTO SAIGON HAD FORCED HIM TO POSTPONE HIS COUP BUT THAT ACTION AGAINST THE DIEM REGIME WAS NEEDED MORE THAN EVER.)

4. FIELD DISSEM. STATE (AMBASSADOR LODGE) USMACV (GENERAL HARKINS) CINCPAC PACFLT ARPAC PACAF.

END OF MESSAGE

CLASSIFICATION – DISSEMINATION CONTROLS

FORM 1-63 USE PREVIOUS EDITIONS

C.I.A. DIEM REPORT 1963

A C.I.A. telegram dated September 16, 1963, speaks of assassination attempts on President Diem by plotters seeking to overturn the government. The C.I.A. supported this activity.

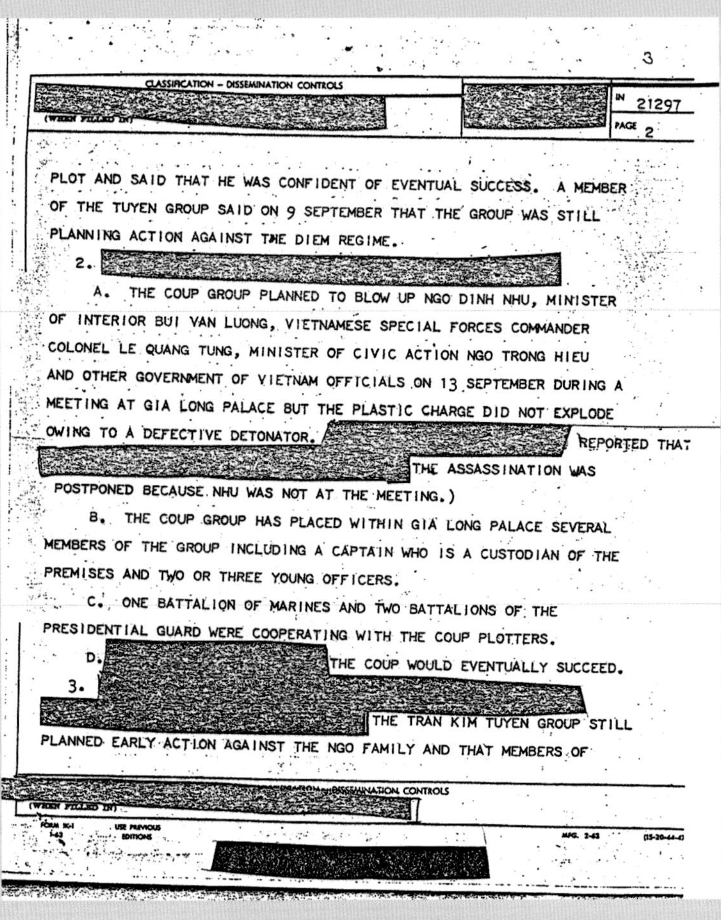

3

CLASSIFICATION – DISSEMINATION CONTROLS

(WHEN FILLED IN)

IN 21297

PAGE 2

PLOT AND SAID THAT HE WAS CONFIDENT OF EVENTUAL SUCCESS. A MEMBER OF THE TUYEN GROUP SAID ON 9 SEPTEMBER THAT THE GROUP WAS STILL PLANNING ACTION AGAINST THE DIEM REGIME.

2.

A. THE COUP GROUP PLANNED TO BLOW UP NGO DINH NHU, MINISTER OF INTERIOR BUI VAN LUONG, VIETNAMESE SPECIAL FORCES COMMANDER COLONEL LE QUANG TUNG, MINISTER OF CIVIC ACTION NGO TRONG HIEU AND OTHER GOVERNMENT OF VIETNAM OFFICIALS ON 13 SEPTEMBER DURING A MEETING AT GIA LONG PALACE BUT THE PLASTIC CHARGE DID NOT EXPLODE OWING TO A DEFECTIVE DETONATOR. REPORTED THAT THE ASSASSINATION WAS POSTPONED BECAUSE NHU WAS NOT AT THE MEETING.)

B. THE COUP GROUP HAS PLACED WITHIN GIA LONG PALACE SEVERAL MEMBERS OF THE GROUP INCLUDING A CAPTAIN WHO IS A CUSTODIAN OF THE PREMISES AND TWO OR THREE YOUNG OFFICERS.

C. ONE BATTALION OF MARINES AND TWO BATTALIONS OF THE PRESIDENTIAL GUARD WERE COOPERATING WITH THE COUP PLOTTERS.

D. THE COUP WOULD EVENTUALLY SUCCEED.

3. THE TRAN KIM TUYEN GROUP STILL PLANNED EARLY ACTION AGAINST THE NGO FAMILY AND THAT MEMBERS OF

DISSEMINATION CONTROLS

(WHEN FILLED IN)

FORM 1-63 USE PREVIOUS EDITIONS

BUDDHIST MONK REVOLT

The Buddhist "revolt" began on May 8, 1963, when Diem troops fired into a crowd of Buddhists protesting a government law prohibiting flying religious flags. President Diem, his family and political cronies were Catholic and had begun a campaign of oppression against the powerful Buddhists. He blamed the shooting on the Viet Cong. The monks rioted in the streets causing more bloodshed. One afternoon, Thich Quang Duc, an elderly monk, sat in the busy street and set himself afire. World-wide scorn fell on Diem and on the U.S. for supporting Diem. Diem refused to end the persecution, bringing himself closer to assassination and ruin for his regime.

Below: Another Buddhist monk follows Thich Quang Duc's example to make a political statement against the Catholic regime of President Diem by immolating himself with gasoline in a busy street in downtown Saigon. Diem feared the power of the Buddhist monks and began persecuting them. A number of riots occurred and monasteries were closed.

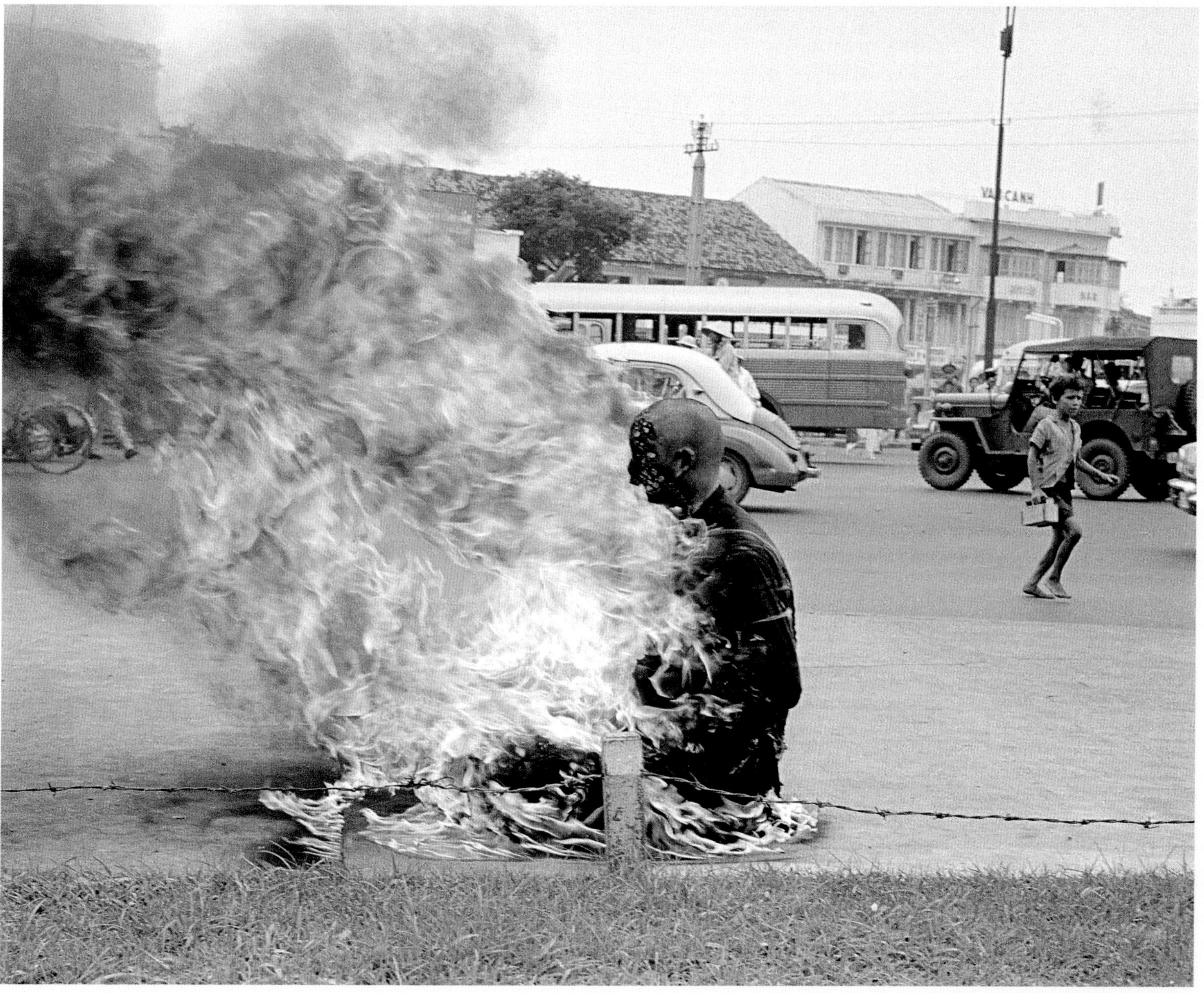

BEIBU GULF (GULF OF TONKIN)

AT 16:30 HOURS ON AUGUST 2, 1964, THE DESTROYER U.S.S. *MADDOX* CRUISED THE BEIBU GULF (GULF OF TONKIN) 28 MILES OFF THE COAST OF NORTH VIETNAM. THE THIRD PHASE OF OPLAN-34A—RETALIATORY RAIDS AGAINST THE NORTH VIETNAMESE BY ELEMENTS OF THE A.R.V.N.—CALLED FOR A.R.V.N. COMMANDO ATTACKS AGAINST NORTH VIETNAMESE COASTAL INSTALLATIONS. A RAID HAD OCCURRED TWO DAYS EARLIER NEAR THE PORT OF VINH AND TWO OFFSHORE ISLANDS, HON ME AND HON NGU. THE *MADDOX* WAS ON STATION AS PART OF AN ONGOING SERIES OF PATROLS, CODE-NAMED "DESOTO," TO MONITOR ELECTRONIC ACTIVITY ALONG THE COAST. ON THIS DAY, THAT MONITORING HAD A DUAL PURPOSE "...SPECIFICALLY TO RECORD NORTH VIETNAMESE RADAR AND OTHER ELECTRONIC EMISSIONS WHICH COULD BE EXPECTED TO SPIKE AFTER AN (OPLAN) 34-A RAID."

The destroyer's radar reported that apparently hostile contacts moving at high speed were closing. The *Maddox* increased speed from 10 to 25 knots but the contacts continued to close. At a range of eight miles they were identified as three North Vietnamese P-4 patrol boats mounting torpedoes and 12.7mm machine guns and approaching at their top speed of 40 knots. Fire control radar took over. At 9,800 yards, *Maddox* fired three warning shots from a five-inch gun. Ignoring the shots, the patrol boats swung from line astern and began their attack.

Below: The U.S.S. *Maddox* (DD-731) is an Allen M. Sumner-class destroyer named for Captain William A. T. Maddox, U.S.M.C. She was laid down by the Bath Iron Works Corporation at Bath in Maine on October 28, 1943, launched on March 19, 1944. As she cruised in international waters in the Tonkin Gulf on August 2, 1964, she was reportedly attacked by three North Vietnamese torpedo boats, an action which became known as the Gulf of Tonkin Incident and led to the escalation of U.S. involvement in Vietnam.

Opposite: The U.S.S. *Ticonderoga* (CV-14) refuels from Navy tanker U.S.S. *Ashtabula* in the Tonkin Gulf. The *Ticonderoga* sent F-8E Crusader jets to the aid of the U.S.S. *Maddox* following the destroyer's reported brief firefight. Planes from the *Ticonderoga* also attacked North Vietnamese shore installations and a torpedo boat base at Vinh, sinking eight boats at the dock.

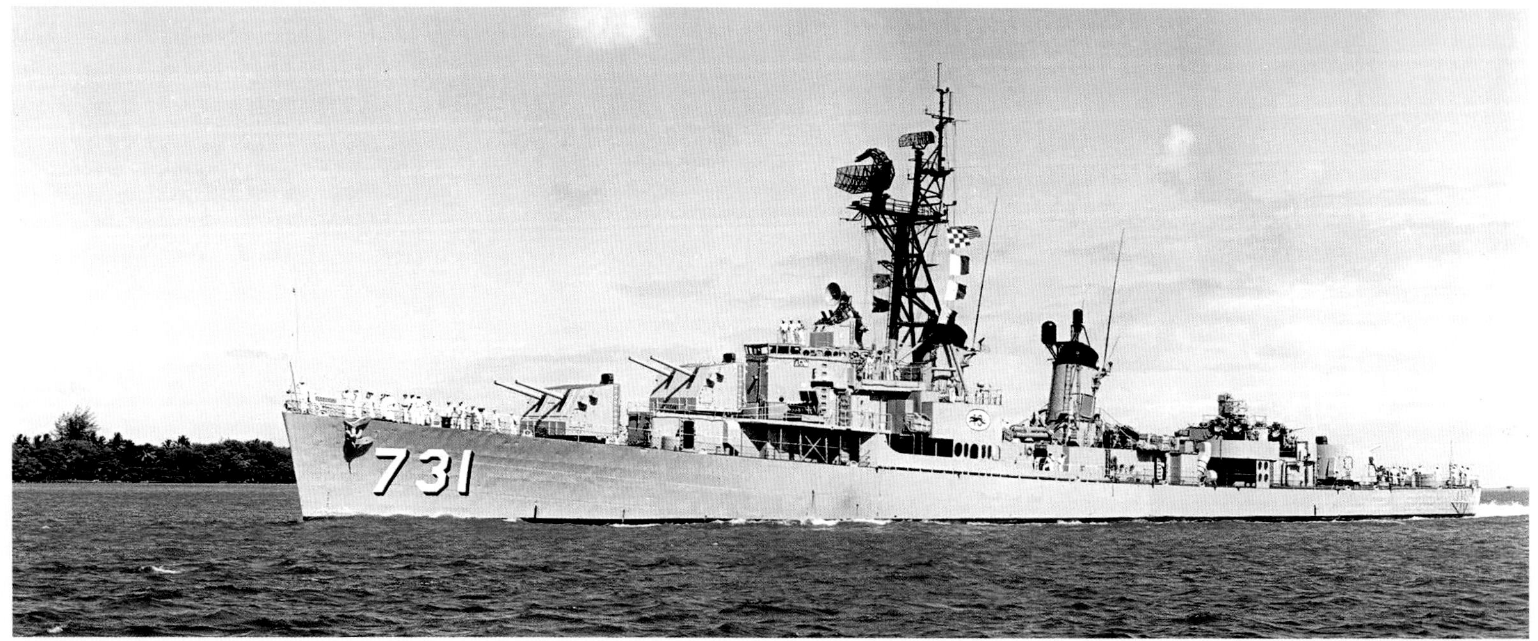

NAVAL SHIPS PROFILES

Patroling the Tonkin Gulf on August 2, 1964, was the U.S.S. *Maddox*, a 2,200-ton Allen M. Sumner Class destroyer. This World War II veteran carried six five-inch guns, six three-inch anti-aircraft guns, 11 20mm AA guns and ten torpedoes at a top speed of 34 knots. The *Maddox* was attacked by two N.V.A. Swatow gunboats based on the Soviet P-6 design. These were armed with four Chinese 37mm guns, four Chinese 14.5mm heavy machine guns and one Chinese 81mm recoilless gun. The *Maddox* was joined by the U.S.S. *Turner Joy*, a Forrest-Sherman class destroyer launched in 1958 and the U.S.S. *Ticonderoga* CV-14 aircraft carrier—another World War II veteran—which launched support aircraft.

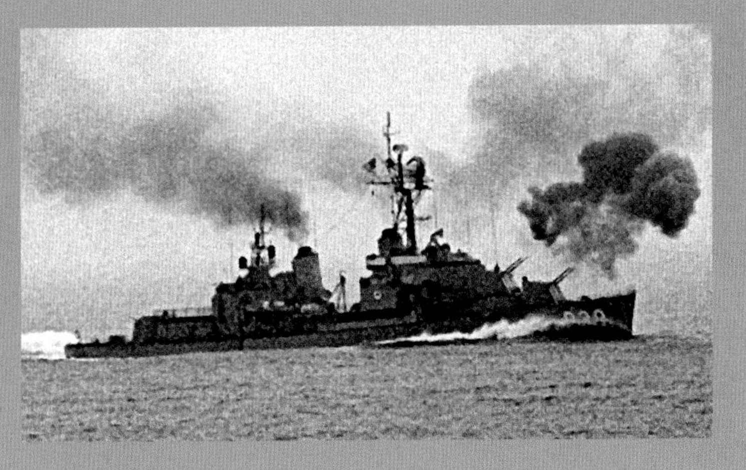

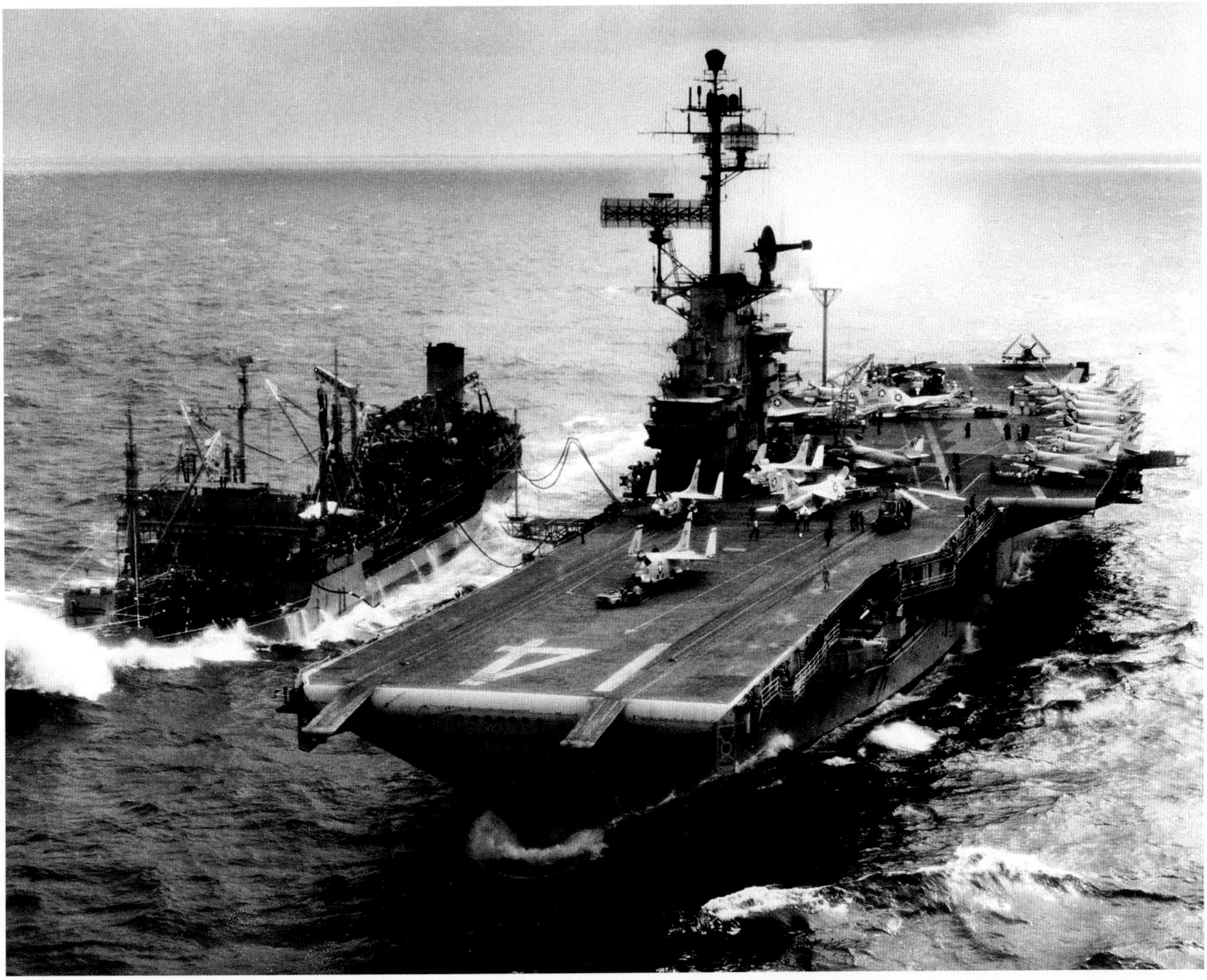

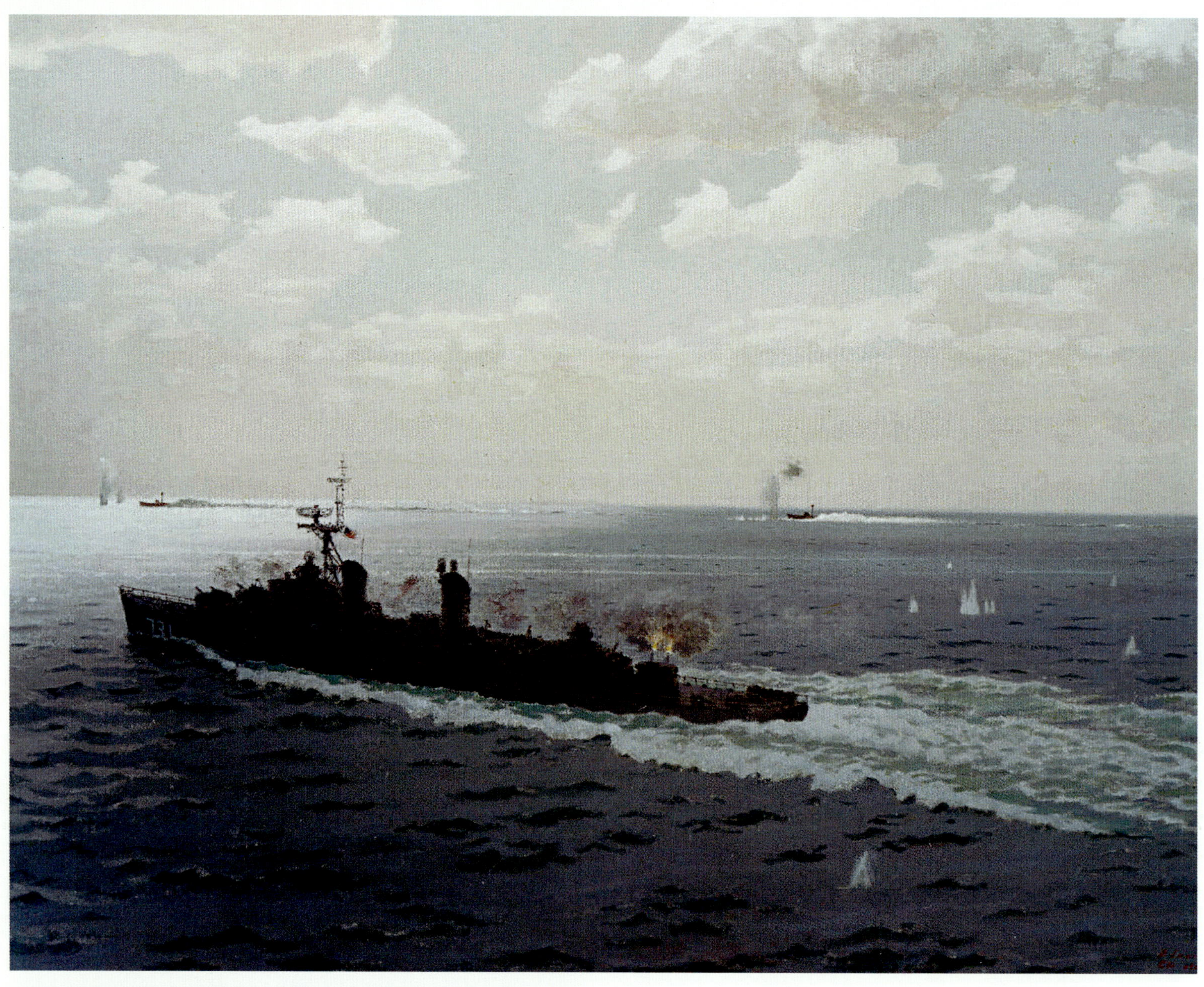

The U.S.S. *Maddox* ripped continuous fire from her five-inch and three-inch guns, pumping almost 300 rounds at the small zig-zagging craft.

Amid the pounding, all the boats fired torpedoes. The number two boat was shot to pieces as its torpedo fired but failed to run. Another P-4 halted dead in the water from a direct hit. The *Maddox* turned into the boats, combing the wakes of the torpedoes that sped down the destroyer's starboard side. A single cannon shell lodged in one of the destroyer's steel screens.

At 17:29 hours, the attack was broken off. Steaming nearby, the fleet aircraft carrier U.S.S. *Ticonderoga*, had launched F-8E

Above: A painting showing the U.S.S. *Maddox* under attack by two North Vietnamese torpedo boats and returning fire. She was struck once by a light cannon shell that lodged in a forward screen. Torpedoes were seen in the water, but none hit.

NAVAL AIRCRAFT DEPLOYED IN THE TONKIN GULF

The U.S.S. *Ticonderoga* Essex Class aircraft carrier dispatched four rocket-armed F-8E Crusaders to assist the U.S.S. *Maddox*. Upon arrival, the Crusaders launched five-inch Zuni unguided rockets and strafed the North Vietnamese craft with their 20mm cannons. The Vought Crusader was the first production carrier-borne supersonic aircraft. It was also called "The Last Gunfighter." The F-8E was the last fighter of the Vietnam era to rely primarily on four 20mm guns. The Phantom F-4 that followed it into service carried only missiles until late in the conflict when North Vietnam employed MiG-21 fighters.

H. J. Res. 1145

Eighty-eighth Congress of the United States of America

AT THE SECOND SESSION

Begun and held at the City of Washington on Tuesday, the seventh day of January, one thousand nine hundred and sixty-four

Joint Resolution

To promote the maintenance of international peace and security in southeast Asia.

Whereas naval units of the Communist regime in Vietnam, in violation of the principles of the Charter of the United Nations and of international law, have deliberately and repeatedly attacked United States naval vessels lawfully present in international waters, and have thereby created a serious threat to international peace; and

Whereas these attacks are part of a deliberate and systematic campaign of aggression that the Communist regime in North Vietnam has been waging against its neighbors and the nations joined with them in the collective defense of their freedom; and

Whereas the United States is assisting the peoples of southeast Asia to protect their freedom and has no territorial, military or political ambitions in that area, but desires only that these peoples should be left in peace to work out their own destinies in their own way: Now, therefore, be it

Resolved by the Senate and House of Representatives of the United States of America in Congress assembled, That the Congress approves and supports the determination of the President, as Commander in Chief, to take all necessary measures to repel any armed attack against the forces of the United States and to prevent further aggression.

Sec. 2. The United States regards as vital to its national interest and to world peace the maintenance of international peace and security in southeast Asia. Consonant with the Constitution of the United States and the Charter of the United Nations and in accordance with its obligations under the Southeast Asia Collective Defense Treaty, the United States is, therefore, prepared, as the President determines, to take all necessary steps, including the use of armed force, to assist any member or protocol state of the Southeast Asia Collective Defense Treaty requesting assistance in defense of its freedom.

Sec. 3. This resolution shall expire when the President shall determine that the peace and security of the area is reasonably assured by international conditions created by action of the United Nations or otherwise, except that it may be terminated earlier by concurrent resolution of the Congress.

Speaker of the House of Representatives.

Acting President pro tempore of the Senate.

TONKIN GULF RESOLUTION

On January 7, 1964, President Lyndon Johnson signed this resolution. Passed by Congress, it allowed U.S. troops to be deployed for combat in South Vietnam.

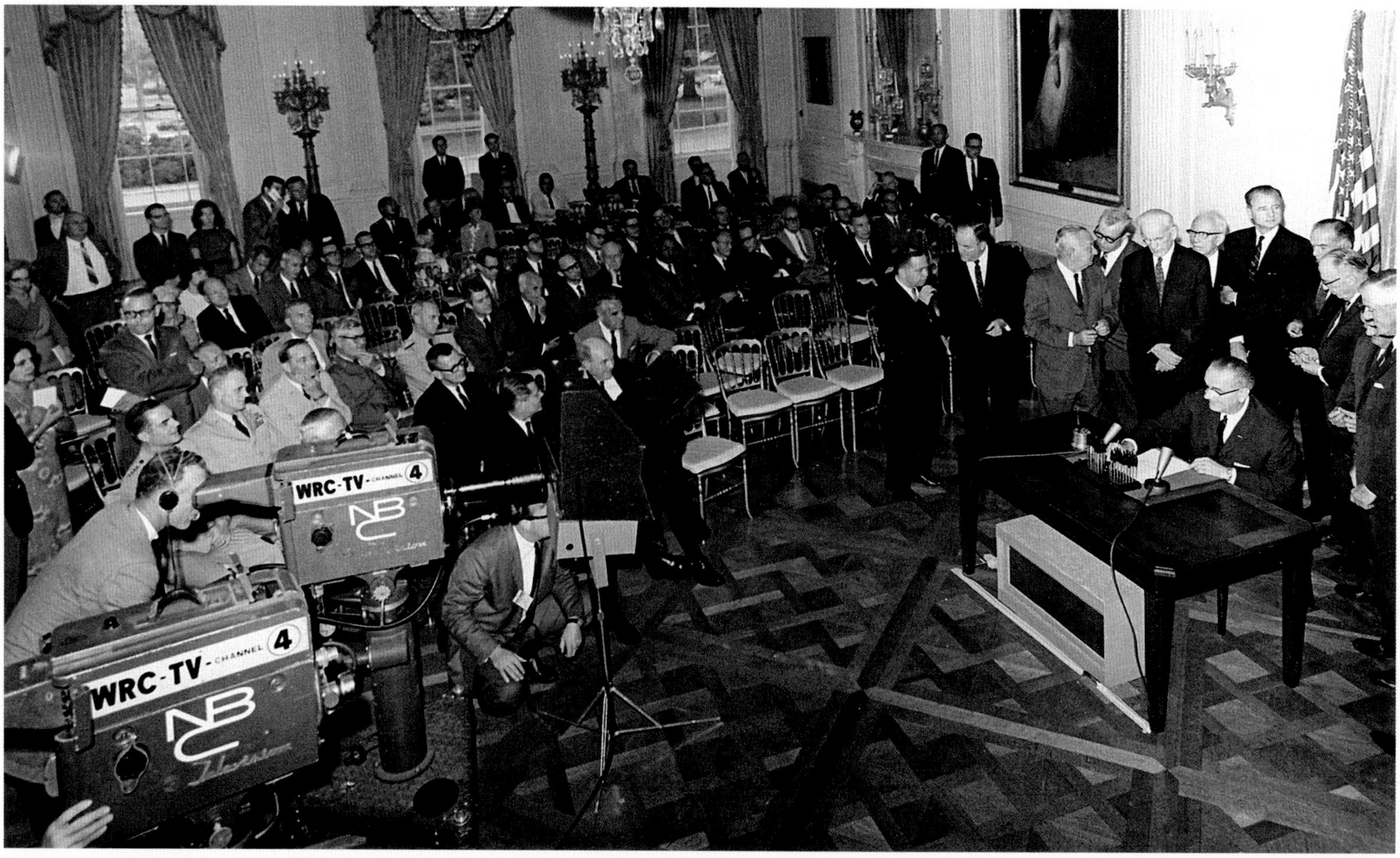

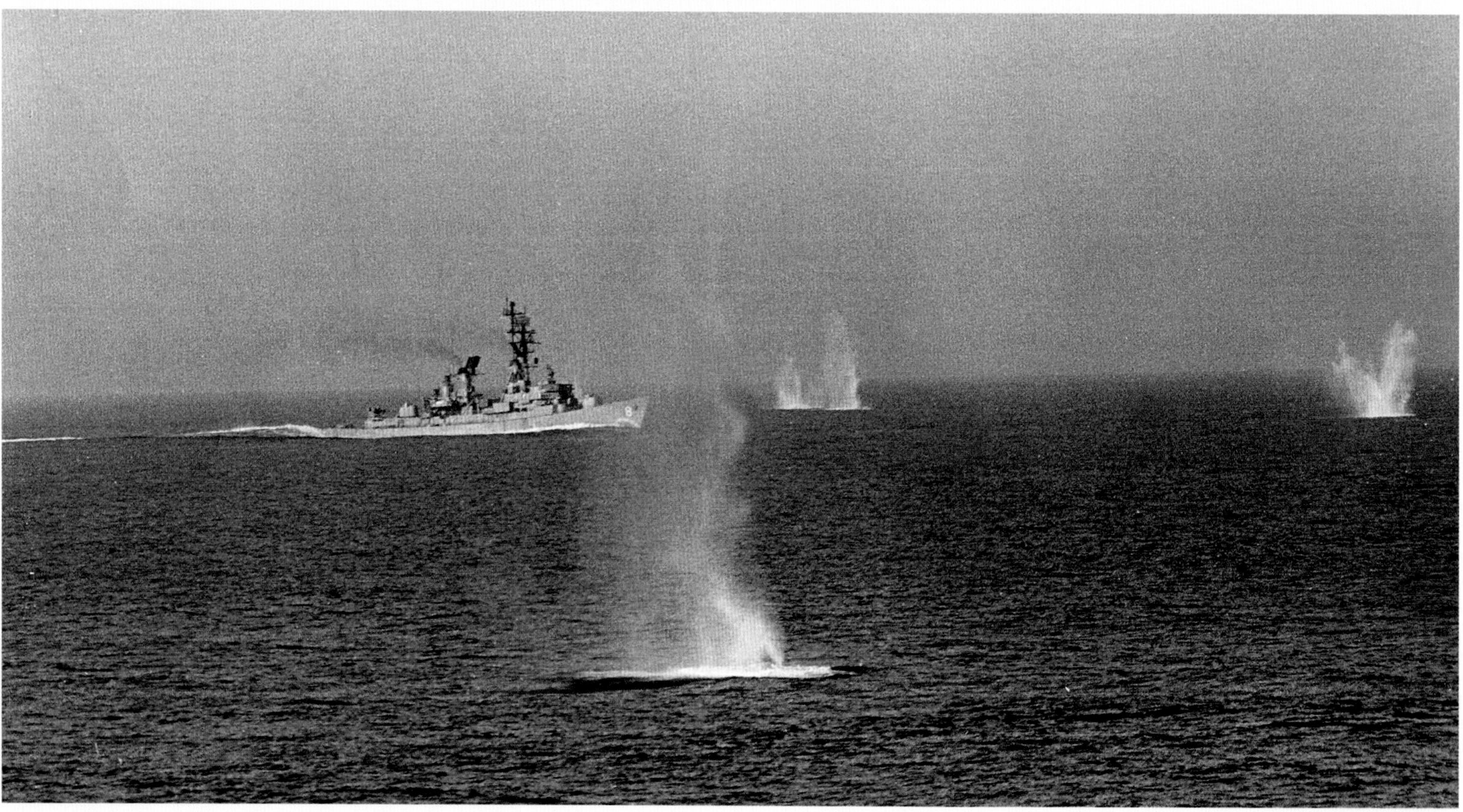

Crusader fighter-bombers which caught up with the battered P-4 boats and added to their battle damage and casualties.

On 4 August, the *Maddox* was joined by the destroyer U.S.S. *Turner Joy*. The two ships claimed another patrol boat attack was made, but owing to bad weather at night and no visual or physical confirmation, that claim was set aside.

President Lyndon Johnson, despite lack of positive evidence of the second attack, cited both hostile acts as reasons to launch an air strike on August 5 which destroyed the torpedo boats' base at Vinh. The navy planes sank eight boats and set afire the nearby fuel storage facility.

Two days after that attack, the American House of Representatives voted 416 to zero and the Senate voted 88 to two to adopt a Tonkin Gulf Resolution that allowed the President to "...take all necessary measures to repel attacks against the forces of the United States and to prevent further aggression."

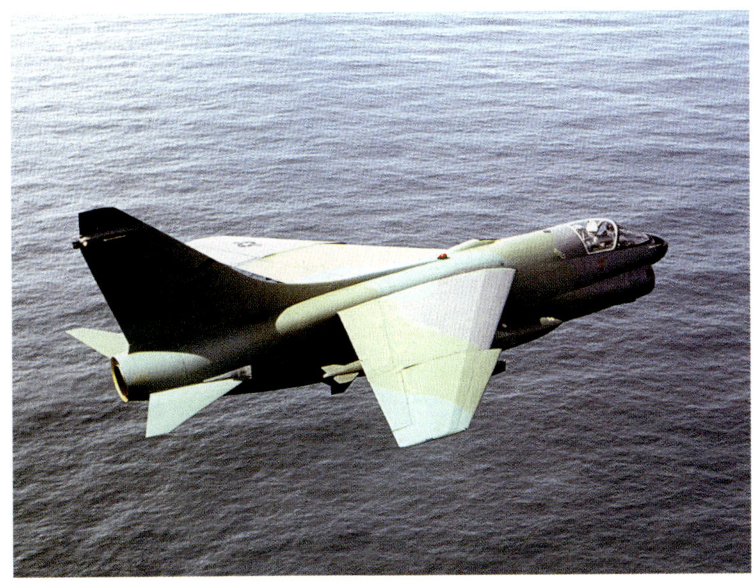

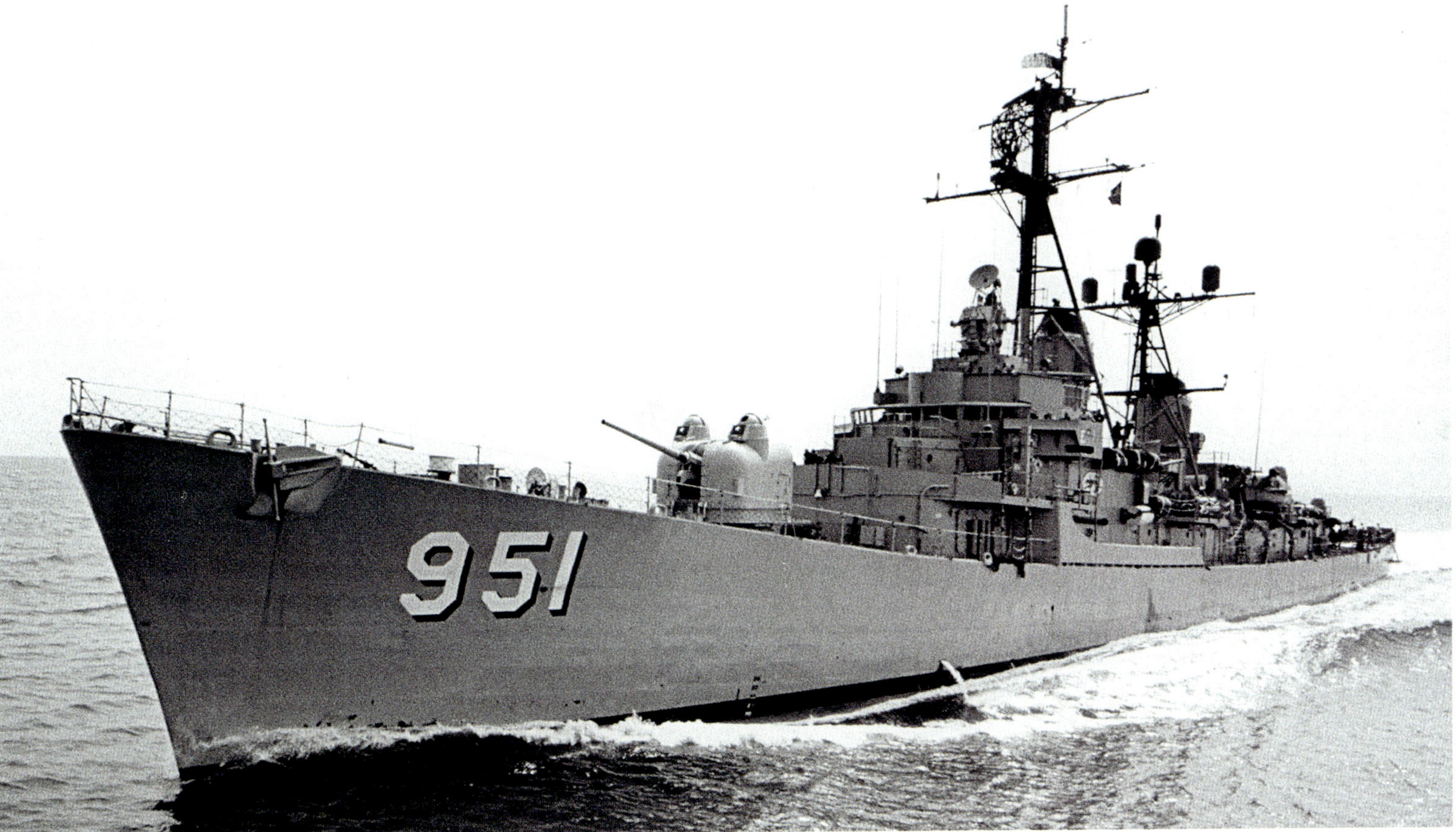

Opposite above: President Lyndon Johnson signs the Tonkin Gulf Resolution that increased the United States' commitment to aiding South Vietnam against North Vietnam's Communist aggression. The attacks by torpedo boats on U.S. Navy ships sealed his decision to send in the U.S. Military in combat strength.

Opposite below: An overhead view of two U.S. destroyers under fire in the Beibu Gulf.

Above top: A Vought F-8E Crusader jet fighter-bomber, the aircraft type fought from Navy aircraft carriers such as the U.S.S. *Ticonderoga* and U.S.S. *Constellation* in the Tonkin Gulf and with Marine Squadrons. It could carry a mixed armament of bombs and rockets besides mounting a 20mm cannon for dogfighting MiG-17 fighters and strafing.

Above: The U.S.S. *Turner Joy* (DD-951) was a Forrest-Sherman class destroyer in the United States Navy. She was named for Admiral Charles Turner Joy U.S.N. (1895–1956). In the Tonkin Gulf on August 2, 1964, *Turner Joy* raced to *Maddox* to provide additional surface strength. By the time she reached *Maddox*, the remaining boat had fled. *Turner Joy* remained with *Maddox*. Less than 48 hours later, the *Turner Joy* reported hostile boats on radar and later saw torpedo wakes, but they failed to contact the boats.

BUFFS, THUDS, & CRUSADERS

THE JUNGLE IS NEVER REALLY SILENT, BUT ALL THE SOUNDS ARE FAMILIAR: THE SHRIEKS, THE CRIES, THE BARKS, AND THE CHIRPS. THEN THE RUSH OF AIR, CRASH OF TORN BRANCHES, AND CRUMP, CRUMP, CRUMP OF EXPLOSIONS AS A LOAD OF 500-POUND BOMBS TEARS THROUGH THE GREEN TRIPLE CANOPY INTO THE RED MUD OF THE HO CHI MINH TRAIL. ABOVE THE BLASTING CHAOS, AT 30,000 FEET, A FLIGHT OF B-52 "BUFFS" (BIG UGLY FAT FELLOWS) RISES AS EACH ONE EMPTIES ALL ITS LOAD OF 84 IRON BOMBS INTO NORTH VIETNAM. TO THE SOLDIERS BENEATH THE 54,000 POUNDS OF HIGH EXPLOSIVE, THE B-52S ARE "WHISPERING DEATH." TO THE PLANNERS IN WASHINGTON, D.C., THE MISSION LAUNCHED IN FEBRUARY 1965 IS THE OPENING ROUND OF OPERATION "ROLLING THUNDER." IT IS AN AIR OFFENSIVE OF LIMITED GOALS DESIGNED TO DRIVE THE NORTH VIETNAMESE TO THE NEGOTIATION TABLE WITHOUT BRINGING CHINA INTO THE FIGHT.

Following the Gulf of Tonkin Incident, the news from Vietnam spiraled downward. On November 1, 1964, guerrillas hit the Bien Hoa air base, destroyed five B-57 Hustler bombers and killed four Americans. In December, at Binh Gia, the 9th V.C. Division trapped and destroyed the A.R.V.N. 33rd Ranger Battalion, and 4th Marine Battalion. Saigon, meanwhile, was hopelessly mired in the Buddhist struggle with the Catholics, student riots, and government officials anxiously packing their bags. President Johnson and his advisors watched as N.V.A. regular units marched into South Vietnam's Central Highlands—the final invasion phase of their strategic plan.

Following an attack on Pleiku Air Base that destroyed 16 helicopters and killed nine Americans, the aircraft carriers U.S.S. *Ranger*, U.S.S. *Hancock*, and U.S.S. *Coral Sea* launched Crusader F-8E fighter bombers reprisal attacks that were only marginally effective. A larger—but controlled—response was needed. On February 13, 1965, President Johnson announced the beginning of "Rolling Thunder."

This mission was designed in Washington to strike specific military and supply targets, gradually increasing in violence,

B-52 FROM 1952

The B-52 "Buff" (Big Ugly Fat Fellow) was in its prime during the Vietnam War and is still flying missions today. Created by Boeing, the eight-engine bomber took its first flight on April 15, 1952, and was an immediate success. Flown with a crew of five and capable of flying up to 50,000 feet, the B-52 carries 27 conventional bombs, cluster bombs, precision guided missiles, cruise missiles, and many more types of ordnance. Fifteen "Buffs" were lost to S.A.M.s (surface-to-air missiles) in 1972 during Operation Linebacker. These bombers could not be replaced because the last B-52 (Model H) was delivered in 1962.

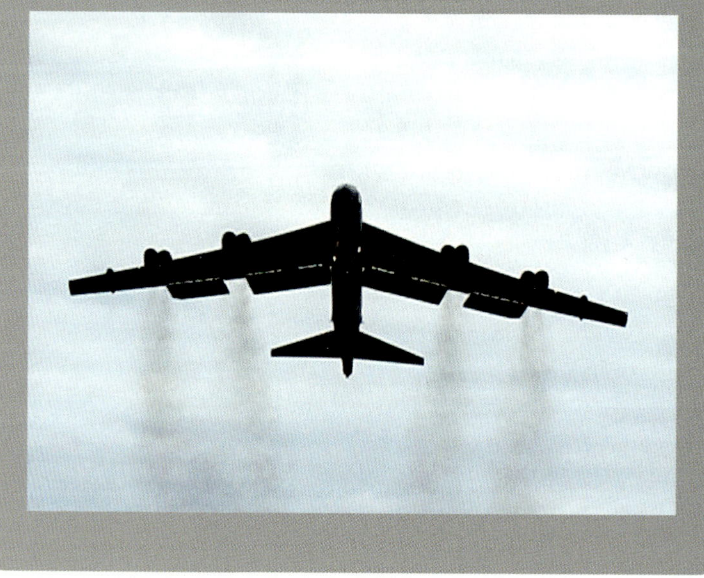

Right: A B-52 bomber lifts off the runway at Anderson Air Force Base in Guam. The first B-52, the City of El Paso, arrived from the 95th Bomb Wing at Biggs Air Force Base, Texas, in March 1964, followed by KC-135 Stratotankers. With the start of Operation Arc Light in June 1965, B-52s and KC-135s began regular bombing missions over Vietnam, and continued in that capacity until 1973, with a break between August 1970 and early 1972.

Opposite: A flight of F-105 Thunderchiefs engage in horizontal bombing through the clouds. Called "Thuds," the F-105 were versatile aircraft and the fastest American jets in Vietnam. They carried a gun for dogfighting, but were at a disadvantage with the more nimble MiGs. They operated over a variety of missions from down on the deck to high level bombing. Toward the end of the conflict they were largely replaced by the F-4.

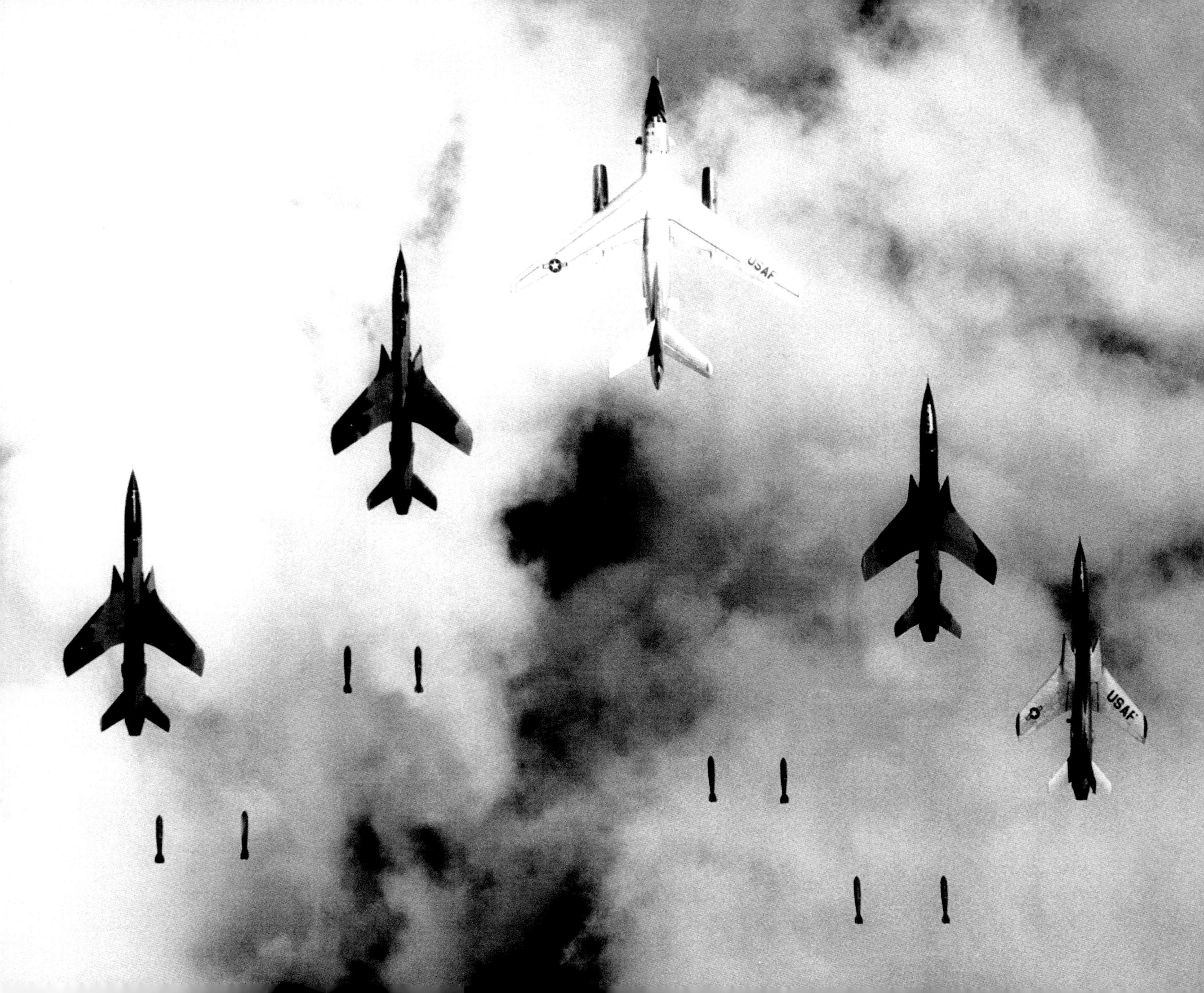
USAF
USAF

forcing the North Vietnamese to retreat back to their own borders and resume negotiations. The B-52s plastered large area targets and supply routes with carpet bombing while F-100 Super Sabres and F-105 Thunderchiefs ("Thuds") made precision attacks on bridges, supply depots, and anti-aircraft sites.

Instead of retreating, the North Vietnamese acquired from the Soviet Union S-75 S.A.M.s, which shot down an F-4 Phantom jet on July 24, 1965. Responding to this threat, the Air Force created the "Wild Weasels," pilots flying the fastest fighter in Vietnam, the workhorse F-105 Thunderchief. They sought out S.A.M. sites by becoming targets. When a S.A.M. was fired at the "Weasel", revealing the site, accompanying planes bombed the N.V.A. anti-aircraft target. By December 1965, the Wild Weasel program was in full operation.

To deal with N.V.A./V.C. already in South Vietnam, General William Westmoreland, Commander-in-Chief M.A.C.V., was given command of two battalions of U.S. Marines sent to defend Da Nang air base —the first American troops shipped to Vietnam as an aggressive ground force.

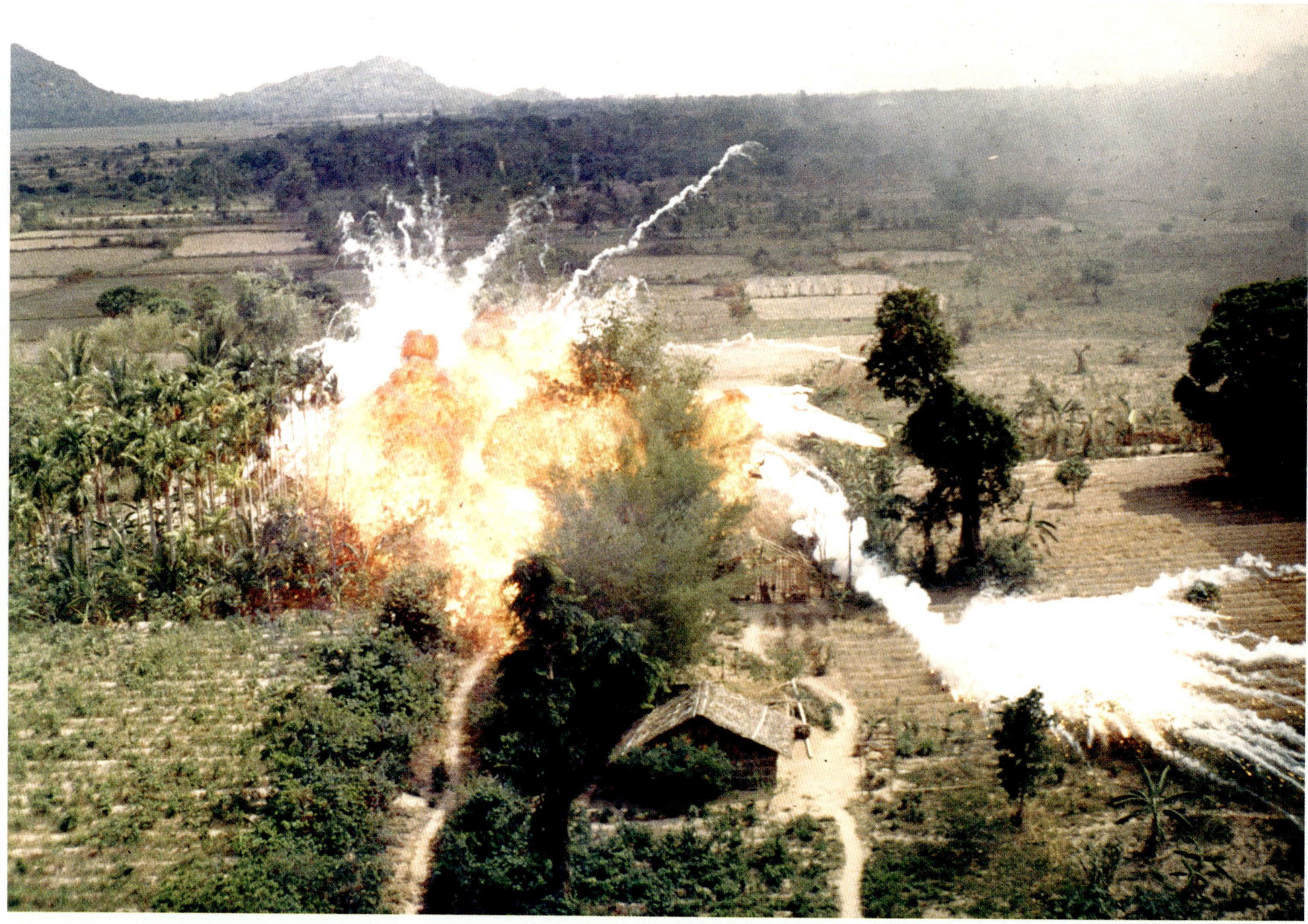

Above: An aerial camera exposes a direct low-level hit on a Vietnamese road, possibly triggering a secondary explosion as munitions ignite.

Opposite above left: A flight of A.R.V.N. T-28 prop aircraft with rockets and bombs attached to hard points beneath their wings act as troop support for A.R.V.N. infantry units on the ground. Later, they were supplemented by the jet A-37 Dragonfly and the Skyraider.

Opposite below left: American troops cross a series of rice paddies in central Vietnam as they patrol, seeking information on V.C. or N.V.A. units operating in the vicinity. They are very exposed to enemy fire and keep their separation in case of mortar or machine-gun attack.

Opposite above right: An F-100 Super Sabre unloads rockets on a target fired from hard points beneath the fighter-bomber's wings. They initially carried four 20mm cannon in a package beneath the nose for dogfighting MiG-17s, but were outclassed by the MiG-21.

Opposite below right: A young U.S. Marine who has just landed on a Vietnamese beach with his unit as part of the first contingent of American troops to land for combat in 1965. When the Marines came ashore, a large body of American press, photographers, and film cameramen were on hand to record the landing, making it look more like a publicity stunt than a combat manuever.

JET AND PROP AIRCRAFT DEPLOYED

Early in the Vietnam conflict, propeller fixed-wing aircraft for ground support included the A-37 Dragonfly and the Air Force Skyraider delivering low-level bomb and gun attacks. The C-47 Dakota was armed with electric Gatling guns and re-named "Spooky" for highly effective ground strafing. Century-series jet fighters arrived, beginning with the F-100 Super Sabre and the F-105 Thunderchief ("Thud")—the fastest aircraft of the war. It delivered bombs and later became the first two-seat "Wild Weasels"—knocking out S.A.M. sites. Though the Navy F-4 Phantom was also adopted by the Air Force, it only carried missiles for dogfighting MiG-17 and later MiG-21 fighters. Other Navy jets, the F-8E and A-4D Skyhawk kept their cannons.

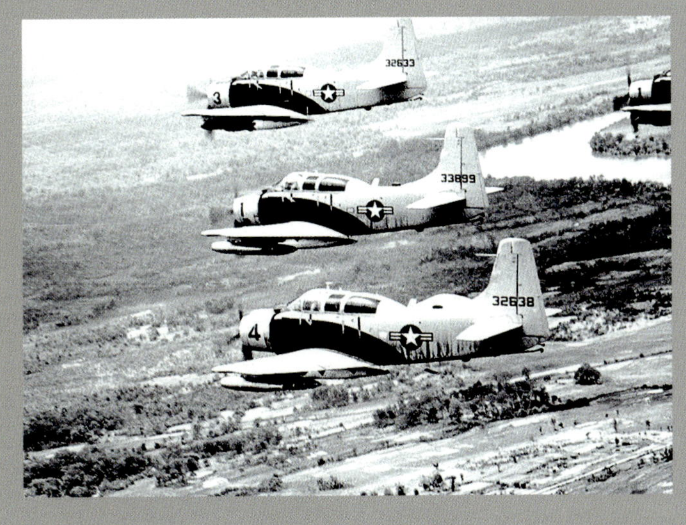

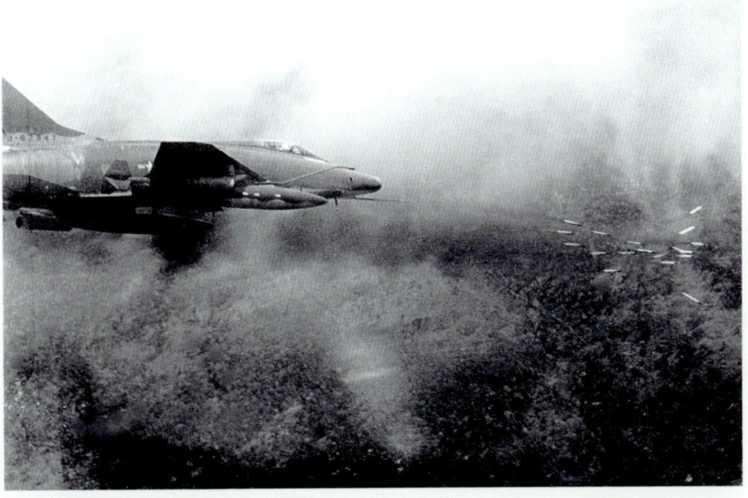

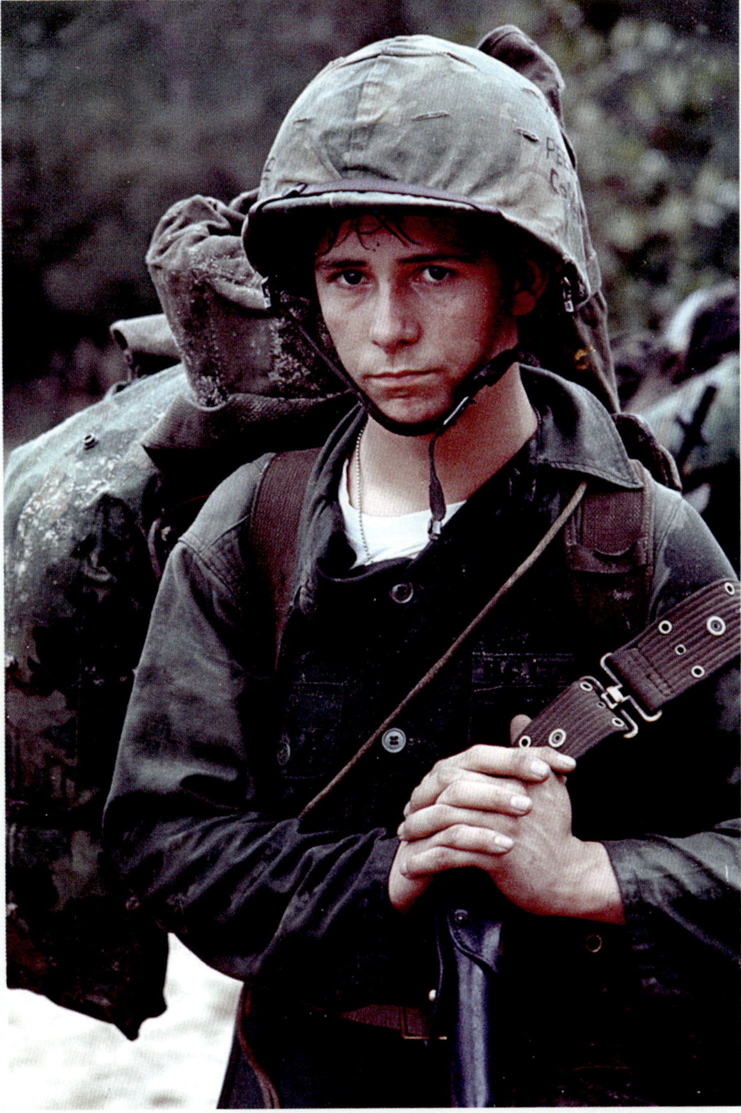

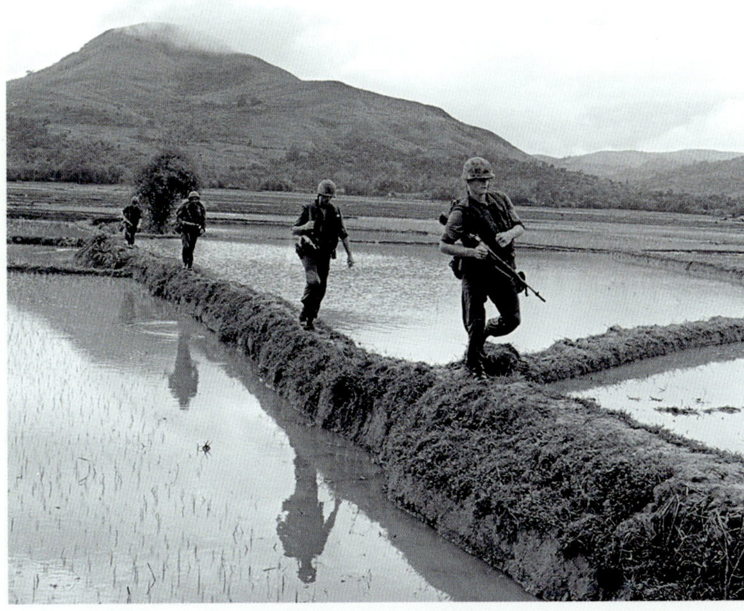

SLICKS INTO X-RAY

SIXTEEN "SLICKS" DROPPED OUT OF THE COOL, CLEAR MORNING SKY TO TREETOP LEVEL. THE SLICKS WERE TROOP-CARRYING UH-1D HUEY HELICOPTERS FLYING WITH THEIR DOORS OPEN. CRAMMED INTO EACH WERE TEN TROOPERS OF THE 1ST BATTALION, 7TH CAVALRY. NO ONE SPOKE BECAUSE NO ONE COULD HEAR OVER THE WHINE OF THE TURBO ENGINE AND THE WIND BUFFETING IN THE OPEN DOOR. THEIR ROTORS' DOWNDRAFT THRASHED AT THE TREES AS THE HUEYS RUSHED TOWARD THEIR LANDING ZONE (L.Z.), THE SIZE OF A FOOTBALL FIELD, NAMED "X-RAY." THE HELICOPTERS TRAVELED IN FOUR GROUPS OF FOUR. TWO GUNSHIP FLANKERS STOOD OUT TO THE SIDE AND SLIGHTLY AHEAD OF THE FORMATION.

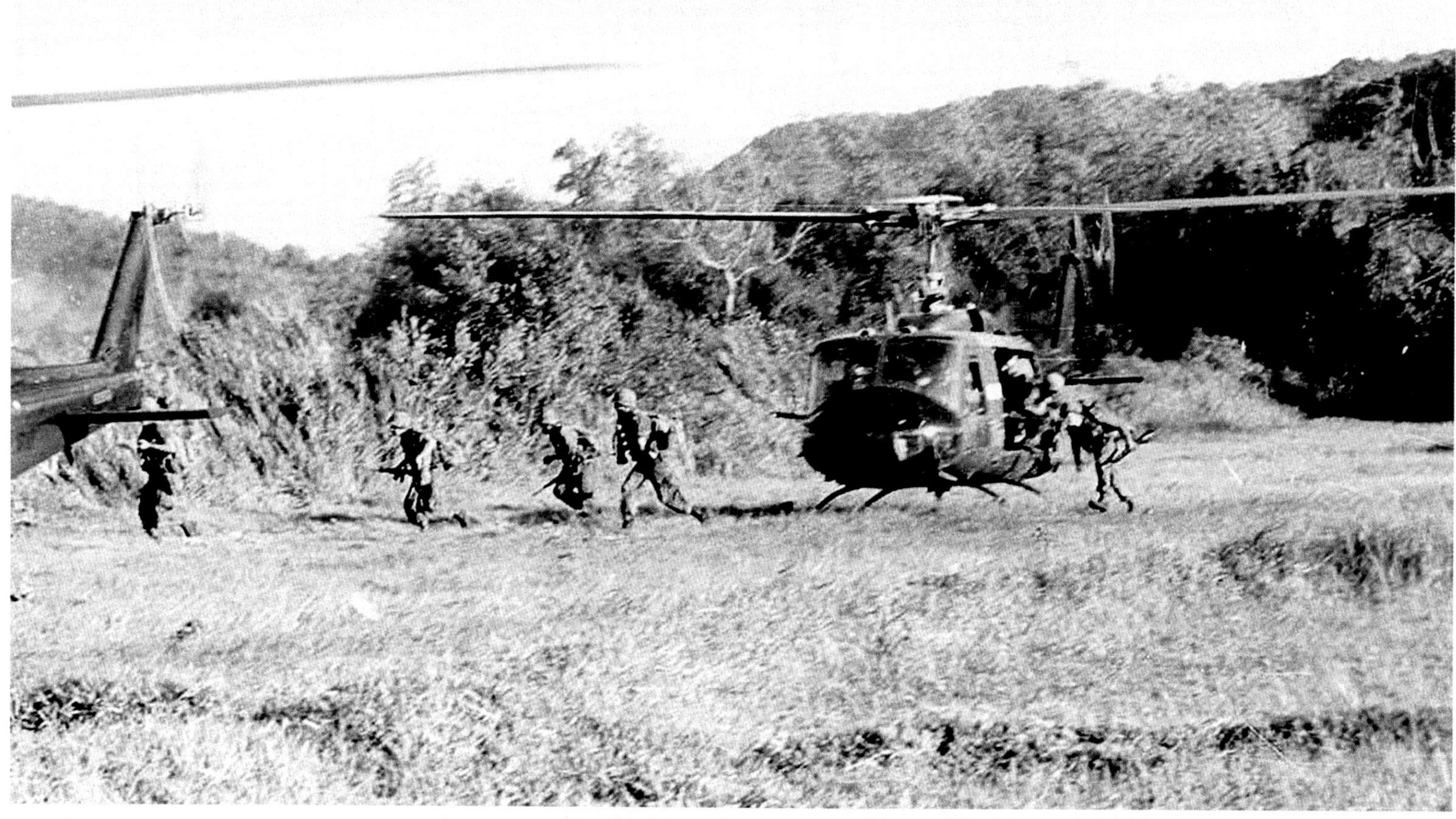

The L.Z. was first hammered by a battery of 105mm howitzers, then a barrage of aerial rocket artillery (A.R.A.) helicopters worked over X-Ray's perimeter. Machine guns, rockets, and grenades blasted grass and shrubs, probing for mines and scything down nearby trees. The helicopters banked away to hover close by. The firing of the howitzers stopped and the first group of eight slicks churned in low and flared to land just above the blasted dirt. Each trooper clicked his M16 rifle selector switch to fully automatic. The men piled out, hit the ground, and followed their officers, shooting bursts into the surrounding bushes and trees.

On November 14, 1965, at the foot of the Chu Pong mountain's eastern slope in the Ia Drang Valley, the troopers of the 7th Cavalry came to "search and destroy." Hurrying to meet them

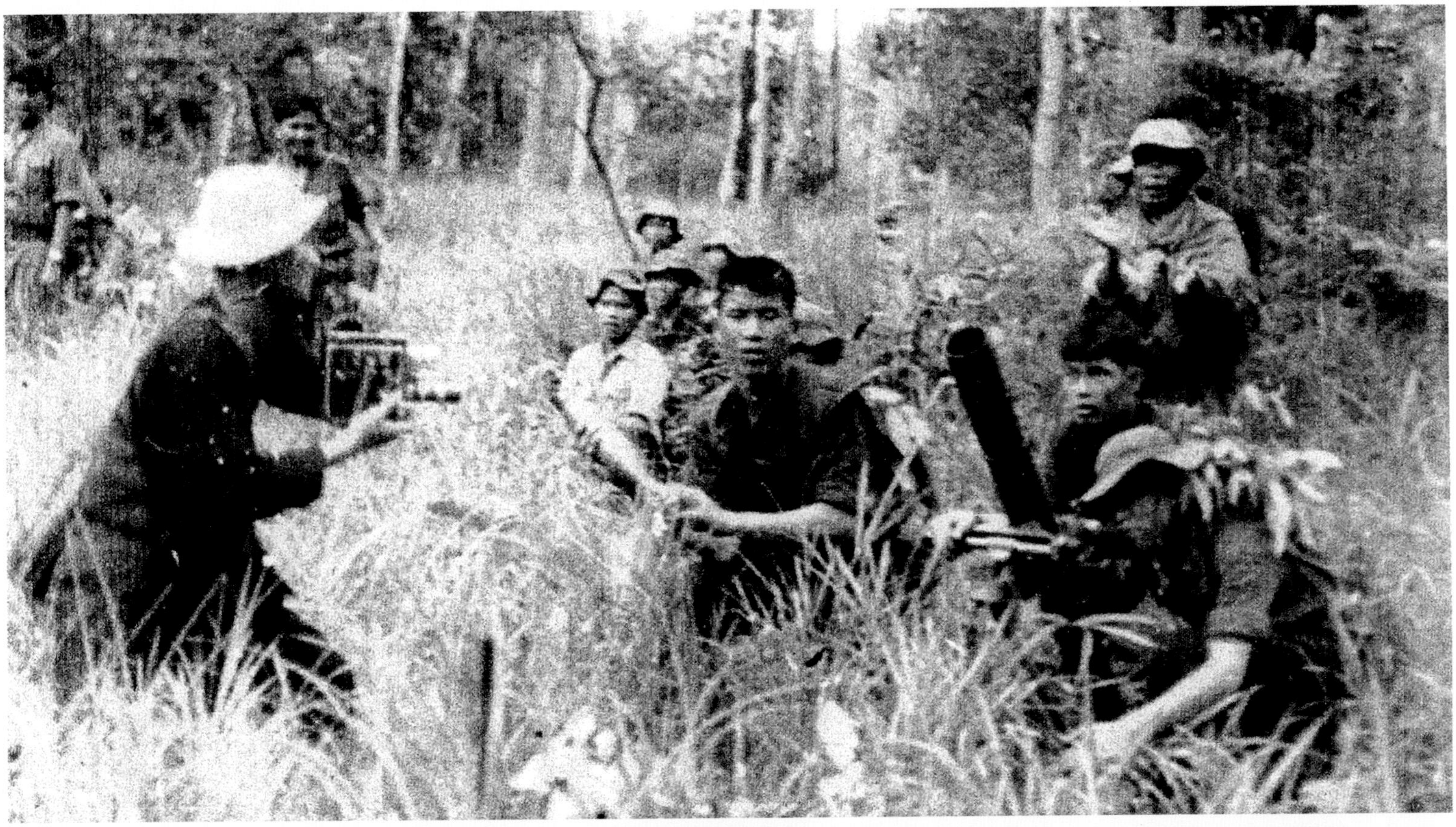

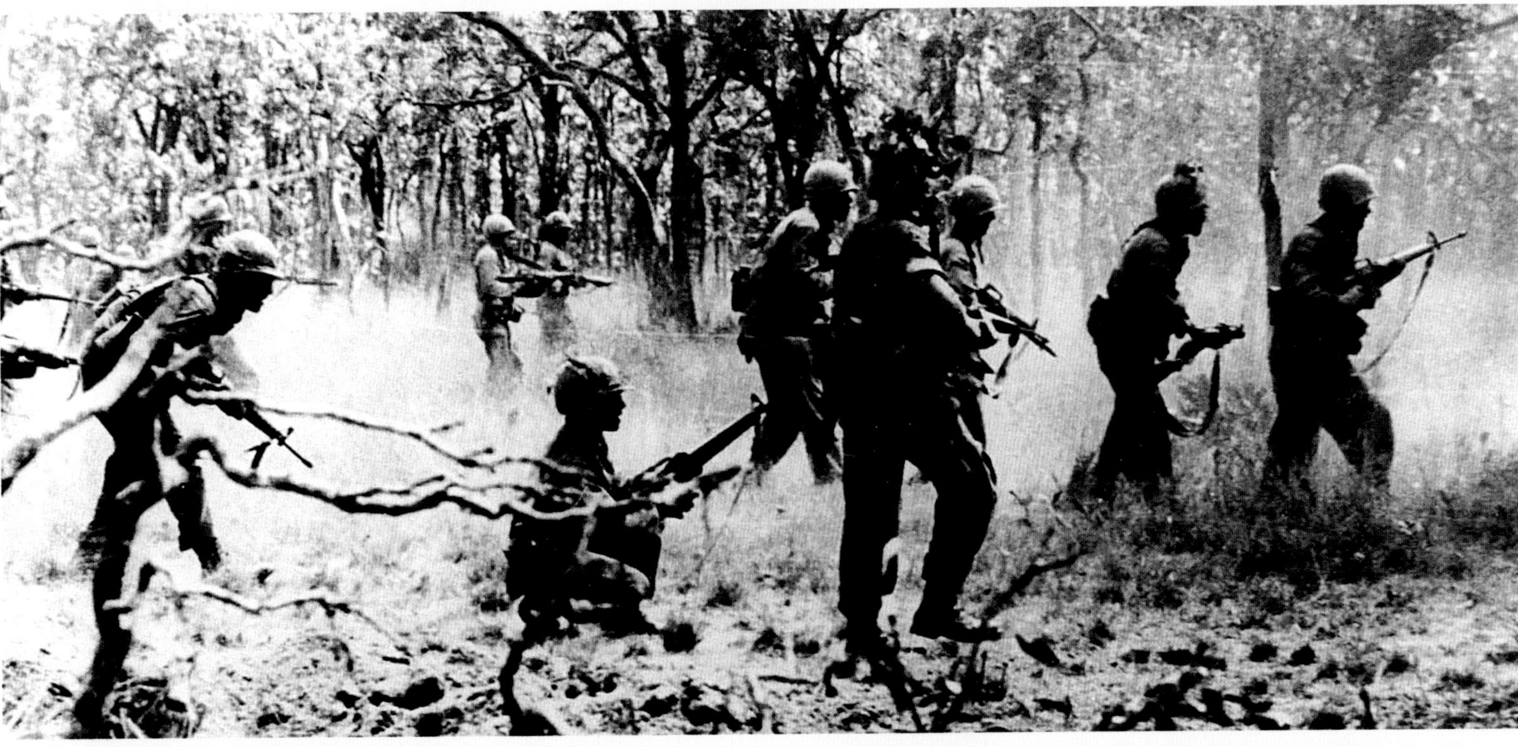

Opposite: Troops of the 7th Cavalry scramble out of their UH-1 Huey "slick" (transport helicopter) under fire from N.V.A. troops on L.Z. X-Ray at the start of the Ia Drang Valley battle. The airmobile force was heavily outnumbered by a growing N.V.A. force.

Above top: A mortar crew zeros in on U.S. targets with a Soviet 82mm M1937 mortar—Chinese model 53—with its 48-inch tube that fires a hand-dropped bomb held by the other crew member for a maximum range of 3,040 meters.

Above: Once on the ground, the airmobile infantry moved forward clear of the L.Z. to drive back the N.V.A. troops, who virtually surrounded their position. Artillery from nearby firebases supported their advance.

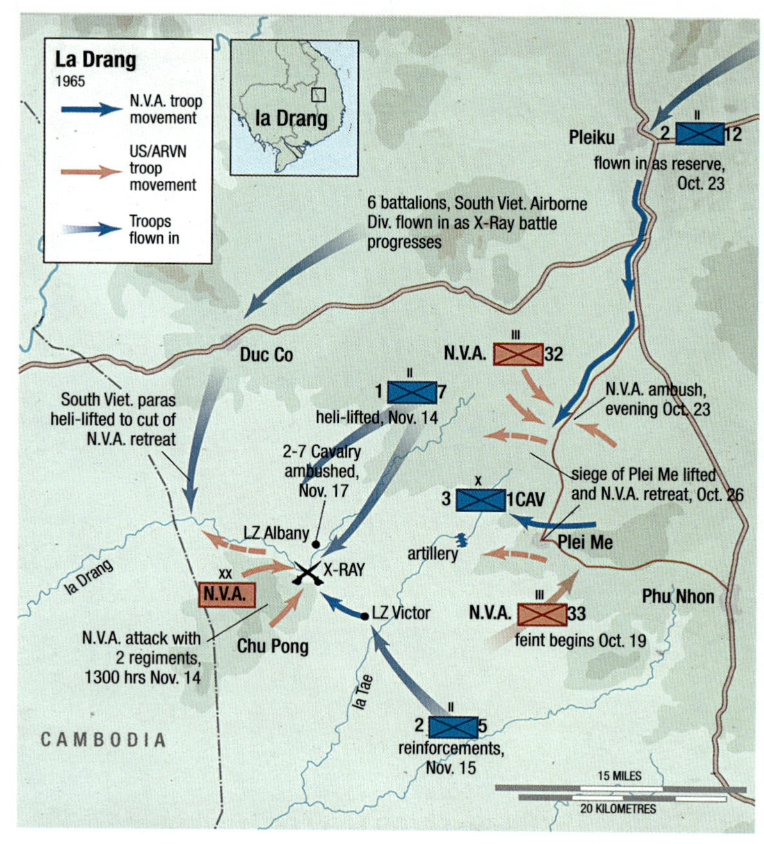

IA DRANG 1965

Map of Ia Drang Battle in 1965. The battle in Ia Drang Valley was set up by The N.V.A. attack on a Special Forces camp at Plei Me in October 19-26. That attack failed and General Chu Huy Man withdrew to his fortress on the Chu Pong mountain above the Ia Drang Valley. In its first battle of the Vietnam War, the 1st Cavalry Division flew into three LZs on November 14 and fought the surprised N.V.A. troops in a savage battle ending in victory for the U.S. forces.

were the 66th and 33rd N.V.A. regiments under the command of Brigadier General Chu Huy Man. His men needed to learn how to fight Americans. Eventually, over 2,000 would hurl themselves at Lt. Colonel Harold Moore's 456 troopers.

The "search and destroy" mission was originally conceived to sweep through regions of the South known to contain V.C. guerrillas, and win over the local populace. Whatever-it-takes firepower and troop numbers were aimed at stubborn bands of guerrillas who melted away from the threat. At the Ia Drang, the value of airmobile cavalry was at stake, but this time against battle-trained North Vietnamese regulars eager to test the Americans' fighting skills. Lessons were learned on both sides.

Succeeding lifts of slicks dropped into the "hot" L.Z. beneath arcing 60mm and 81mm mortar rounds, sniper, and machine-gun fire. Accompanying gunships couldn't fire on areas along the 1st Cavalry's perimeter for fear of hitting American troopers

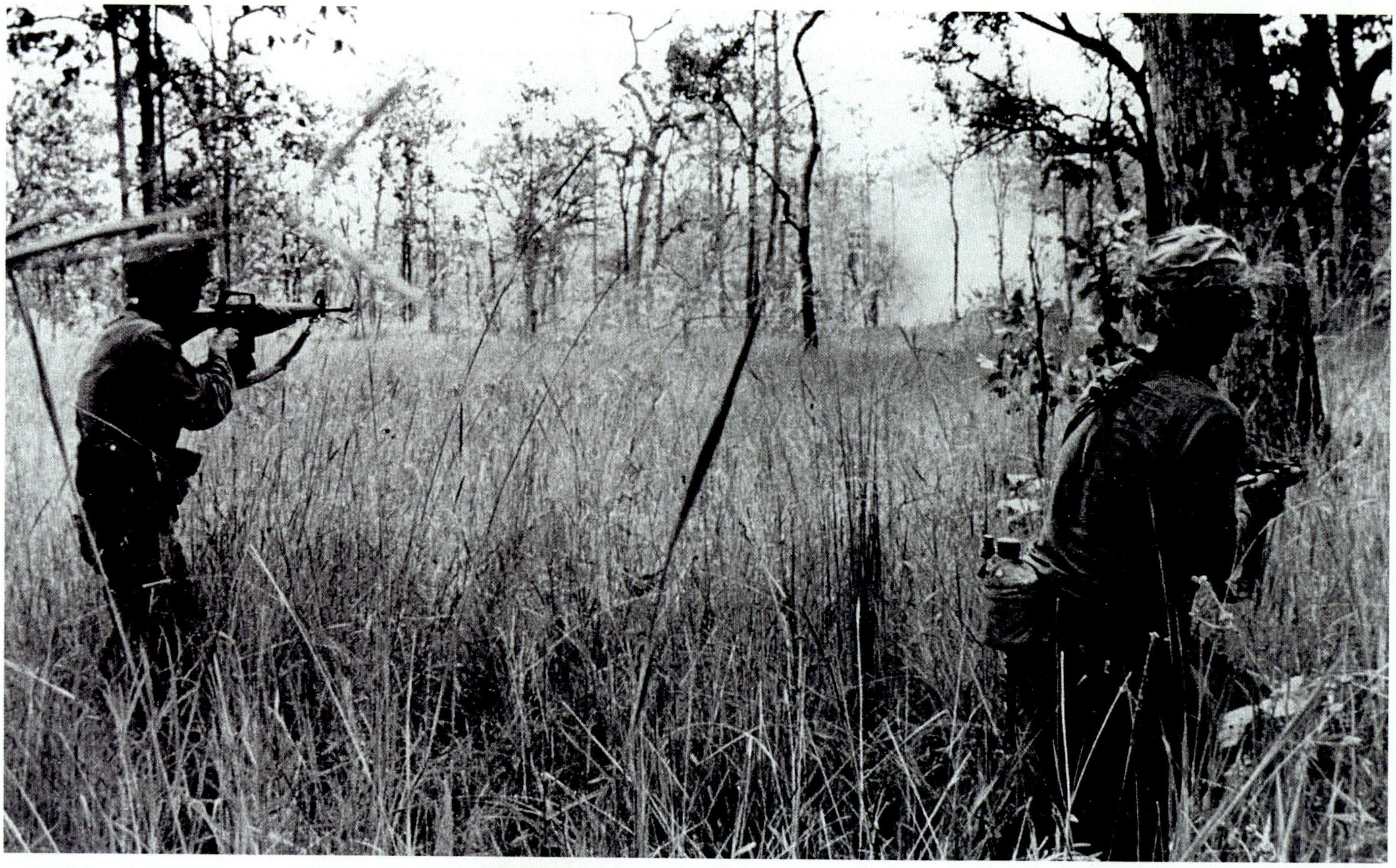

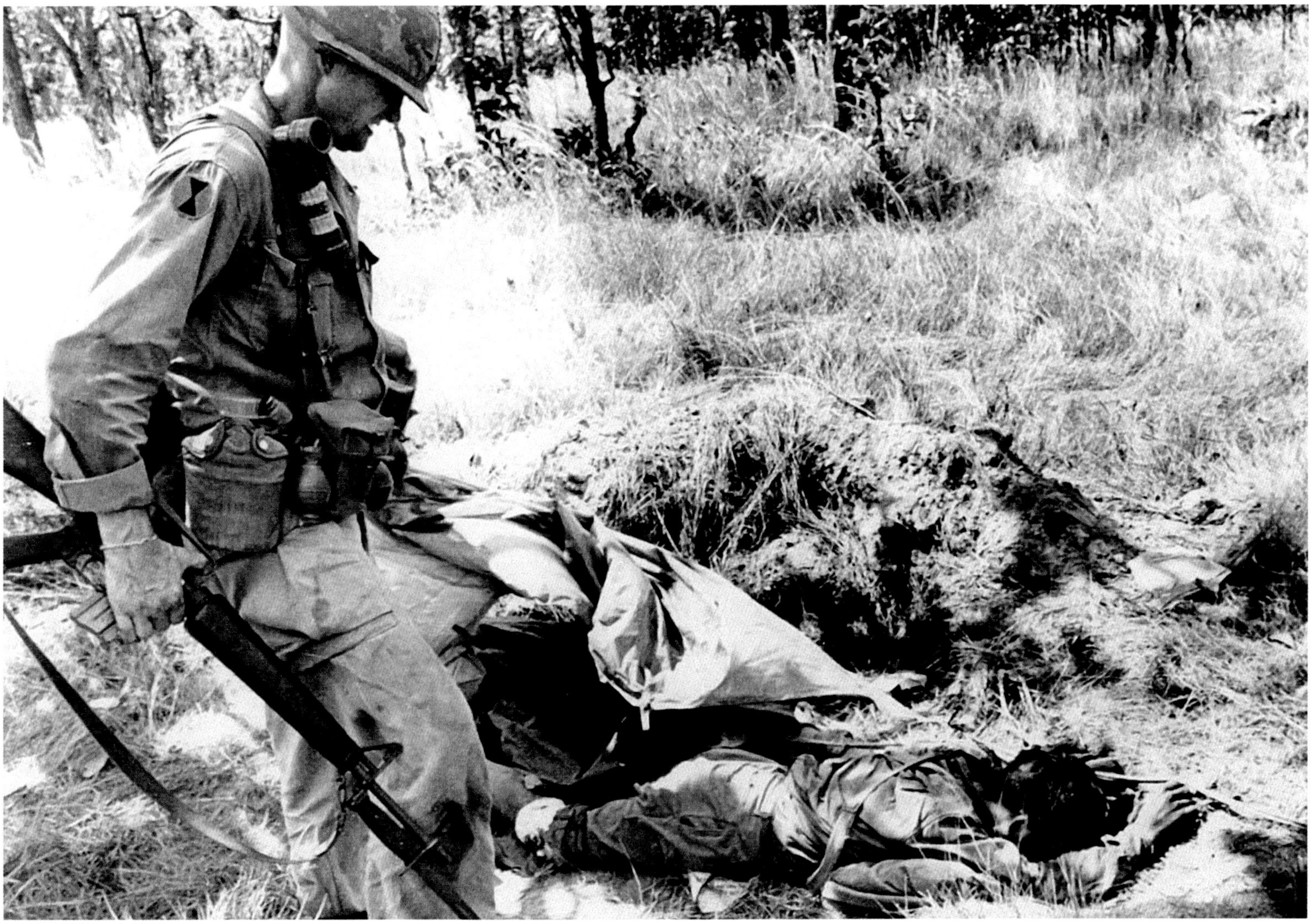

COL. HAROLD G. MOORE

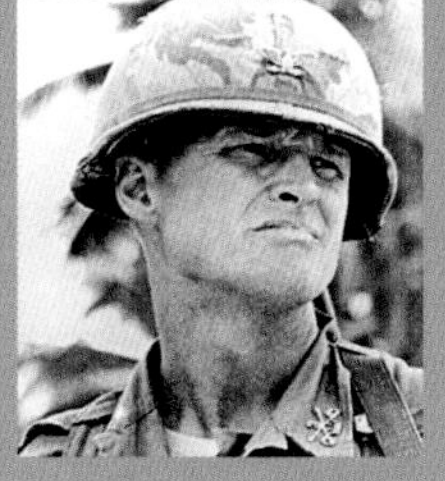

Lieutenant Colonel Harold "Hal" Moore is a West Point graduate, class of 1945, and was lucky enough to get into the early phases of airmobile cavalry created to transport large numbers of soldiers into strategic locations, carrying the fight to the enemy. The Huey UH-1 helicopter made these coordinated attacks possible. Moore's outfit was the 1st Cavalry Division (Airmobile). His command was the 1st Battalion, 7th Cavalry—the unit George Armstrong Custer lead in 1876. During the charge into Landing Zone X-Ray, Moore was the first man in and later, after a bloody see-saw defense and offense, he was the last man of his battalion to leave. His command, supported by artillery and air, attacked and repelled a much larger N.V.A. force.

probing for enemy positions. General Man's N.V.A. swept into the area. These soldiers were met with a barrage of accurate artillery fire and it was the 12 guns lifted into a nearby L.Z. by bigger Chinook helicopters that eventually turned the tide in the fierce, often hand-to-hand struggle.

In three days of fighting, the defenders of L.Z. X-Ray lost 79 troopers dead and 121 wounded. Their sacrifices proved the effectiveness of helicopter assaults. The North Vietnamese carried off their wounded, leaving behind 643 dead. General Man would never again send his men with such abandon against American firepower.

Opposite: Near the end of the conflict, forward elements of the U.S. force cleared their front of remaining N.V.A. troops by blazing away with their weapons on full automatic for two minutes, a hail of bullets called a "mad minute."

Above: Lieutenant Colonel Harold Moore, commander of the units landed at L.Z. X-Ray checks out a dead N.V.A. soldier in a camouflaged sniper dugout during a lull in the fighting. Note that Moore's M16 has its bayonet attached. Hand-to-hand fighting was frequent during the savage encounters of the survive-or-die battles.

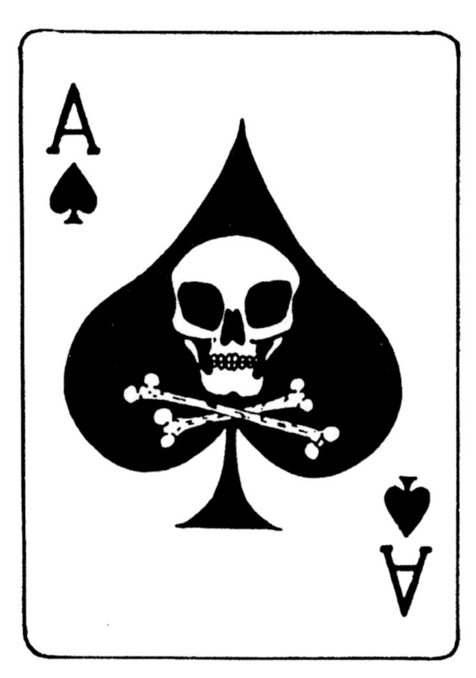

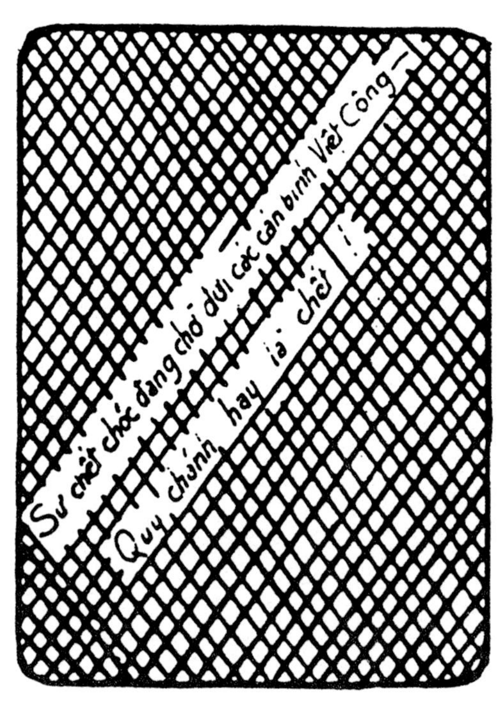

U.S. ARMY CALLING CARD

This playing card was left on the bodies or in the mouths of dead Viet Cong on the battlefield as a warning to others. For translation, see page 156.

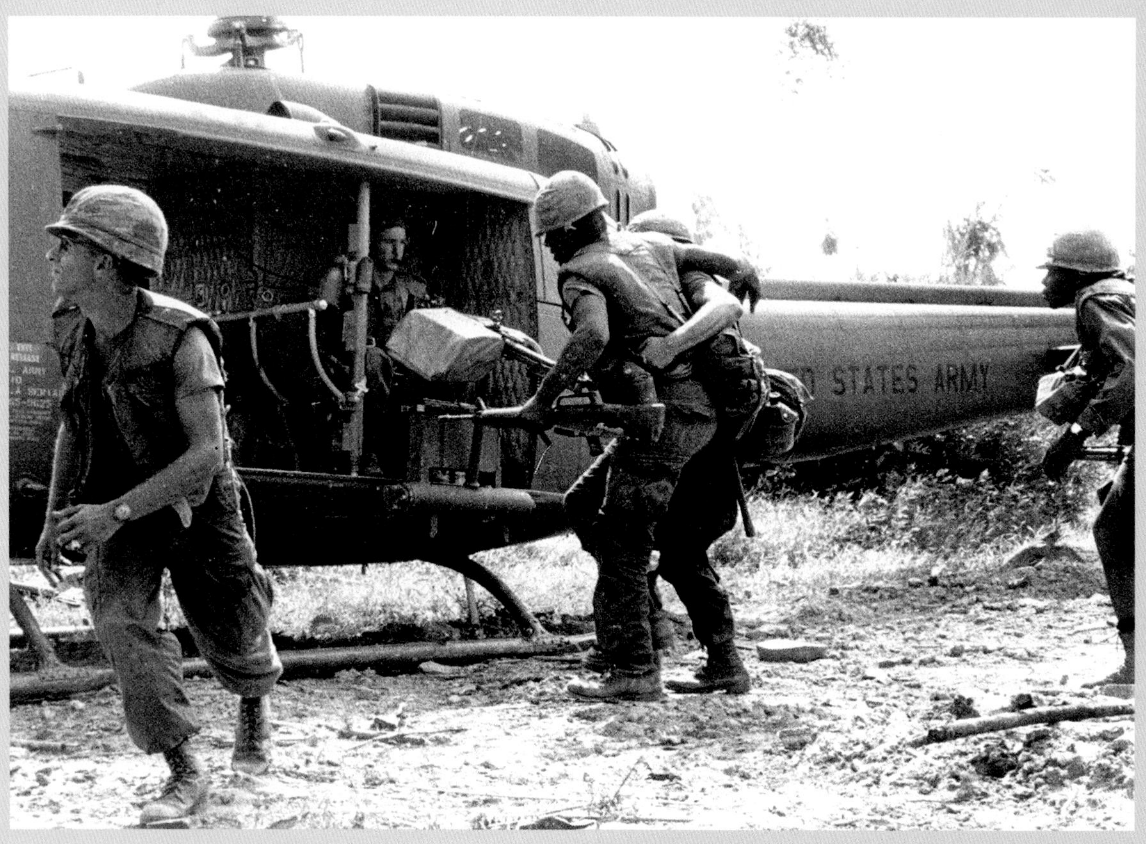

Left: The versatility of the Huey helicopter proved invaluable. At a moment's notice, the crew and their machine could adapt their mission to meet the most pressing need of the moment—whether delivering troops and supplies to the battlefield, providing firepower, or evacuating wounded soldiers.

HUEY UH-1 HELICOPTER

The most familiar symbol of the Vietnam War is the Bell UH-1 (Huey) helicopter. As delivered in 1963 and used in the Ia Drang Valley battle, the Huey had room for 10-12 soldiers with weapons and field packs plus a crew of two. It was a stretch version of the original with wide side doors for quick exit and room for an M60D door machine gun and a gunner. The troop transport models (UH-1D) were called "slicks." There were Medevac versions, command and control, and some with slings for medium-weight combat loads. Gunships and Aerial Rocket Artillery (A.R.A.) models carried side-mounted 2.75-inch rockets, 20mm cannon, and quad M60Cs. Their top speed when loaded was 110 knots.

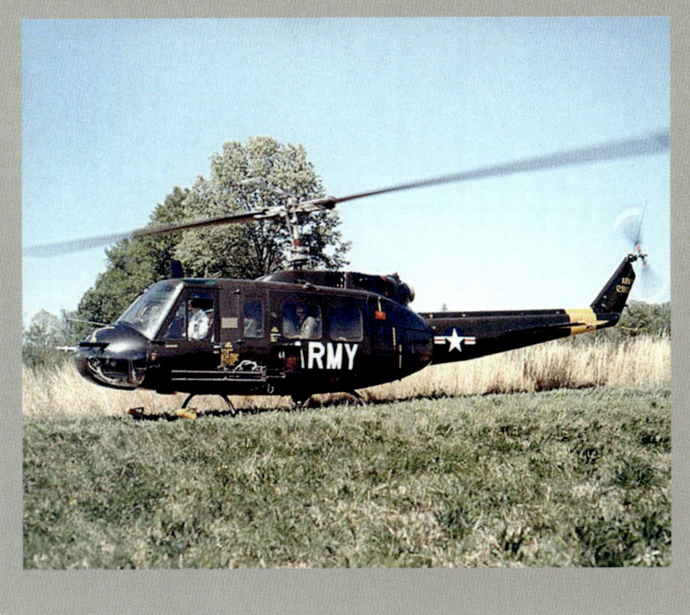

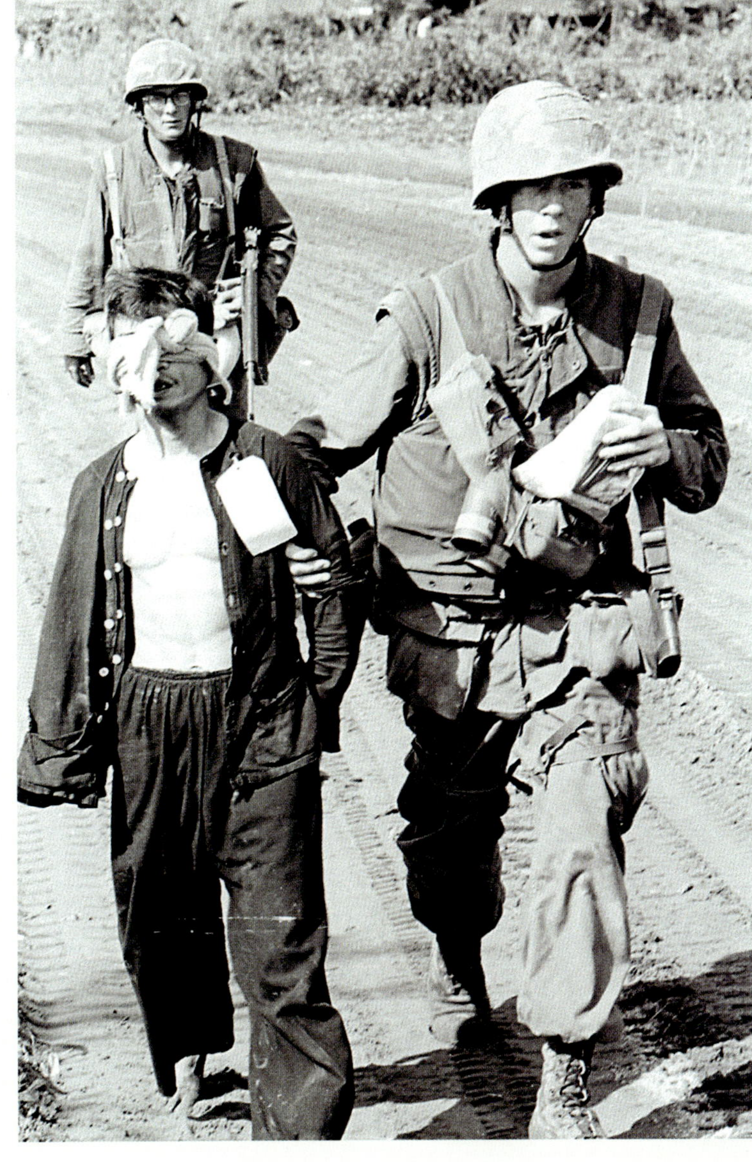

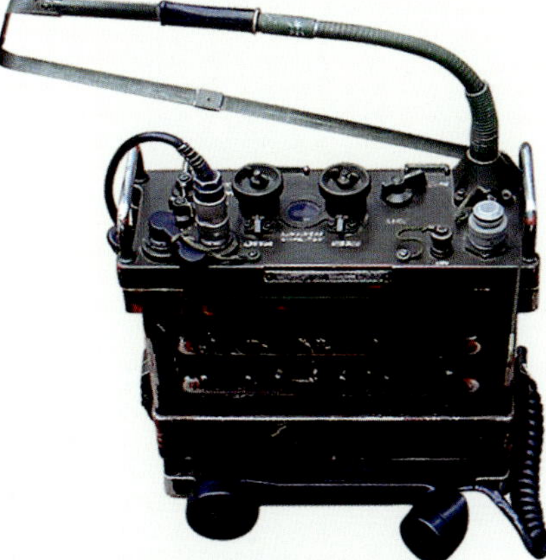

Right: The U.S. Army RT-505/PRC-25 FM receiver/transmitter was developed by the Radio Corporation of America during the 1950s as a replacement for the PRC-10. The "Prick 25" boasted a recommended range of five "clicks" (kilometers) with the short tape antenna, up to eight clicks with the seven-section long-range (fish-pole) antenna, and was powered by a dry cell battery that had an average life of 20 hours.

Top right: A wounded Viet Cong wearing the black pajamas uniform is escorted from an aid station to the waiting prisoner stockade.

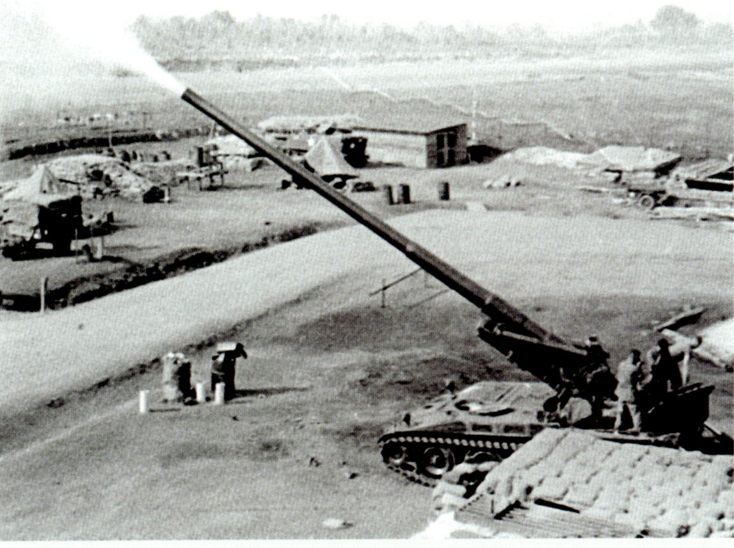

Bottom right: Heavy and medium artillery shared troop ground support with U.S.A.F. and Navy fighters and bombers. This M107 175mm self-propelled gun with its crew of 13 fired a 148 pound projectile nearly 19 miles and sped along at 35m.p.h. Coupled with the ubiquitous 105mm howitzers, Allied forces provided harassing and counter-battery firepower in a variety of tactical situations.

BROWN WATER NAVY

DAWN ARRIVES AS A RED LINE ACROSS THE SOUTH CHINA SEA'S HORIZON. THE USUAL JUNGLE CACOPHONY, AS NATURE YAWNS TO GREET ANOTHER DAY, IS BROKEN BY THE RUMBLE OF MARINE DIESEL ENGINES TURNING OVER. WATER BURBLES AT THE STERNS OF FOUR RIVER PATROL BOATS (P.B.R.s), AND THEY NOSE FROM THEIR SHORE BASE INTO THE CURRENT OF THE MEKONG RIVER. THE LEAD BOAT HELMSMAN GOOSES HIS WATER JET PROPULSION. THE BOW LIFTS AND A WAVE PLANES ALONG THE CRAFT'S MOLDED SIDES PAST THE AMIDSHIP'S 40MM GRENADE LAUNCHER AND THEN THE 7.62MM MACHINE GUNS IN THEIR PORT AND STARBOARD GUN MOUNTS. THE RATING ON THE BOW TWIN .50 CALIBER MACHINE GUNS GRABS A HANDHOLD. AND THEN THE HELMSMEN ACCELERATE TO HIGH SPEED. LIKE THE BOATS OF BASS FISHERMEN HEADING FOR A FAVORITE FISHING SPOT, FOUR OF THE NAVY'S "BROWN WATER FLEET" GO ON THE HUNT.

Following its participation in the OPLAN-34 raids and "Desoto" monitoring missions of North Vietnamese coastal facilities, the U.S. Navy was tasked with interdiction of supplies and weapons being provided to the Viet Cong through the maze of islands formed by the Mekong River delta. These shipments arrived in sampans, junks, and steel-hulled motor barges loaned to the North Vietnamese by China. While fighters and bombers flew off Navy aircraft carriers and Marine units stormed into beaches and coves on tactical raids, it was the riverine force that laid American naval vessels alongside the enemy shipping. The

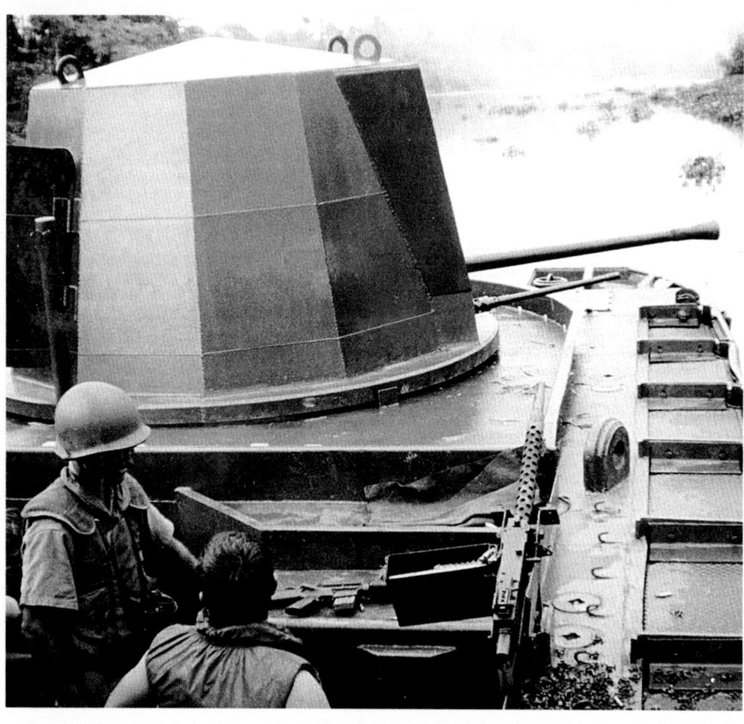

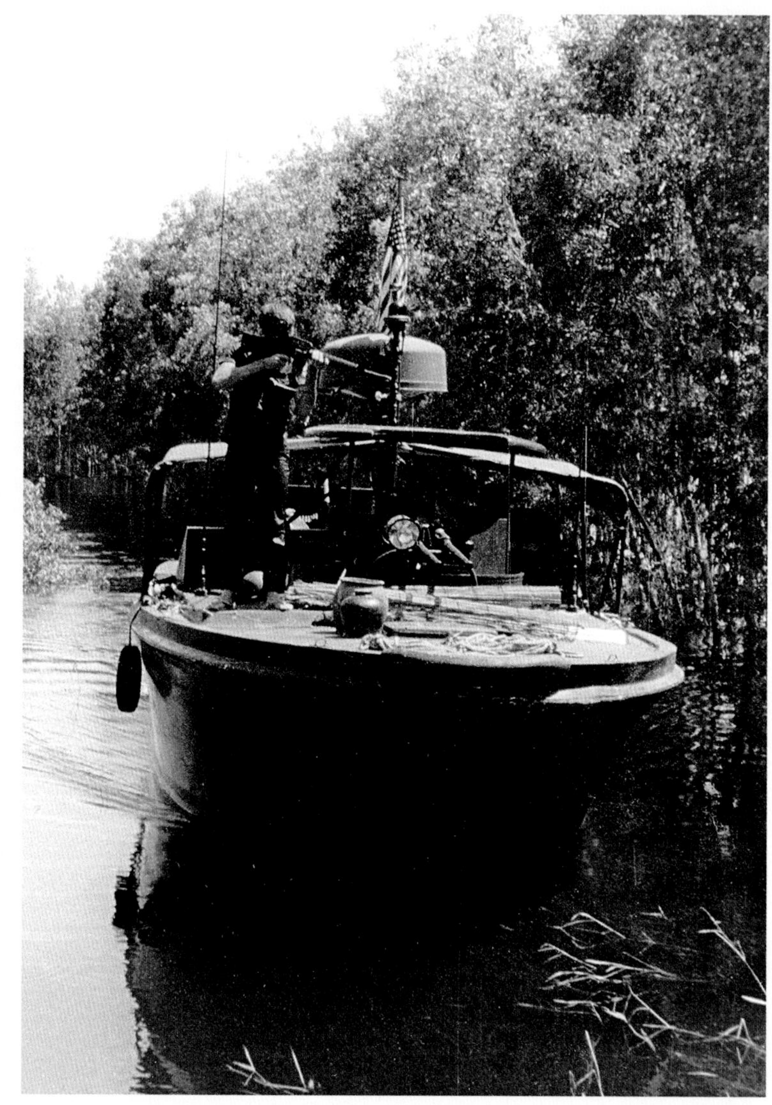

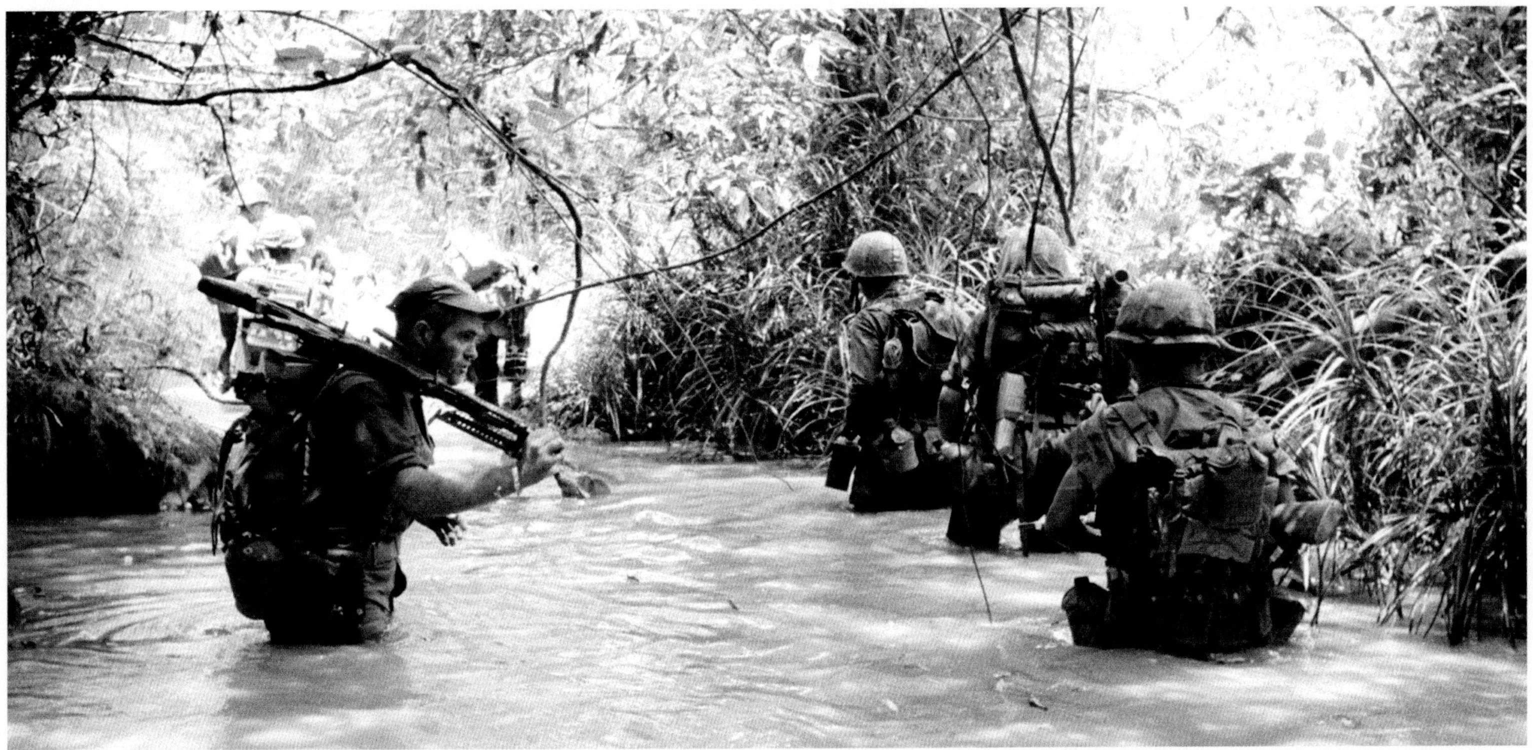

boats were shot up from ambush, destroyed by sunken contact mines, and crippled by hidden rocket-propelled grenade attacks. V.C. small arms and heavy machine gun fire caromed off the boats' steel bar armor with a staccato clatter.

To survive in enemy waters an amazing variety of motor craft was needed. Aluminum-hulled "Swift boats" and 35-foot P.B.R.s constituted the first supply interdiction force when the Seventh Fleet initiated Operation "Market Time" in March 1965. Almost 80,000 V.C. were in the delta against a force of 40,000 A.R.V.N. including infantry, Rangers, and armored cavalry. Patrolling 1,491 miles of natural waterways and 2,485 miles of artificial canals required a strong naval presence. In 1966–67 the task shifted to coordinated boat-air-infantry attacks to clear the V.C. from the delta.

Assault support boats (A.S.B.s) mounted 40mm quick-firing guns and .50 caliber machine guns in rotating turrets called "monitors." Armored troop carriers (A.T.C.s) transported companies of Marines to shore landings while other "Zippo" (nicknamed after the popular cigarette lighter) A.S.B.s scourged the riverbank with flame throwers. Support vessels included rebuilt World War II tank landing ships, fueling ships, and self-propelled three-story barracks ships.

Riverine brown water assaults and ambushes were usually slugging matches pitting Viet Cong rocket-propelled grenades and massed small arms fire against the boats' armor and weapons. Air Force A-37 attack fighters added napalm and their Gatling guns to the missions. By 1969, the Mekong Delta was virtually cleared of major V.C. forces.

SPECIAL NAVAL WEAPONS AFLOAT

Patrol boats and specialized water craft were developed for combat in the Mekong Delta and along the length of the Saigon River. These important supply and troop movement routes were crucial to the Viet Cong. Infantry and naval weapons were modified for use against V.C. soldiers, or enemy watercraft. "Monitor" turrets firing 40mm quick-fire guns or .50 caliber machine guns were common, as were 81mm mortars on rotatable pedestals. Typical 40mm grenade launchers supported flame throwers (called "Zippo" boats) and water cannon to destroy shoreline bunkers. One unit, the Mobile Riverine Force (M.R.F.) was made up of two reinforce brigades—all afloat making use of Armored Troop Carriers (A.T.C.s) and other specialized craft.

Opposite left: "Monitor" turret on the deck of a river patrol boat working the Mekong Delta. These remote-control turrets housed a 40mm rapid-fire gun. The Monitor name comes from the Civil War invention of the first U.S. Navy ironclad ship. That *Monitor* used a two-gun turret and fought the Confederate C.S .*Virginia* (*Merrimac*) to a draw at Hampton Roads in 1862.

Opposite right: Sighting with his M16 rifle, a P.B.R. (River Patrol Boat) crewman searches for possible V.C. in ambush as his fiberglass and aluminum craft noses along the river bank. These P.B.R.s carried twin .50 caliber machine guns forward and a single .50 caliber M.G. in the stern.

Above: Marines wading down one of the many tributaries of the Vietnam river system. All these South Vietnam rivers and creeks were possible Viet Cong and N.V.A. supply routes. Those waterways, too narrow and shallow for patrol boats, had to be checked by foot soldiers.

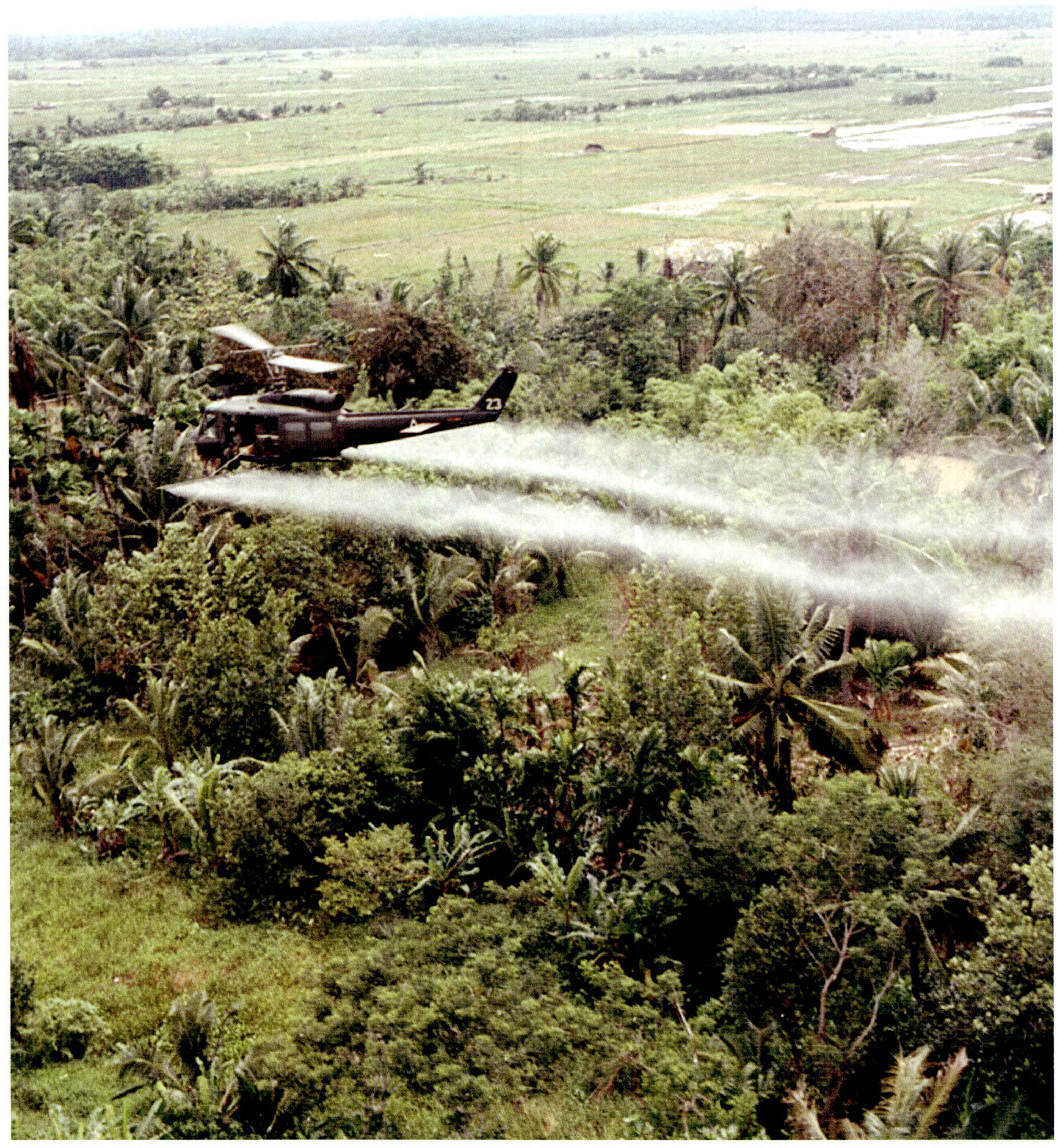

MARINE TROOP SUPPORT MISSIONS

Making use of the river and minimizing casualties required a steep learning curve for the U.S. Marines. Interdicting supplies and destroying V.C. bases and camps along the Mekong Delta required coordinating the P.B.R.s—considering both their firepower and vulnerability—and close air support. After taking heavy casualties during beach landings, Marines learned to let Skyraider aircraft or Huey gunships soften the ground with firepower, land from Hueys or Sikorsky helicopters, destroy the V.C. position, and then pull out aboard the waiting A.T.C.s. Using these tactics, M.R.F. units eventually cleaned out the Delta.

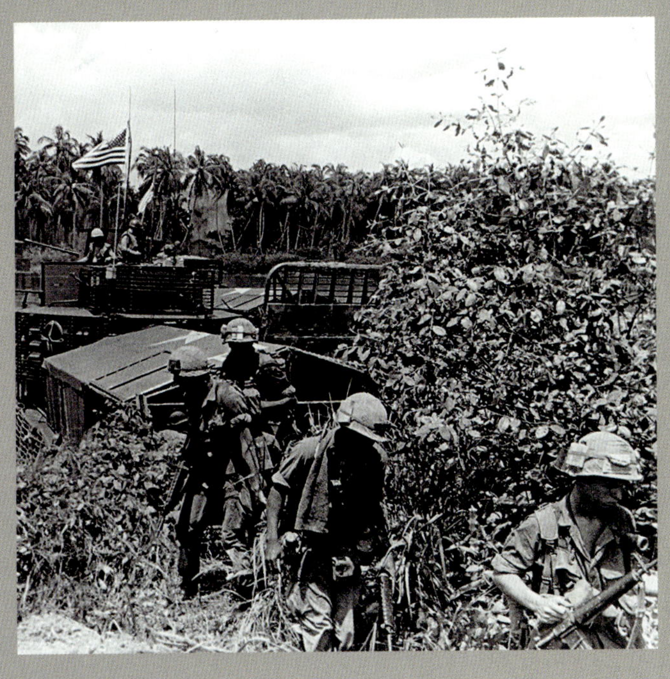

Opposite: A defoliant called "Agent Orange" was sprayed over enemy trails and known positions to kill foliage and expose enemy activities. Later it was learned that the chemical compound released dioxins that became carcinogens and many American and Allied military personnel who came in contact with it contracted various kinds of cancer.

Above: This aluminum-hulled "Swift Boat" fast patrol craft (P.C.F.) was used by the Navy in 1965 for river patrol. It depended on three .50 caliber machine guns and an 81mm mortar plus speed for its defense and ability to cover the patrol area. These craft were used to stop suspected V.C. sampans and boats to be searched for contraband weapons and supplies. By 1968, such searches had severely curtailed the V.C. river supply lines.

Above right: Marines go ashore, landed by armored and sheltered riverine troop ships. Most landings were preceded by heavy aerial bombing or artillery fire support to clear V.C. from the landing area. Earlier in the war, heavy casualties were sustained by the Marines when fire support was not used.

Right: A Marine machine gunner works over the shoreline with his .50 caliber machine gun aboard a Navy river patrol boat. Heavy firepower was a key to survival for the vulnerable boats.

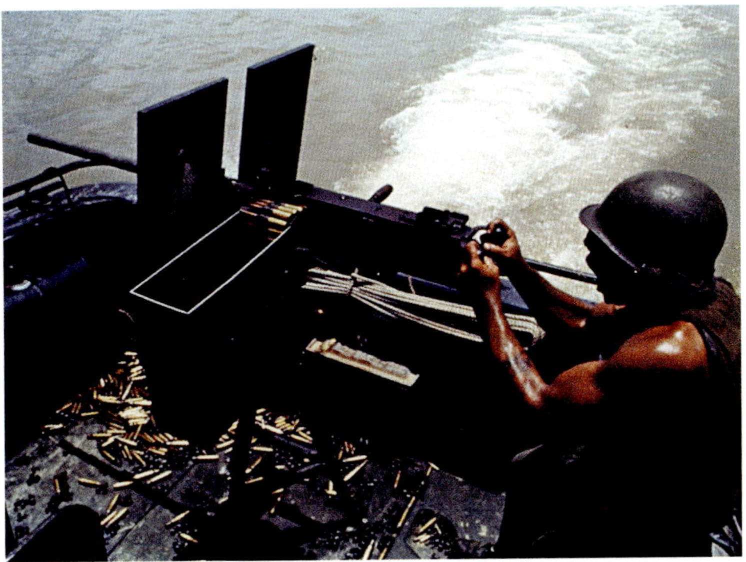

THE "BORDER BATTLES"

IN LATE 1967, N.V.A. GENERAL VO NGUYEN GIAP BEGAN A SERIES OF BATTLES ALONG THE BORDERS OF SOUTH VIETNAM BEGINNING AT THE 17TH PARALLEL, A THREE-MILE DEEP BUFFER BETWEEN THE TWO COUNTRIES REFERRED TO AS THE "DEMILITARIZED ZONE." THESE "BORDER BATTLES" FOLLOWED THE COURSE OF THE HO CHI MINH TRAIL AS IT WOUND SOUTH THROUGH LAOS AND CAMBODIA TO DAK TO IN KONTUM PROVINCE AND THEN TO JUST ABOVE SAIGON IN THE DISTRICT CAPITAL, LOC MINH. THE BATTLES WERE PLANNED TO DRAW AMERICAN FORCES FROM URBAN AREAS SO THAT V.C. UNITS COULD INFILTRATE HIDING PLACES AND CREATE SUPPLY DUMPS FOR THE UPCOMING TET OFFENSIVE PLANNED FOR JANUARY 1968. THEIR DISTRACTION ALSO GAVE N.V.A. AND V.C. COMMANDERS A CHANCE TO SLIP INTO HUE AND SAIGON TO RECONNOITER EACH LOCATION FOR WEAK POINTS AND TROOP PLACEMENTS.

The U.S. Army command under General William Westmoreland had given A.R.V.N. forces the main role in the defense of Saigon. American troops moved to outlying bases as N.V.A. activity seemed to be building in the border areas.

In Quang Tri Province near the D.M.Z., U.S. Marines battled during the summer as N.V.A. units moved troops and artillery down toward the Marine firebase at Khe Sanh. Waves of N.V.A. units flowed down across the 17th Parallel and up into the hills surrounding the artillery compound. For 12 days Marine counter-battery fire enfiladed the N.V.A. positions and prevented them from dominating the hilltops. Further south, on October 29, the 273rd V.C. Regiment attacked Loc Ninh to gather training experience in using V.C. guerrillas in military methods and attack operations against American troops.

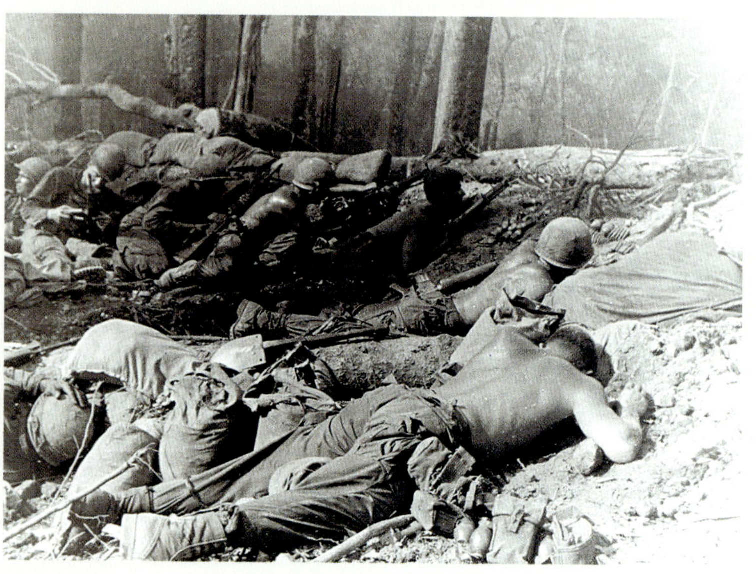

GENERAL WILLIAM WESTMORELAND

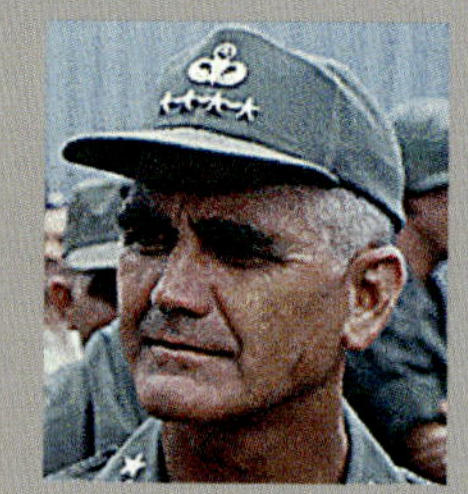

Born in 1914, General Westmoreland fought through World War II with distinction and assumed command of all military forces in Vietnam in 1964. At that time the Viet Cong changed from small-scale guerrilla attacks to N.V.A. full-scale battles, moving forces along the Ho Chi Minh Trail in Cambodia. Management of the war shifted to Washington as large-scale bombing was introduced along with increased numbers of U.S. combat forces. Westmoreland became the media focus for "body count" and "search and destroy" stories, and although the V.C. Tet Offensive was a U.S./A.R.V.N. victory, the scope of the attacks turned many in the U.S. against the escalating war. General Westmoreland left Vietnam in 1968 to become Army Chief of Staff in Washington.

Left: Troops of the 173rd Airborne Brigade under fire at Dak To on Hill 823. Dak To was a high casualty defense against heavy N.V.A. attacks in the mountainous country. The preparation for the planned Tet Offensive made these attacks necessary to draw U.S. forces away from urban areas in the south.

Right: The M61 fragmentation antipersonnel grenade was standard issue. The circular safety pin was pulled free, releasing the safety handle that armed the fuse. Fragmentation effect came from the coil of serrated wire wrapped tightly around the explosive within the thin metal shell.

Opposite: A demolitions soldier leaves a village as hooches that disguised tunnel openings and V.C. bunkers detonate in smoke and flames from his C-4 explosives.

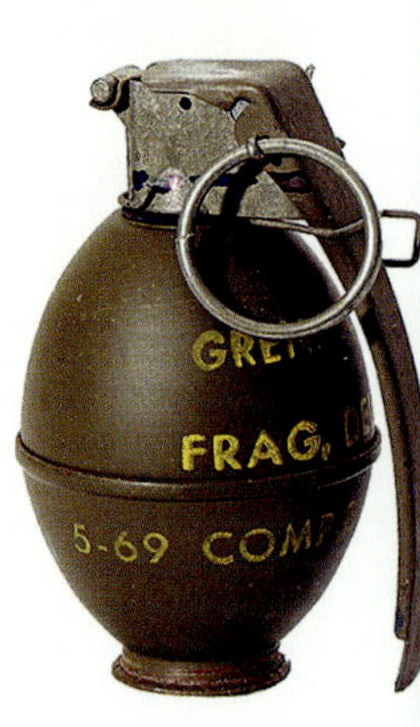

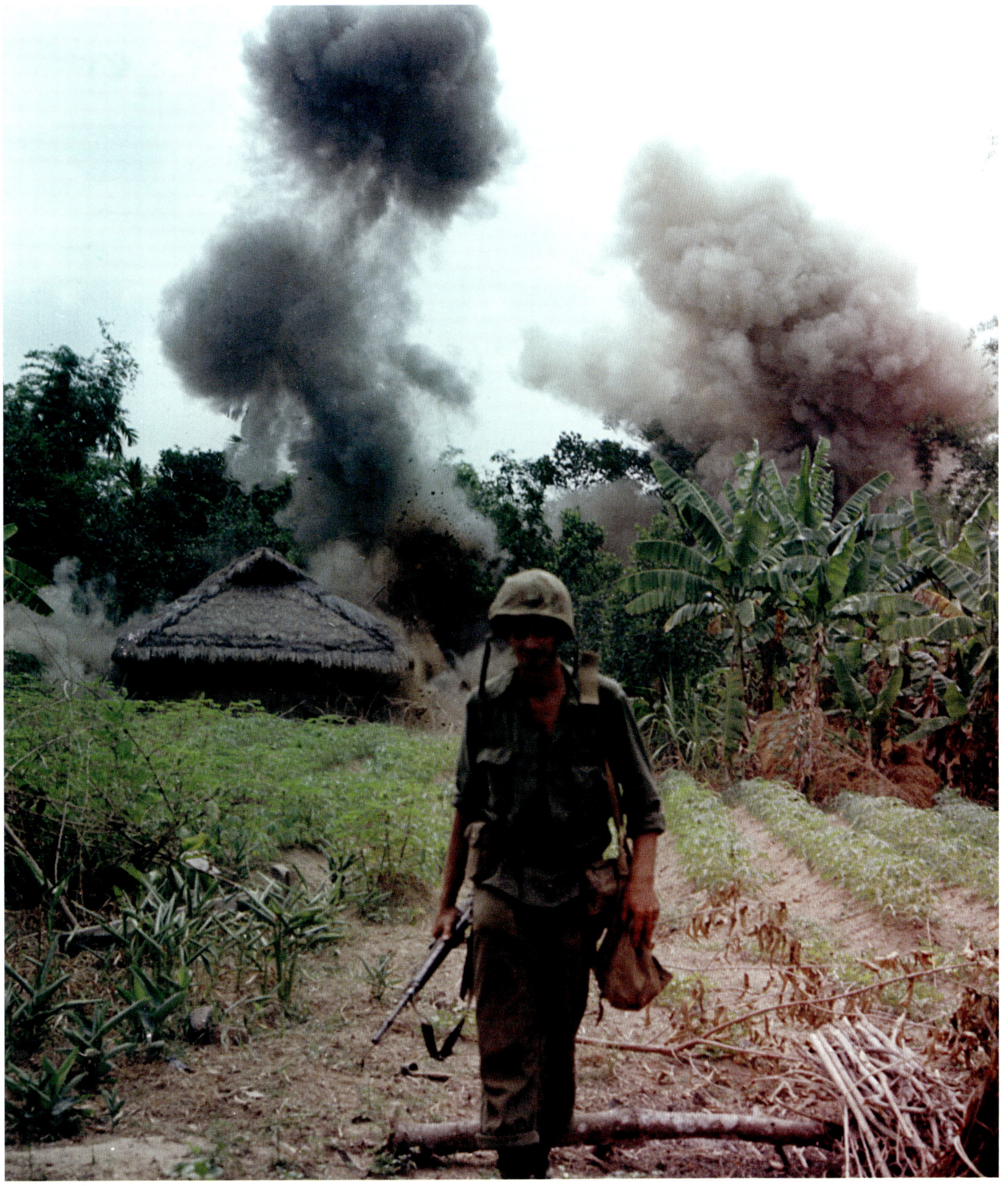

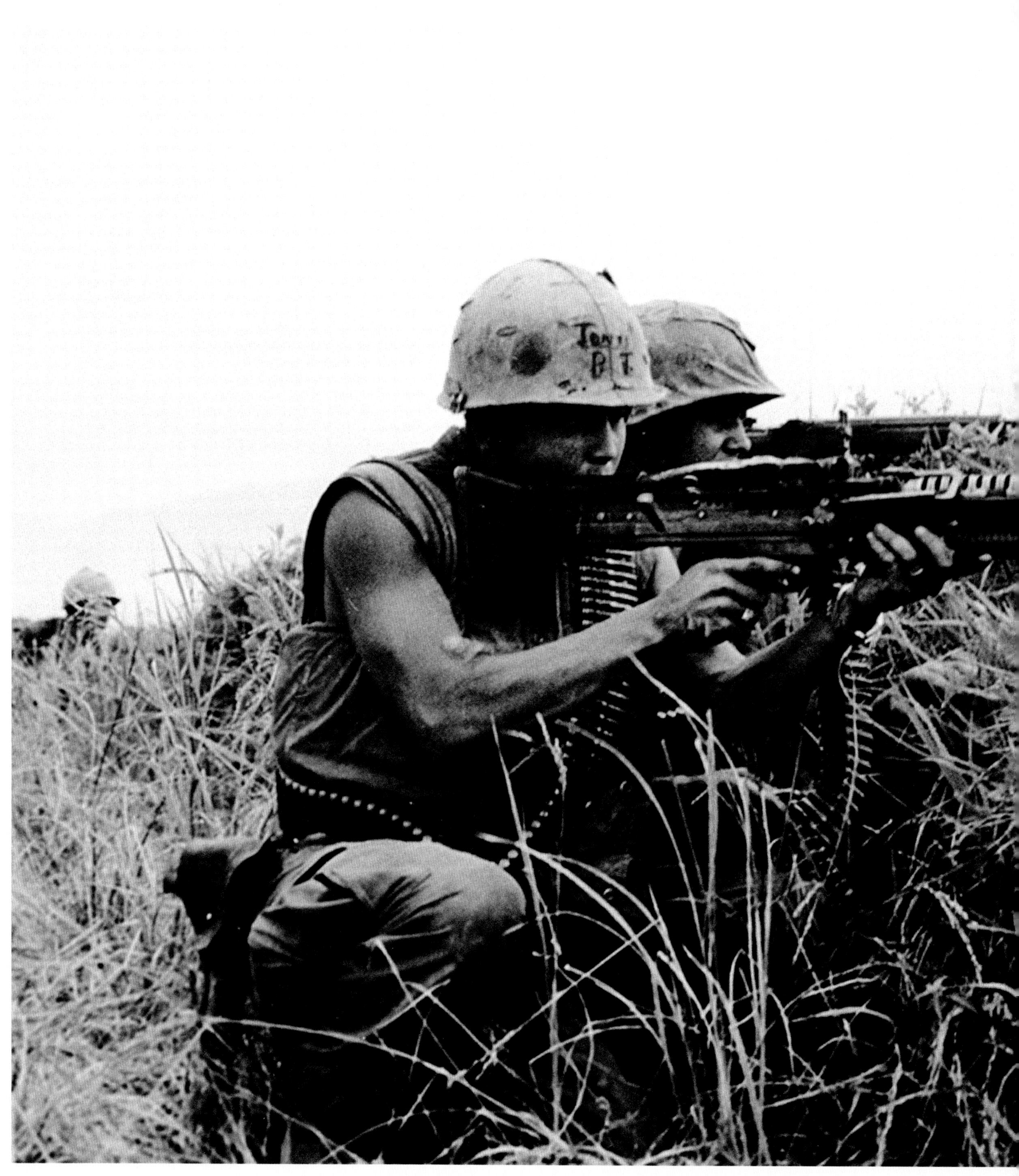

"STARLIGHT" NIGHT VISION SCOPES

"Passive" detection systems were under development in 1961, and by 1965 reached the battlefields as "Starlight" rifle and spotting scopes. Previous infra-red night vision systems could be seen by the N.V.A., but these Starlight units gathered ambient moon- and star- light and magnified it electronically to produce an image on a screen within the optical tube. The AN/PVS-2 Night Vision Sight was available by 1967 and weighed six pounds with its battery operating for 100 hours.

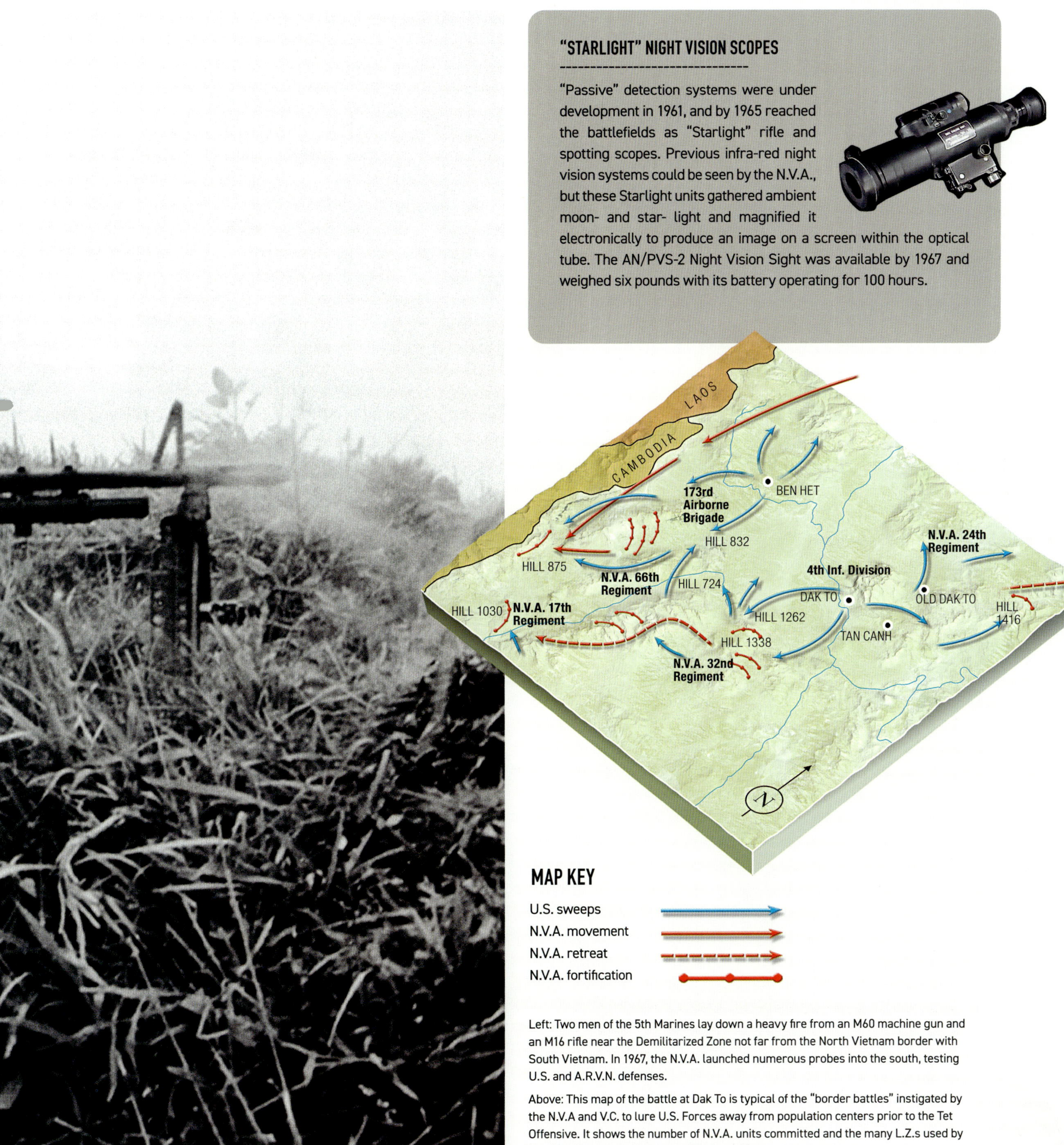

Left: Two men of the 5th Marines lay down a heavy fire from an M60 machine gun and an M16 rifle near the Demilitarized Zone not far from the North Vietnam border with South Vietnam. In 1967, the N.V.A. launched numerous probes into the south, testing U.S. and A.R.V.N. defenses.

Above: This map of the battle at Dak To is typical of the "border battles" instigated by the N.V.A and V.C. to lure U.S. Forces away from population centers prior to the Tet Offensive. It shows the number of N.V.A. units committed and the many L.Z.s used by the Allies to counter the strong N.V.A. positions.

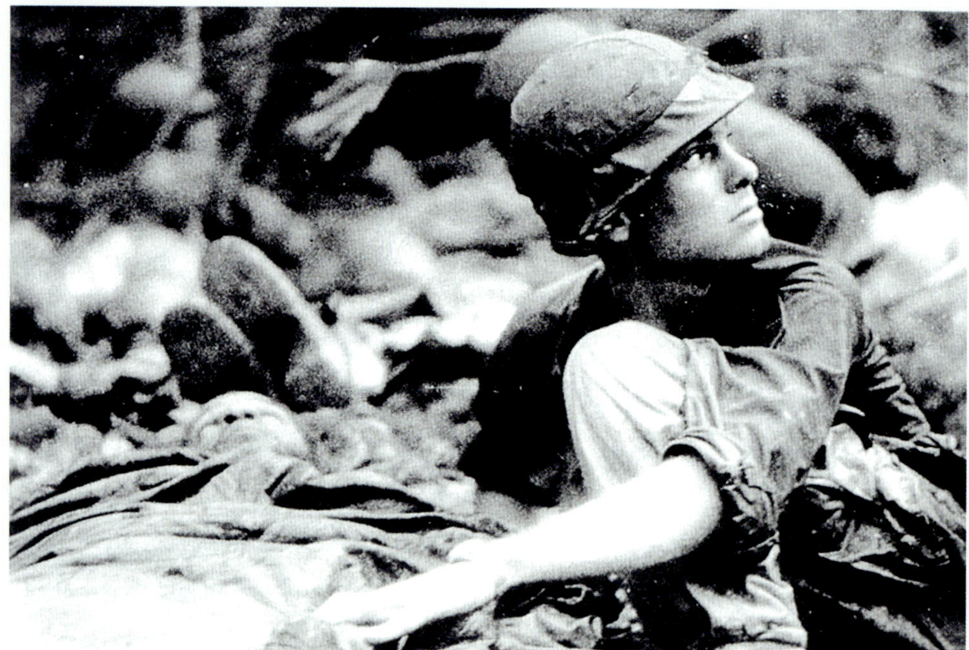

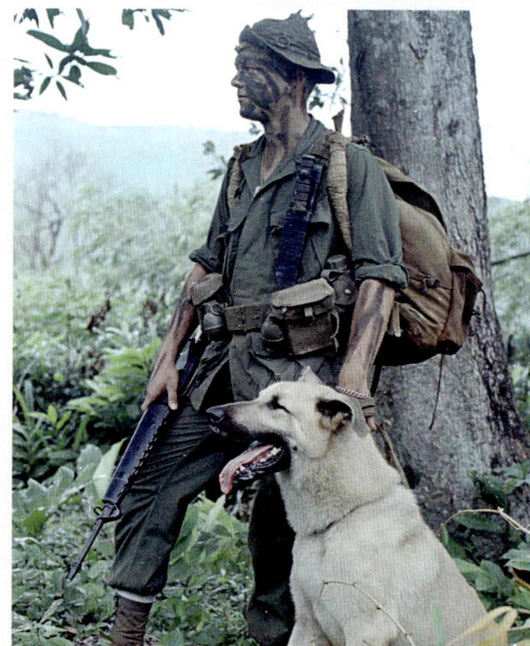

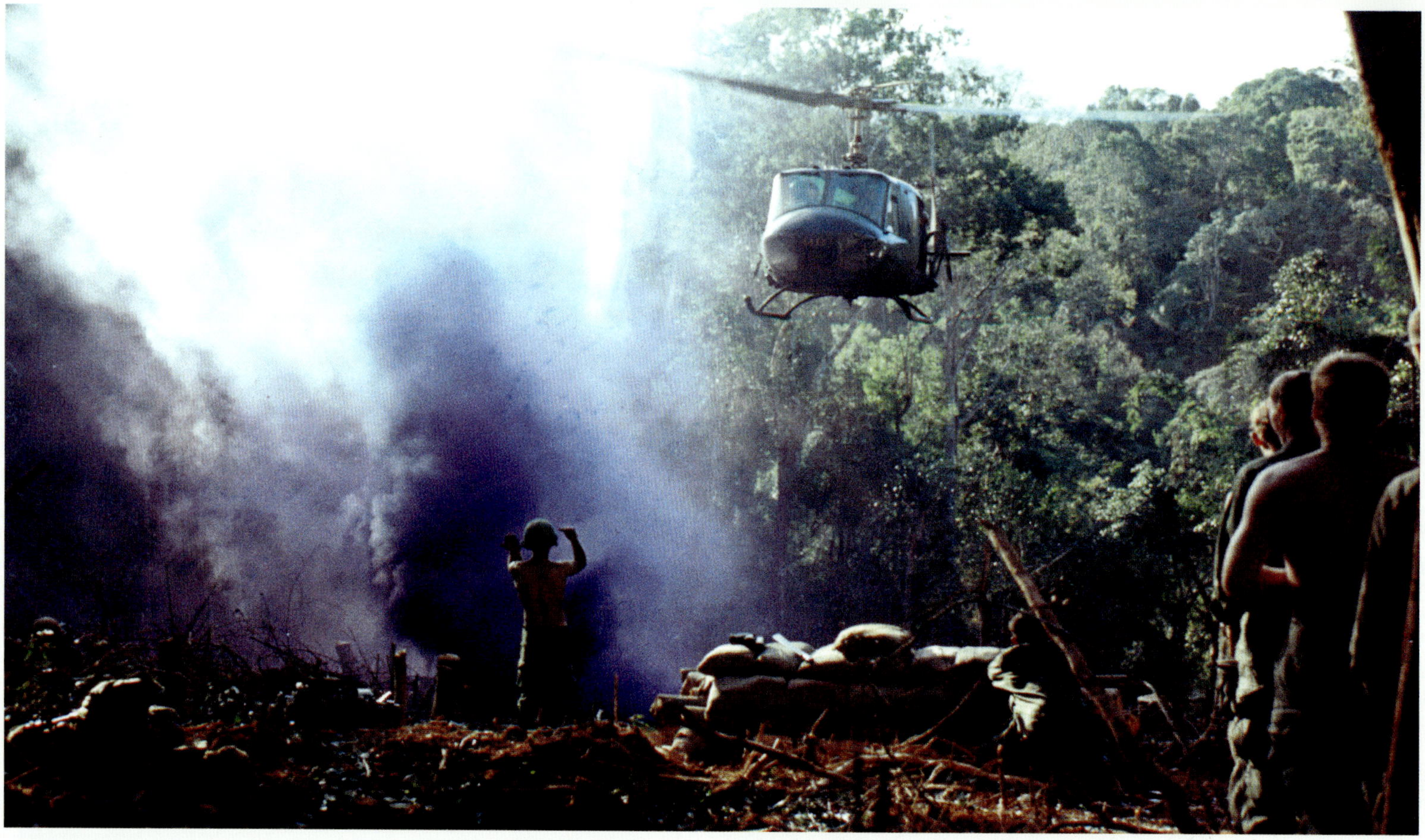

Top left: A soldier at Dak To listens for incoming artillery. N.V.A. mortars frequently harassed soldiers between attacks.

Top right: Corporal McWilliams takes a break with his scout dog, Major. Discovering N.V.A. and V.C. infiltrators required many different approaches. These dogs were trained to scout, others sniffed out explosives. The bond between the soldier and his dog was critical to their job.

Above: A Huey UH-1B(D) resupply helicopter comes into a friendly L.Z. at Dak To marked by colored smoke in 1967.

Opposite: A C-47 "Spooky" aircraft, built for transport use in World War II, banks left over an N.V.A. position in Kontum Province as electrically fired, rotating barrel miniguns in its side-winds rain down a hail of lead. Also called "Puff the Magic Dragon," the planes orbited a target in a left "pylon turn" to concentrate their fire into a small space.

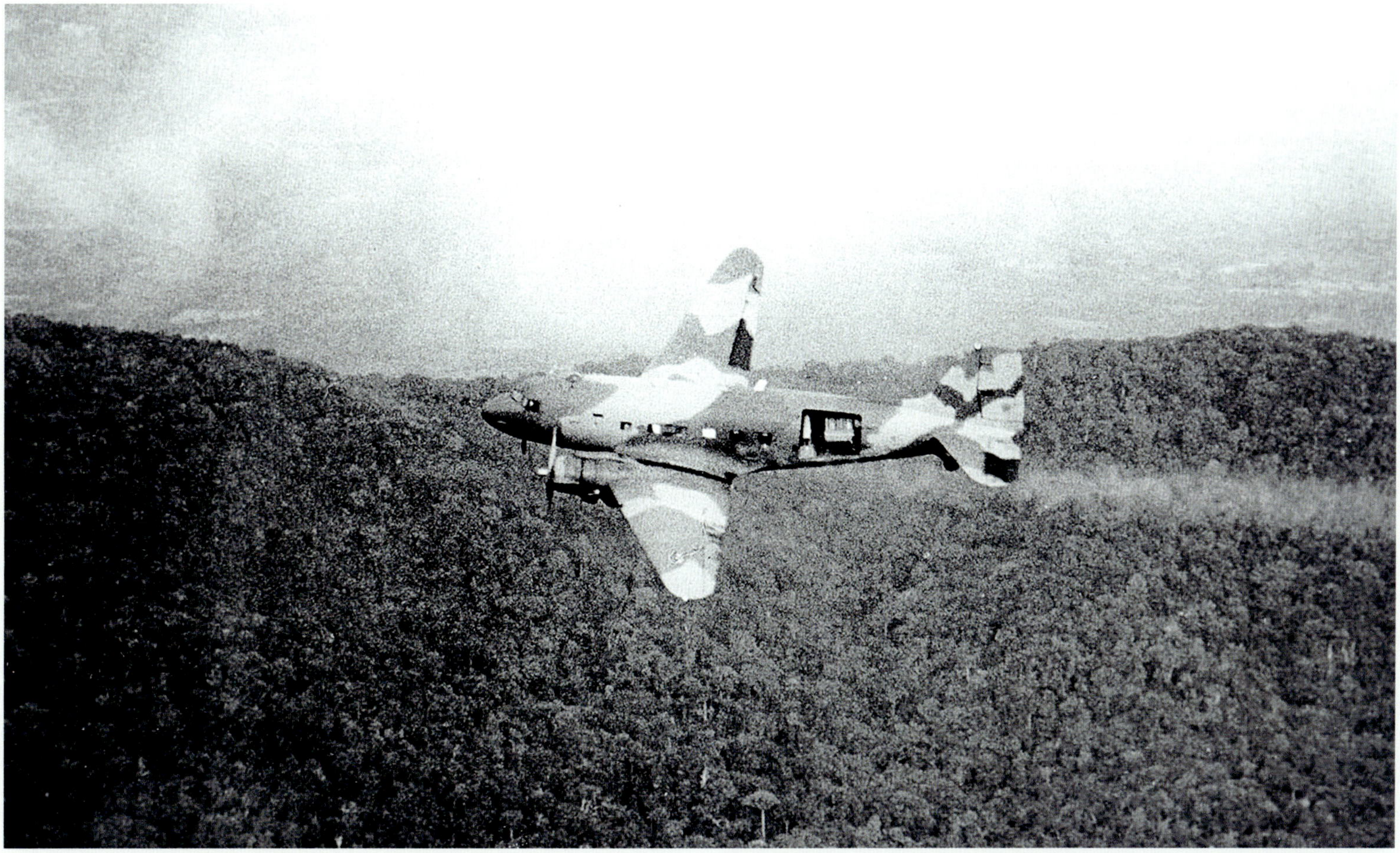

The V.C. were hopelessly outclassed by American military technology and skills. Their attempts were easily discovered by American electronic anti-intrusion devices, guard-dog patrols, and reconnaissance units using Starlight night vision spotting scopes. Once detected, the attackers found themselves under fire from devastating artillery barrages and the guns and rockets of Army aviation. The ability to react quickly to the V.C. attackers in battalion-strength with new tactics and technology overwhelmed the guerrillas.

In the north, the 174th N.V.A. Regiment, reinforced to 6,000 troops, began an attack on Dak To airfield on November 3, in a battle that would last 20 days. Heavy and costly skirmishing had been raging well before the battle, drawing in additional American and Allied forces before finally totaling 4,500 soldiers. Assaults on fortified bunkers, prepared well in advance, were necessary to clear the hills of the N.V.A. The cost to the N.V.A. and to the U.S. 4th Division and the 173rd Airborne Brigade amounted to 1,455 N.V.A. and 285 Americans, with 985 American wounded. It was one of the bloodiest battles of the war.

One result of the "border battles" was the return of U.S. troops to the Saigon area to bolster the A.R.V.N. garrison—a reversal of Giap's plan. Alerted U.S. and Allied forces would be better prepared for the Tet Offensive that would erupt at the beginning of 1968.

ELECTRONIC ENEMY SENSING DEVICES

Keeping track of V.C./N.V.A. troop and supply movements—especially during these Cambodian border battles—was aided by motion sensors planted along paths and roads frequented by troop and supply convoys. Recon teams planted camouflaged miniature TRC-3 detectors on trails that broadcast any movement. The Air Force also delivered ADSIDs (Air-Delivered Seismic Intrusion Detectors) dropped from aircraft to spike into the ground like lawn darts. The N.V.A. used counter measures such as running a truck back and forth past the sensor while their supplies crossed on another distant trail. Sensor monitors also had to differentiate between moving troops and mating frogs.

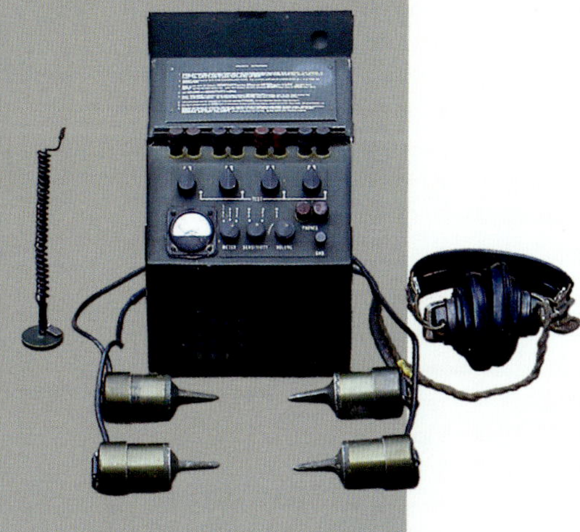

CHAPTER 12

U.S. SOLDIER

MORE THAN A THIRD OF THE ENTIRE UNITED STATES' MILITARY FORCE WAS COMMITTED TO THE WAR IN VIETNAM FROM 1965 TO 1973. ESSENTIALLY, THE VIETNAM CONFLICT WAS A LAND WAR AND THE ARMED SERVICES WERE DEPLOYED TO SUPPORT THE "GROUND POUNDERS," THE "GRUNTS," THE "STRAIGHT-LEG INFANTRY"—ARMY OR MARINES—WHOSE ULTIMATE SUCCESSES OR FAILURES DETERMINED THE COURSE OF EVENTS.

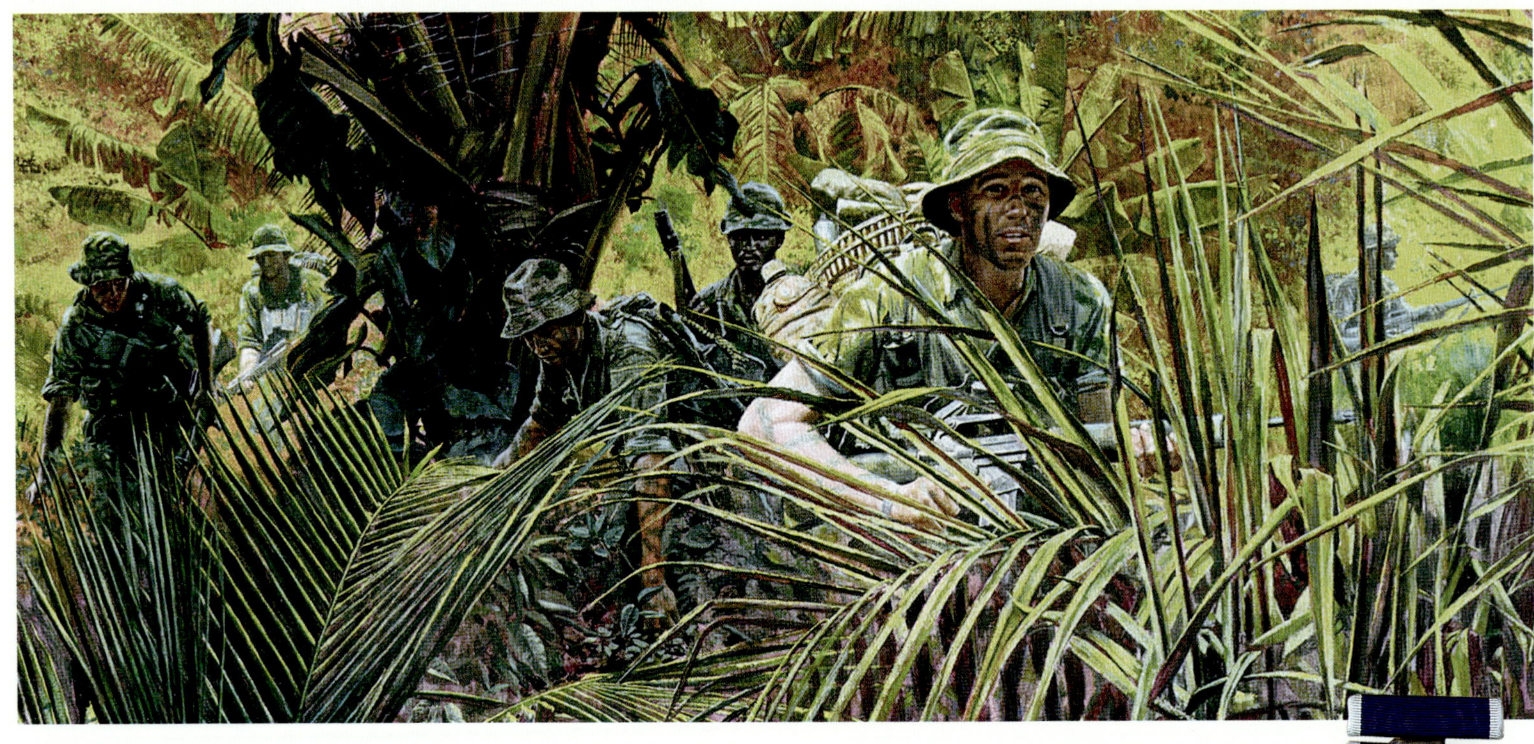

In a war of mobility with no real "front lines" or "rear area," combat required a tough mind as well as fighting skills and a fit body. The American military provided every technological assistance and logistical need, months of training—and re-training as conditions changed or new tactics evolved. However, it was tough-minded, resilient, and innovative leadership that kept men alive and won battles.

The average soldier was 19–20 years old and most were unmarried. About 76 percent came from working class or lower income families, and only 26 percent were draftees. Most who went into combat carried a rifle, or manned a crew-served weapon, such as a mortar or heavy machine gun, and lived and fought from day to day with what he carried with him.

"In-country," he could be self-sufficient for days at a time. Most wore no body armor because practical body armor had not been perfected for grunts. Only the heavy, nylon flak vest was occasionally worn. Ceramic-aluminum oxide "chickenplate" armor went to door gunners in helicopters. The soldier's shirt and fatigue uniform, however, were 98 percent mosquito proof. The World War II design M-1 helmet weighed three-and-a-

Right: The Purple Heart award, presented to any soldier or sailor wounded in any action against an enemy of the United States.

Above: Over 7,000 Army National Guardsmen served in the war zone. Company D (Ranger), 151st Infantry, Indiana Army National Guard arrived in December 1968. The Indiana Rangers were assigned reconnaissance and intelligence-gathering missions. Operating deep in enemy territory, Ranger patrols engaged enemy units while conducting raids, ambushes, and surveillance missions. Delta Company members were awarded 510 medals for valor and service.

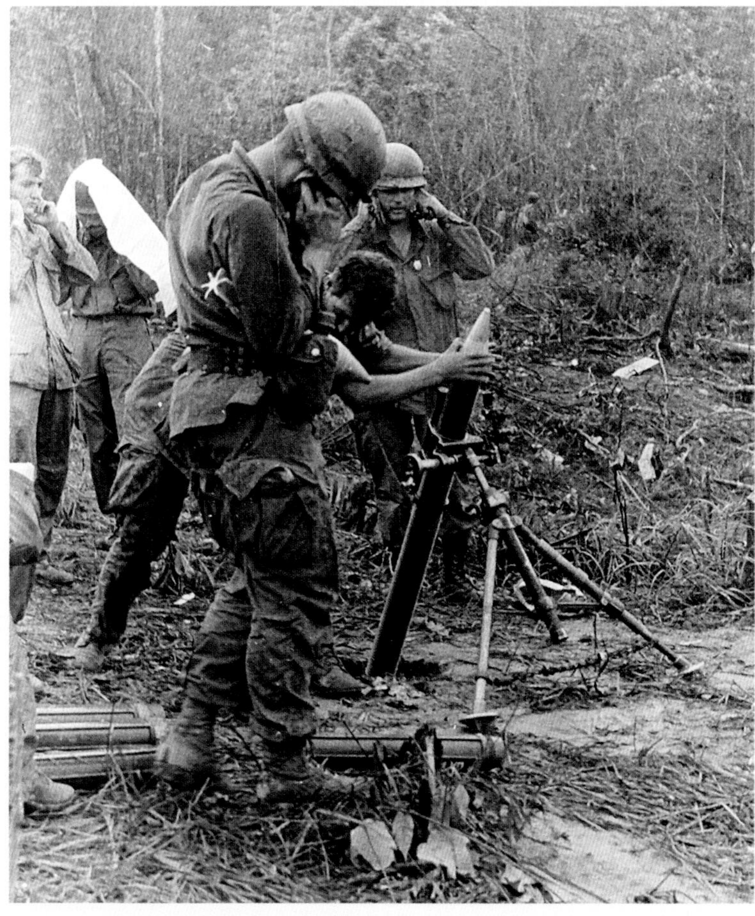

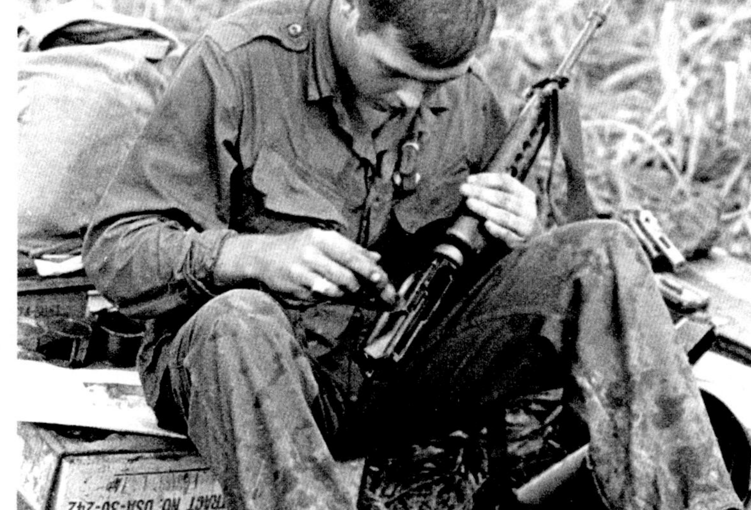

Above: A light 60mm mortar team loads mortar bombs to lob at a high angle on an N.V.A. target. The 60mm mortar is part of a weapons platoon attached to an infantry company. The mortar tube and tripod are carried separately and the bombs are distributed among members of the platoon.

Above right: The fully automatic M16A1 assault rifle arrived in Vietnam in 1965. Under jungle combat conditions the first rifles jammed because mud and damp gummed up the bolt operation and corroded the breech.

Right: A soldier applies L.S.A. lubricant to his M16 rifle's receiver and bolt channel. Troops were issued a comic book that stressed weapon cleaning three to five times a day.

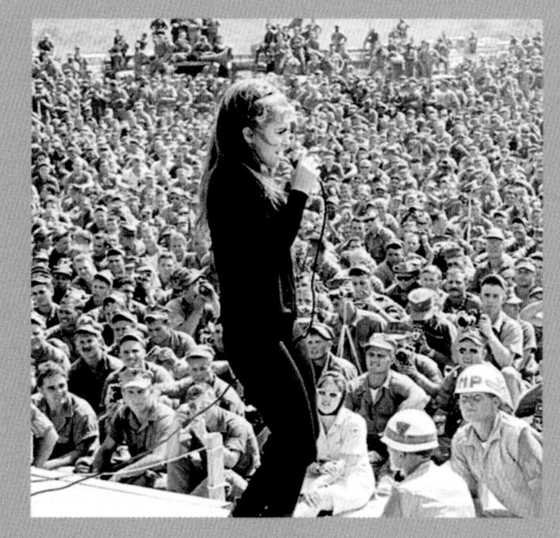

U.S.O. SHOWS FOR R.&.R TROOPS

Formed in 1941, the U.S.O. (United Service Organization) is a privately operated non-profit company created at the request of President Roosevelt to give troops a touch of home. They opened U.S.O. centers in combat areas for the first time in Saigon, 1963. Seventeen Vietnam centers and six serving Thailand were visited by a million service members a month. In 1964, Bob Hope brought his U.S.O. Christmas Show to Vietnam for the first time; he kept coming back for the next ten years. During the Vietnam years, about 5,559 performances took place. When the U.S.O was threatened with disbanding in 1974, a review concluded, "If there were no U.S.O., another organization would have to be created... isolation of the military from civilian influence is not, we believe, in the best interest of this nation."

half pounds and came with a canvas cover slotted for adding camouflage.

Meals were canned C-rations that came in a "meal" package weighing two-and-a-half pounds. The main course, such as meatballs and beans, could be heated over a pinch of C-4 explosive set alight with a match. He had an aluminum mess kit, at least two water bottles, first aid kit, cigarettes, poncho (ground sheet) and poncho liner for sleeping. Bottles of insect repellent were stuck in the band around his helmet. His nylon and leather boots were as waterproof as possible. Over his green or camouflage fatigues he wore a harness and often extra bandoliers of ammunition for his M16A1 rifle or M79 grenade launcher.

Fragmentation grenades were carried in canvas pouches. Hooking them to a belt by the handle was too dangerous, as the grenade handles could break unnoticed, setting the grenade off. Claymore directional mines were packaged two to a canvas bag that, once emptied, was used to hold more ammunition for the soldier's rifle. His bayonet fit in a belt scabbard and a "shelter half" (half of a tent) was rolled just above his butt. The load averaged 50–60 pounds, but was usually taken by helicopter or truck from one bivouac to another and virtually never carried.

He went to war in helicopters or trucks, and aboard armored personnel carriers (A.P.C.s). Once he arrived at his bivouac he walked into battle. Rotation out of the "boonies" (areas remote from the main bases at Da Nang or Saigon) to showers and maybe a U.S.O. stage show was a welcome relief, but each day he woke up alive was a gift.

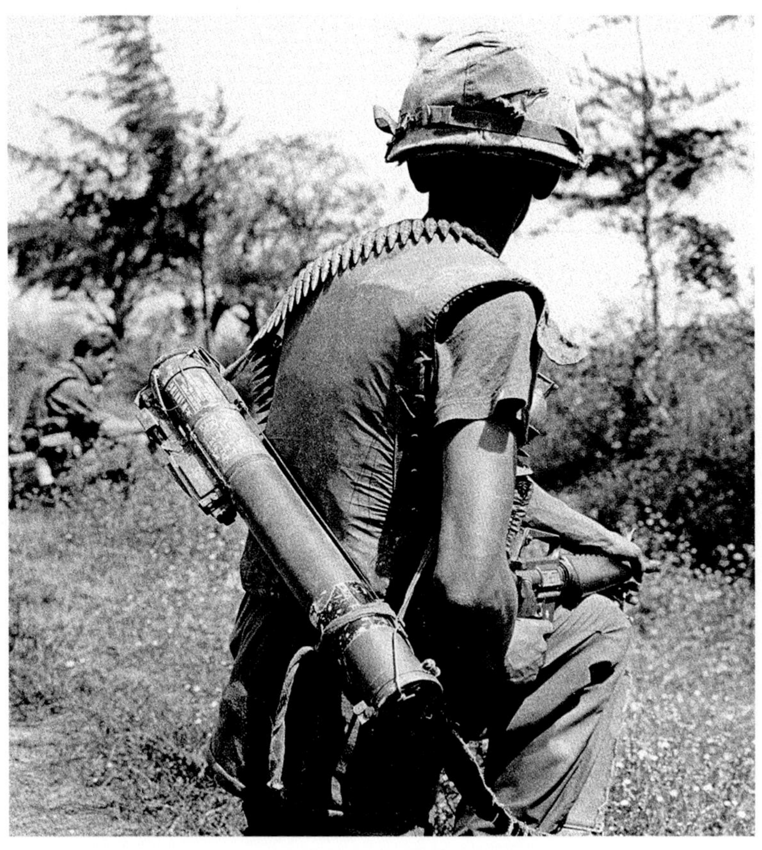

Above and below: Two photos showing the L.A.W. (light anti-tank weapon), a use-once-and-discard shoulder-fired weapon that fires a high-explosive warhead that can penetrate light armor.

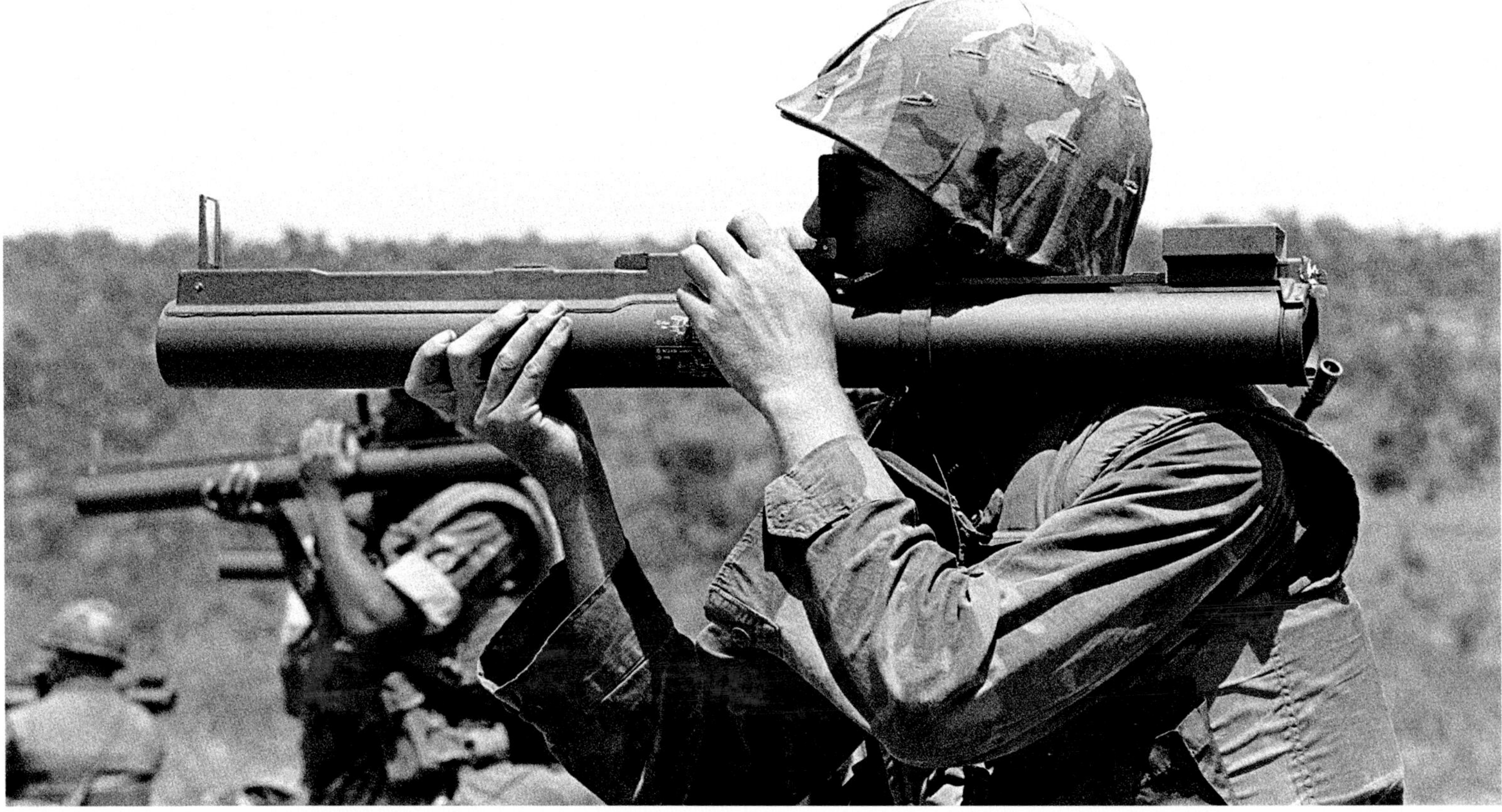

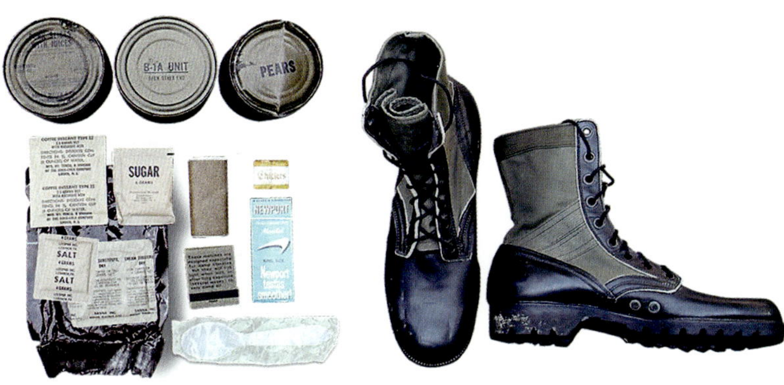

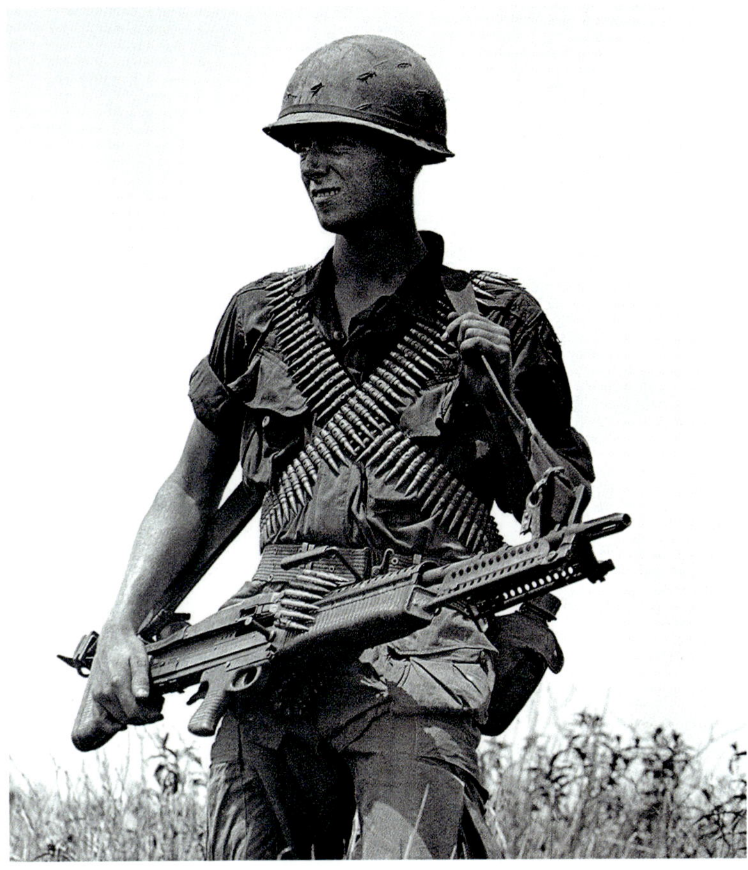

Above left: The Individual Combat Meal weighed approximately 2 pounds and was available in 12 different menus. Each meal consisted of a canned meat course, a canned fruit course, and a B-unit tin containing one of the various types of crackers. Soldiers opened the cans with the P-38 can opener. C-rations were issued throughout the Vietnam War.

Above right: Tropical jungle boots, issued in 1962 with a direct molded sole (D.M.S.), overcame the problems of the previous boot, eliminating its rotting and leaking. The D.M.S. boot had nylon and leather uppers with improved durability. Originally designed for Special Forces in 1960, it became a general issue pattern.

Right: This lethal young soldier in tropical greens carries his M60 light machine gun with its bipod folded ready for action, with a few 7.62 rounds trailing from its closed breech. He wears more ammunition for easy access in case of a sudden firefight. Additional ammo in sealed waterproof cans was carried by other members of the squad.

Below right: A soldier loads his single-shot M79 grenade launcher. The shoulder-fired weapon (pictured far left) fires a 40mm grenade used against personnel, or to launch smoke grenades and flares.

COMPOSITION OF AMERICAN SQUAD/PLATOON

The American Army (and Marines) went to war with a highly structured table of organization. In Vietnam the platoon was usually the largest unit directly engaged. It was made up of from two to four squads, and led by a lieutenant, a sergeant first class, and the squad leaders (usually sergeants), and included a radio operator. Its number of men depended on the number of squads, since each squad had eight to ten men. A weapons squad with light machine gun, mortar, anti-tank weapons, grenade launchers, and any specialty equipment such as a sniper team was also available.

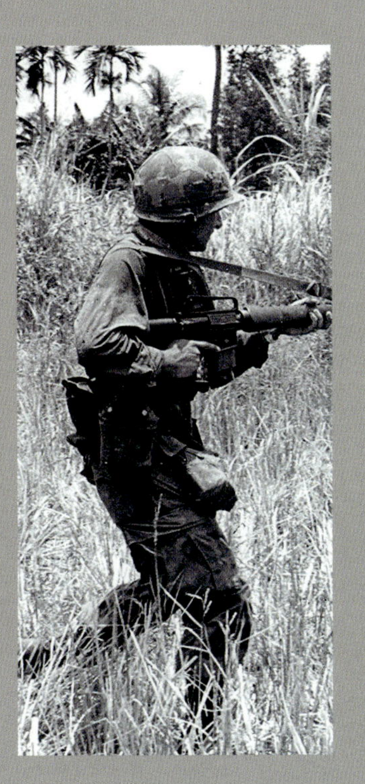

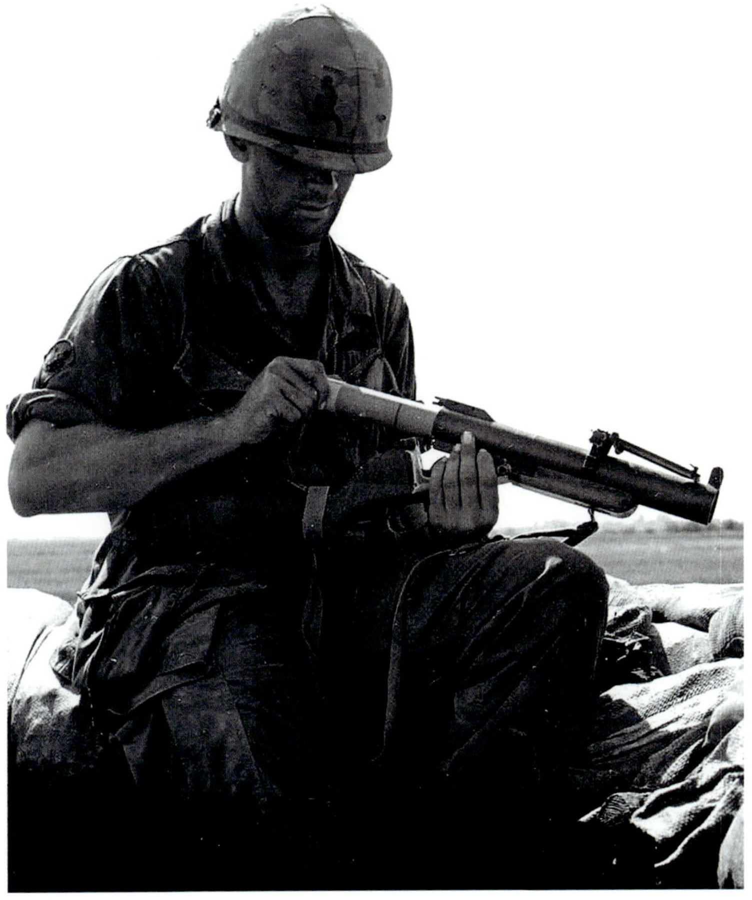

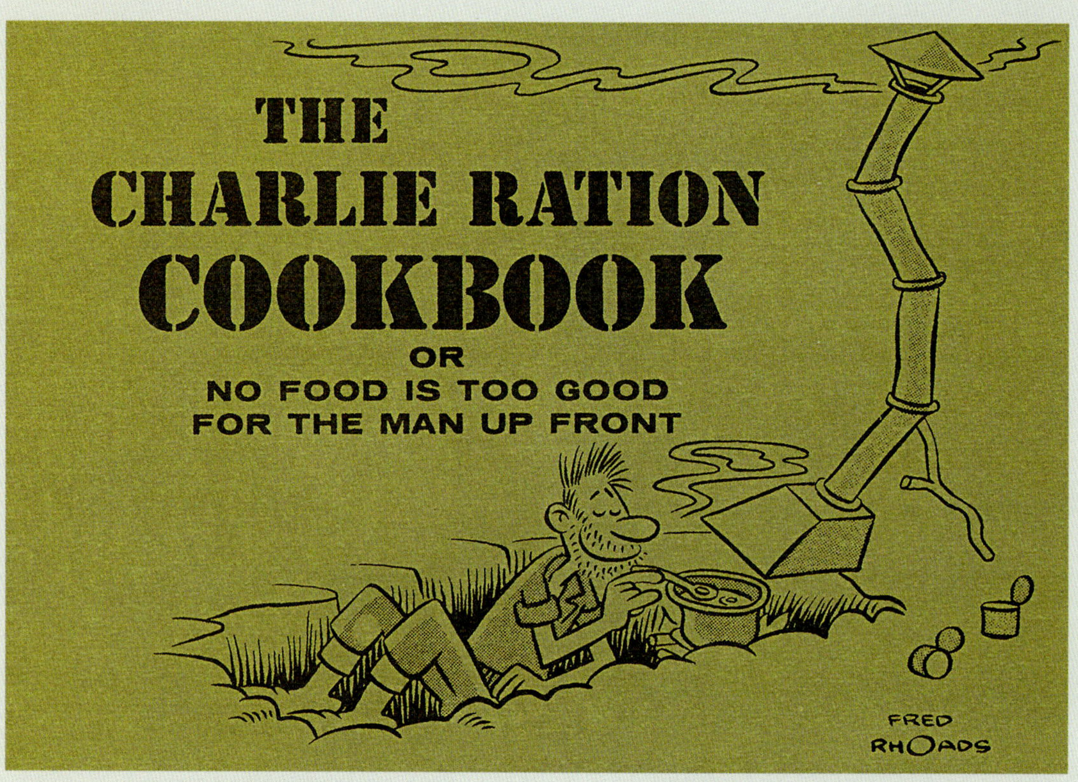

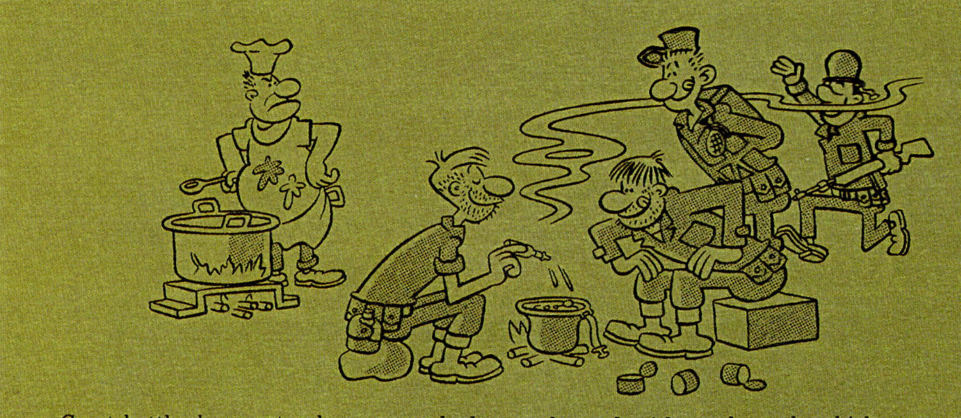

Great battles have not only produced famous generals, but gourmet dishes as well. Chicken Marengo was named after the battle of Marengo, in which Napoleon Bonaparte defeated the Austrians on the 14th of June, 1800. This dish was first cooked on the battlefield itself by Dunand, chef to Napoleon.

Bonaparte, who ate nothing until after a day's battle was over, had gone forward with his general staff and was a long way from his supply wagons. Seeing his enemies put to flight, he asked Dunand to prepare dinner for him. All the chef could find were three eggs, four tomatoes, six crayfish, a small hen, a little garlic, some oil and a saucepan. He then and there created the Chicken Marengo.

The dish was served on a tin plate, the chicken surrounded by the fried eggs and crayfish, with the sauce poured over it, the water being laced with brandy borrowed from the General's flask. Bonaparte, having feasted upon it, said to Dunand, "You must feed me like this after every battle."

The American fighting man today does not have a personal chef, but he does have his C-

Rations. The contents of these remarkable packages contain far more nutriments than normally required for any man in the field and offer solid, good-tasting meals that are the envy of fighting men all over the world. Occasionally, though, a trooper will find it necessary to depend on C-Rations for a prolonged period of time . . . and it is with this in mind that TABASCO brand pepper sauce thought of a recipe book to help add dash and variety. There is no telling what gastronomic creations can be concocted with the C-Rations as a basic, combined with what the American trooper can find in the field or village near the combat zone. All he needs is imagination and a buddy who will act as assistant chef.

Whether eaten alone, with a buddy or two or in a group, the recipes found in this book are predominantly based on the single units and various combinations of the basic C-Rations. Outside ingredients may help, but they are not essential to the menus. (Another thought: when combat situations make it impossible to do anything with your C-Rations except open them up and eat them cold, adding Tabasco right from the bottle will always add a distinctive bright flavor.)

G.I. Joe has gone gourmet. These recipes were created for the fighting man in the field. Bon appétit.

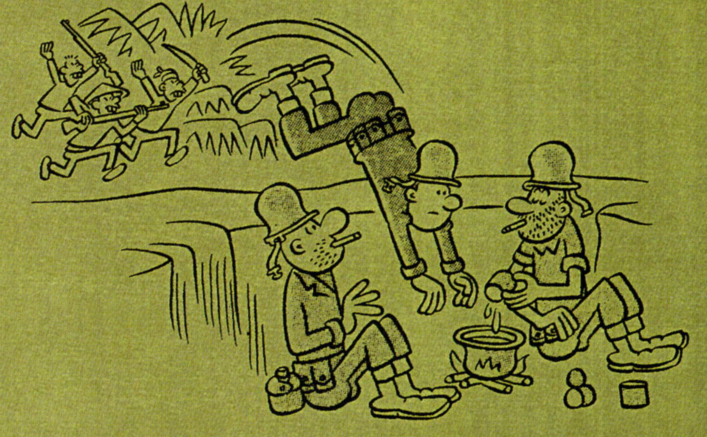

FOX HOLE DINNER FOR TWO
(*Turkey and Chicken Poulette*)

Two spoons butter or oil or fat
Two spoons flour
***One can chicken and noodles**
***One can turkey loaf, cut up into pieces**
Three dashes TABASCO pepper sauce
***Salt and pepper to taste**
***One can cheese spread**
***12 spoons milk**
***Crackers from one C-Ration can, crumbled**

No one likes to dine alone, and this recipe is ideal to combine a variety of C-Ration Units.

Melt butter or oil or fat, add flour and stir until smooth. Add milk and continue to cook until sauce begins to thicken. Add cheese spread and cook until cheese melts and sauce is even. Empty cans of turkey loaf and chicken noodles into the cheese sauce. Season with Tabasco, salt and pepper to taste and continue cooking. Cover poulette with crumbled crackers and serve piping hot.

**This is from your Basic C-Ration*

SOUP DU JOUR

***One can ham and lima beans, mashed**
One equal can hot water
***Salt and pepper to taste**
A generous dash TABASCO pepper sauce
Three spoons green onions, chopped and sautéed in butter or oil or fat
Two spoons butter or oil or fat for the onions
Four spoons butter or oil or fat for the bread croutons or crumbled crackers
***Fried bread croutons or crumbled crackers**

There is a soup du jour on every menu in every American restaurant from Maine to Frisco. There is no reason why the Armed Forces should be an exception. The front line fighting man has one advantage. He knows what goes into his soup du jour.

Mash the ham and lima bean mixture to a pulp. Combine with a can of hot water and bring to a boil, stirring briskly all the time. Add Tabasco and salt and pepper to taste. Serve piping hot, garnished with fried white bread croutons (pieces of white bread cut up into cubes) or crumbled crackers sautéed in butter or oil or fat.

**This is from your Basic C-Ration*

BREAST OF CHICKEN UNDER BULLETS

***One can boned chicken**
***One can cheese spread**
***Salt and pepper to taste**
One dash TABASCO pepper sauce
***White bread**
Two spoons butter or oil or fat, if available

Breast of chicken under glass was never intended for areas where glass and shrapnel fly. This dish can be prepared in quick time, using only the Basic C-Ration.

Heat the can of boned chicken in a meat can. Melt the cheese spread. If butter or oil or fat is available, add two spoons. Season with salt and pepper and Tabasco. Cut loaf of white bread in half, trimmed if so desired. Place a mound of chicken over each half of white bread and cover each with the hot melted cheese sauce. This should stick to your ribs.

**This is from your Basic C-Ration*

BATTLEFIELD FUFU
(*Chicken with Peanut Butter Sauce*)

***One can boned chicken**
***One can peanut butter**
Two spoons butter or oil or fat
One spoon soya sauce
Two dashes TABASCO pepper sauce
***Two to three spoons milk**

Ham slices or pork steaks may be substituted for the boned chicken. No matter what you do to it, though, it is still Battlefield FuFu.

Melt the butter or oil or fat and add the peanut butter. Stir until well blended. Add the milk and continue cooking until sauce is smooth. Now add the can of boned chicken, pulled apart, and the soya sauce and Tabasco. Continue cooking until hot and smooth. This may be served over boiled rice or crumbled crackers or with white bread.

**This is from your Basic C-Ration*

HAM WITH SPICED APRICOTS

***One can fried ham, sliced with juices**
***One can apricots with juice**
***One can jam**
Three spoons flour
Three spoons butter or oil or fat
One spoon lemon juice
One spoon soya sauce
Generous dash TABASCO pepper sauce
***Salt and pepper to taste**

Melt butter or oil or fat, add flour and stir until well blended. Add the jam and cook until melted. Now add the juices from the ham and the apricots as well as the lemon juice, soya sauce and Tabasco. Salt and pepper to taste. Con-

C-RATION COOKBOOK

C-rations were an improvement on World War II "K" rations, but even with the variety of canned entrées and snacks, this cookbook was welcome.

CHAPTER 13

N.V.A. SOLDIER

THE OPPONENTS OF THE AMERICANS AND A.R.V.N. WERE TWO SEPARATE ARMIES. THE PEOPLE'S LIBERATION ARMED FORCES (P.L.A.F.), THE MILITARY ARM OF THE NATIONAL LIBERATION FRONT (N.L.F.), WAS CREATED IN 1961 FROM PARAMILITARY UNITS OPERATING IN THE CENTRAL HIGHLANDS AND MEKONG DELTA OF SOUTH VIETNAM. THE DIEM GOVERNMENT CONTEMPTUOUSLY REFERRED TO THEM AS "VIET CONG," WHICH MEANS "VIETNAMESE COMMUNISTS." ALTHOUGH OSTENSIBLY A SEPARATE ORGANIZATION FROM HANOI'S WORKERS' PARTY OF VIETNAM AND PEOPLE'S ARMY OF NORTH VIETNAM (P.A.V.N.), THE LEADERSHIP OF THE N.L.F. AND V.C. BASICALLY TOOK THEIR ORDERS FROM THE NORTHERN CAPITAL.

The V.C. were a true guerrilla insurgency. Their uniform was a black "pajama" top and trousers, cinched with a web belt and cloth shoulder braces. The V.C. guerrilla carried personal items and food in cloth pouches hung from the belt and in shoulder bags. A linen tube of dry rice looped over his shoulder like a bandolier. He could subsist for days on boiled rice spiced with *nouc mam*, a fermented fish paste. A hearty family-like atmosphere of sharing pervaded each squad. Every regular

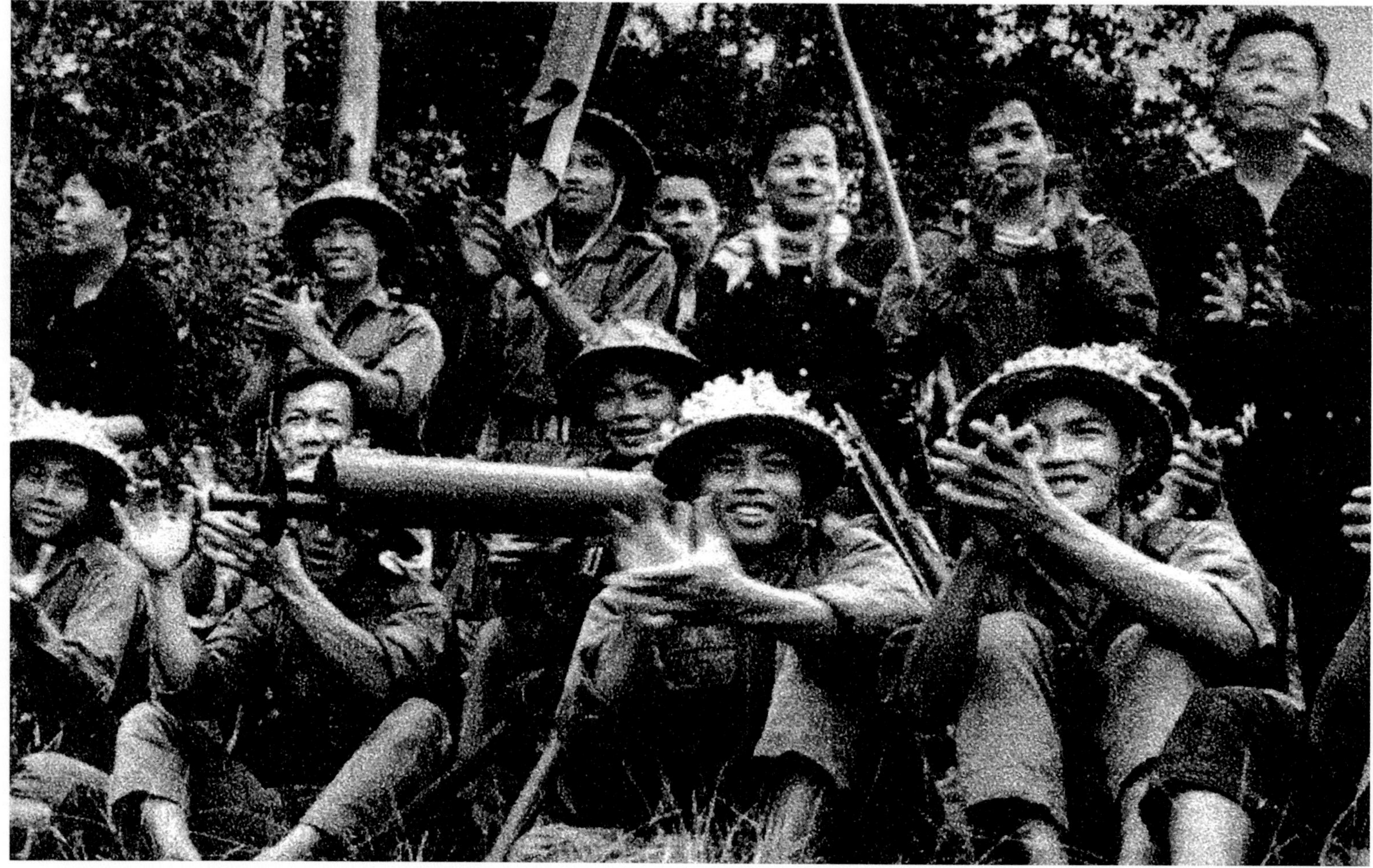

or "main force" V.C. carried a rice bowl, water canteen, and spoon, and some had a collapsible mess kit. Their shoes were "Papa Ho" (slang for Ho Chi Minh) sandals cut from old truck tires.

V.C. weapons were a mixed lot, from French and Chinese submachine guns and rifles to rocket-propelled grenade launchers and crew-served heavy machine guns and mortars, even home-made rifles and pistols. By 1968, the "main force" V.C. units of battalion strength and larger were often staffed and led by P.A.V.N. officers and used the Russian- or Chinese-made AK-47 assault rifle as a standard arm.

Dedicated, trained, ideologically stiffened in the field by political commissars, and led by trained officers, the P.A.V.N., also known as the N.V.A., was a disciplined force, skilled in handling heavy weapons, artillery, anti-aircraft weapons, and, eventually, Russian-made T-54 tanks. Their crew-served heavy machine guns were mostly wheeled 7.92mm and 7.62mm Soviet weapons, themselves modeled on World War I-era equivalents. Individual arms were a mix of Chinese-copied sub- and light

Opposite: A mixed group of N.V.A. and Viet Cong soldiers photographed in camp around a Chinese Type 54 crew-served, water-cooled machine gun. It is a 1935 copy of the Maxim MG-08 in 7.92 caliber. The men wear a variety of uniforms from black "pajamas" to khaki shirts and trousers. All wear sandals and the helmets are made of plastic-covered bamboo studded with leaves for camouflage.

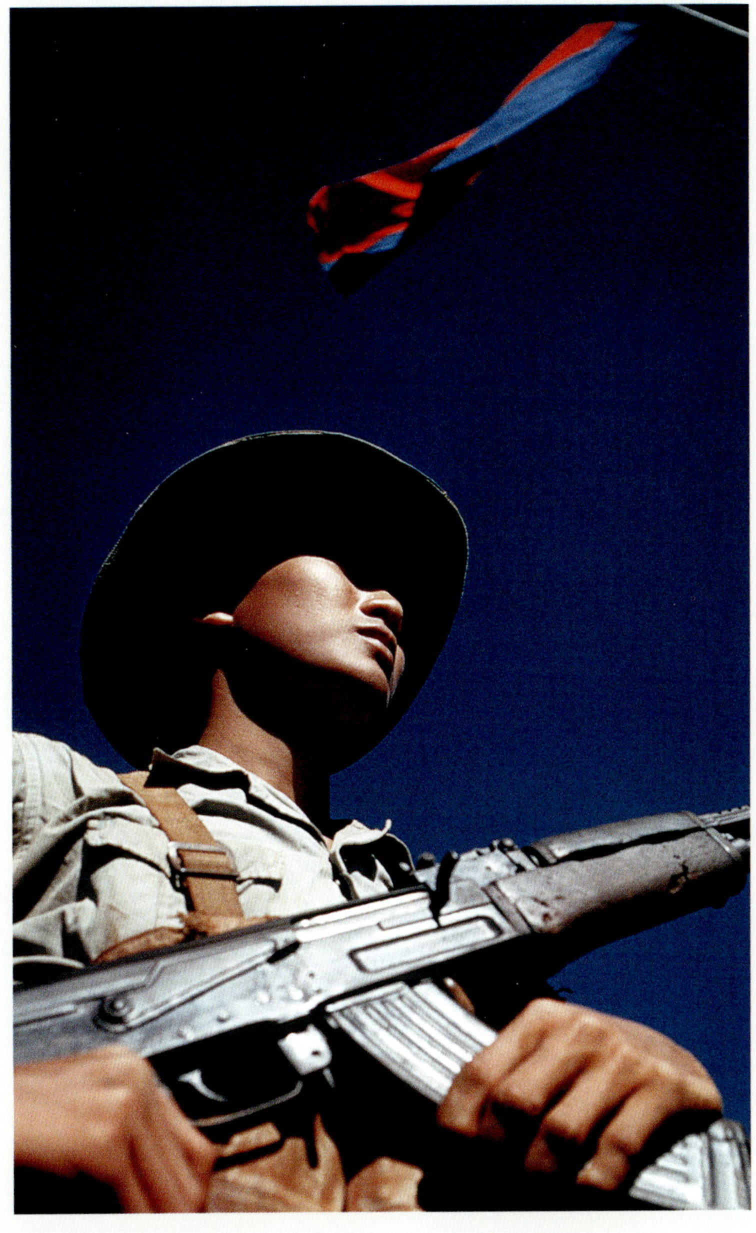

Right: An N.V.A. regular soldier in khaki uniform carrying his 7.72mm AK-47 assault rifle. He wears a soft jungle hat in place of a helmet. The North Vietnamese Army soldier was tough and highly motivated due to strict education in the Communist cause to liberate Vietnam from foreign armies and the corruption of the South Vietnam political regimes. If ordered, he would hold his ground until killed, and gave little quarter in the field.

Below, box: Ta Thi Kieu, heroine of the National Liberation Forces (N.L.F.). Her military career began as a Viet Cong squad leader in Bentre Province and, through her bravery in combat, she rose to become an international symbol for the N.L.F. She wears a cloth "Emulation" badge and an early V.C. war badge on her black tunic.

Below right: A Viet Cong "Emulation" badge. The cloth "medals" were created early in the war until the North Vietnamese could create their own metal medal awards.

WOMEN IN THE V.C./N.V.A./P.A.V.N.

Women played important roles in the N.V.A./V.C./P.A.V.N. armies from the conquest of Dien Bien Phu to the fall of Saigon. They hauled disassembled artillery components over jungle hills and across rivers. Women poled waterborne supply rafts down the rivers and pushed bicycles loaded with rice and ammunition along rocky trails. They toiled in jungle repair shops set up for weapons maintenance and worked alongside doctors in makeshift hospitals. In combat they carried ammunition, took their places on 37mm anti-aircraft guns, and won medals for bravery for blowing up tanks. Their very presence in combat bolstered the resolve of many male soldiers.

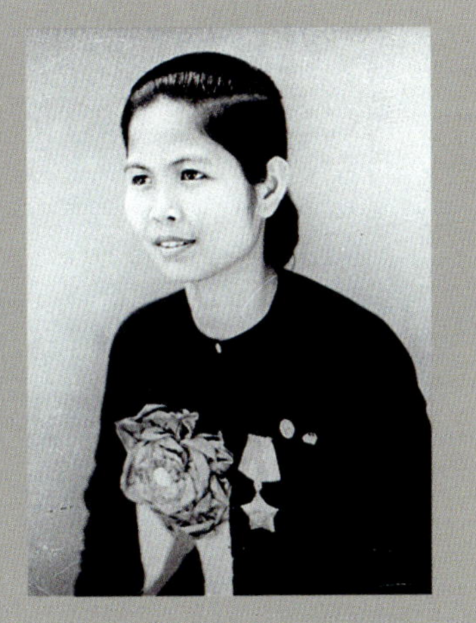

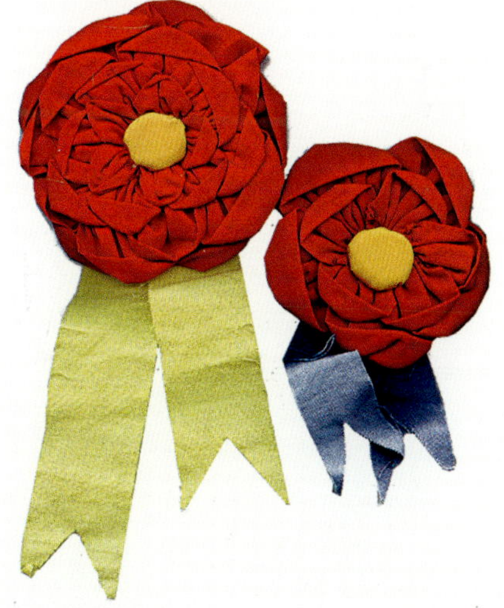

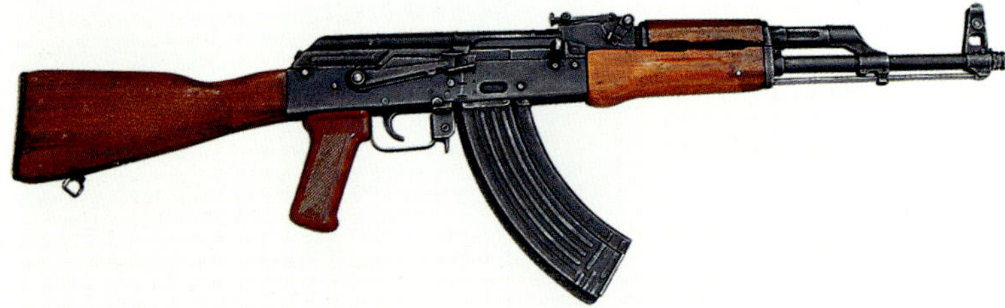

machine guns. The AK-47 became their most effective weapon.

Women occasionally served alongside men in both V.C. and N.V.A. units, hauling heavy equipment over mountain trails, sharing rough camps, and manning anti-aircraft weapons. Although few in number, they were a favorite subject for Communist propagandists, often shown in photos escorting American prisoners at gunpoint, but were a tough, effective force in their own right.

N.V.A. uniforms were mostly tan fabric topped with a floppy field hat or pith helmet made of wood or woven palm leaves over a conical frame. While more formal, they still wore sandals or canvas tennis shoes. Because of their familiarity with the country, N.V.A. fieldcraft and survival skills were more finely tuned than the Americans'. However, officers sometimes depended on "human wave" charges in which many young men and women were slaughtered. The toughness and resilience of the N.V.A. and V.C. made them formidable opponents to Allied and A.R.V.N. forces.

Above: An AK-47 Assault Rifle, acclaimed internationally as the finest weapon of its type in the world. The build is extremely durable, accurate enough for most combat situations, and easy to repair and clean in the field. Its rate of fire is 90–100 rounds per minute in single shots or bursts of 400 rounds per minute on full automatic firing from a 30- or 40-round box magazine or a 75-round drum. It has a unique "pop-pop-pop" firing sound that sets it apart on the battlefield.

Right: N.V.A. soldiers firing a Chinese Model 56 (Soviet PPSh) submachine gun and an R.P.G. launcher. The rocket-propelled grenade could penetrate medium armor and disable tanks by blowing off a tread and destroying bogey wheels.

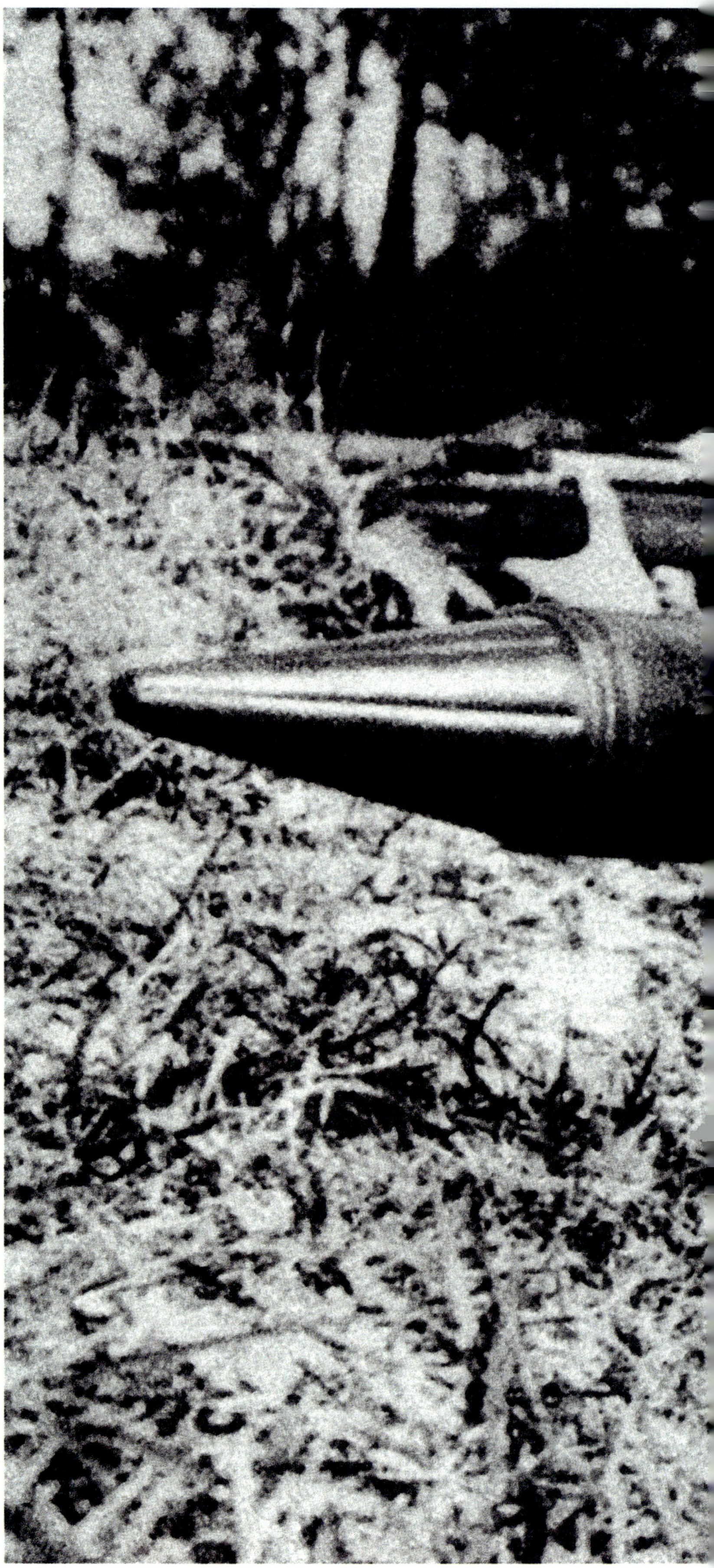

BOOBY TRAPS

Early on in the conflict, the Viet Cong discovered that a well-placed booby trap could be worth a squad of soldiers. Sharpened bamboo spikes, smeared with water-buffalo or human excrement, called "*punji* sticks" placed point-up at the bottom of a small camouflaged hole could wound one soldier and require two more to carry him to an aid station. Trip wires caused window-size racks of sharpened bamboo sticks to swing down from tree branches into a soldier. Simple wedged grenades with their safety pins pulled made opening doors very dangerous. Americans affixed Claymore mines chest-high on trees facing up a trail to wipe out a squad of V.C.

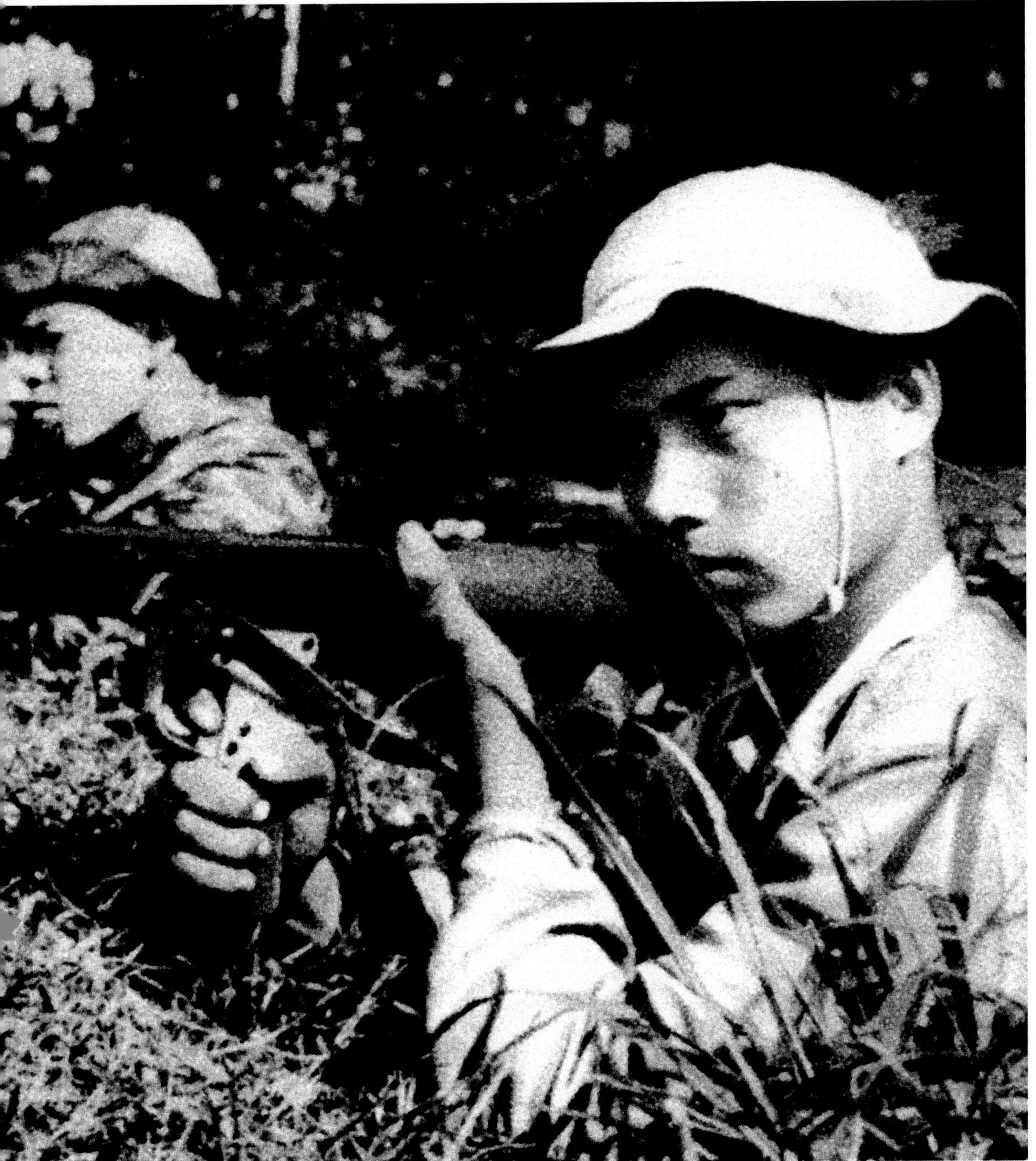

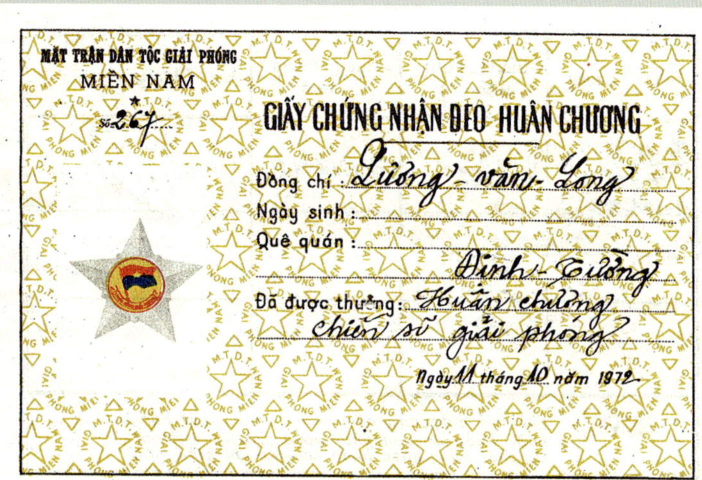

MẶT TRẬN DÂN TỘC GIẢI PHÓNG
MIỀN NAM

Số 267

GIẤY CHỨNG NHẬN ĐEO HUÂN CHƯƠNG

Đồng chí : Lương văn Long
Ngày sinh :
Quê quán : Định Tường
Đã được thưởng: Huân chương chiến sĩ giải phóng

Ngày 11 tháng 10 năm 1972

Huân chương	Quyết_nghị định số	Ngày, tháng năm	Chứng thực
chiến sĩ giải phóng hạng ba	433/42	11/10/1972	[illegible]

GHI CHÚ : Phải giữ giấy này cẩn thận — Khi phát bằng hoặc huân chương phải đóng dấu và viết chữ: Đã phát bằng hoặc huân chương vào giấy này.

V.C. ORDER OF SOLDIER OF LIBERATION AWARD

Certificates issued by military or civilian authorities to confirm a medal or order were typically carried by recipients as verification. The N.L.F. Order, established on August 9, 1965, was for units or individuals serving the cause of liberation in combat, production, or official capacity.

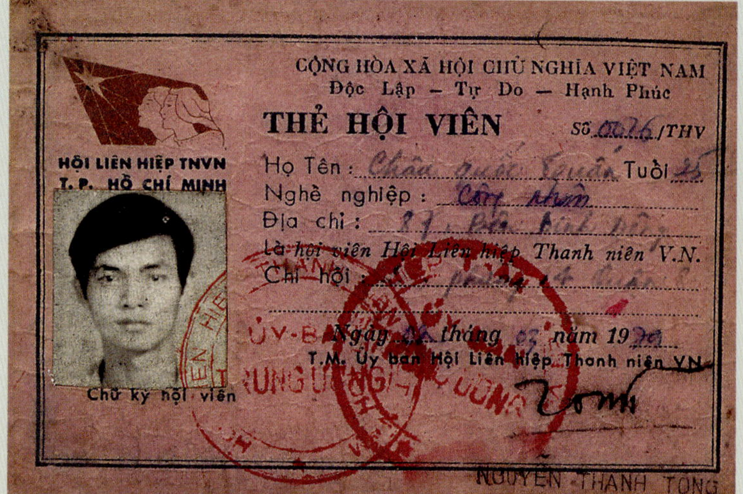

CỘNG HÒA XÃ HỘI CHỦ NGHĨA VIỆT NAM
Độc Lập — Tự Do — Hạnh Phúc

HỘI LIÊN HIỆP TNVN
T.P. HỒ CHÍ MINH

THẺ HỘI VIÊN Số 0076/THV

Họ Tên : Tuổi 25
Nghề nghiệp : Công nhân
Địa chỉ :
Là hội viên Hội Liên hiệp Thanh niên V.N.
Chi hội :

Ngày tháng năm 19
T.M. Ủy ban Hội Liên hiệp Thanh niên VN

Chữ ký hội viên

NGUYỄN THANH TONG

VANGUARD YOUTH I.D.

This I.D. card is for a youth organization, Thanh Nien Tien Phong (Vanguard Youth), founded in Saigon by the Communists under Japanese occupation in 1942. It became the focus for the Communist effort in the south and soon expanded from 200,000 to over a million members, who worked at non-combat jobs until late in the war when they were drafted into the P.A.V.N. For translation, see page 156.

HO CHI MINH'S ARMY BOOKLET

Not unlike Chairman Mao Tse Tung's Little Red Book, the Van Nghe Quan Zo was studied by V.C. and N.V.A. soldiers and civilians for its Communist-based wisdom.
For translation, see page 156.

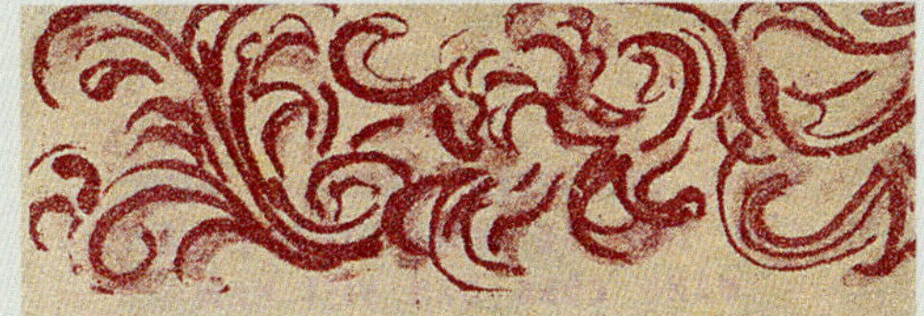

QUÂN ĐỘI TA TRUNG VỚI ĐẢNG, HIẾU VỚI DÂN, SẴN SÀNG CHIẾN ĐẤU HY SINH VÌ ĐỘC LẬP, TỰ DO CỦA TỔ QUỐC, VÌ CHỦ NGHĨA XÃ HỘI, NHIỆM VỤ NÀO CŨNG HOÀN THÀNH, KHÓ KHĂN NÀO CŨNG VƯỢT QUA, KẺ THÙ NÀO CŨNG ĐÁNH THẮNG

Chủ tịch
HỒ CHÍ MINH

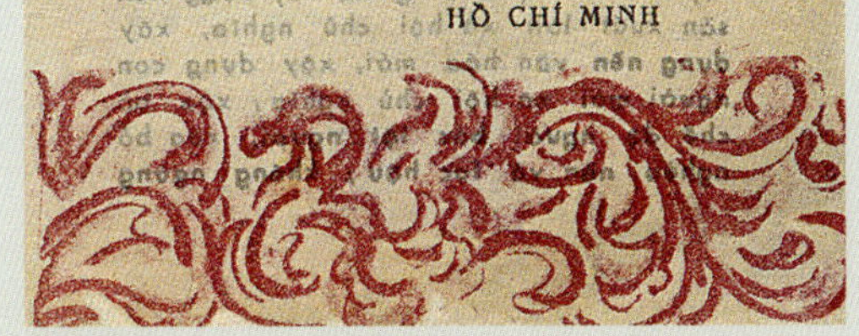

NHIỆT LIỆT CHÀO MỪNG KỶ NIỆM LẦN THỨ 50 NGÀY THÀNH LẬP ĐẢNG CỘNG SẢN VIỆT NAM

NGHỊ QUYẾT
ĐẠI HỘI LẦN THỨ TƯ CỦA ĐẢNG

(Trích)

— Nắm vững chuyên chính vô sản, phát huy quyền làm chủ tập thể của nhân dân lao động, tiến hành đồng thời ba cuộc cách mạng: cách mạng về quan hệ sản xuất, cách mạng khoa học – kỹ thuật, cách mạng tư tưởng và văn hóa, trong đó cách mạng khoa học – kỹ thuật là then chốt; đẩy mạnh công nghiệp hóa xã hội chủ nghĩa là nhiệm vụ trung tâm của cả thời kỳ quá độ lên chủ nghĩa xã hội; xây dựng chế độ làm chủ tập thể xã hội chủ nghĩa, xây dựng nền sản xuất lớn xã hội chủ nghĩa, xây dựng nền văn hóa mới, xây dựng con người mới xã hội chủ nghĩa; xóa bỏ chế độ người bóc lột người, xóa bỏ nghèo nàn và lạc hậu; không ngừng đề cao cảnh giác, thường xuyên củng cố quốc phòng, giữ gìn an ninh chính trị và trật tự xã hội; xây dựng thành công Tổ quốc Việt Nam hòa bình, độc lập, thống nhất và xã hội chủ nghĩa; góp phần tích cực vào cuộc đấu tranh của nhân dân thế giới vì hòa bình, độc lập dân tộc, dân chủ và chủ nghĩa xã hội.

— Trung thành với chủ nghĩa Mác – Lênin, Đảng ta không ngừng giáo dục đảng viên và nhân dân ta thấm nhuần những tình cảm cách mạng trong sáng của Hồ Chủ tịch, tiếp tục giương cao ngọn cờ độc lập dân tộc và chủ nghĩa xã hội, kết hợp nhuần nhuyễn chủ nghĩa yêu nước chân chính với chủ nghĩa quốc tế vô sản, chống mọi khuynh hướng cơ hội chủ nghĩa và mọi biểu hiện của chủ nghĩa dân tộc tư sản và tiểu tư sản, giữ vững độc lập, tự chủ, ra sức làm tròn nhiệm vụ đối với dân tộc và làm tốt nghĩa vụ quốc tế đối với nhân dân các nước.

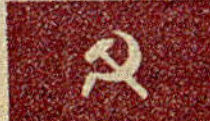

2

11	Thứ hai	25
12	Thứ ba	26
13	Thứ tư	27
14	Thứ năm	28
15	Thứ sáu	29
16	Thứ bảy	*Th. Giêng Canh Thân (đ)*
17	CHỦ NHẬT	2

Ý CHÍ MẠNH
CHẤT LƯỢNG CAO
ĐOÀN KẾT TỐT
KỶ LUẬT NGHIÊM
QUYẾT CHIẾN
QUYẾT THẮNG

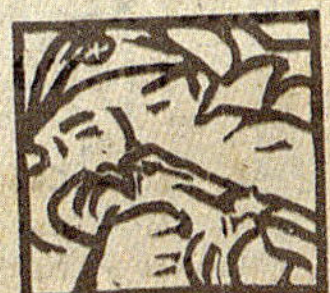

Doan Thượng	141 km	Lang Thíp	228 km
Văn Phú	149 —	Bảo Hà	237 —
Yên Bái	154 —	Thái Văn	248 —
Cổ Phúc	166 —	Cầu Nhỏ (trạm)	255 —
Ngòi Hóp	177 —	Phố Lu	262 —
Mậu A	187 —	Lạng (trạm)	271 —
Mậu Đông	195 —	Thái Niên	278 —
Trái Hút	203 —	Làng Giàng	284 —
Lâm Giang	211 —	Phố Mới	293 —
Mỏ Đá	215 —	Lao Cai	295 —
Lang Khay	219 —		

LÀNG GIÀNG — PÒ HÀN: 5 km

ĐƯỜNG XE, TÀU LIÊN VẬN TRONG NƯỚC

Hà Nội — Cao Bằng	281 km
Hà Nội — Lai Châu	509 km
Hà Nội — Nghĩa Lộ	239 km

TET OFFENSIVE

GENERAL GIAP MUST HAVE SAVORED THE AUDACITY OF HIS COMBINED ASSAULTS PLANNED FOR THE TET HOLIDAY AT THE BEGINNING OF THE LUNAR NEW YEAR IN JANUARY 1968. IN HONEYCOMBS OF TUNNELS AND DEEP GALLERIES DUG BENEATH STRATEGIC LOCATIONS IN SOUTH VIETNAM, TONS OF WEAPONS AND SUPPLIES HAD BEEN STORED IN SMALL QUANTITIES TO ENABLE QUICK DISTRIBUTION. BATTALIONS OF TROOPS IN CIVILIAN CLOTHES INFILTRATED THE CITIES AND VILLAGE AREAS TO MINGLE AND CELEBRATE.

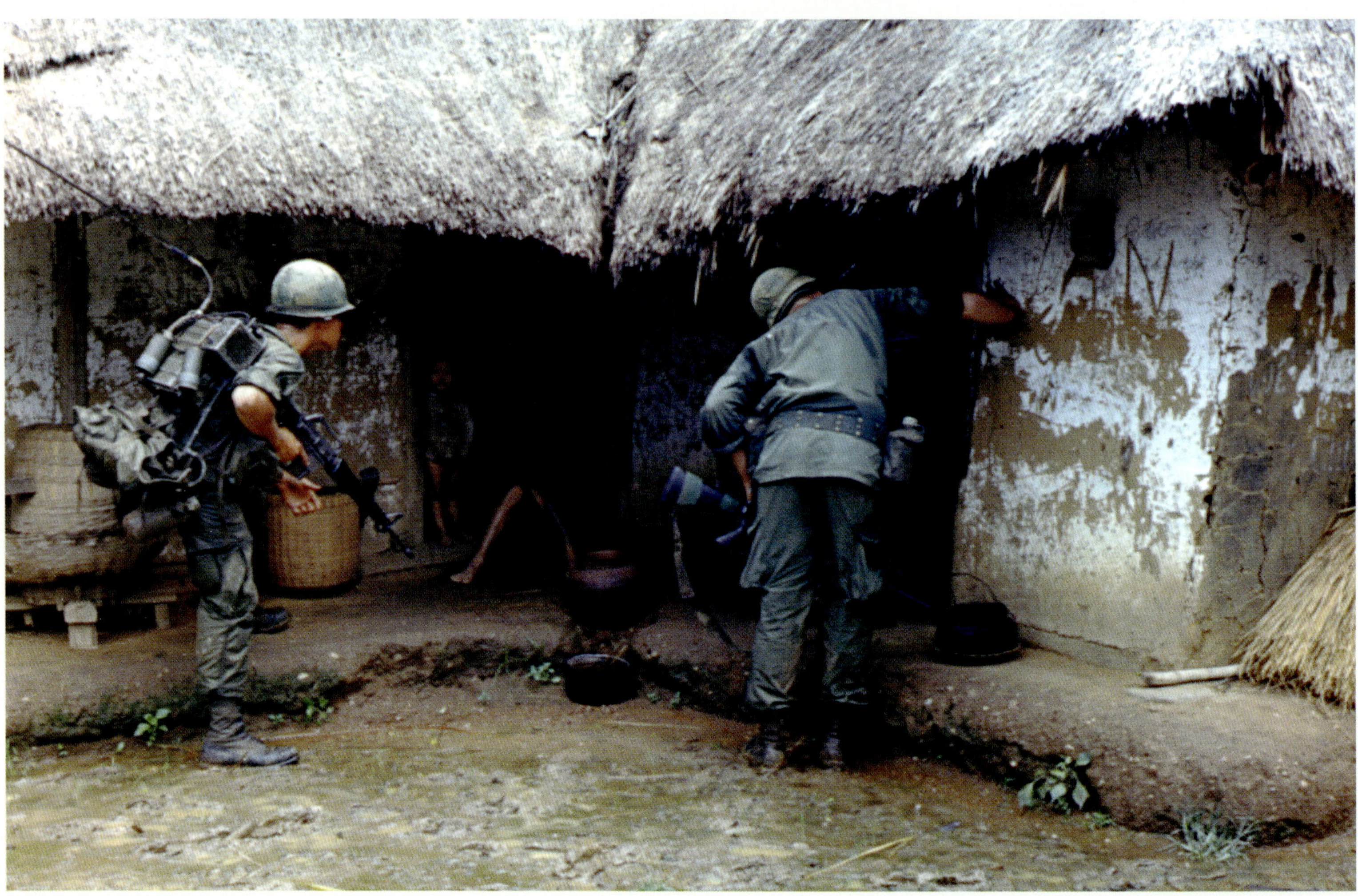

The Viet Cong declared a truce lasting from January 27 through to February 3, while the Americans and South Vietnamese instituted a 36-hour cease-fire. However, when preparations for the celebration got under way, the Viet Cong prepared to jump off in coordinated attacks on 39 provincial capitals, 71 district capitals, and five major cities including Saigon. Giap had

Above: A rifle team of U.S. soldiers begins the search of a village "hooch" looking for Viet Cong, weapons caches, explosives, or even a tunnel entrance to underground shelters. The V.C. had established hidden weapons and troop hide-aways long before the Tet attacks began.

Opposite: Black smoke covers Saigon as fire trucks rush to contain blazes caused by the Viet Cong's surprise attacks. Specially trained squads of Viet Cong sappers—demolitions experts—targeted key military and government buildings in the capital.

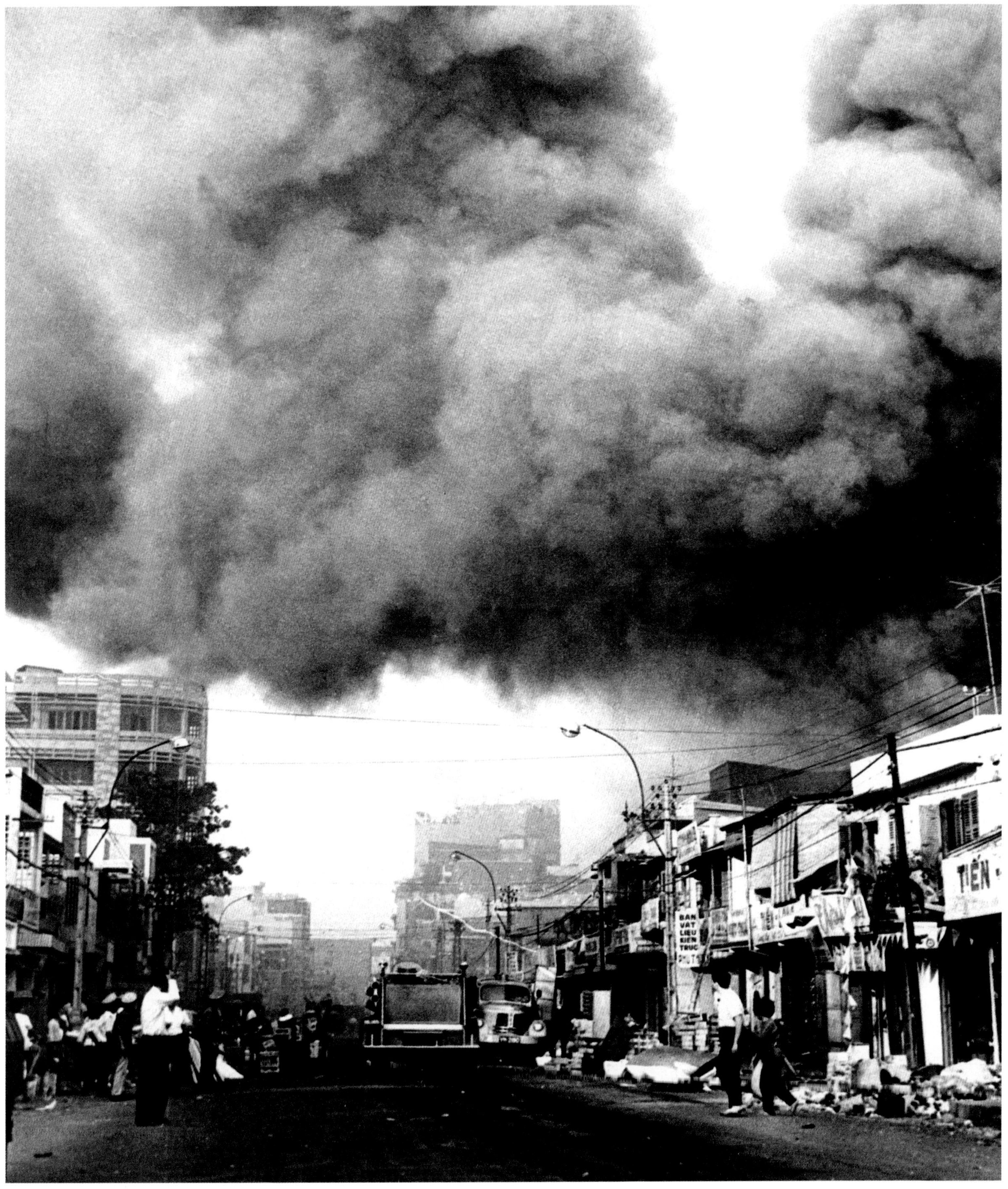
BAN
VAT
LIEU
KIEN
TRUC
TIẾN

TET OFFENSIVE 1968

Map of Tet Offensive 1968. Depicts the scope of the Tet Offensive as it erupted in a coordinated attack against key villages, towns and large population centers in South Vietnam. Weapons and troops had been hidden for deployment as U.S. and A.R.V.N. forces were lured to battles along the Cambodian border and jungle firebases. The Tet attacks were beaten back, resulting in the destruction of the Viet Cong as a fighting force.

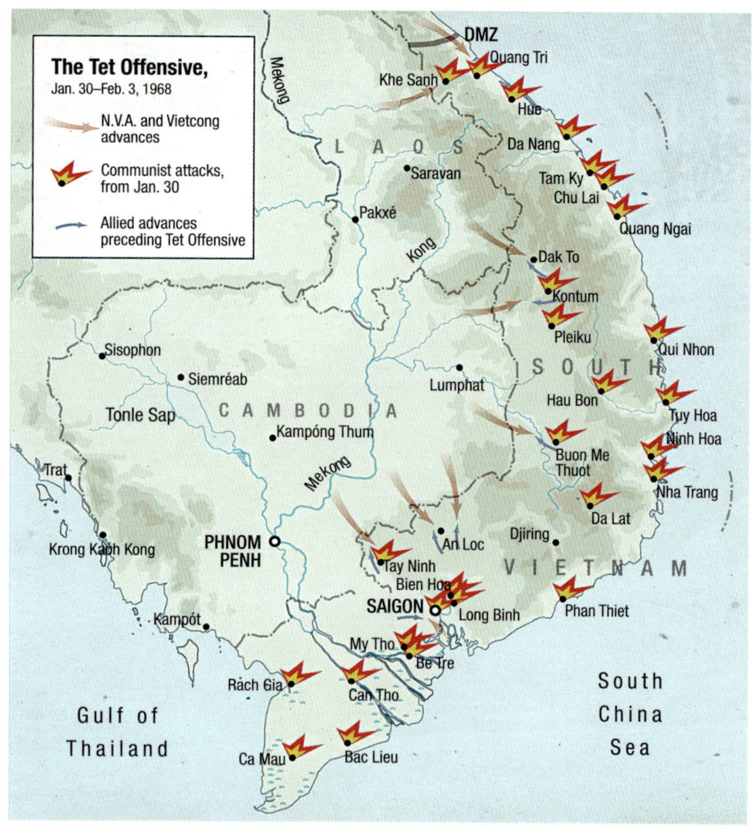

U.S. WEAPONS AVAILABLE

While the scope of the Tet Offensive surprised the Allies, they had the firepower to cope, from their M16 rifles, M60 light machine guns, L.A.W. anti-tank weapons, and 60mm mortars. They were supported by "Duster" 40mm-tracked vehicles, quad 50-caliber machine-gun vehicles, M48 tanks, and M113 A.P.C.s with recoilless rifles. For artillery, howitzers from 75, 105, 155, and 175mm were available. Overhead, F-105 Thunderchief, F-8E Crusaders, A-4D fighter-bombers, propeller-driven Skyraiders, and devastating C-47 "Spookies," with their electric Gatling guns, offered close troop support. The ubiquitous Huey UH-1 and Sikorsky helicopters provided both transport and firepower.

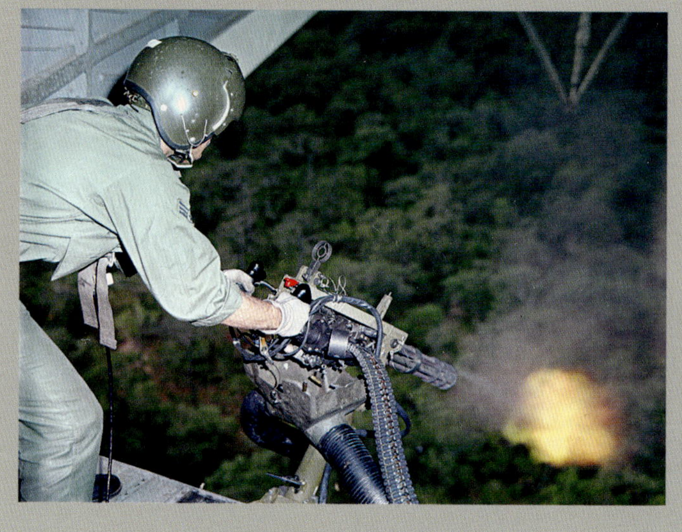

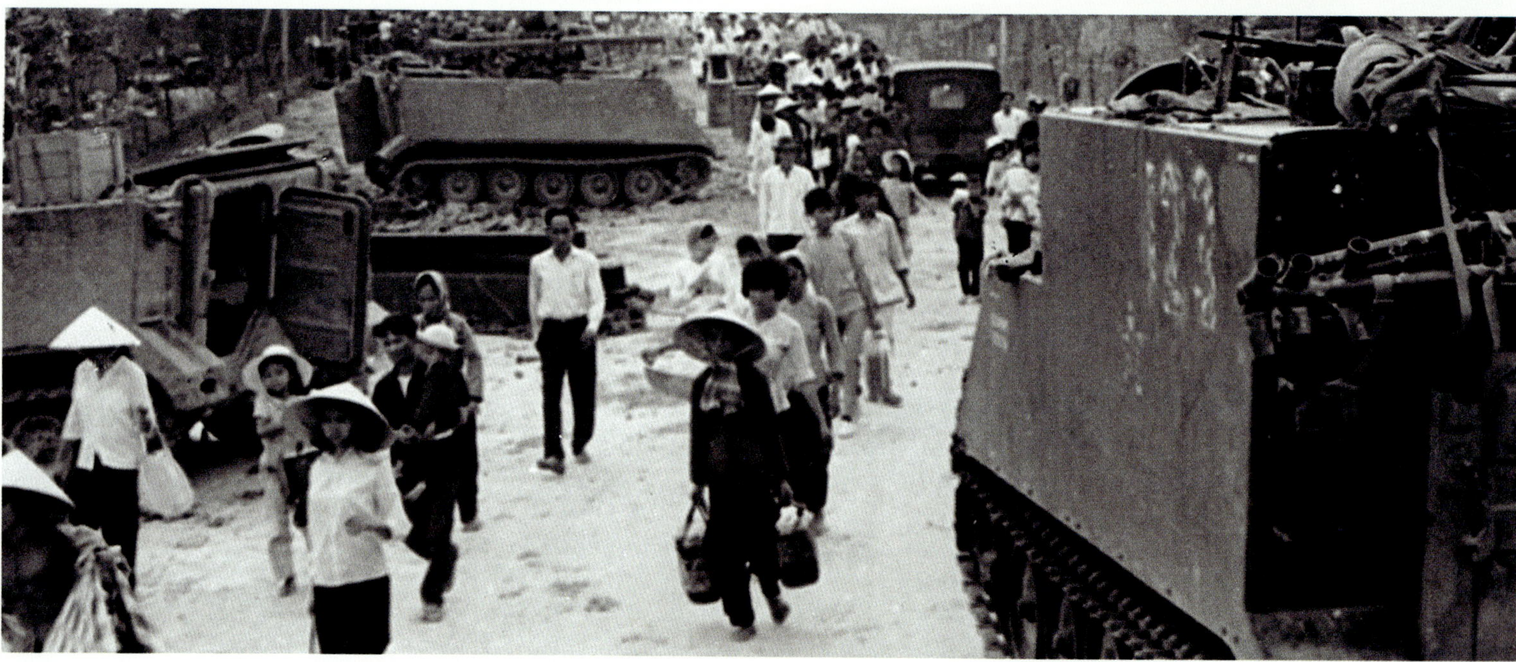

originally decided on the early hours of January 30, but then postponed until January 31. However, the Viet Cong Military Region Five kept to the original plan and jumped off on the 30th.

American Intelligence was aware that some kind of offensive was likely to happen over Tet, but had little precise information. Their suspicions were only confirmed when the V.C. began their attacks. By January 31, when the other cadres of V.C. exploded from their tunnels and gathering points all over South Vietnam—at Da Nang, Hoi An, Ban Me Thuot, Hue, and Pleiku—they found fully alerted American and A.R.V.N. forces. But still the scope of

Opposite, box: A helicopter aircrewman mans a rotary-barrel, electrically operated 7.62 minigun, sending a hail of bullets down into attacking forces in support of U.S. ground troops.

Opposite below: South Vietnamese flee attacks on their villages from infiltrated Viet Cong as the Tet holidays become a brutal slaughter for men, women, and children in outlying provinces. M113 armored personnel carriers protect the road against further attacks.

Below: On January 31, 1968, three Vietnamese women move back into the Cholon area of Saigon in hopes of salvaging some belongings after V.C. leveled a two-block area of homes and buildings.

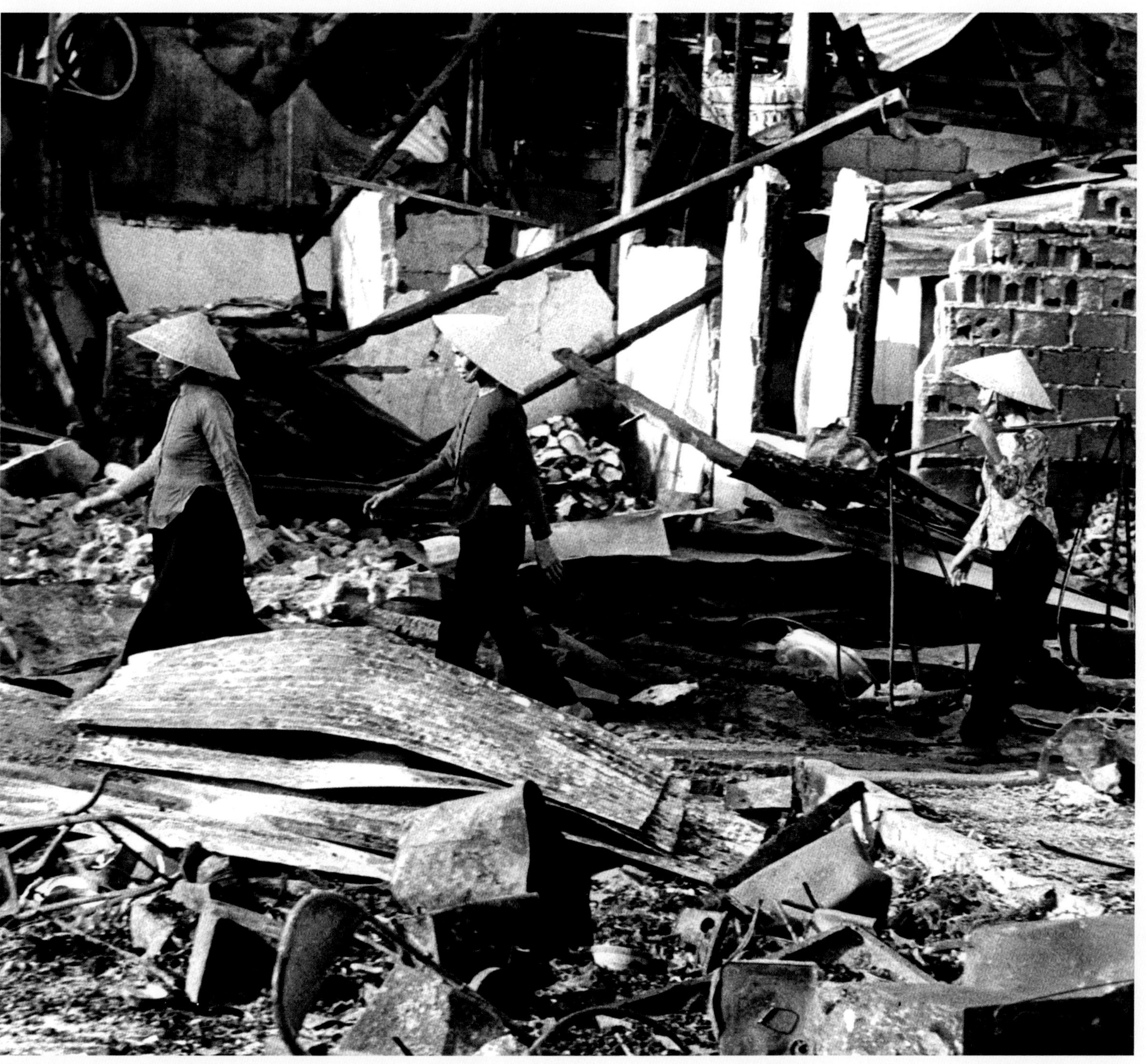

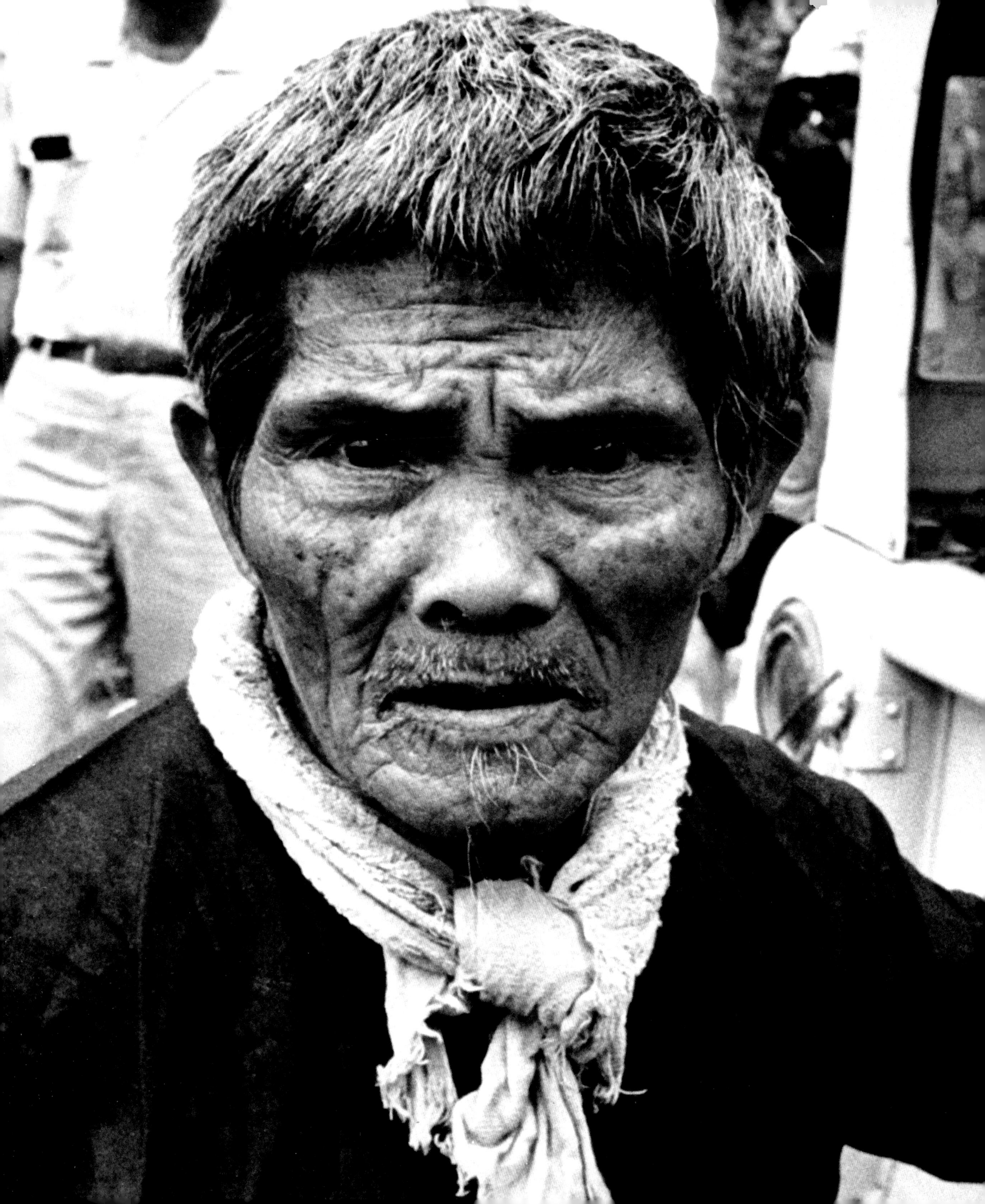

N.V.A. WEAPONS

General Giap launched many attacks with different forces throughout South Vietnam. By 1968 the Viet Cong had supplemented their older Chinese weapons and those captured during early victories over the A.R.V.N.—M1 carbines, Browning light machine guns, and M1 rifles—with the AK-47 and R.P.D. machine guns, standbys of the N.V.A. Crew-served weapons included Soviet DsHK 12.7mm heavy machine guns and Soviet 50mm mortar. The 82mm mortar, 105mm and 155mm howitzers, and 122mm rockets provided long and heavy barrages at the Marines' Khe Sahn firebase.

the attacks astounded the Allies. In Da Nang a battalion of the 2nd North Vietnamese Division had infiltrated the city and began hammering away with heavy mortars. At Nha Trang on the coast, mortar rounds landed on the South Vietnamese Naval Training facility and a major attack was launched. The North Vietnamese attackers were immediately crushed by prepared defenders.

Outside Saigon, at Tan Son Nhut Air Base, fuel depots and parked aeroplanes went up in geysers of flame, destroyed by mortars and bazookas by two battalions of the 9th Viet Cong Division.

In all, some 68,000 V.C. and North Vietnamese swept across South Vietnam in the first 24 hours. Since they attacked heavily defended locations, the enthusiastic but not well-trained V.C. suffered very heavy losses. In Saigon, however, the "Paris of the Orient" was defended not by combat-experienced forces, but by spit-and-polish garrison troops and military police, who suddenly found themselves in major firefights and hand-to-hand combat at the U.S. embassy, the Presidential Palace, and the radio station offices. TV crews found themselves dodging grenades and bullets, and the impression that went out round the world was very different from the experience of the average American or A.R.V.N. soldier.

By February 3, the well-planned, poorly executed offensive was over, leaving between 35,000 and 50,000 Communists dead and wounded. The Americans lost 1,500 killed, the A.R.V.N. buried 3,000, and South Vietnamese civilians counted almost 10,000 dead. Militarily, the Allies had won, but politically the victory was far from clear cut. And the year had just begun.

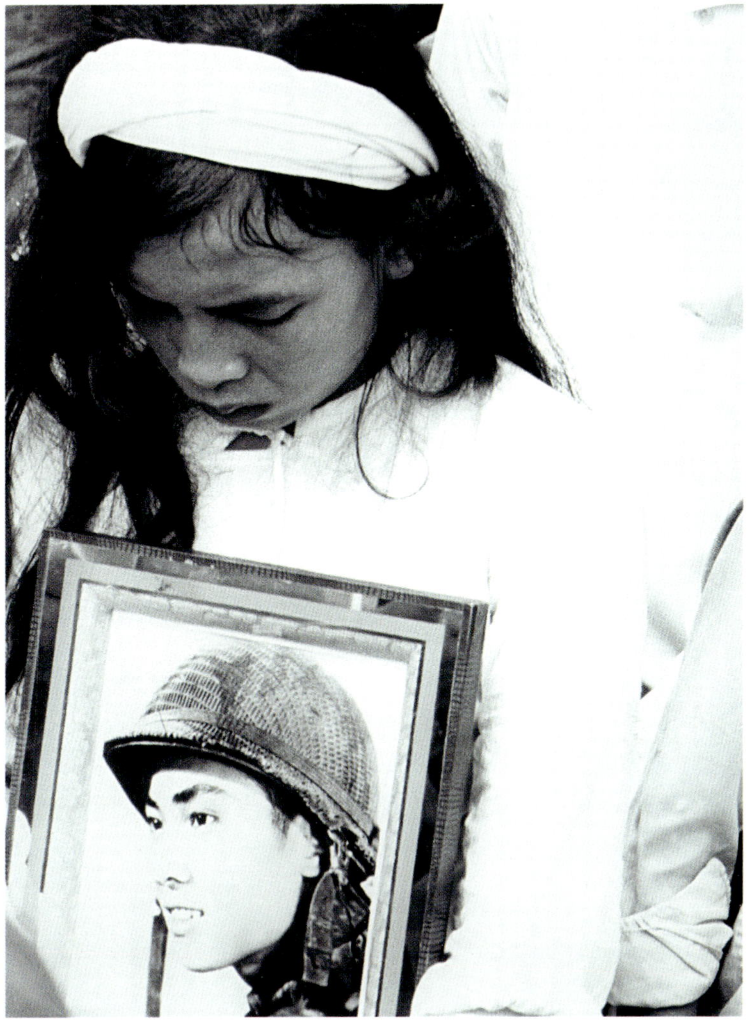

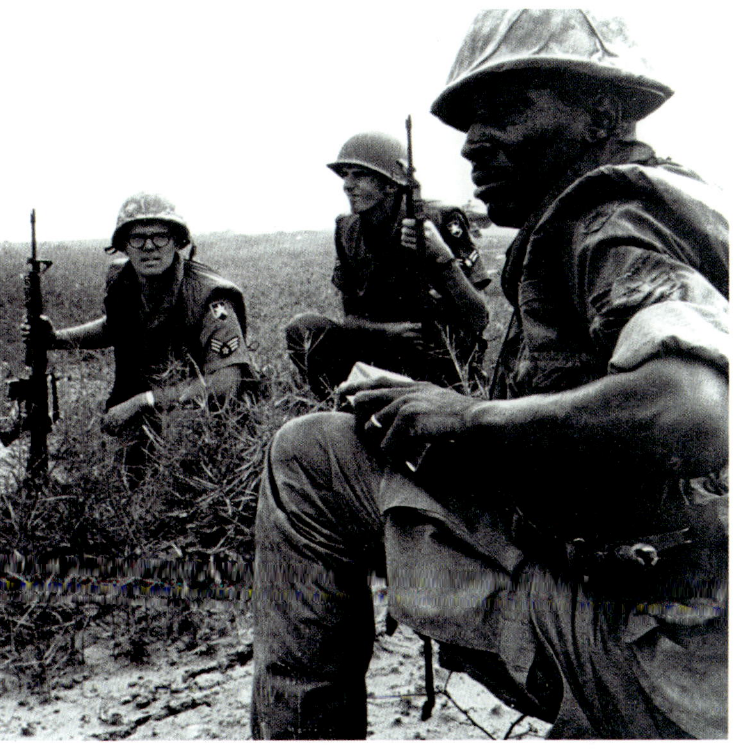

Opposite: The strain shows on a farmer, one of 4,500 who fled from their homes in South Vietnamese hamlets that had been family homes for generations.

Above right: A young wife mourns the death of her husband, killed during the Tet battles. The A.R.V.N. distinguished themselves in defending and retaking the city of Hue.

Right: U.S. troops watch and wait as V.C. pour from previously infiltrated positions. Eventually, defense turned to offense and the V.C. threat in the South was virtually wiped out, leaving the fight to the regular N.V.A. troops.

RECAPTURING HUE

HUE IS THE THIRD-LARGEST CITY IN VIETNAM AND STRADDLES THE HUONG (PERFUME) RIVER. WITHIN HUE THE CITADEL IS AN OLD WALLED CITY THAT SURROUNDS THE IMPERIAL PALACE ON THE RIVER'S NORTH BANK. A RAILWAY BRIDGE AND THE HIGHWAY 1 BRIDGE JOIN THE SECTIONS OF THIS ANCIENT CITY. BECAUSE OF THE LOCAL VIET CONG'S NUMEROUS TRUCE VIOLATIONS, 1ST A.R.V.N. DIVISION COMMANDER GENERAL NGO QUANG TRUONG KEPT HIS MEN AT THEIR POSTS AS THE TET LUNAR NEW YEAR CELEBRATIONS GOT UNDERWAY. WHEN THE MORTAR ATTACK ON THE CITY BEGAN IN THE EARLY MORNING HOURS OF JANUARY 31, A.R.V.N. AND AMERICAN TROOPS AND STAFF WERE ON 100 PERCENT ALERT.

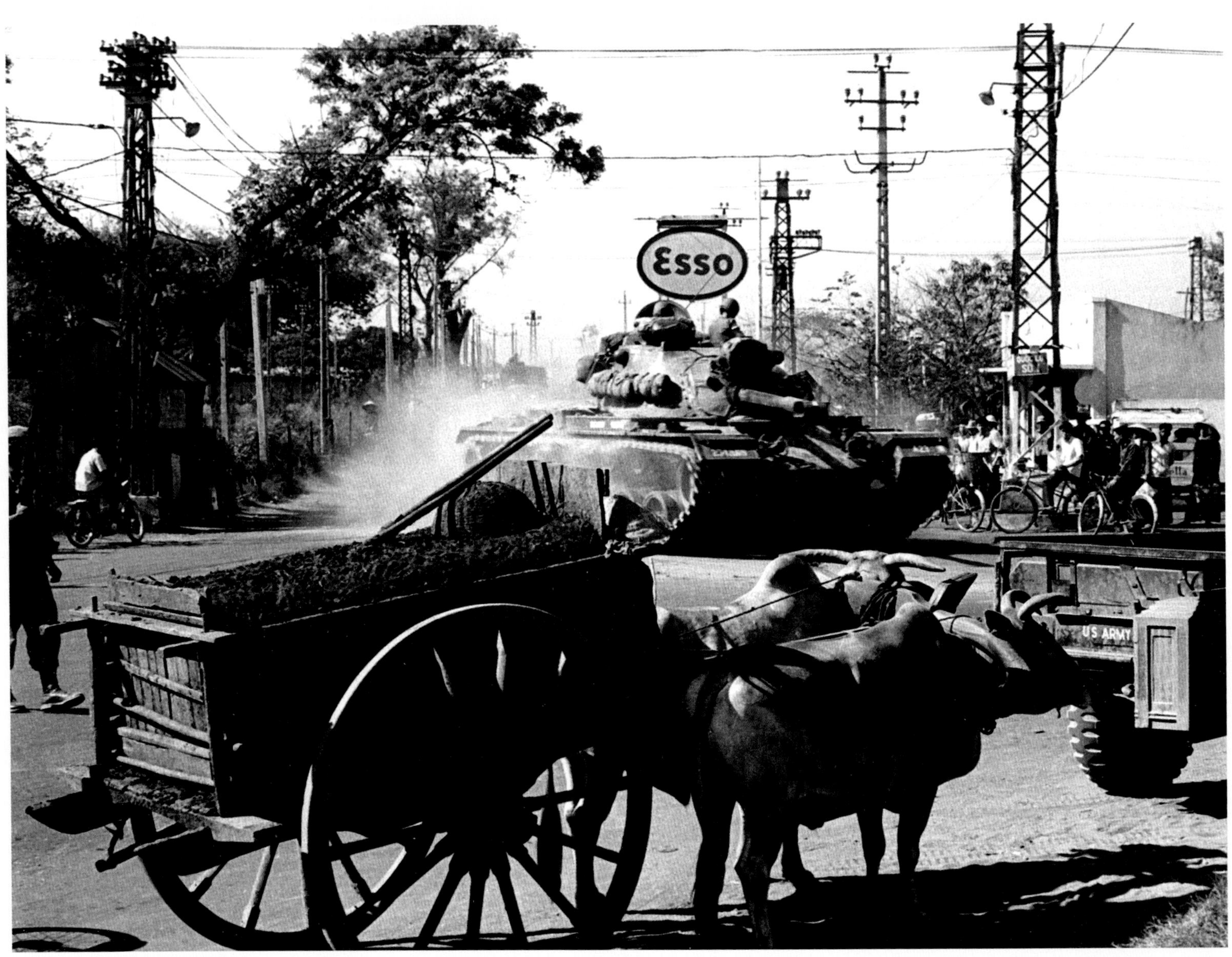

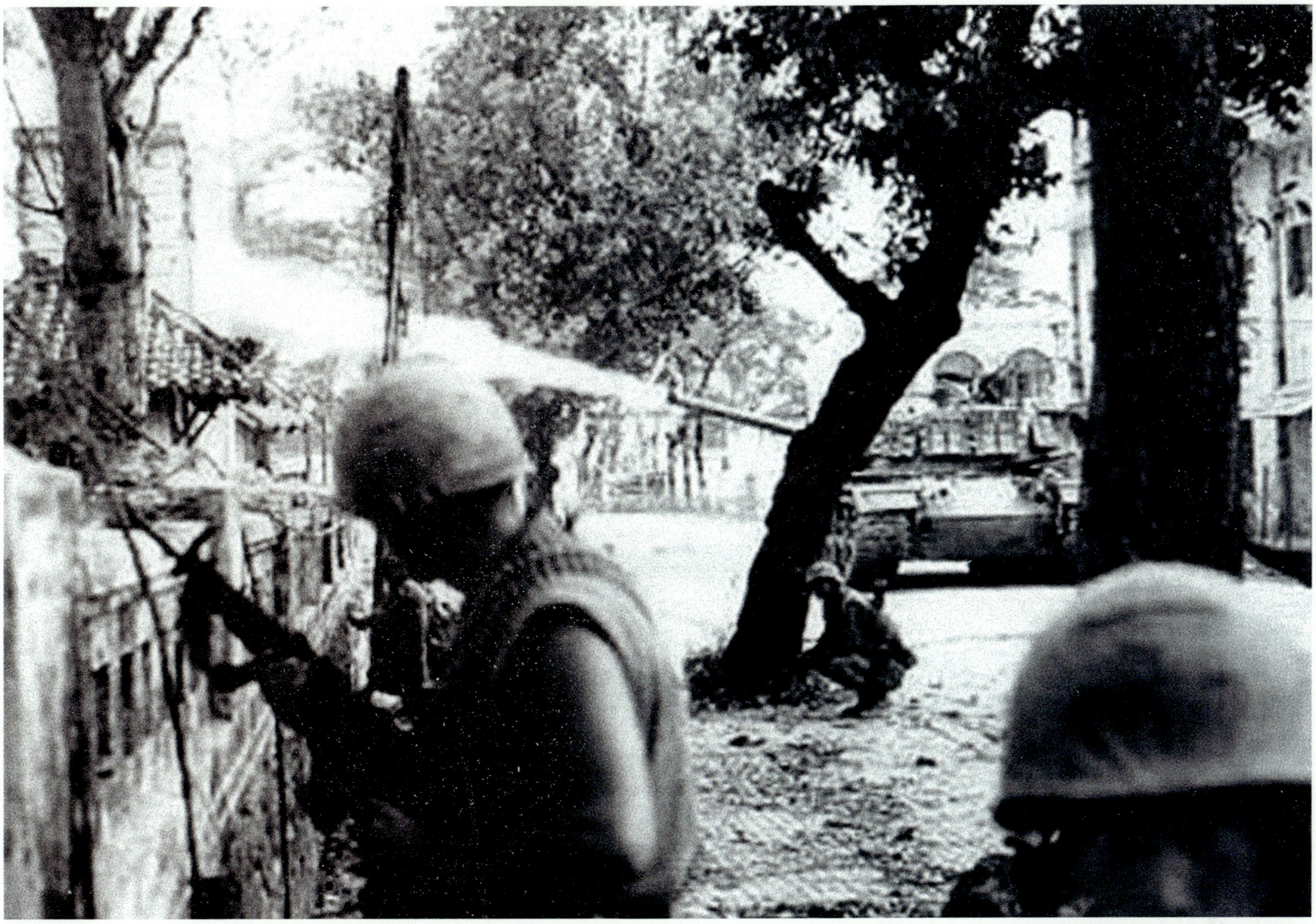

American advisors and A.R.V.N. troops held their ground against V.C. and N.V.A. ground attacks. The 4th North Vietnamese Division staged a second attack, striking the south-east side of the M.A.C.V. compound just before sunrise. Small arms fire drove them off.

The cultural significance and densely populated neighborhoods of the city prevented the use of air strikes or heavy artillery. The Citadel had been quickly overrun by the 802nd and 800th battalions of the 6th North Vietnamese Regiment and, as dawn broke, only the A.R.V.N. 1st Division and M.A.C.V. compounds remained in Allied hands. The V.C. and N.V.A. had set up blocking positions surrounding Hue to prevent rescue attempts. Two companies from the 1st and 5th Marines plus some M48 tanks gunned their way through to the M.A.C.V. defenders, but when the strike force attempted to cross the river to relieve the A.R.V.N. compound they were driven back from the walled city.

Opposite: A U.S. Army M48 tank hurries down a city street past a waiting ox cart on the way to a defensive position. Tanks played an important part in dislodging clusters of V.C. from buildings and fortified positions.

Above: U.S. Marines wait for an M67A1 flamethrower tank, the "Zippo." This M48 variant performed well in the recapture of Hue. The M48 was the last U.S. tank to offer a flamethrower option.

Right: The shoulder patch of the 101st Airborne (Air Assault) "Screaming Eagles." Formerly a paratrooper division, in World War II it was the 101st that held Bastogne during the Battle of the Bulge in December, 1944 and told the Germans, "Nuts," when asked to surrender. In Vietnam, helicopters swept the troops into the recapture of Hue where they performed with gallant distinction.

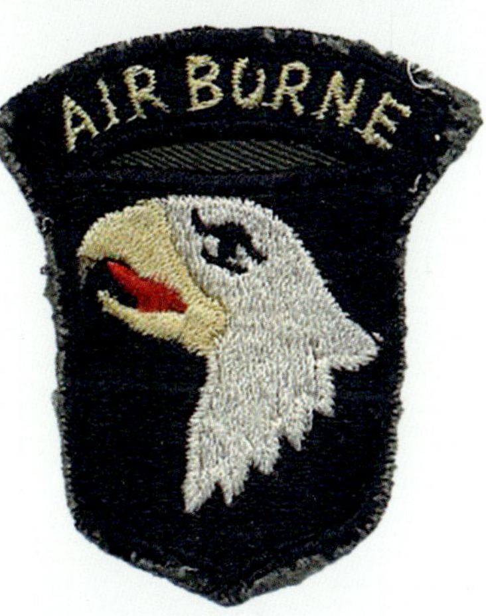

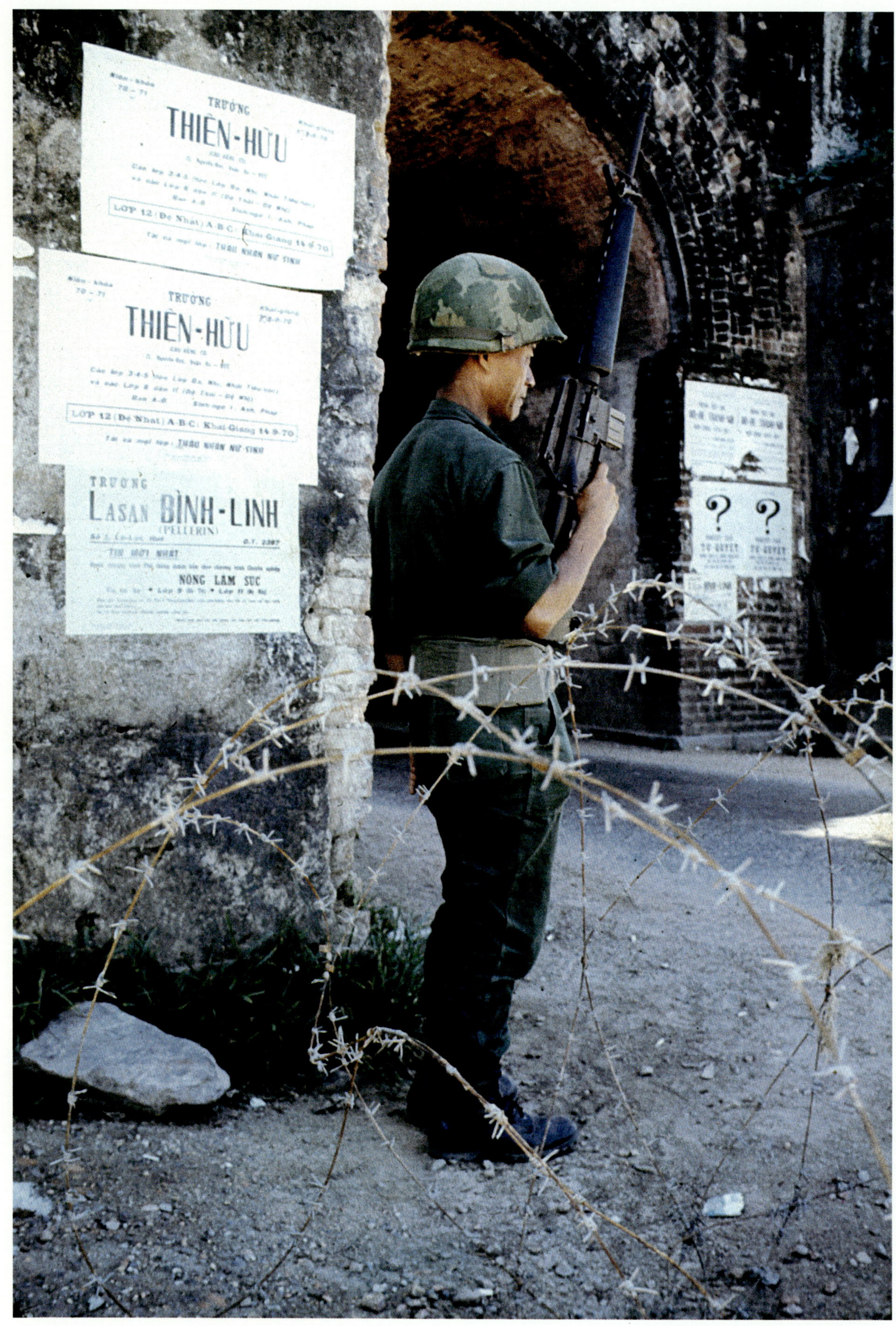
TRƯỜNG
THIÊN-HỮU
LỚP 12 (Đệ Nhất) A.B.C. Khai-Giảng 14-9-70
TRƯỜNG
THIÊN-HỮU
LỚP 12 (Đệ Nhất) A.B.C. Khai-Giảng 14-9-70
TRƯỜNG
LASAN BÌNH-LINH
(PELLERIN)
NÔNG LÂM SÚC

CITADEL, THE OLD CITY/PALACE

As the Tet Offensive crashed into A.R.V.N. and U.S. Marine resistance in Hue, the very heart of Vietnam was threatened with destruction. The old city (its name a mispronunciation of Hoa) was created in 1307, but it was not until 1687 that the city became the political center of Vietnam and it was named the capital in 1778 by the Tay Son dynasty. Gia Long, first emperor of the Nguyen dynasty, began construction of the Hue royal architecture complex. By 1876, the French had their "European Quarter" built opposite the Royal Citadel. For 300 years the walled city was expanded and improved, and was finally inhabited by Bao Dai, the last emperor. Though ancient walls were breeched and holed, they remained standing and are being restored today.

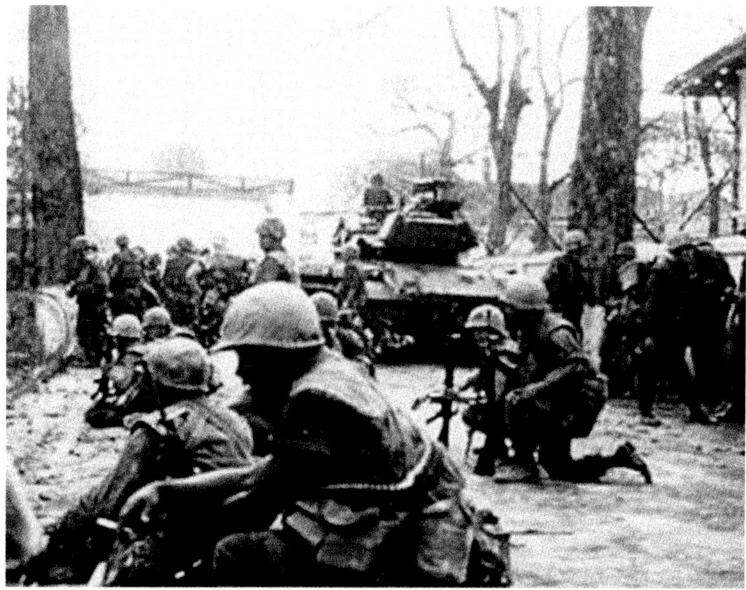

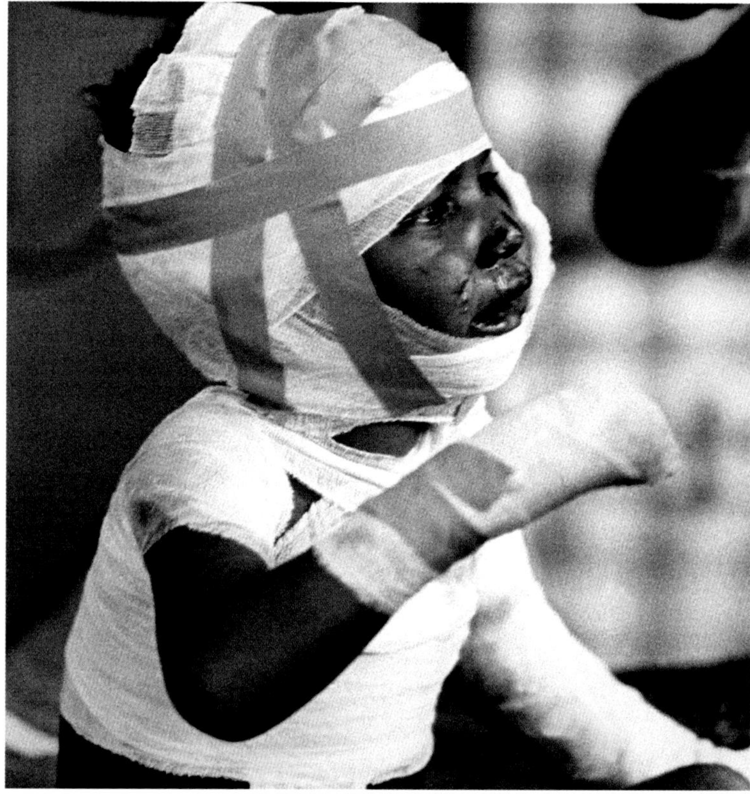

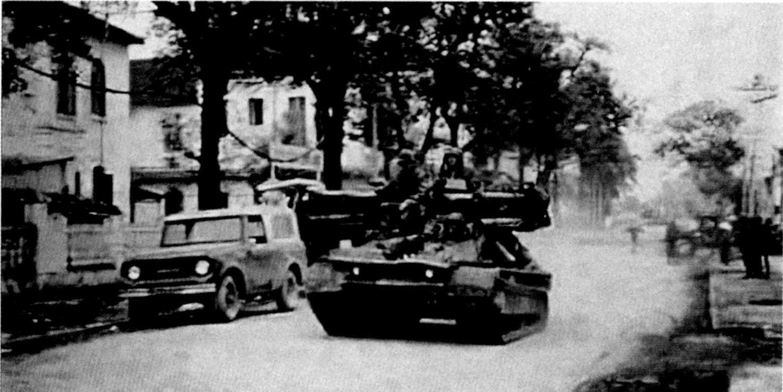

Opposite: The venerable city of Hue surrounded the Citadel, former residence of the Emperor and now a center of government. The defense of Hue during the Tet Offensive of January, 1968 was an A.R.V.N. garrison fight, but U.S. Marines and Army Airborne joined the battle.

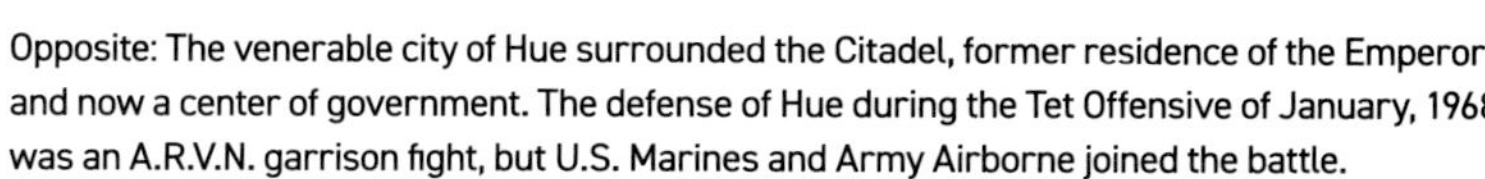

Above: A three-year-old Vietnamese boy in an aid station where his wounds have been bandaged, but no field dressing can repair the loss of his parents in a V.C. attack. Thousands of civilians were left dead and homeless as Viet Cong soldiers rampaged through the cities and countryside spreading terror.

Top right: Waiting to begin an attack on a bridge crossing the Perfume River in Hue, U.S. Marines and an M48 Patton tank wait in a side street for the order to move out.

Right: Marine Corps "Ontos"—122mm recoilless multibarrel tracked vehicle—used in Hue to clean out pockets of V.C. resistance during the Tet Offensive.

The 101st Airborne and 1st Cavalry (Airmobile) troops began sealing off Hue from further reinforcements or escape while the U.S. Marines and A.R.V.N. had the dirty job of fighting snipers and those determined to hold out to the death street by street. A.R.V.N. troops had retaken the airfield inside the Walled City. By February 10, airborne units from Quang Tri and Dong Ha were landed there. As the battle in the Citadel continued, U.S. Marines on the south side of the river managed to stage a helicopter assault on V.C. units operating in Hue, and returned the city to the South Vietnamese government.

For nine more days, the V.C. sent in reinforcements and supplies as artillery from both sides pounded Hue's beautiful buildings into rubble heaps. When the 1st Cavalry (Airmobile) managed to stop supplies feeding in through a breech in the Citadel's west wall to the defenders, the battle was over for the V.C. and N.V.A. in the old city. A.R.V.N. sweeps and attacks killed and captured the survivors and 25 days of savage battle ended.

The V.C. and N.V.A. left 8,000 dead, but Hue civilians paid the highest price. Some 116,000 were left homeless, and the V.C. shot, bludgeoned, or even buried alive more than 2,800 in mass graves surrounding the city.

AIRMOBILE—U.S. AIRBORNE CAVALRY

While the battle for Hue during the Tet Offensive was basically a Marine and A.R.V.N. fight, the mobility of U.S. troops was once again called upon. Sealing off N.V.A. supplies to their besieged troops in the Old City by the 101st Airborne and the 1st Cavalry Division (Airmobile) proved again the value of fast response, helicopter-borne fighting units. First tried at An Khe in the Central Highlands in 1965, then again at the Ia Drang Valley in 1966, these team-based assaults continually kept the V.C. and N.V.A. off balance.

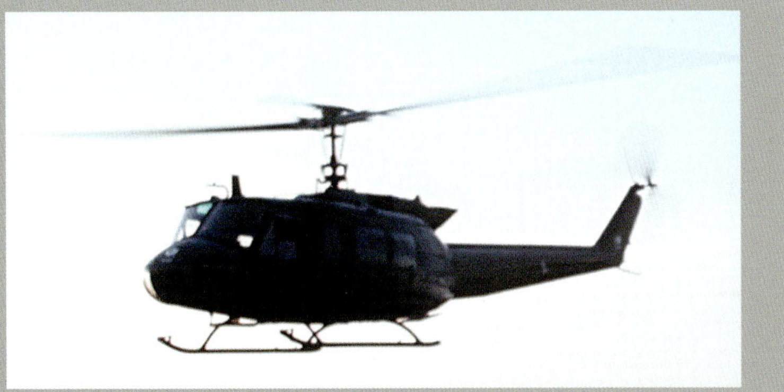

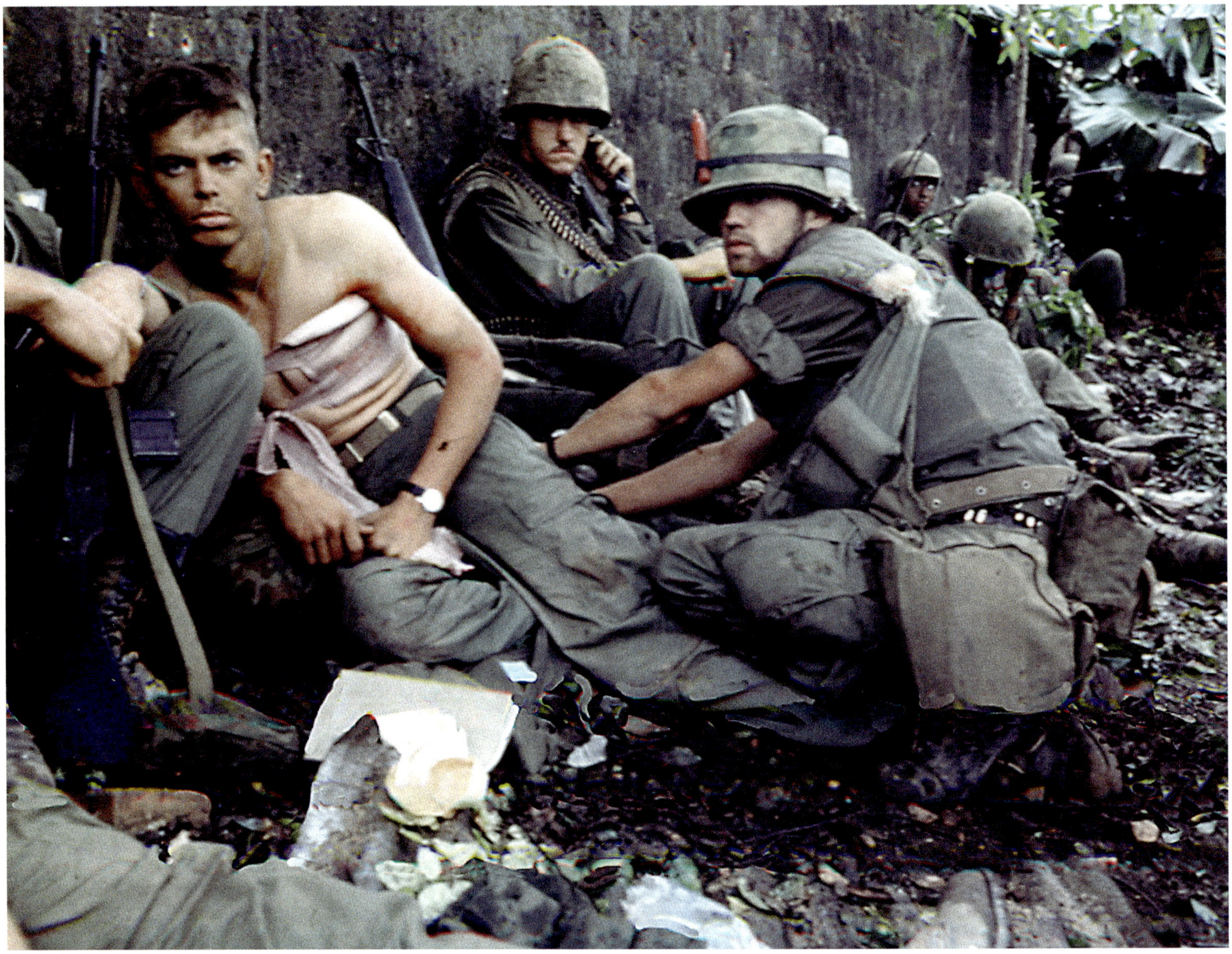

Above: Hue was a city-fought battle unlike the jungle campaigns. Walls and buildings became barricades for fighting and shelter. Here, a medic treats a wounded soldier as the squad takes a break from the fighting, but with weapons within reach.

Opposite: Two children peer around the wrecked wall that was once part of their home in Saigon after the Tet Offensive was driven back. Whole villages were massacred by V.C. troops.

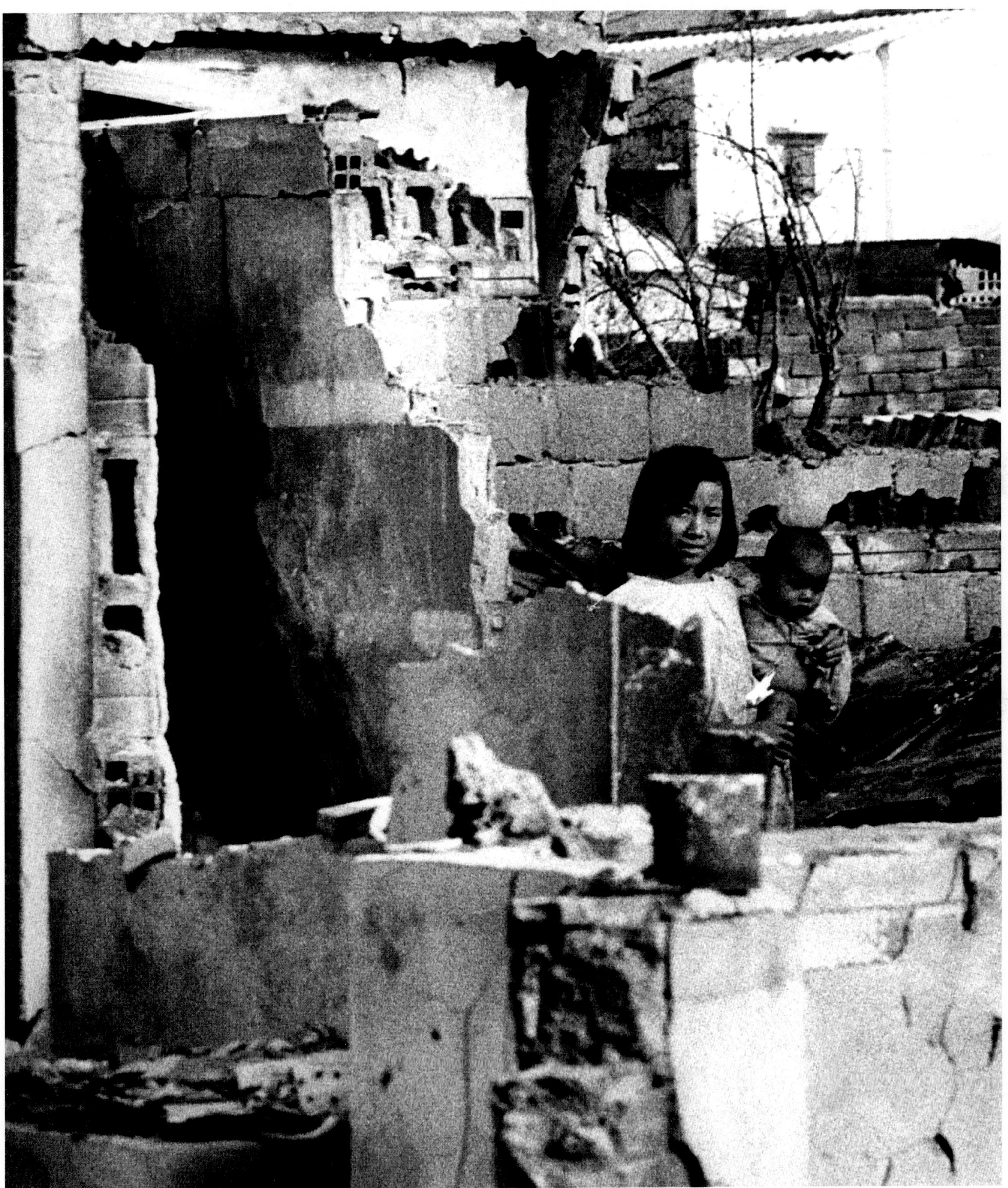

SIEGE OF KHE SANH

WITH THOUSANDS OF TROOPS COMMITTED TO THE TET HOLIDAY SURPRISE ATTACKS ACROSS SOUTH VIETNAM, GENERAL VO NGUYEN GIAP COULD CONCENTRATE ON HIS MASTERPIECE. THE AMERICANS HAD CREATED AN ISOLATED OUTPOST NEAR THE LAOTIAN BORDER MANNED BY A MERE 6,000 TROOPS AND SUPPLIED TOTALLY BY AIR. IT WAS DIEN BIEN PHU ALL OVER AGAIN. SINCE NOVEMBER HE'D BEEN MOVING TROOPS INTO THE HILLS NEAR THE FIREBASE AT KHE SANH. ALTOGETHER, THE FORCE NUMBERED CLOSE TO 40,000 SOLDIERS WITH ATTENDANT ROCKETS, ARTILLERY, MORTARS, HEAVY MACHINE GUNS, AND SOVIET PT-76 TANKS.

The troops manning Khe Sanh were U.S. Marines and A.R.V.N. Rangers. The camp had been set up in the early 1960s by Special Forces advisors making use of an old French airfield. When the Marines took over the base in 1966, they fortified the airstrip to handle heavier Air Force cargo planes. As with Dien Bien Phu, the base was divided into satellite positions surrounding the main fortification. Sand-bagged trenches ringed the perimeters connecting heavily built bunkers and an extensive communications system. Acoustic sensors and seismic detectors intended to monitor movement along the Ho Chi Minh Trail, the main supply route from North Vietnam that ran through Laos, had shown that large forces of North Vietnamese were on the move and seemed to be heading toward Khe Sanh.

Unlike the French in 1954, the defenders of Khe Sanh had plenty of supporting heavy weapons. There were 18 105mm howitzers and six 155mm guns, with more 155mm and 175mm guns on call at a nearby base. Six M48 tanks had 90mm guns. There were also four tracked M42 "Dusters," each mounting twin 40mm rapid-fire guns. And above all this was the United States Air Force: B-52 bombers, F-105 Thunderchiefs, and F-8E

N.V.A. AND BO DOI

The North Vietnamese Army was made up of many levels of soldiers, guerrillas, and support personnel. In a major attack such as at Khe Sanh, most troop movements were managed by uniformed and well-equipped N.V.A. soldiers and officers trained in the North to deal with complex situations, communications, weapons, and coping with the fog of war. The basic foot soldiers were the Bo Doi, who were Viet Cong recruited from villages in South Vietnam, armed with a hodge-podge of weapons (some home-made), and led by N.V.A. officers or V.C. who had shown aptitude for leadership. At the bottom were coolies who hauled supplies and, like the V.C., were recruited from villages—often at gunpoint.

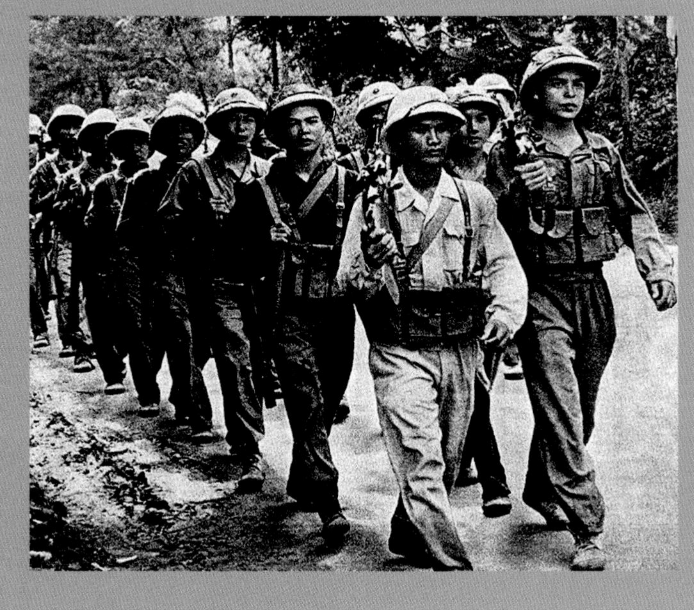

Right: Two squads of regular N.V.A. troops march along a jungle trail. The lead soldier carries a Czech ZB-26 light machine gun. They wear formal uniforms, combat shoes, and Chinese combat harnesses. All wear canvas pith helmets and some wear P.A.V.N. cap badges.

Opposite above: A C-130 Hercules makes a high-speed, low-level supply drop at Khe Sanh off its lowered ramp. Supplies were packed on wooden skids and a parachute pulled them from the rear of the plane. This allowed big loads to be delivered without the risk of landing while under artillery fire.

Opposite below: Huey UH-1 slicks slide into a hot L.Z. to lift off a patrol. The Khe Sanh airfield was targeted by the N.V.A., but they were unable to shut down air resupply to the Marines as they had with the French in 1954.

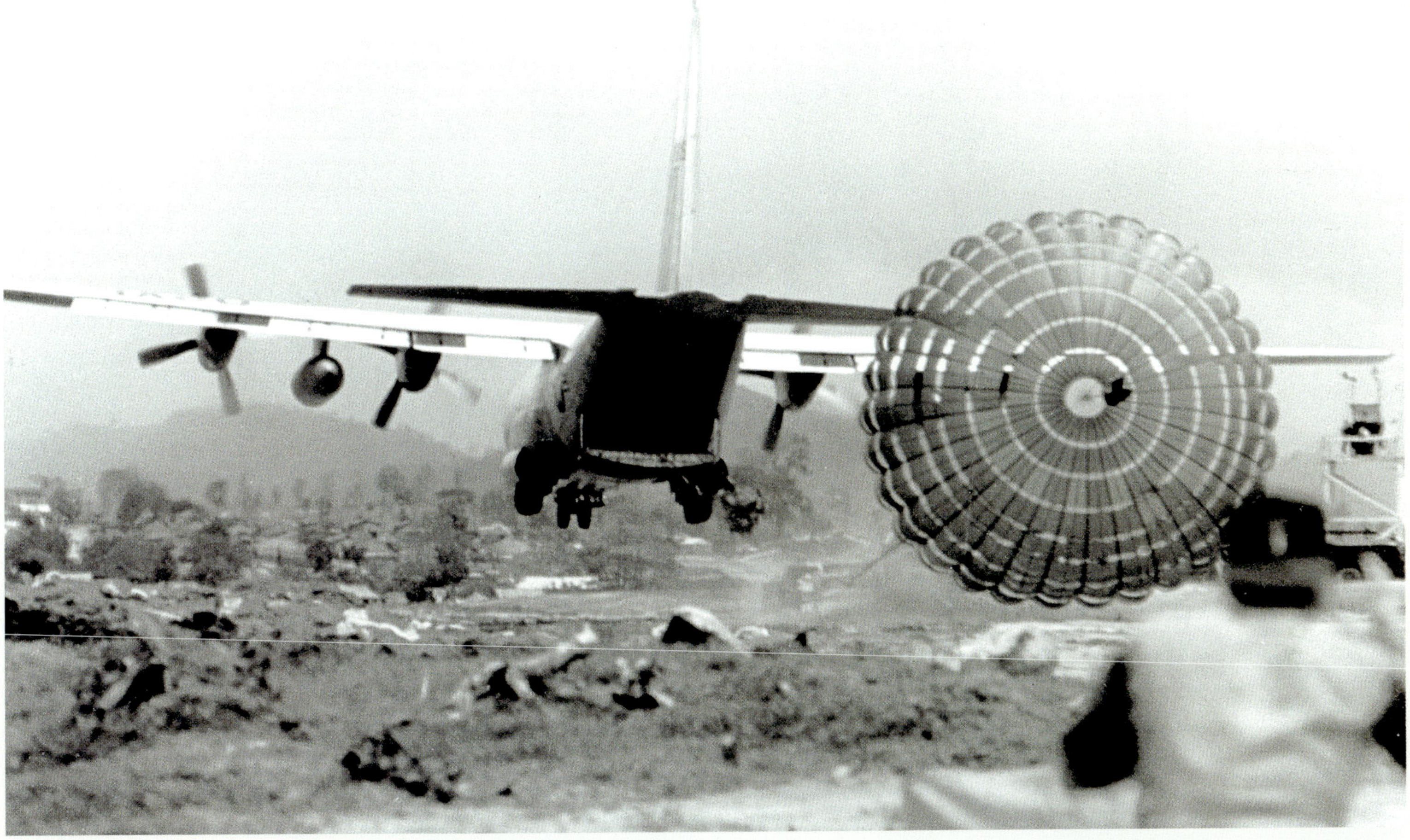

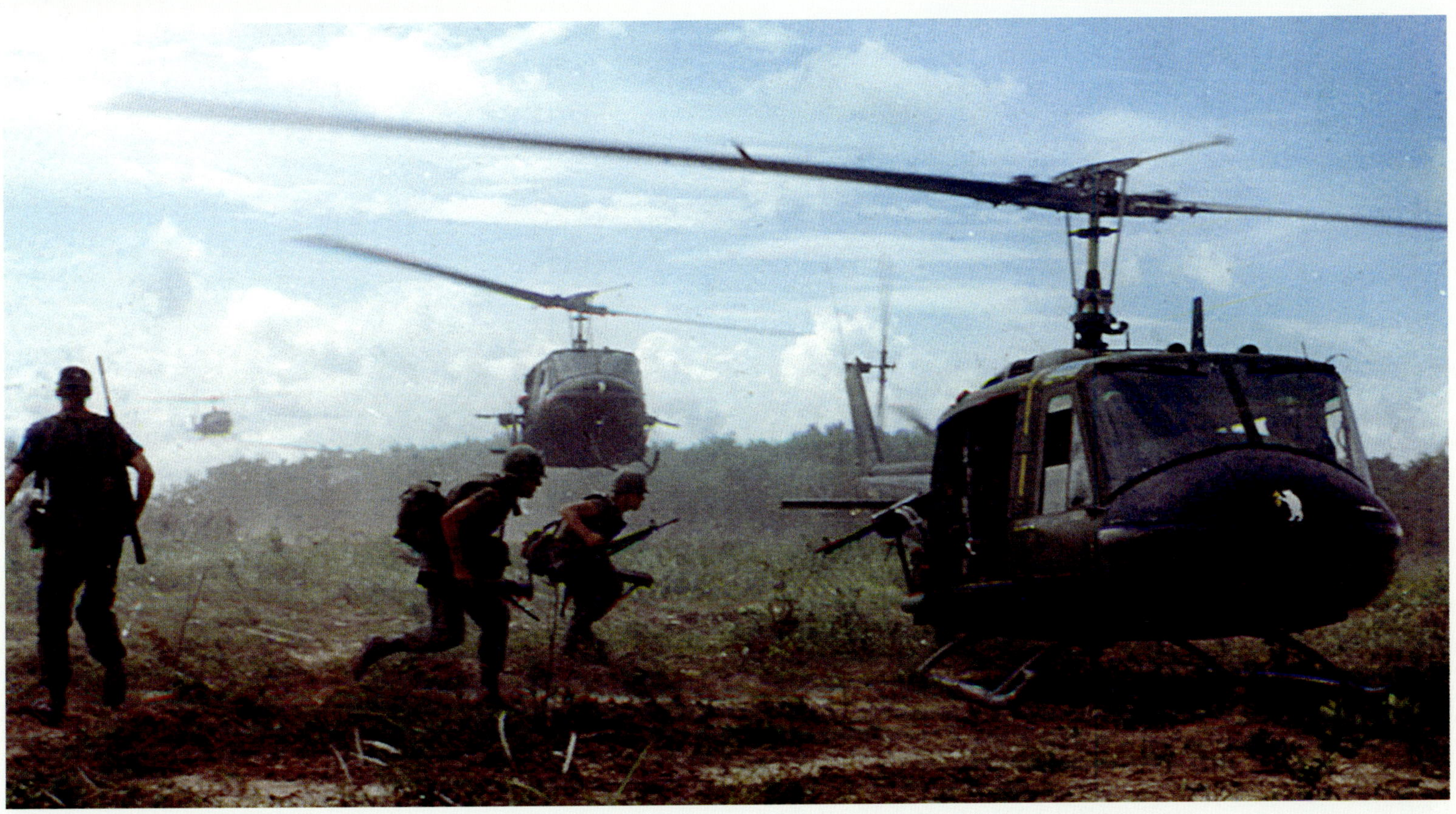

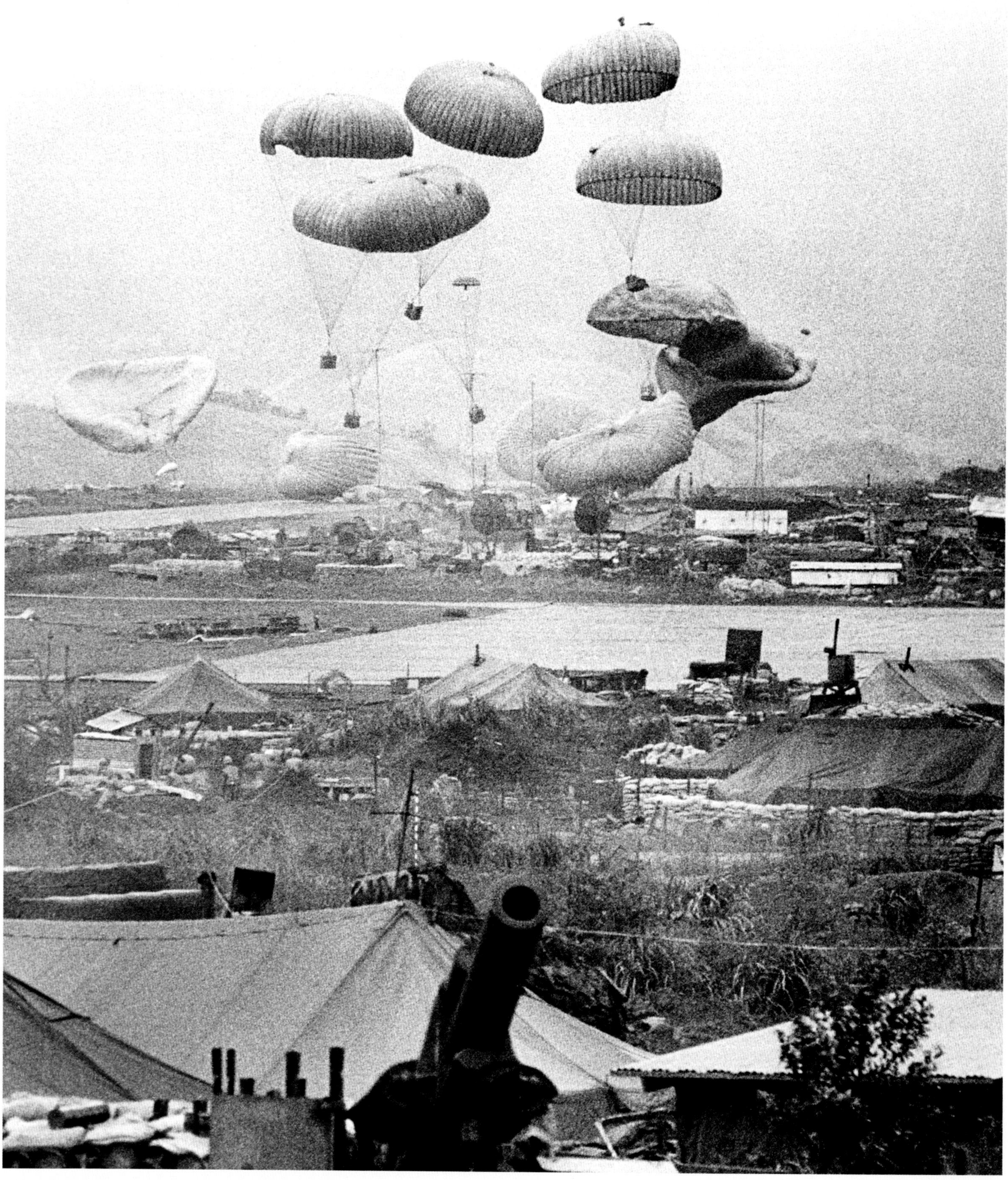

Crusader fighter-bombers. The U.S. Marines and the A.R.V.N. Rangers were ready for a fight.

Giap opened with a mortar bombardment on January 21. When one of the mortar bombs blew up 1,500 tons of ammunition, a flight of B-52 bombers silently appeared and pounded everything flat around the perimeter. After that, a line of small C-123 cargo planes made touch-and-go landings delivering 130 tons of ammo before dark. Also arriving was the 1st battalion of the 9th Marines to reinforce the base perimeter. Eventually, by the last week in January, the big C-130 cargo planes were once again able to use the airfield.

The siege raged back and forth. Giap committed some Soviet PT-76 light tanks in February and overran a Special Forces camp at nearby Lang Vei, losing five of 12 tanks to recoilless rifles and L.A.W.S. anti-tank rockets. When another ammo dump blew up, an AC-47 "Spooky" arrived overhead and orbited the base unleashing a broadside of Gatling guns, each spewing 3,000 rounds of 20mm bullets per minute.

More Marine reinforcements flew in. Counterattacks were effective and by April, Khe Sanh was secure. Giap lost 9,000–13,000 troops at the firebase and an unknown number churned into the earth beneath the B-52 bombs. The Marines lost 199 killed.

C.I.A. STALKS THE V.C./N.V.A.

The name of the game in Vietnam was to win the allegiance of the people. Achieving this goal for the V.C. often meant using fear, torture, and executions in the villages and cities. To counter these acts—when propaganda failed—Provincial Reconnaissance Units ("P.R.U.s") were created. These American-led, C.I.A.-financed paramilitary forces numbered about 5,000 Vietnamese in counter-guerrilla units. Operating out of regional safe houses, they practiced all the arts of guerrilla warfare. Leading these P.R.U.s were Special Forces Green Berets. Thousands of V.C. spies, double-agents, and provocateurs were eliminated, but as the war wound down for the U.S., P.R.U. operations were left to the South Vietnamese, resulting in some tragic massacres.

Opposite: Supply drops arrived regularly to keep the Marines' artillery, small arms, and tanks operating throughout the siege. General Giap threw many "human wave" charges of V.C. and N.V.A. forces at the Marine firebase, but the tactics failed.

Below: A recon squad has captured a suspected Viet Cong. As they interrogate him an attempt is made to recruit him to the A.R.V.N. The V.C. feared being taken captive because of the activities of the P.R.U.s.

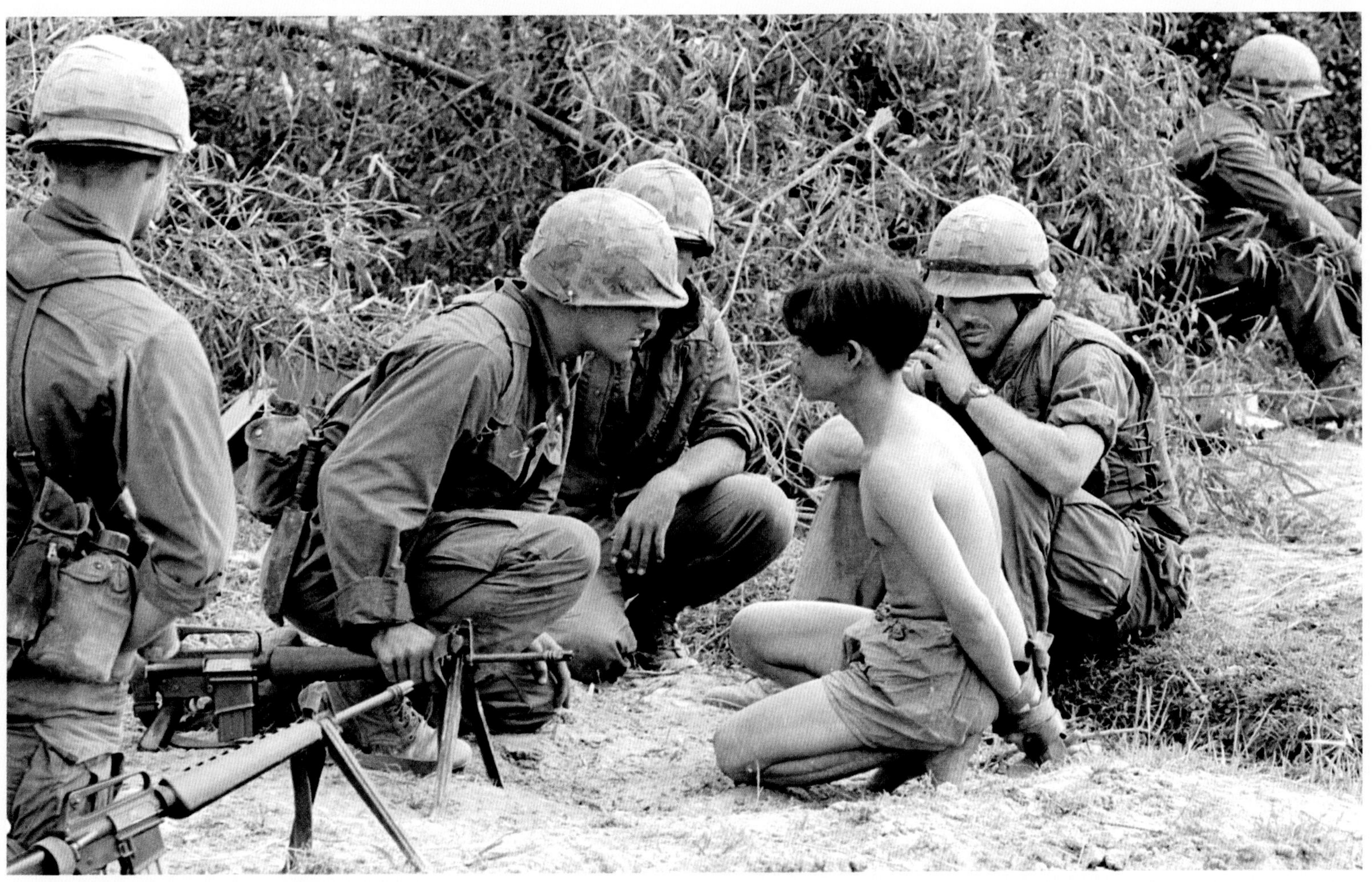

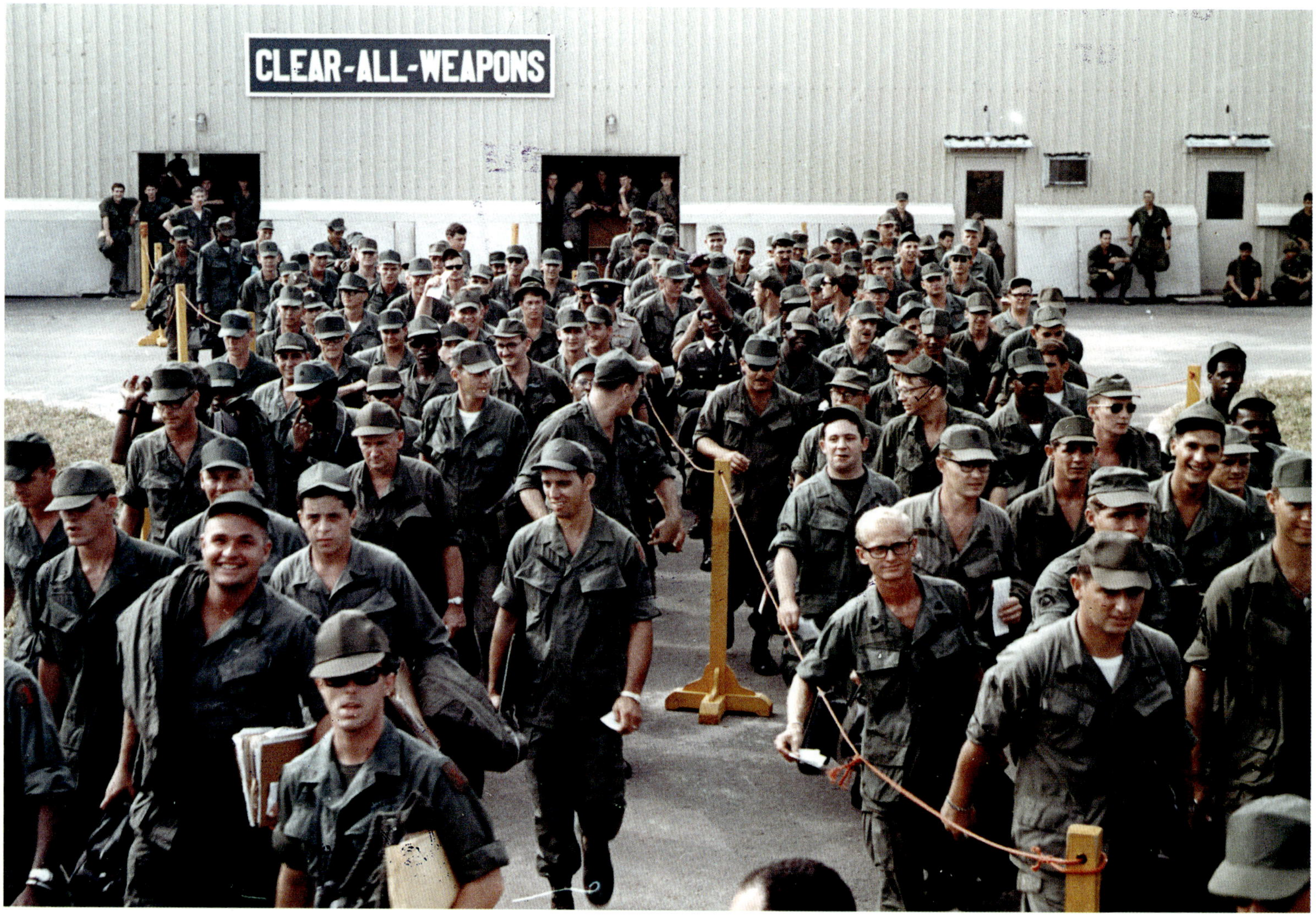

RATS OF KHE SANH

The Siege of Khe Sanh was not unlike sieges of ancient times when living conditions produced new enemies within. The rats were huge and vicious: According to Peter Bush, "Theoretically there could have been one hundred thousand rats by day 27 of the siege, one-half million rats on day 43, and over one million by day 50. Whatever their number, the rats at Khe Sanh were like the rain and the shrapnel—always irritating, always present, always threatening." Eventually some Marines, tiring of the rats scampering across them at night, loaded their rifles with tracer rounds, and sharpened their shooting skills on the rat population living off the distant garbage pits.

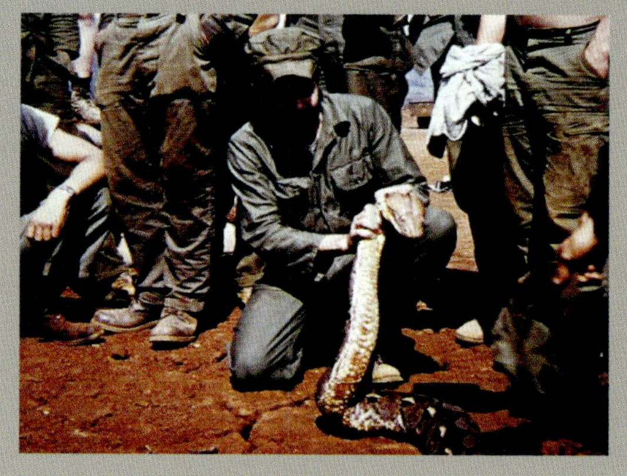

Above top: Troops with their personal gear heading for waiting transport aircraft on the first leg of their trip home to the States. Those soldiers or Marines who decided to "ship-over" signed up for a second "tour" of combat.

Above, box: A squad of Marines at Khe Sanh gathers around a boa constrictor snake that had crawled into a bunker during the siege. The only thing the troops hated more than marauding snakes were packs of huge dog-size rats that scurried across them when they tried to sleep at night. Many Marines used pistols, rifles, and machine guns to dispose of the bold scavengers.

Opposite: During a lull in combat, a soldier entertains his buddies with some tunes on his guitar. Soldiers found diversions wherever they could to ease the tension between battles.

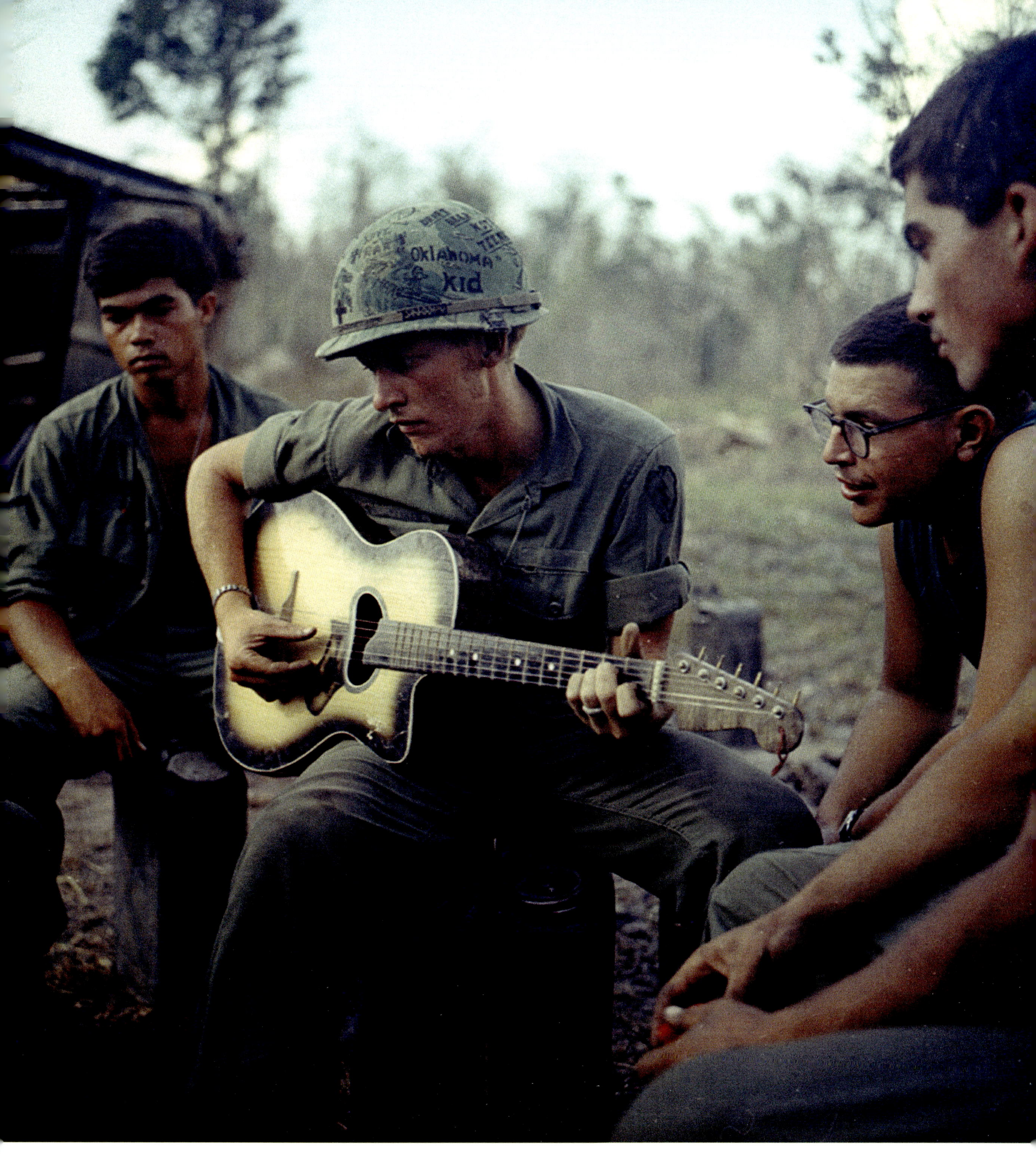
OKLAHOMA
Kid

CHAPTER 17

THE AIR WAR

SECRETARY OF STATE HENRY CABOT LODGE WROTE TO PRESIDENT JOHNSON ON JANUARY 5, 1966, "THE VIETNAMESE NEWSPAPER *TIEN VANG* SAW THE BOMBING PAUSE AS AN INVITATION FOR HANOI TO APPRAISE THE UNITED STATES AS WEAKENING IN ITS DETERMINATION TO CARRY ON THE WAR."

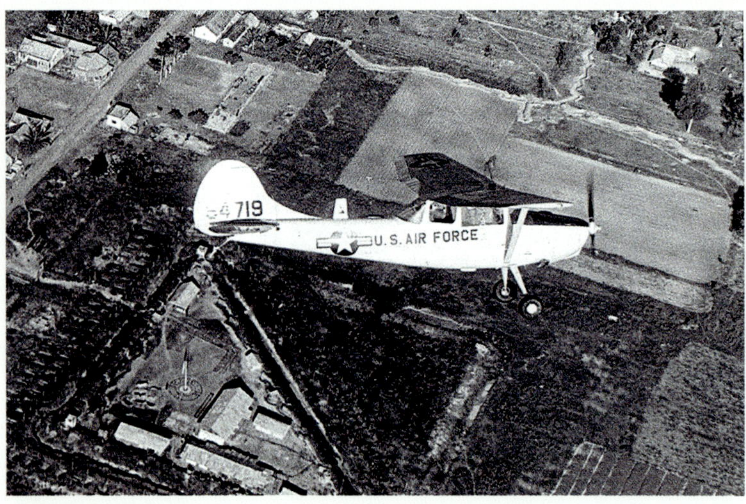

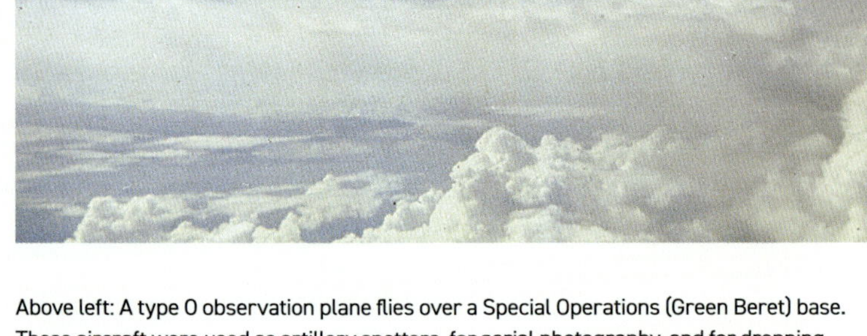

Above left: A type O observation plane flies over a Special Operations (Green Beret) base. These aircraft were used as artillery spotters, for aerial photography, and for dropping flares to illuminate the battlefield and identify friend or foe.

Above right: An F-105 Thunderchief gains altitude. This fighter, a member of the high-speed "Century Series" that began with the F-100 Super Sabre, was the fastest supersonic fighter in Vietnam. It carried a variety of weapons for close ground support, horizontal bombing, and a gun for dogfighting with MiG fighters. The "Thud" could not turn with a MiG-17 or -21, but used its high speed to avoid trouble.

American air power had become a growing factor in the prosecution of the war since President Johnson sent naval aircraft to bomb North Vietnamese coastal facilities in 1964 following the Tonkin Gulf attacks on the destroyer U.S.S. *Maddox*. As North Vietnam incursions and Viet Cong guerrilla attacks increased in scope, American ground commanders came to rely heavily on air support whenever there was risk of losing a ground battle to overwhelming numbers and along the supply lines that snaked down into South Vietnam. American commanders also believed bombing targets in Hanoi and Hai Phong was critical to the war effort.

Besides the supply role of Bell UH-1 Huey and Sikorsky helicopters for ferrying troops to battle zones and CH-47 Chinook or CH-54 Tarhe helicopters to shift artillery to firebases, heavily armed helicopter gunships offered prodigious firepower during ground operations and "dustoffs" (wounded evacuation under fire). Vietnam was principally a land war, requiring fast combat reaction and insertion of troops to meet both small guerrilla and regiment-size North Vietnamese operations. But the American air and naval-air elements added tactical pinpoint and area destruction that was unmatched and almost invariably won the day when called upon.

Down low, just above the jungle canopy, propeller-driven A-1E Skyraiders orbited for long periods over a target, supporting rescue of downed pilots by "Jolly Green Giant" CH-3 helicopters. The AD-1 Skyraider was protected by F-100 Super Sabre and later F-105 Thunderchief and F-4 Phantom fighters which engaged any North Vietnamese MiG fighters that tried to intercept the Skyraiders. In 1967, North Vietnam had 44 MiG-17 fighters, updated versions of the Korean War MiG-15. They also had 16 MiG-21 jets, more up-to-date aircraft that were a match for any Allied plane. Russian S.A.M. sites ringed Hanoi and other targets in the North along with obsolescent—yet still effective—anti-aircraft guns. Captured American pilots received harsh treatment because of their devastating raids and endured severe conditions in prisoner-of-war camps such as the "Hanoi Hilton."

JOLLY GREEN GIANTS

As air operations escalated, the number of N.V.A. anti-aircraft sites increased exponentially resulting in more Allied aerial casualties. The HH-3E former transport helicopter (known as the Jolly Green Giant) was converted to combat rescue missions. Armor, 7.62 machine guns, self-sealing fuel tanks, a rescue hoist, and forest penetrator were standard equipment. Communication was maintained with fixed wing propeller craft such as Skyraiders and A-37 Dragonflies for covering fire during rescues. The Giants were also used as insertion and extraction units during covert Special Forces missions. The HH-3E, which arrived in Vietnam in 1967, was operated by the Aerospace Rescue and Recovery Service (A.R.R.S.) out of Udorn, Thailand.

Below: Looking past a door gunner with his 7.62mm rotating barrel Minigun, an HH-3E Jolly Green Giant twin-engine, heavy-lift helicopter heads out on a rescue mission. The HH-3E rescue crews were responsible for saving the lives of many pilots downed behind enemy lines, working with fixed-wing aircraft for enemy ground-fire suppression.

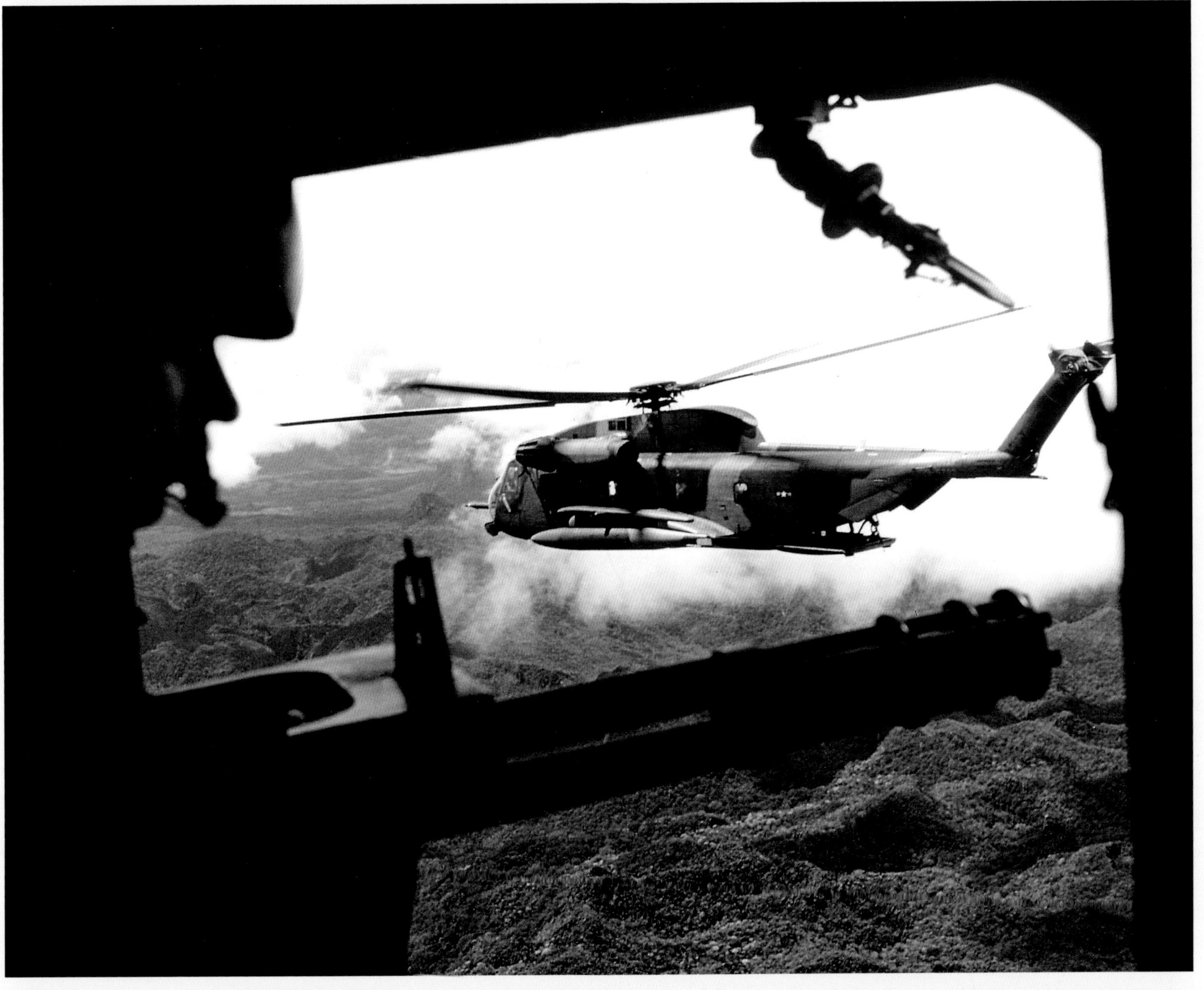

B-52 bombing was the most feared and effective aerial weapon. "Pauses" in their raids were offered to force North Vietnam back to the negotiating table. Hanoi used these reprieves to increase their rush of troops and supplies into the South. Bombing of Hanoi had little effect since there was virtually no strategic manufacturing to destroy. North Vietnam's ability to wage war was provided by China and the Soviet Union. The bombing also produced a negative effect on the people of Vietnam, as illustrated by a Vietnamese newspaper cartoon: two Vietnamese men watch B-52s fly above them. "Are they going north?" asks one. "No," says the other. The first man says, "Let us move north then."

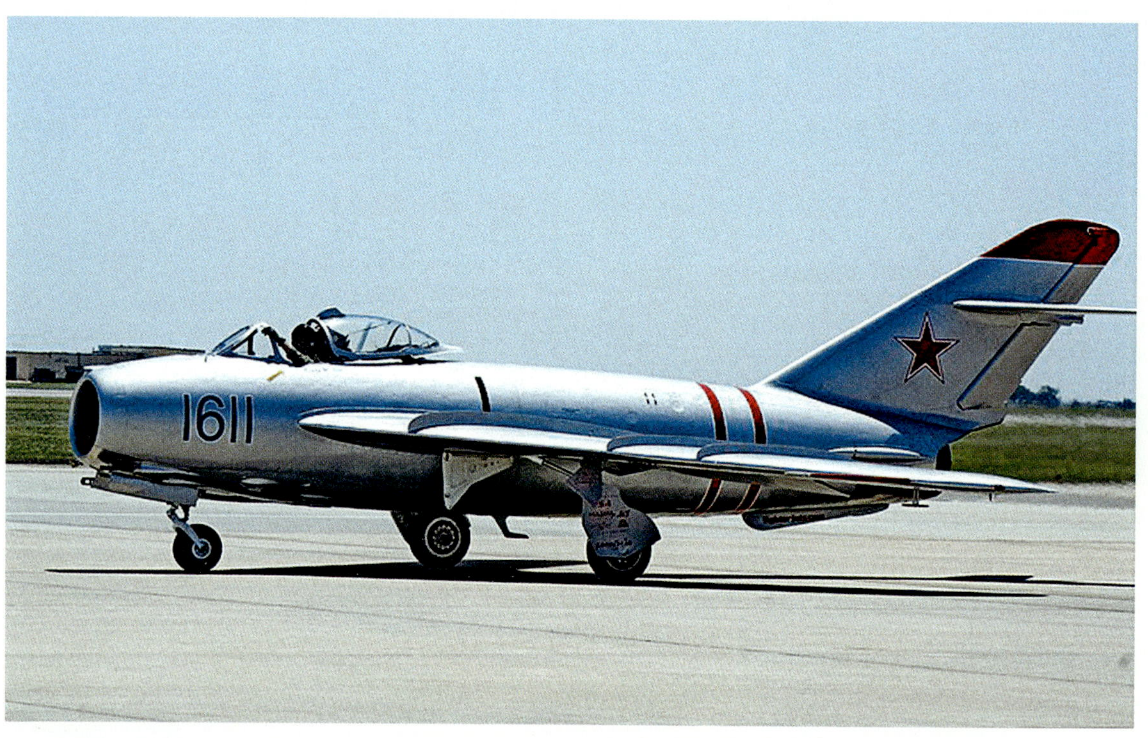

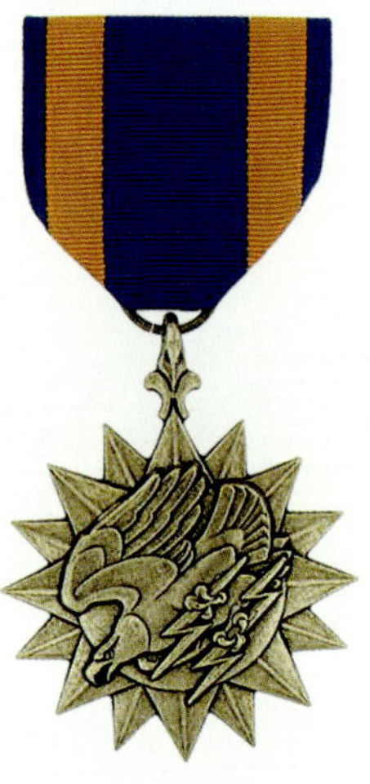

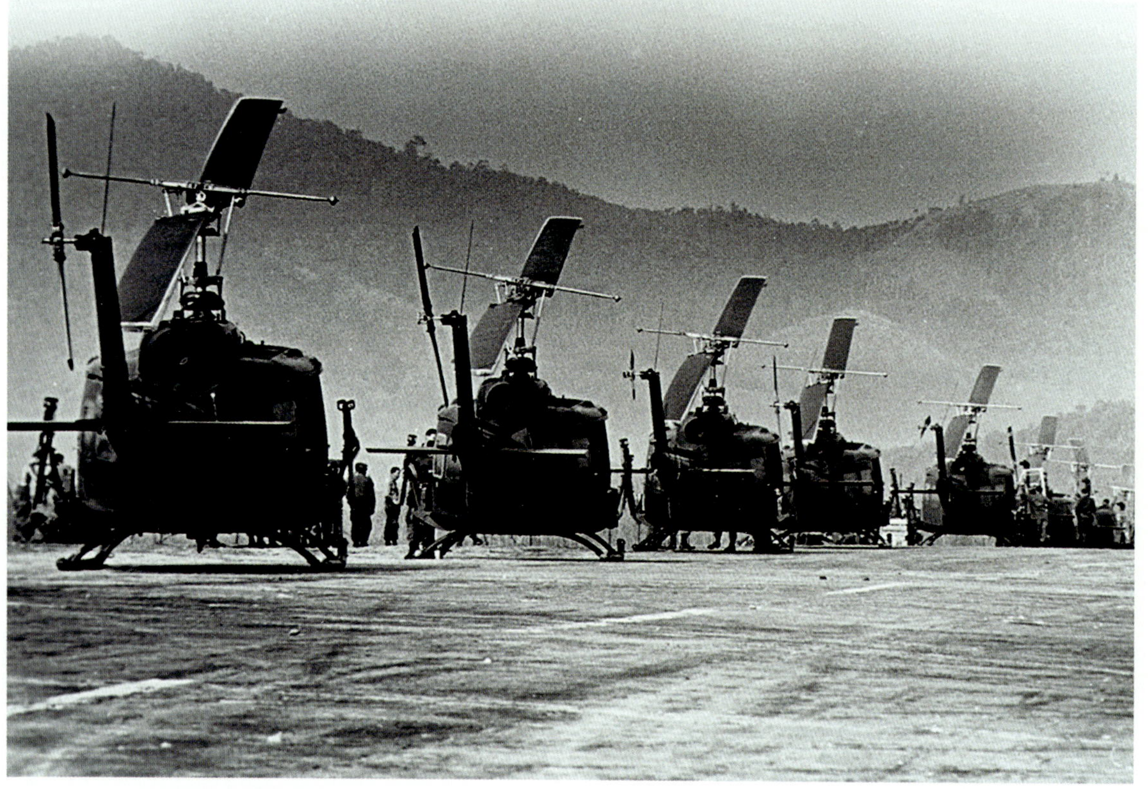

Above left: A Soviet MiG-17 taxis for a take-off. The Mikoyan-Gurevich (MiG) design bureau upgraded the MiG-15 that flew in Korea, employing wing-mounted rockets and an afterburner to achieve supersonic speed bursts. Even though it was considered obsolete by the mid-1960s, the MiG-17 gave a good account over Vietnam, being flown by most of the top North Vietnamese pilots, including the leading Vietnam People's Air Force (V.P.A.F.) ace, Nguyen Van Coc, who scored nine kills while flying with the 921st Fighter Regiment based at Noi Bai, north-west of Hanoi.

Left: A line of UH-1 Huey helicopter "slicks" awaits their airmobile infantry units for delivery to a patrol L.Z. The Huey became one of the signature aircraft of the Vietnam War—alongside the B-52 bomber. Used for troop transport, medical evacuation, and heavily armed for enemy fire suppression, these helicopters gave soldiers complete troop movement flexibility in a war with no front lines.

Above: The U.S.A.F. Air Medal is awarded to U.S. military and civilian personnel for single acts of heroism or meritorious achievements while participating in aerial flight, and to foreign military personnel in actual combat in support of operations.

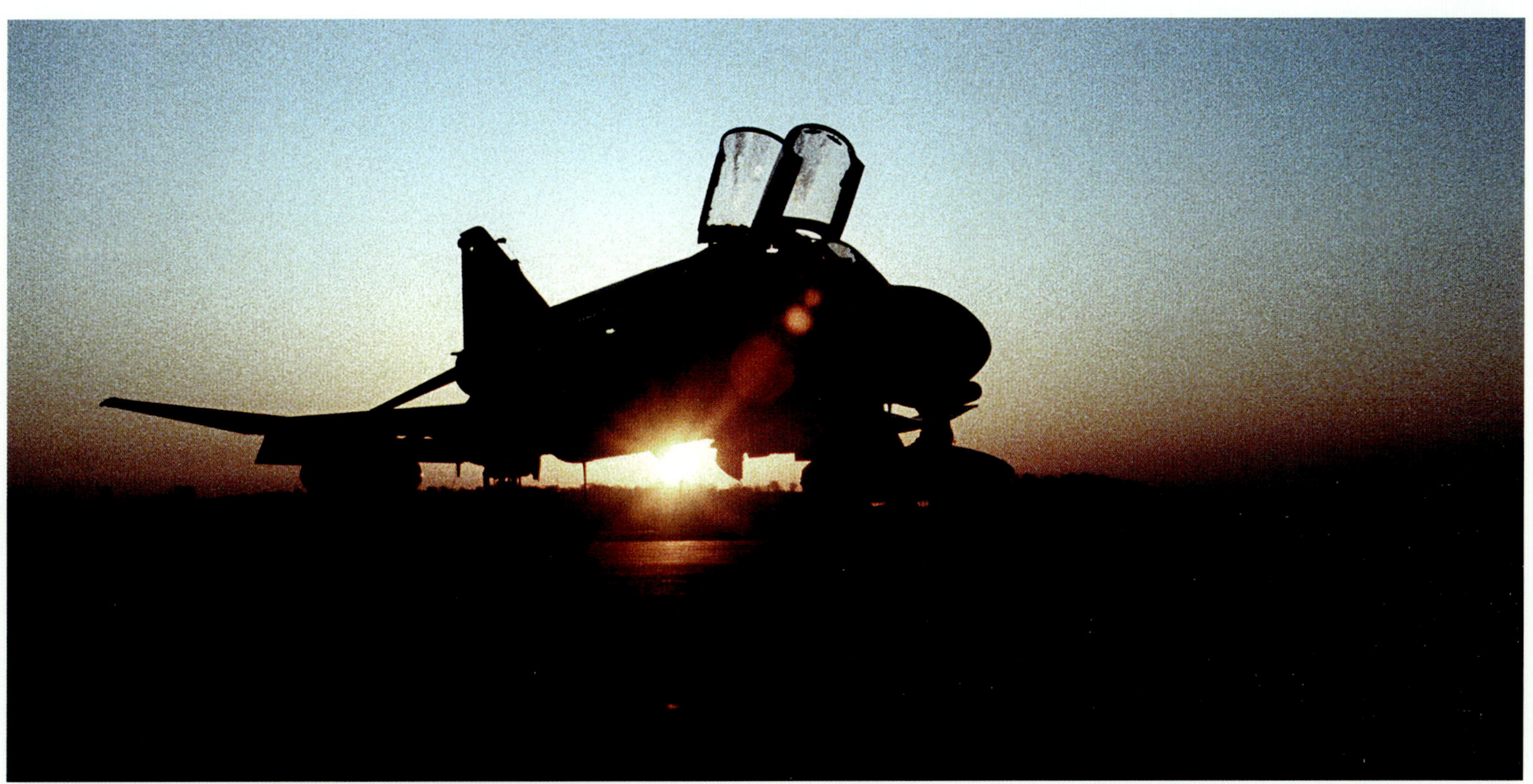

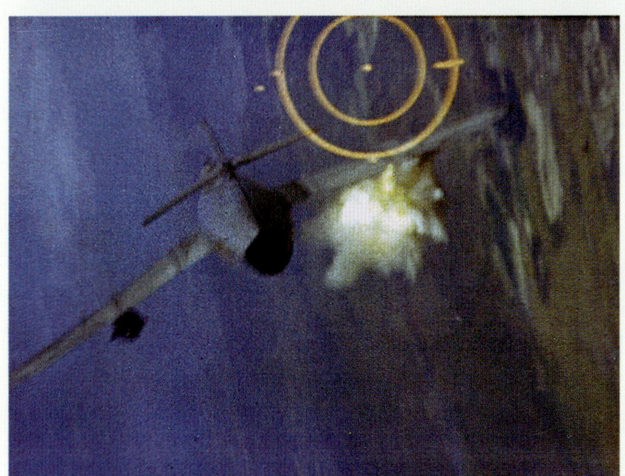

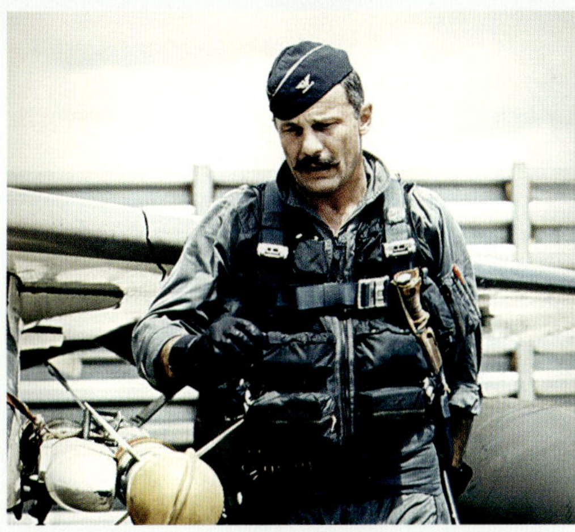

Above: An F-4 Phantom awaits its crew on the ready line at sunrise. Both canopies are open for the pilot and his Electronic Warfare Officer (E.W.O.). The Phantom operated off both Navy carriers and air bases as a supersonic fighter bomber. Early F-4s arrived only with Sparrow and Sidewinder missiles for self-defense, but later a gun was added in an external package to cope with the MiG-21 figters.

Far left: A frame from a gun camera shows a MiG-17 taking a hit on a wing fuel tank in a gun attack by a U.S. fighter. The illuminated heads-up gunsight reticule can be seen lifting above target lock as the pursuing fighter begins to bank away from the kill.

Above left: Major Robin Olds shot down 13 German fighters in World War II. He downed four MiG fighters in Vietnam while commander of the 8th Tactical Fighter Wing at Ubon Royal Thai Air Force Base, Thailand. Olds flew 152 combat missions, 105 of them over North Vietnam, from October 1966 to September 1967. He shot down two MiG-17s and two MiG-21s, two on one mission. His F-4, by now called "Scat XXVII," is at the Air Force Museum, Wright-Patterson A.F.B., Ohio.

Left: An American pilot shot down over North Vietnam receives first aid from a Vietnamese medical corpsman while an N.V.A. soldier guards him.

HANOI HILTON P.O.W. CAMP

Many of the pilots and air crews who were shot down over North Vietnam were imprisoned in a number of prisons scattered around Hanoi. The conditions were terrible. Watery soup and stale bread passed for food and kept the men in perpetual intestinal distress. They were beaten, starved, tortured, and used for anti-American propaganda. The most infamous of these prisons was the "Hanoi Hilton"—actually the Hoa Lo prison. Others were dubbed Alcatraz, Briar Patch, Dirty Bird, and the Zoo. In 1973, all prisoners were supposed to be repatriated, but after the war, in 1975, more than 2,000 were still unaccounted for.

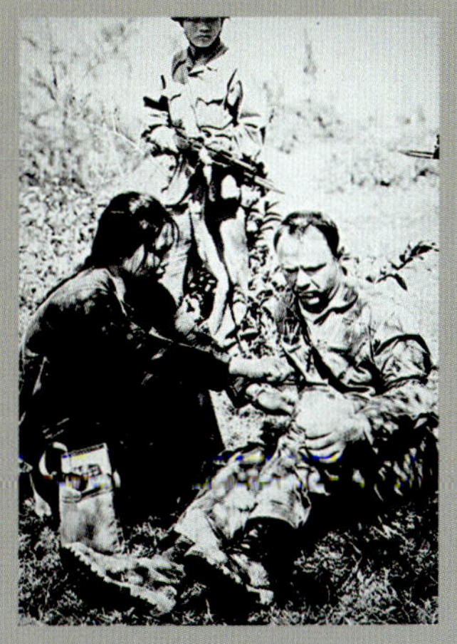

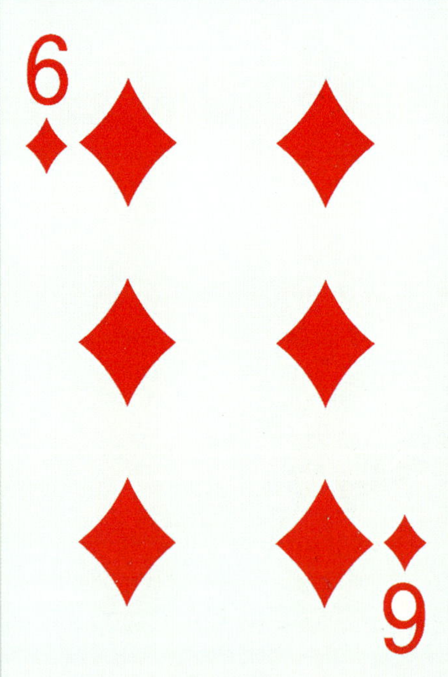

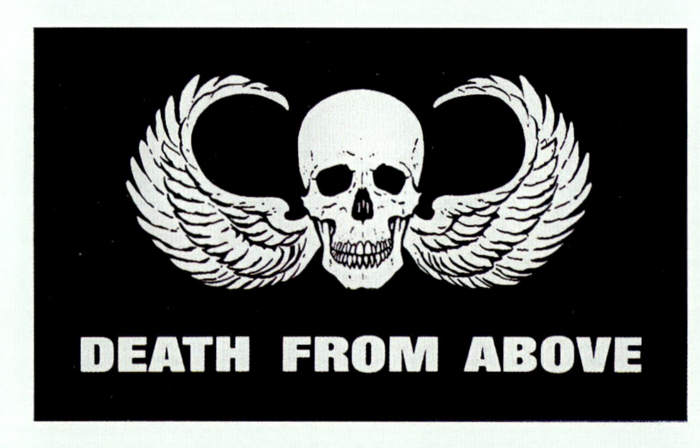

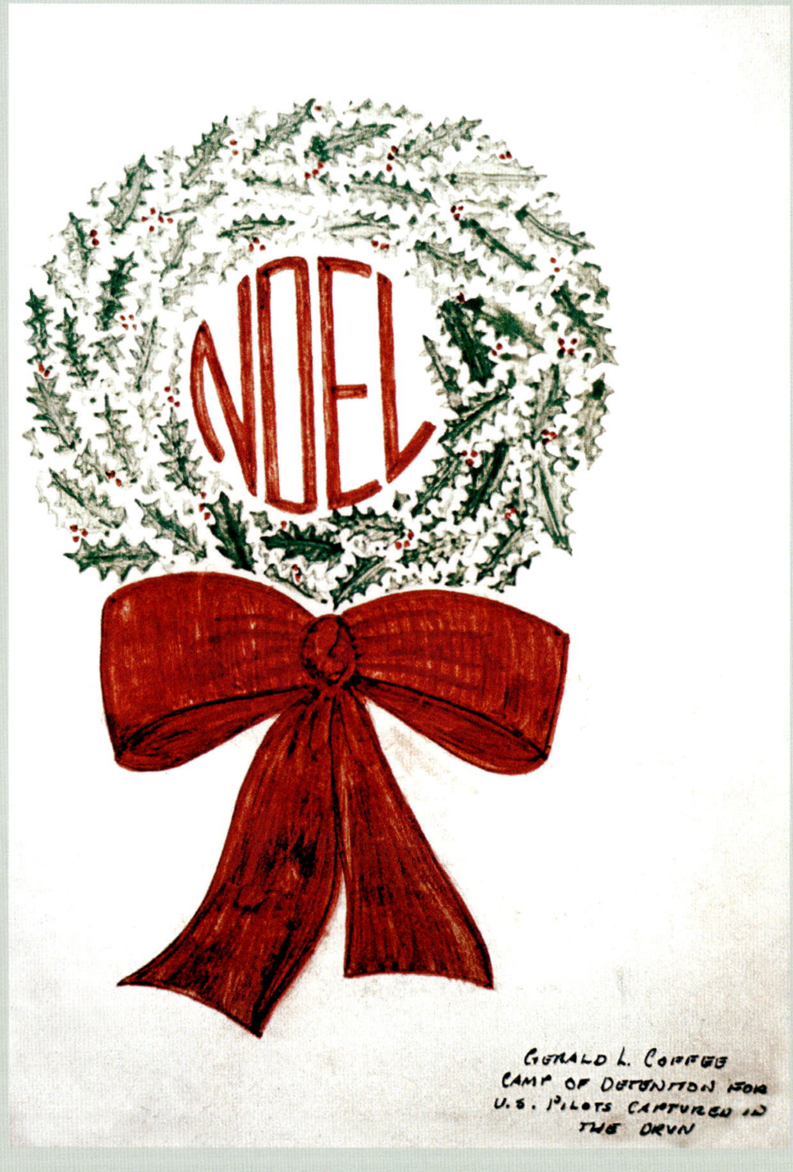

U.S. AIRBORNE CALLING CARD

These cards, part of a psychological warfare program, were often left with slain N.V.A. or V.C. fighters, more often than not placed in the dead person's mouth. They were designed to demoralize survivors who returned to battle scenes to reclaim fallen comrades.

P.O.W. CHRISTMAS CARD

Poignant holiday cards were hand-painted in watercolor by American Prisoners of War in North Vietnamese P.O.W. prisons. They were sent home to the U.S. through the Red Cross and other neutral countries' humanitarian services.

Opposite: An AC-47 flies above a known stronghold of Viet Cong insurgents but, instead of opening fire, the "Spooky" drops psychological warfare leaflets urging the V.C. to surrender and give up the Communist propaganda line.

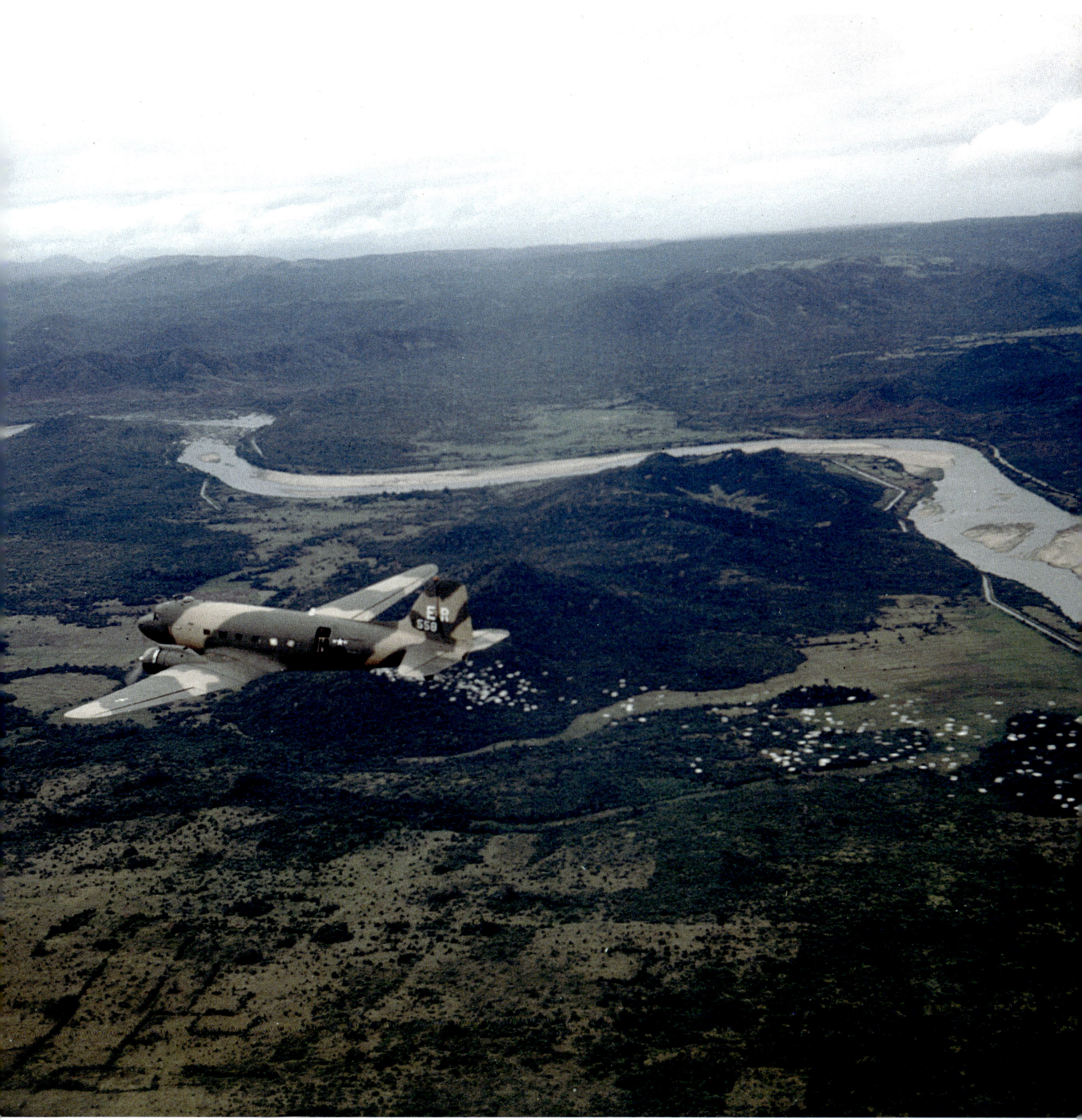
ER

TUNNEL RATS

THE "TUNNEL RATS" WHO CRAWLED THROUGH MILES OF TUNNELS AND GALLERIES DUG BY VIET CONG GUERRILLAS HAD ONE OF THE MOST DANGEROUS JOBS IN VIETNAM. THESE AUSTRALIANS, AMERICANS, AND NEW ZEALANDERS WERE BRAVE BEYOND ANY NORMAL DEFINITION OF THE WORD. THEY WERE ARMED WITH ONLY A PISTOL—PREFERABLY A REVOLVER OF MEDIUM CALIBER WITH A MUZZLE SUPPRESSOR TO REDUCE NOISE—A KNIFE, A TORCH, AND INDIVIDUAL ITEMS SUCH AS INSECT SPRAY FOR USE AGAINST FIRE ANTS. THEY WERE USUALLY MEN OF SMALLER STATURE THAN THE AVERAGE SOLDIER BECAUSE OF THE NARROW TUNNEL WALLS AND CONFINED SPACES, DUG TO ACCOMMODATE THE SMALLER V.C. THEY WORE NO HELMET AND USUALLY ONLY AN UNDERWEAR ("SKIVVY") SHIRT. THE TUNNEL RATS ALSO FOUGHT BATS, POISONOUS SNAKES, AND SUFFOCATING CLAUSTROPHOBIA THAT COULD CAUSE SUDDEN, TERRIBLE PANIC IN THE DAMP DARK FAR BENEATH THE JUNGLE SURFACE. OFTEN, A PIECE OF STRING THAT TRAILED BEHIND THEM WAS THEIR ONLY CONTACT WITH THEIR BUDDIES FAR ABOVE.

Around any bend in any tunnel could be a V.C. trip wire or a waiting trapdoor guard armed with a silent stabbing spear. Booby traps were common, often grenades triggered by unseen watchers. A soldier dropping into a lower-level tunnel could receive an instant knife thrust. Tunnel searchers never knew what enemy lay ahead, or who was coming up behind after slipping silently in from a hidden trapdoor.

The Viet Cong dug storage galleries, living quarters, map rooms, hospitals, and an ever-expanding web of communications tunnels lit by oil lamps. Their ingenuity and discipline while fighting the better-equipped Allies won them respect. The tunnels were entirely unknown to the Allies before "Operation Crimp" uncovered part of the complex in January 1966 while trying to "wipe out" the V.C. command structure at Cu Chi near South Vietnam's "Ho Bo Woods." The operation was a failure except as a wake-up call to the existence of the vast tunnel system.

The American engineers used large tractors with sharp Rome blades to clear away the undergrowth masking tunnel entrances, C-4 explosives to blast it, and C.S. gas piped in to drive out the inhabitants. An entire American divisional headquarters

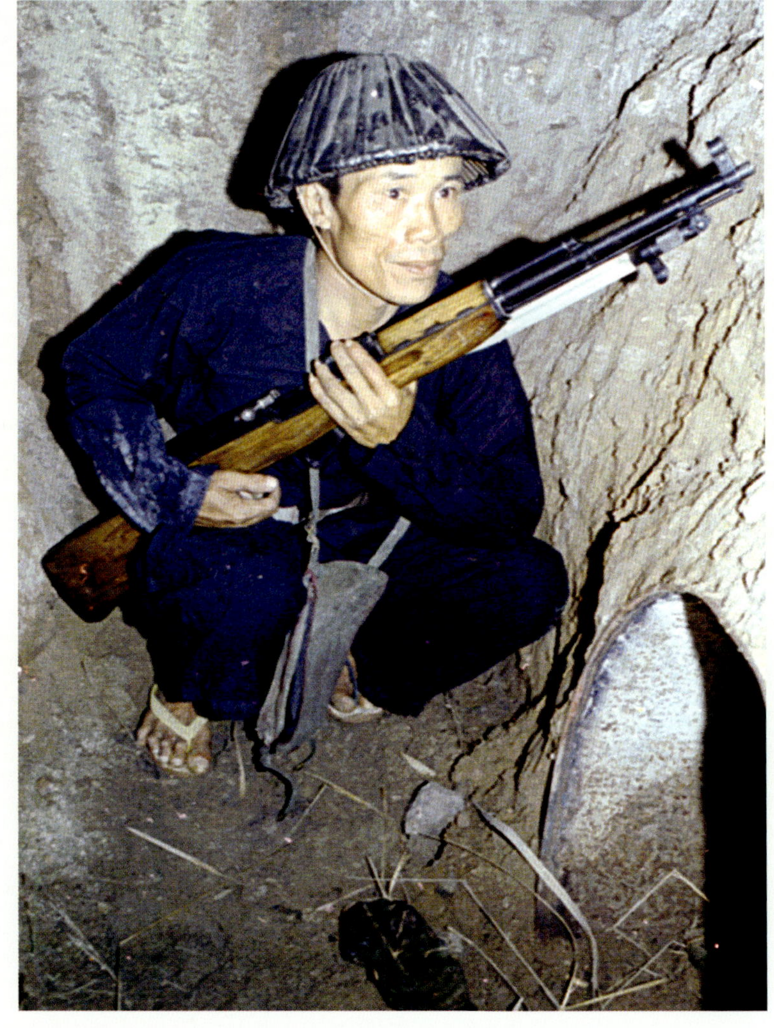

Right: An elderly V.C. crouches in a tunnel with his Simonov SKS rifle. He wears a plastic-covered bamboo helmet and shower flip-flops for shoes. The rifle is a poor choice due to its length in the close quarters, but using the folding bayonet beneath the barrel makes more sense.

Opposite: Four soldiers use a team effort to haul one of their buddies out of a V.C. tunnel entrance after an exploration. V.C. tunnels had many booby traps, trip wires, and hidden spaces where tunnel guards lay in ambush with silent wire garrottes or a quick thrust with a short pointed spear.

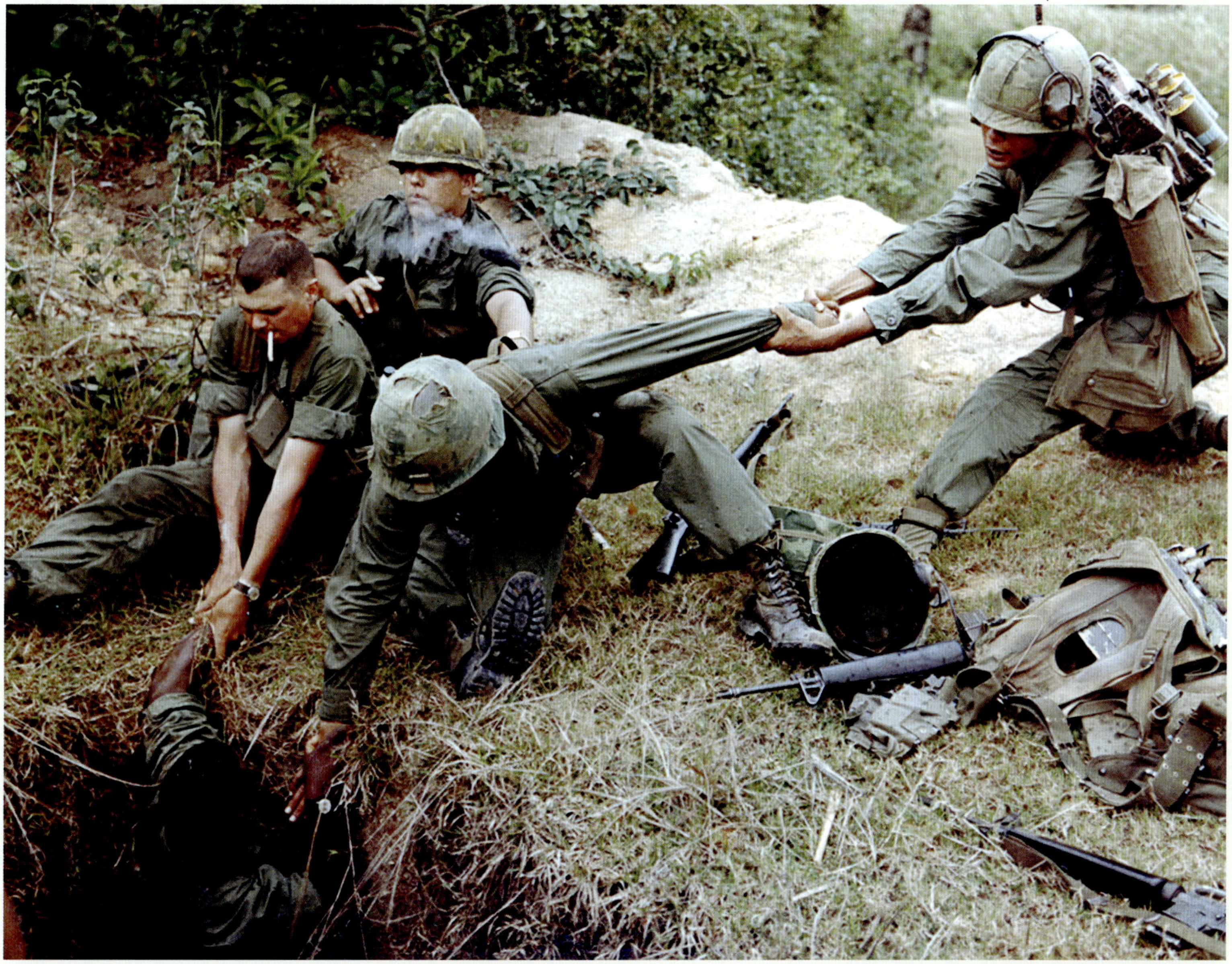

A SPECIAL KIND OF SOLDIER

The tunnel complex that snaked beneath the jungle was critical to the Viet Cong. Camouflaged entrances in hooches and alongside trails led into multi-level galleries. Hidden air ducts protruded just above the jungle floor. Often there were no "tunnel rat" specialists around when an entrance was discovered and the shortest man in the squad was called on. But tunnel exploration was always by volunteers. Prior to the Tet Offensive small caches of weapons were hidden near tunnel entrances for quick access. While the main technology was courage, Smith & Wesson did create a special .44 caliber revolver that fired a bullet which broke into four segments like a shotgun round. While devastating, its muzzle blast was also blinding.

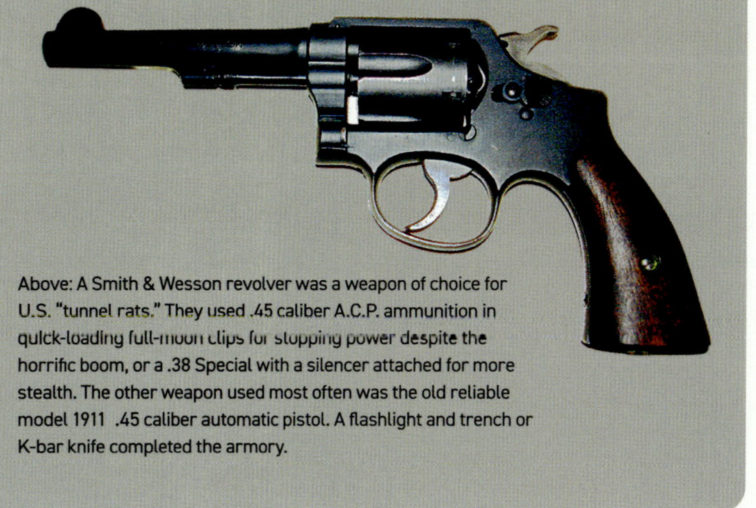

Above: A Smith & Wesson revolver was a weapon of choice for U.S. "tunnel rats." They used .45 caliber A.C.P. ammunition in quick-loading full-moon clips for stopping power despite the horrific boom, or a .38 Special with a silencer attached for more stealth. The other weapon used most often was the old reliable model 1911 .45 caliber automatic pistol. A flashlight and trench or K-bar knife completed the armory.

THE IRON TRIANGLE

The "Iron Triangle" was a 60-square-mile wooded area lying between the Saigon River and Route 13. On January 8, 1967, 16,000 American and 14,000 A.R.V.N. invaded the V.C. stronghold. This headquarters and supply distribution point only 25 miles north-west of Saigon took 19 days of heavy fighting to clear. Large caches of food were seized as well as excavation of a warren of subterranean tunnels that honeycombed the area, often snaking beneath Allied base camps.

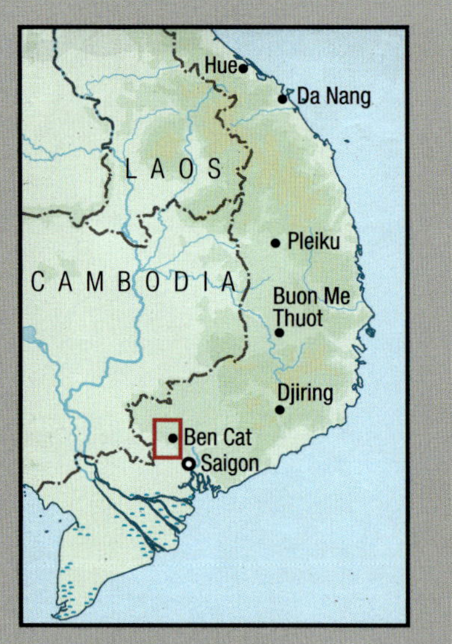

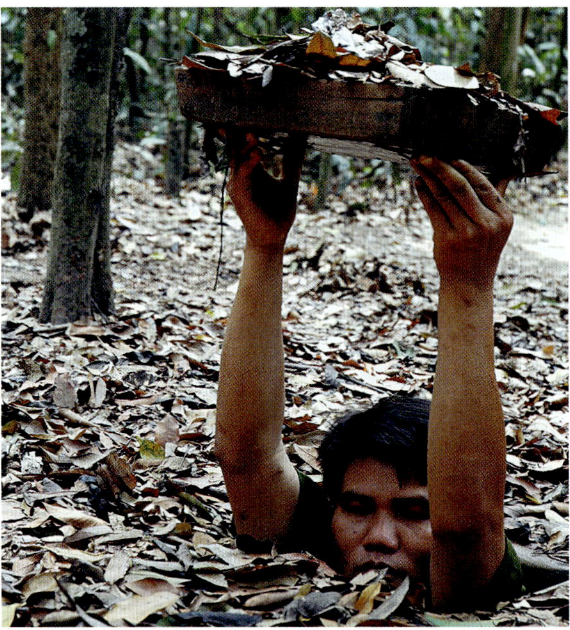

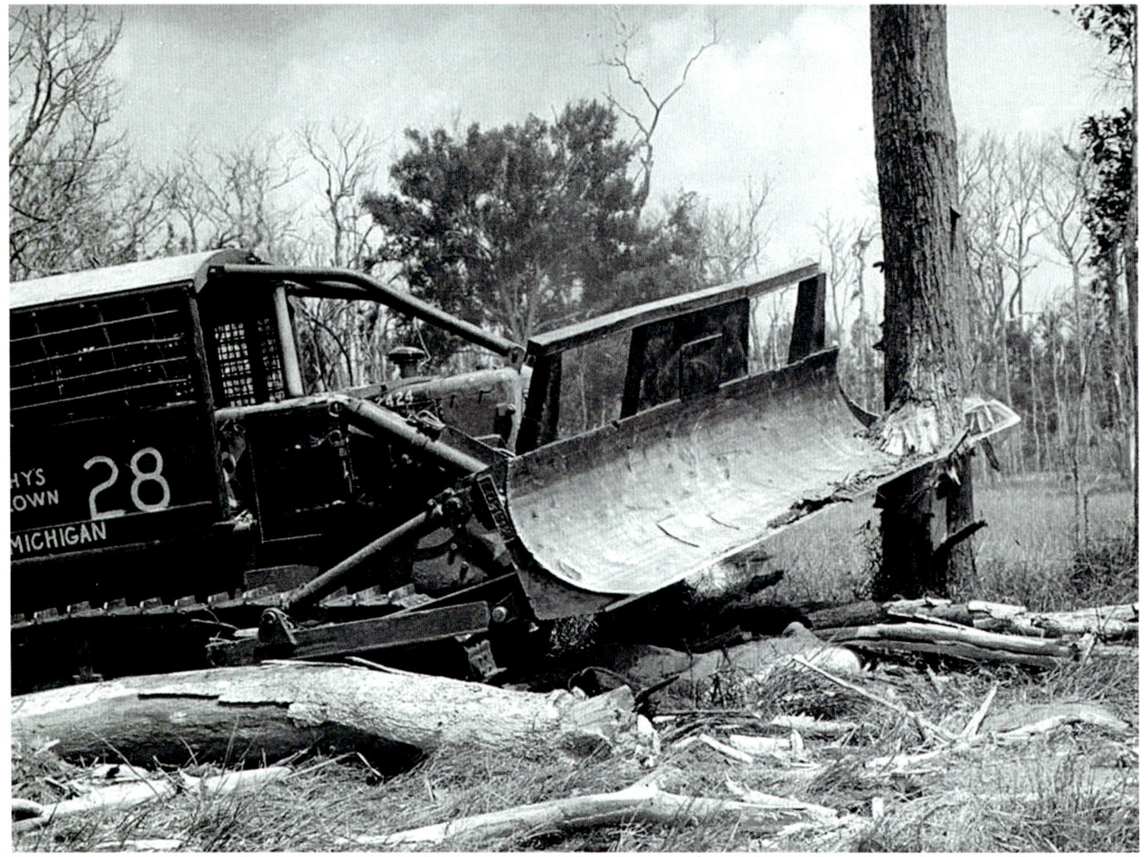

Above: After the war, a young Vietnamese demonstrates one of the hidden tunnel entrances through which whole squads and platoons of V.C. had passed to restock supplies, hide, and wait for the next mission.

Left: A U.S. Army Engineers' Rome Plow built in Rome, Georgia, with its protected cab, slices through a tree with its 10-foot wide blade. These plows, protected by A.P.C. and tank armor, cleared dense jungle from suspected tunnel entrances, carved out landing fields for light aircraft, and buried V.C. and N.V.A. trenches after battles.

Opposite: A team of three army engineers prepare a satchel charge packed with C-2 explosive and long fuses for tunnel demolition. The charge had to be buried as far along the tunnel as possible to cave in galleries further in the complex beneath trapdoors.

was built at Cu Chi above unknown tunnels that thronged with V.C. A complete hospital was located beneath the American compounds. While the Americans dug and blasted, Australian engineers pioneered many tunnel search techniques, building their own legacy of ruthless bravery in the Royal Engineers.

The Cu Chi and other tunnels made possible the Tet Offensive in 1968, but its bloody fighting decimated the Viet Cong and shifted the war to one of conventional, armor-heavy divisions invading from the North. The tunnel complex became superfluous by 1969 and few of the V.C. tunnel fighters survived the war. The Australian, American, and New Zealand "tunnel rats" had difficulty adjusting to normal lives on the surface and many remained loners with their dark memories long after the conflict.

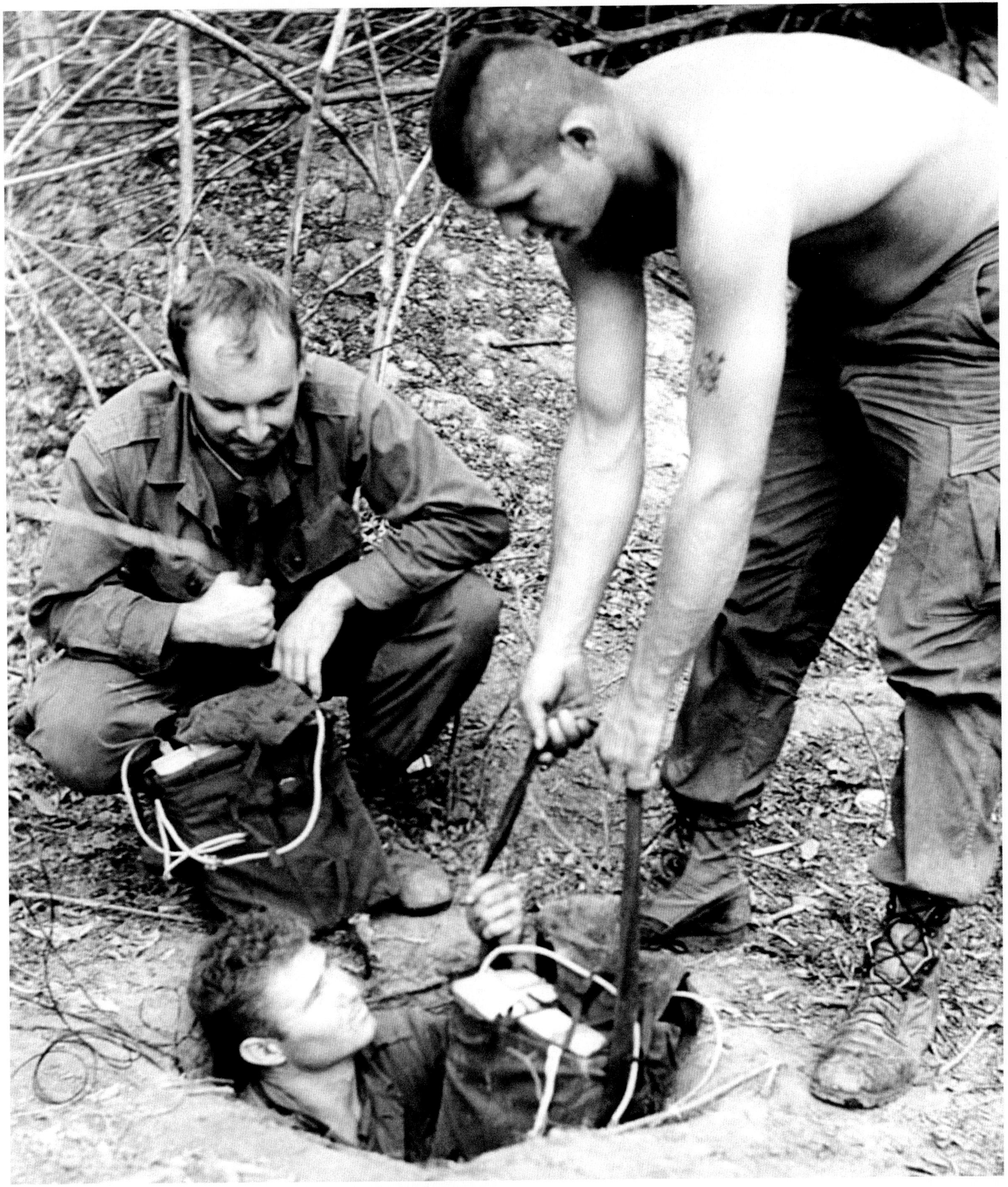

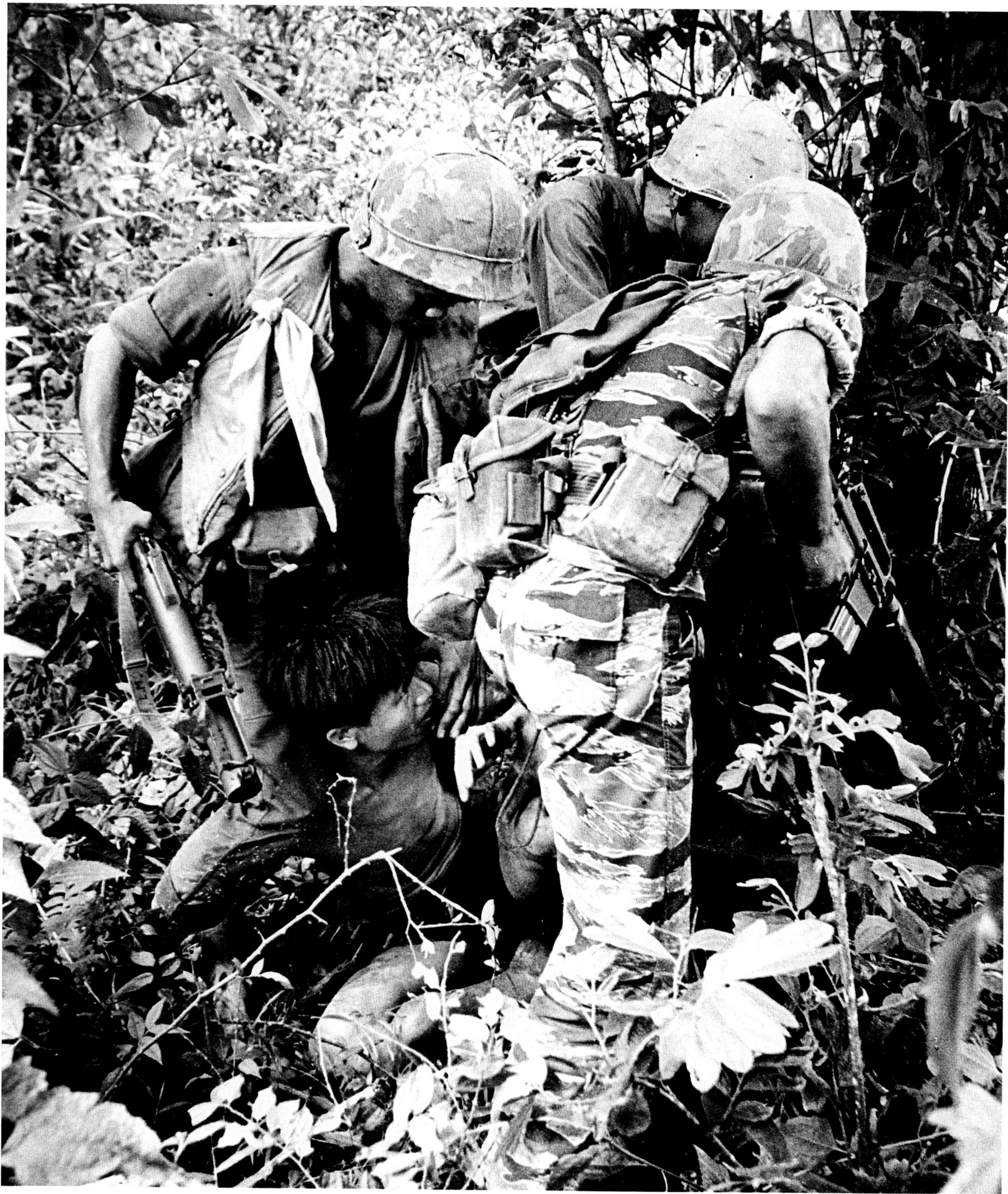

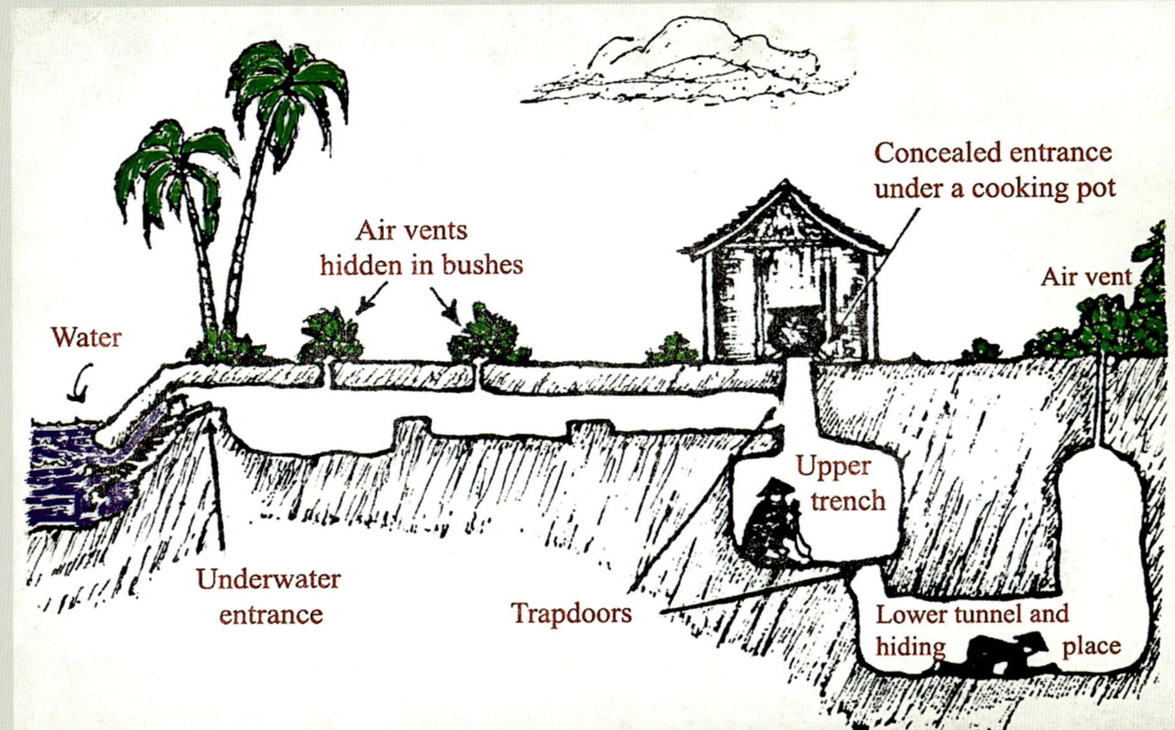

CROSS-SECTION TUNNEL DIAGRAM

The diagram of a cross-section view of a V.C. tunnel complex demonstrates its complexity and many exit and entry options. Some galleries penetrated 50 feet beneath the jungle floor for hospitals and supply storage. Both living in these tunnels and attacking them required considerable courage and discipline.

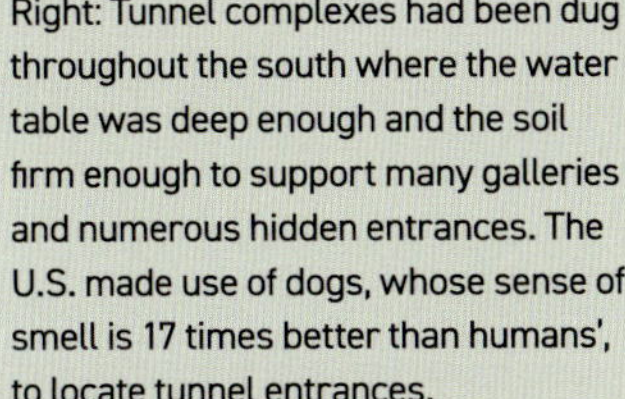

Right: Tunnel complexes had been dug throughout the south where the water table was deep enough and the soil firm enough to support many galleries and numerous hidden entrances. The U.S. made use of dogs, whose sense of smell is 17 times better than humans', to locate tunnel entrances.

Opposite: Two soldiers drag a V.C. from his spider hole. One soldier carries an M79 grenade launcher that might have fired a smoke grenade into the tunnel to flush out the V.C. inside. The third soldier is either an A.R.V.N. interpreter or a Special Operations Green Beret as denoted by his tiger-stripe camouflage.

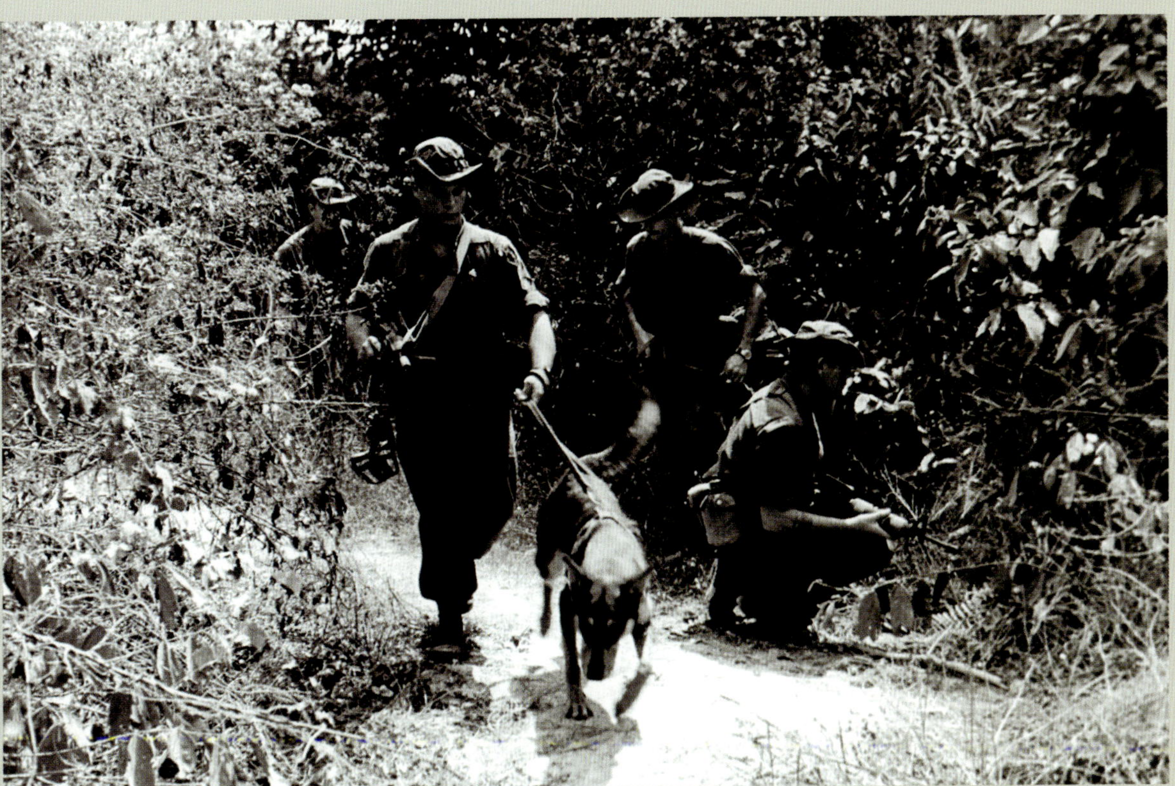

BEN HET

A SOVIET 76MM TANK ROUND EXPLODED AGAINST THE M48A3 PATTON TANK'S OPEN LOADER HATCH. ITS SEARING EXPLOSION CAUGHT TWO AMERICAN TANKERS ON THE HULL, KILLING THEM. FLARES CAST THEIR LIGHT ON THE HILLSIDE SLOPING UP TO THE BEN HET FIREBASE WHERE TWO AS YET UNTOUCHED PATTON TANKS, NUMBERS 13 AND 15, STILL TRAINED THEIR 90MM GUNS DOWN AT THE N.V.A. SOLDIERS WORKING THEIR WAY TOWARD THE BARBED WIRE. THE NORTH VIETNAMESE HAD DRAWN FIRST BLOOD IN THEIR ATTACK.

The Ben Het firebase with its 175mm artillery battery was entrenched on a hill commanding a crucial stretch of Route 512 leading to Dak To and only seven miles from the Cambodian border. The firebase constantly threatened—with both artillery and air strikes—this North Vietnamese supply line to the Central Highlands. It was manned by a dozen Green Berets, 400 tough Montagnards and the 175mm artillery battalion.

Early in February 1969 two platoons each of four M48A3 tanks of the 1st Battalion, 69th Armored Command, moved into the area with the 1st Platoon digging in three of their tanks (numbers 13, 14, and 15) on the crest of the West Hill while the fourth tank remained mobile on the Main Hill facing the supply road. The 2nd Platoon remained at Dak To in reserve six miles distant. Throughout that month Ben Het endured persistent artillery

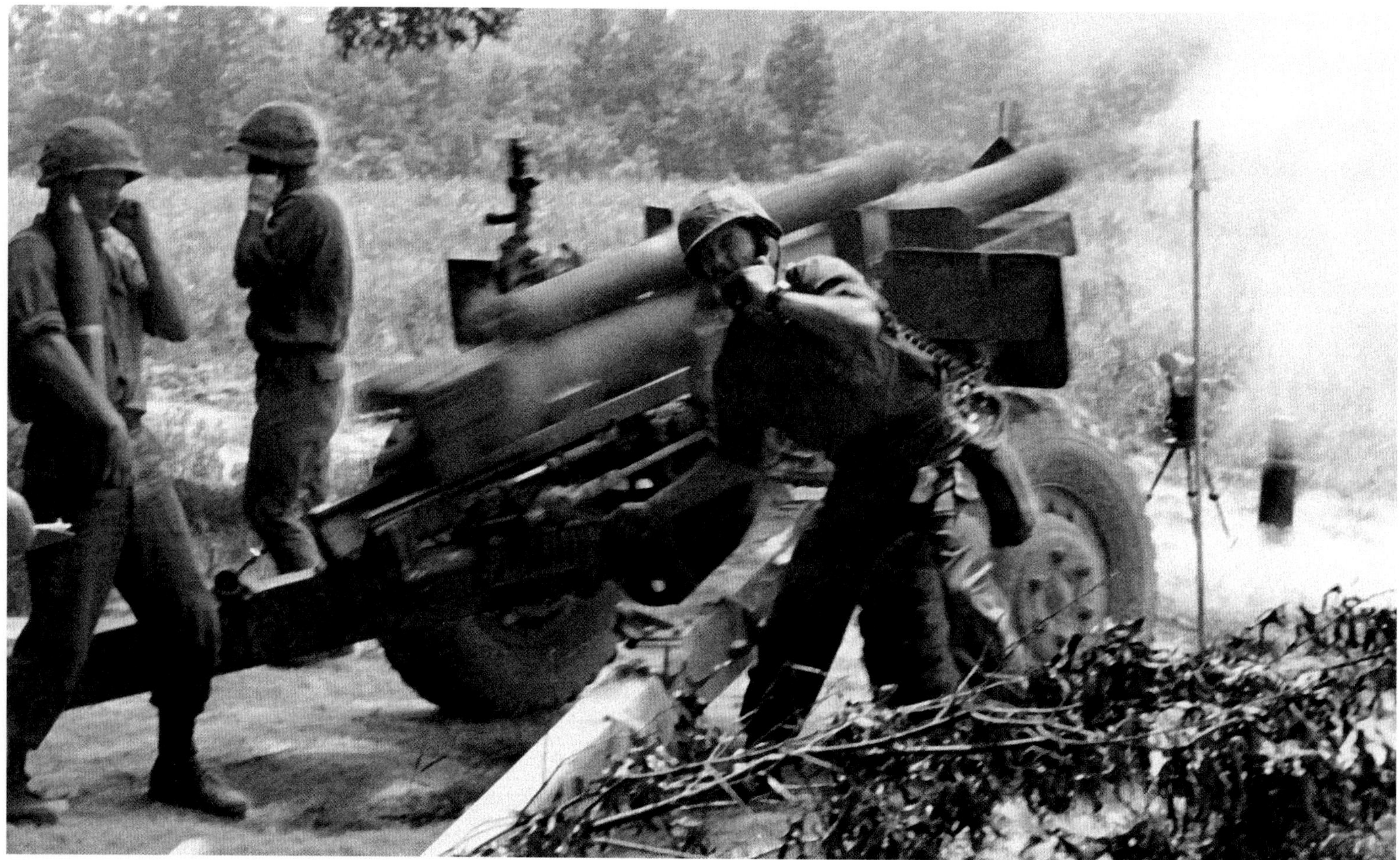

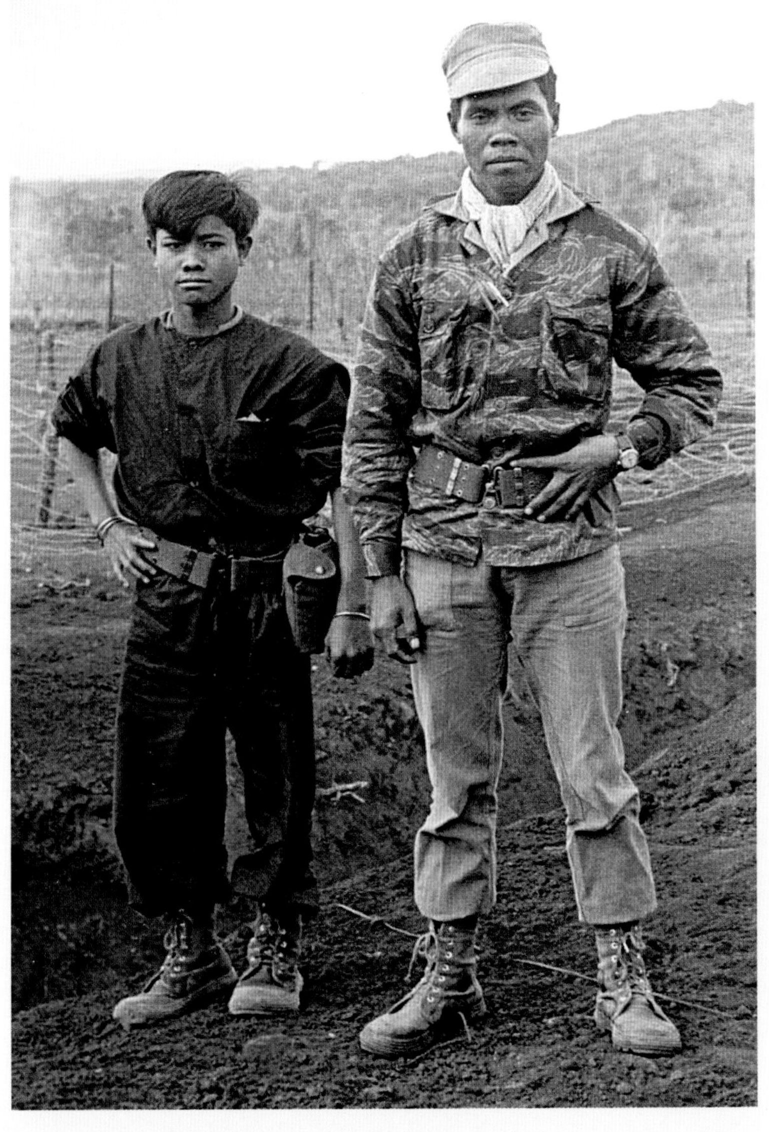

SOVIET PT-76 TANK (N.V.A.)

This Soviet design with a 76mm gun was copied by the Chinese and adopted in 1952 as the PT-76 (Plavayushchy Tank or swimming tank). Produced by the Volgograd tractor factory, about 7,000 were built with 2,000 exported. Its flat, sea-worthy hull allowed it to be amphibious, propelled by water jets in the rear, front, and sides. With a three-man crew, this light tank was effective against troops and light armor, as proved in its successful use at Lang Vei—although with heavy casualties from L.A.W.s and bazookas. The U.S. M48 out-classed it in every department, but toward the end of the war, the N.V.A. was given Chinese models of the Soviet T-54 which out-gunned the M48A3.

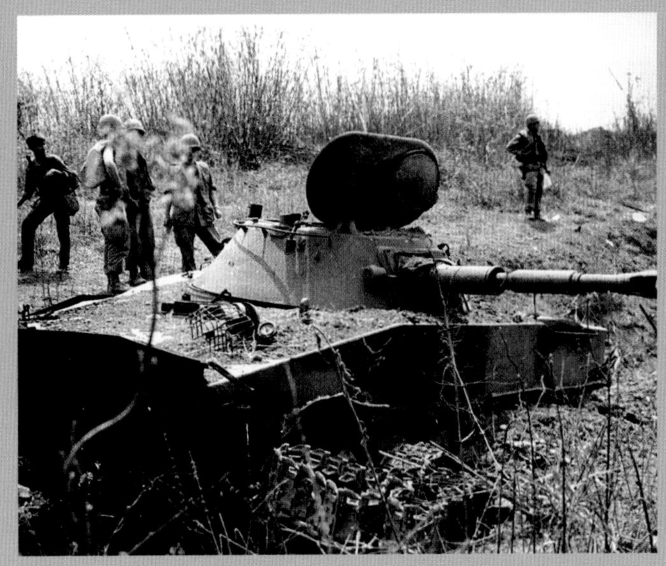

Opposite: A firebase crew man their 105mm howitzer as it fires a fixed round at the enemy. Ben Het was established to enfilade an N.V.A. supply road to the South with artillery. Four U.S. M48 tanks were sent to supplement artillery fire power. Destroying Ben Het was critical to N.V.A. operations.

Above: Montagnards were sometimes referred to as "America's most loyal allies in Vietnam." Considered an inferior minority by the South Vietnamese, these indigenous tribes acted as scouts and fought side by side with U.S. soldiers throughout the war.

Above right: A Soviet-design PT-76 amphibious tank sits knocked out and abandoned by its N.V.A. crew. These tanks were used against the defenders of Ben Het. They had light armor and a 76mm gun and were designed for beach landings and swimming river crossings.

Right: An AC-47 Spooky heads for combat. During the tank battle at Ben Het, Spooky aircraft slashed N.V.A. troops sheltering in the woods with 7.62mm multiple miniguns while orbiting the attacker's postion. The World War II former cargo plane also dropped flares that illuminated N.V.A. shock troops as they tried to crawl up on the U.S. position.

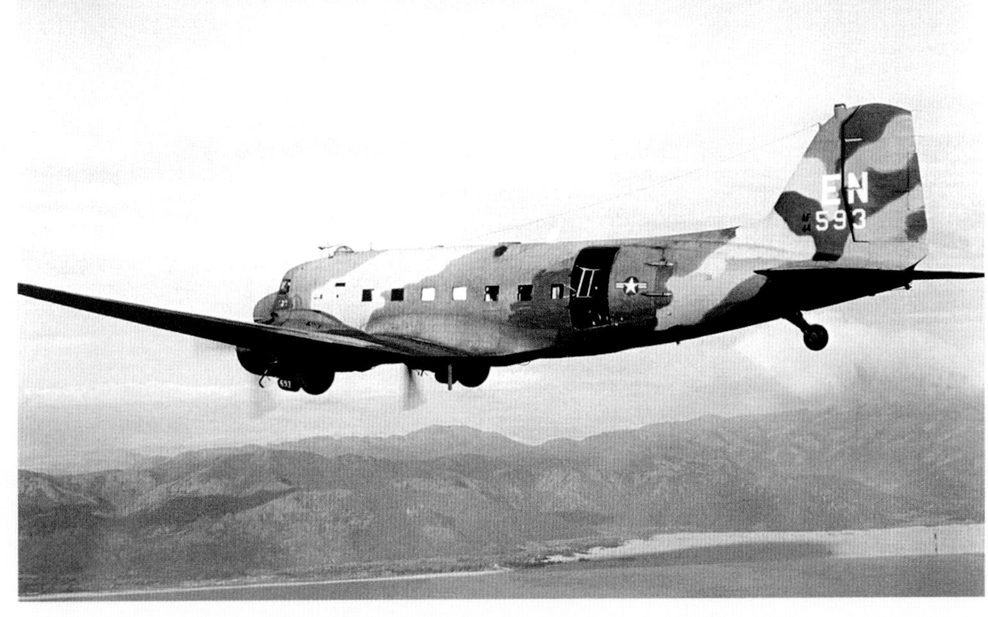

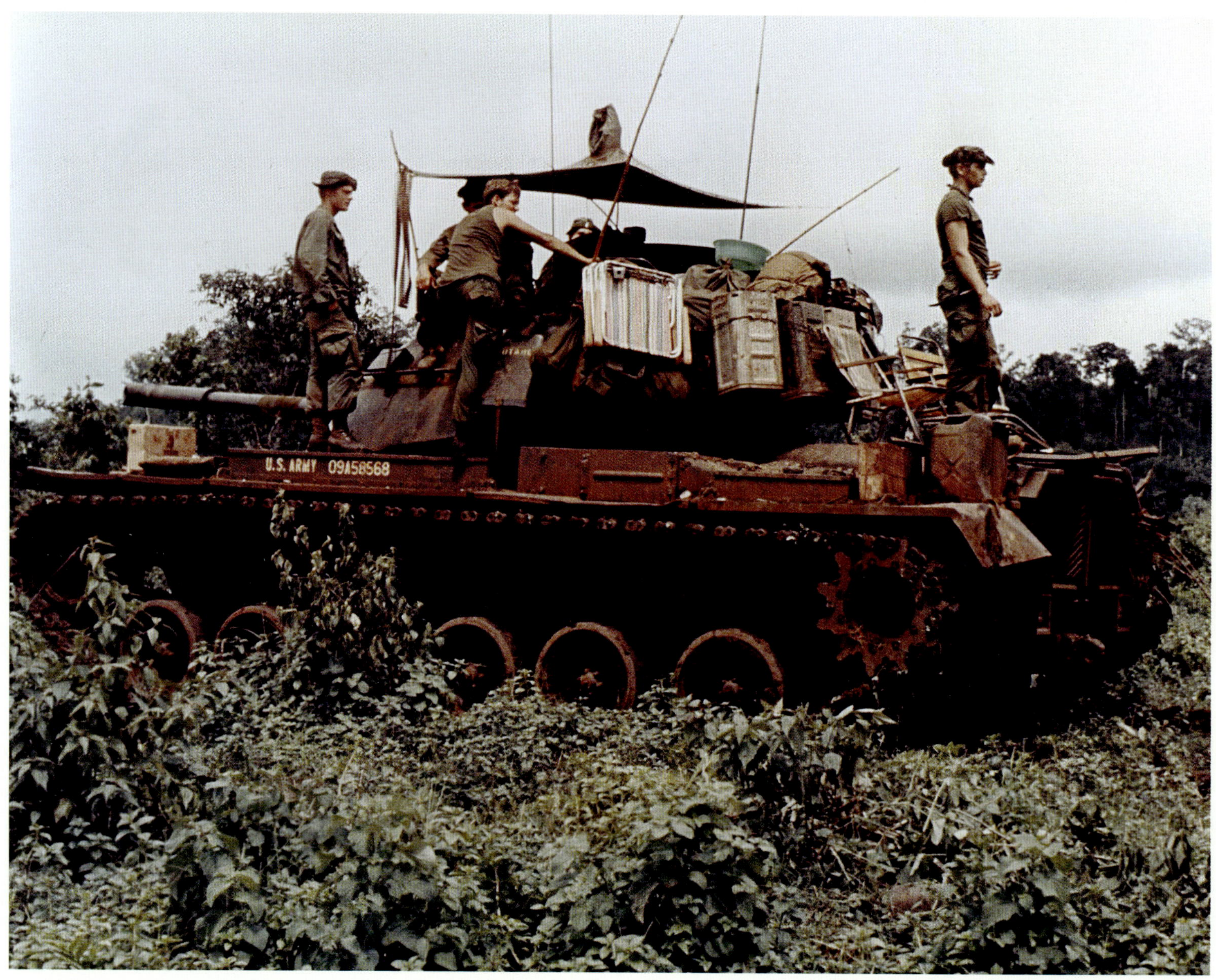

and heavy mortar bombardment. The North Vietnamese were determined to open up their interdicted supply road. And then, at 21:00 hours on March 3, while a mortar barrage rained down, two tank crew reported hearing the clank of tracks and the whine of diesel engines coming from the distant tree line.

A year earlier the N.V.A. had used light, 15-ton PT-76 tanks to overrun a Special Forces base at Lang Vei with heavy casualties, but no North Vietnamese armor had been seen since then. The destruction of M48 tank number 14 left only tank number 13 facing the N.V.A. armor. Since no-one had expected to encounter enemy tanks, number 13 carried only a few anti-tank armor-piercing rounds. Up the hillside came the men of the 16th Company, 4th Battalion, 202nd Armored Regiment, of the N.V.A. The roar of gunfire, thud of grenades, and bark of heavy machine guns filled the night.

As tank 13 fired at PT-76 muzzle flashes, a C-47 Spooky aircraft was called in. The antique propeller plane went into an orbiting bank above the N.V.A. position and a deep "Awwwwwwwww!" rose above the ground. A torrent of 20mm round—every fifth one a tracer—poured from electric Gatling guns into the massed soldiers at 3,000 rounds per minute, halting their advance with heavy casualties.

A fireball burst in the woods as tank 13 scored an armor-piercing hit. Another PT-76 fired and the American gunner pumped high explosive rounds at the muzzle flash. The relatively thinly armored N.V.A. tank burst into flames.

With daylight, a helicopter dust-off flew in and carried out wounded. The 2nd Platoon of four tanks had arrived and the gunfire dwindled away. Two N.V.A. tanks and an armored personnel carrier were smoking hulks. The only tank battle fought by American forces in Vietnam was over.

U.S. M48 TANK

The M48A3 Patton tank used by both the Army and the Marines in Vietnam began life in 1950 when the Detroit Arsenal produced a medium tank with a 90mm gun to replace the M26 Pershings of the post World War II period. Though Vietnam was hardly "tank country" the M48 acted in road security and artillery support roles. Against the only N.V.A. tank used early in the war (the PT-76) the Patton was more powerful and better protected against anti-tank weapons. It was also a match for the Soviet T-54 used in the 1970s when the M48A5 was upgraded with a 105mm gun. Another variant that served in Vietnam was the M67A2 flamethrower tank.

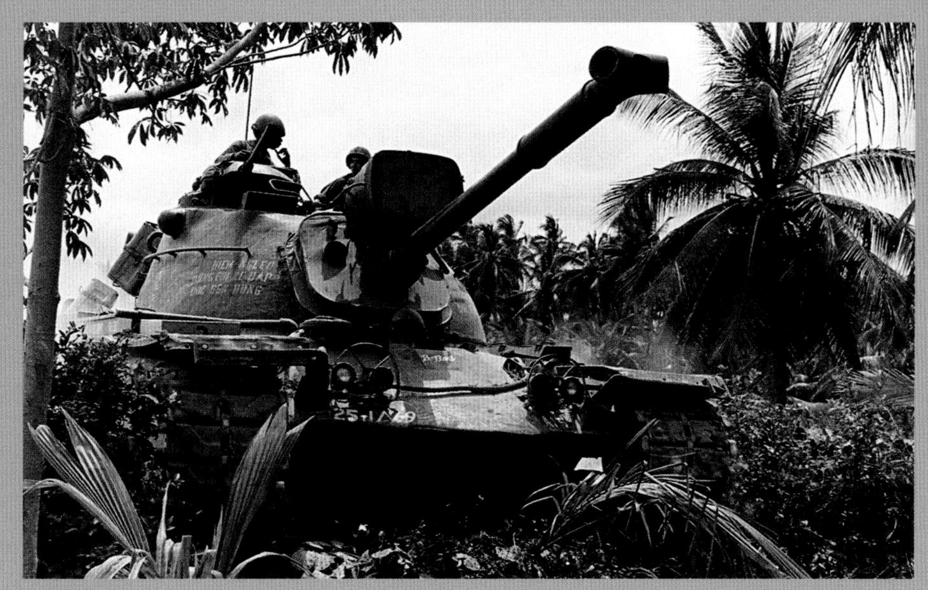

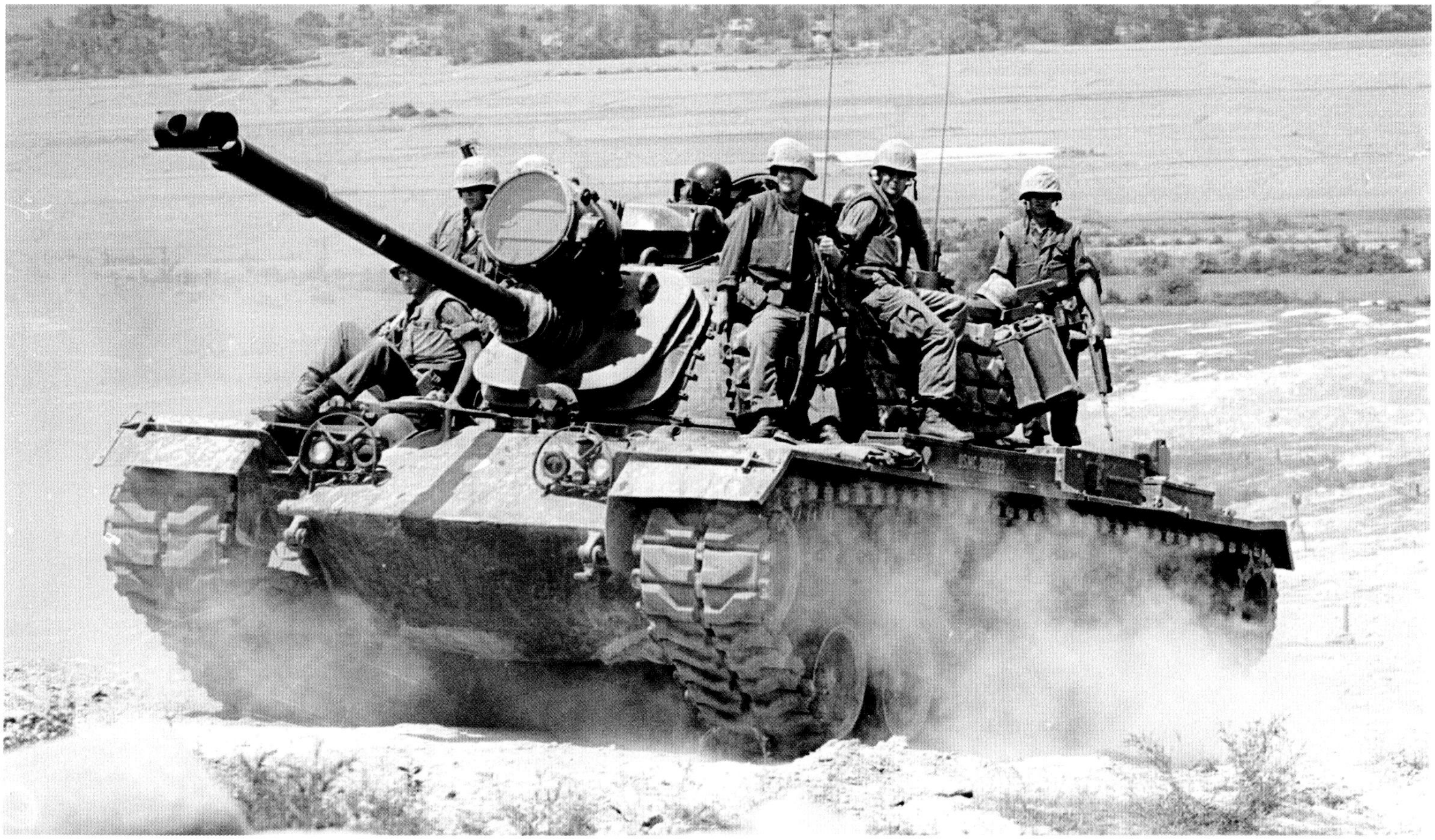

Opposite: This M48 Patton tank was the primary heavy tank used in Vietnam. This tank and crew are on their way to either a firebase or squadron area to begin operations. All the crew's belongings plus extra ammunition, rations, and colorful folding aluminum chairs are hung on the turret.

Top: At Ben Het, where the only tank-against-tank battle was fought during the Vietnam War, four American M48 tanks with their 90mm guns were dug in at two positions overlooking the N.V.A. supply road and a dense forest that concealed the enemy build-up before and during the attack on the firebase.

Above: As the battle developed at Ben Het, a second platoon of four tanks rushed through the night to add their guns to the fighting. They knew the road might be mined, but pressed on regardless. M48 tanks were used by both the U.S. Army and Marines.

HAMBURGER HILL

CARL VON CLAUSEWITZ, MILITARY PHILOSOPHER, ONCE WROTE THAT WAR IS CONTROLLED BY ITS POLITICAL OBJECTIVE: "... THE VALUE OF THIS OBJECT MUST DETERMINE THE SACRIFICES TO BE MADE FOR IT BOTH IN MAGNITUDE AND ALSO IN DURATION. ONCE THE EXPENDITURE OF EFFORT EXCEEDS THE VALUE OF THE POLITICAL OBJECT, THE OBJECT MUST BE RENOUNCED."

In 1969, the United States military fought its last major land battle of the Vietnam War and its bloody result further reduced what remained of support for the war at home. The American military learned that the A Shau Valley near the Laotian border had become an area of high N.V.A. activity. It was an important storage point for matériel brought into South Vietnam via the Ho Chi Minh Trail. In May 1969, army commanders decided to clear out the valley with ten battalions of infantry. The plan, stated by one army historian, required:

"The 3/187th Infantry [to] combat-assault into L.Z. 2, 2,000 meters northwest of Dong Ap Bia (hill 937) and 1,500 meters west of the Laotian border. D, A, C, B Company would act as the brigade reserve until released. D Company would secure the L.Z. until replaced by A Company and then R.I.F. (Reconnoiter in Force) to the high ground 500 meters to the northwest. C Company would secure the L.Z. until the Headquarters element reached the L.Z. and then move 500 meters to the southwest. The Headquarters group would move to link up with C Company, moving toward

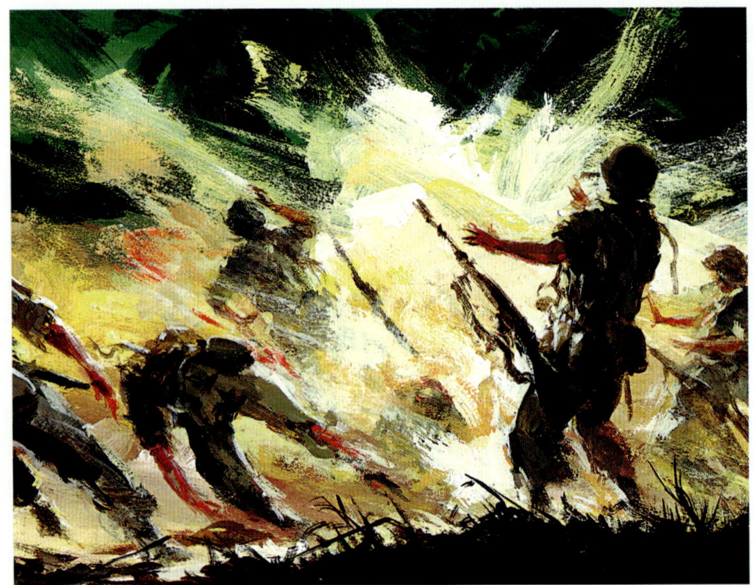

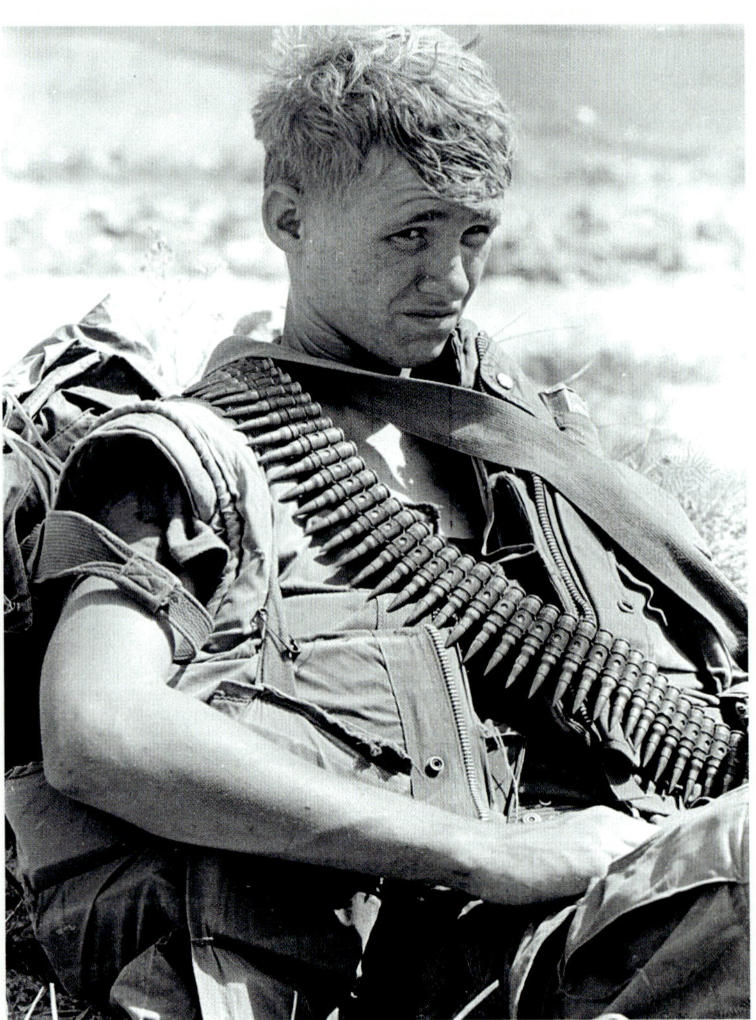

Left: Combat artist John Steel painted this scene of a V.C. mine planted on a trail to catch patrols. A single mine can kill several men and wound others, and requires still further soldiers to remove the wounded to the rear for aid.

Above: An exhausted young American soldier "takes five" during a patrol. The fighting was incredibly intense up and down Hill 937 and the surrounding terrain. Besides his own equipment, the soldier carries a belt of ammunition for a 7.62mm crew-served machine gun. It was common practice to assign quantities of ammunition for mortars and machine guns to members of the rifle squad working with the weapons unit.

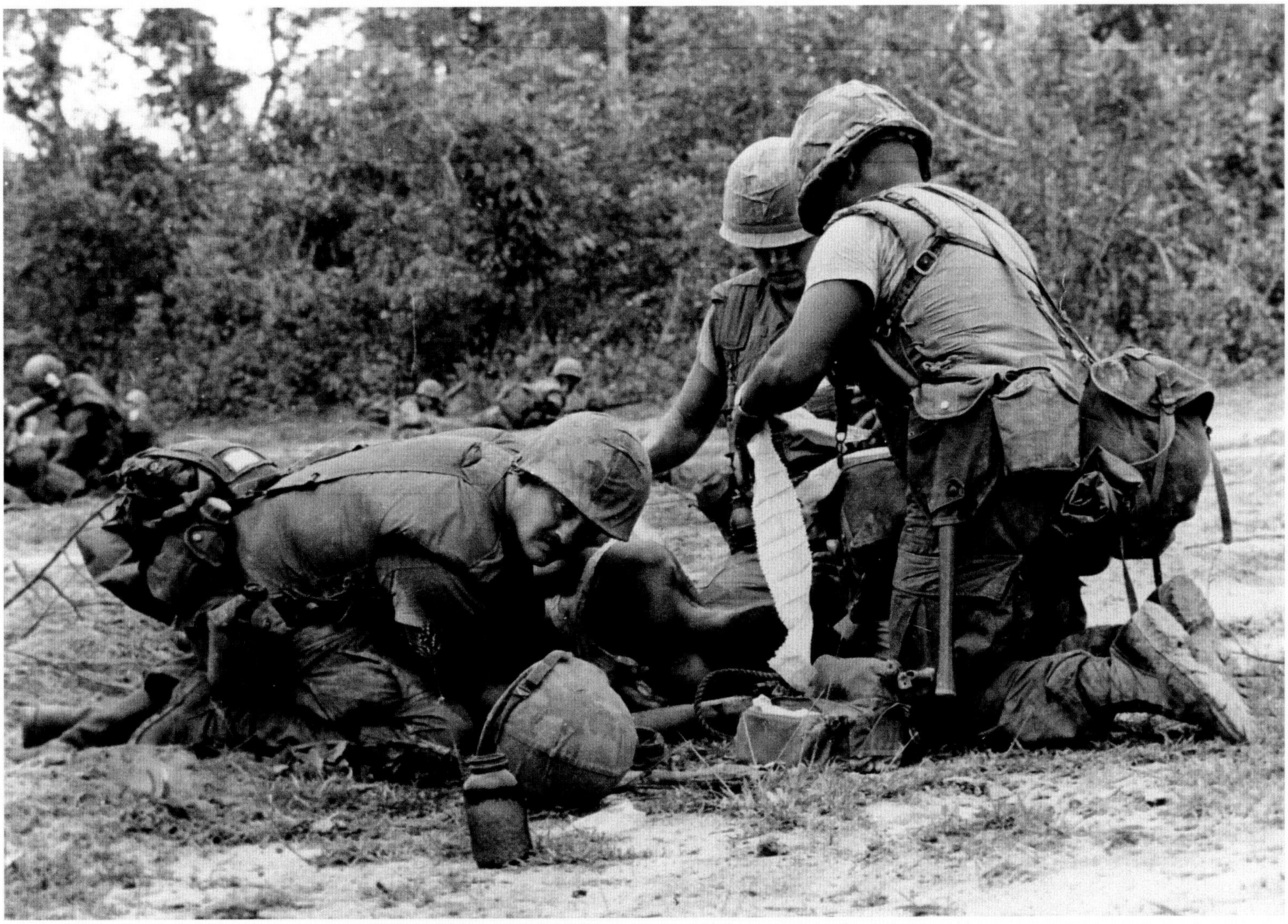

Above: A medic bandages a wounded soldier in the field. Often medics had to work while under fire and just as often the N.V.A. and V.C. targeted medical personnel with mortars and sniper fire. A wounded medic means other soldiers go without care and possibly die from their wounds. Army and Marine Medical Corpsmen had to be both brave and selfless.

Right: A Claymore mine on its stand. The mine could also be taped to a tree at shoulder height and triggered with a trip wire. Inside the convex surface cover was an array of shrapnel that exploded outward in an arc, cutting down advancing N.V.A. troops. It could also be remote-controlled with a button push to defend a perimeter position as at Hamburger Hill.

N.V.A./V.C. DEFENDING FORCE

The N.V.A. had moved into the Ap Bia area to recover after battling Marines in February. They had ample warning of the impending attack and had constructed camouflaged bunkers and tunnels, and knew the terrain. They were also a much larger force than expected. With ineffective air and artillery support on the initial approach to the summit, the American and A.R.V.N. troops were at every disadvantage. N.V.A. anti-aircraft guns shot up helicopters from hidden positions while N.V.A. troops scurried unseen down the flanks of the attacking Army and Marines. Eventually, 720 Air Force sorties dropping 450 tons of bombs and 69 tons of napalm cleared the way for the American and A.R.V.N. battalions. Secured on May 20, Hamburger Hill was abandoned on June 5.

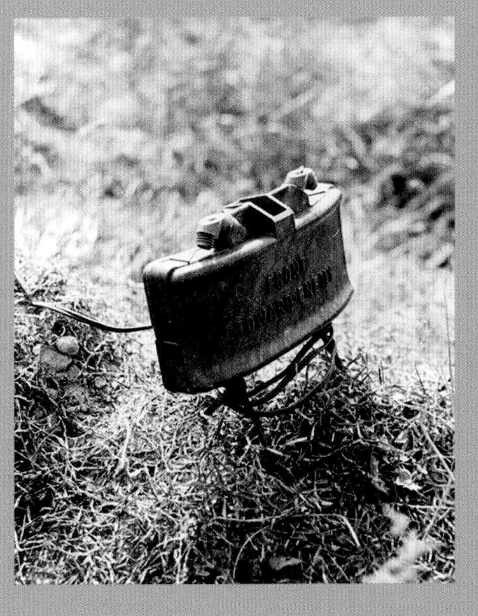

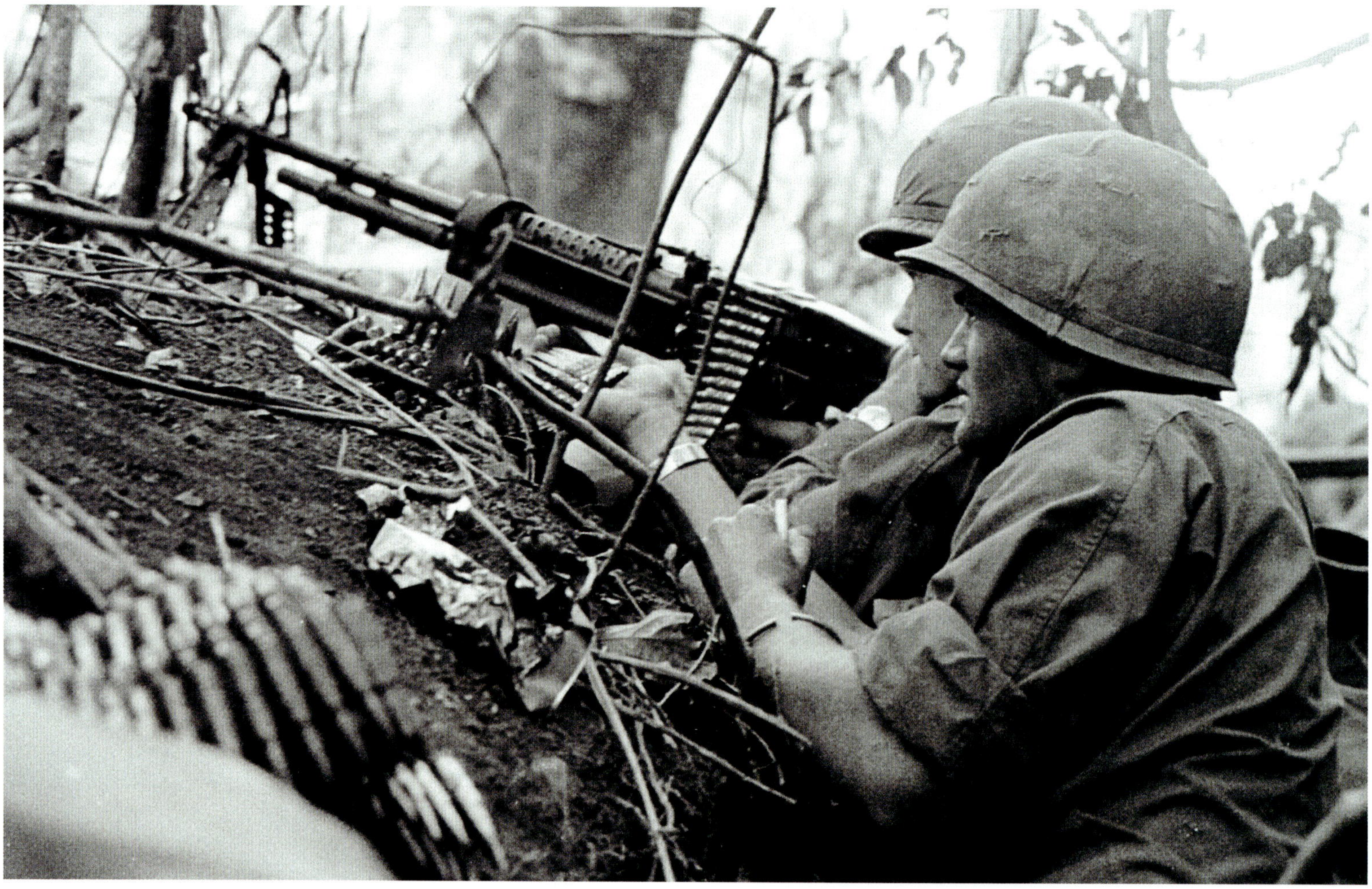

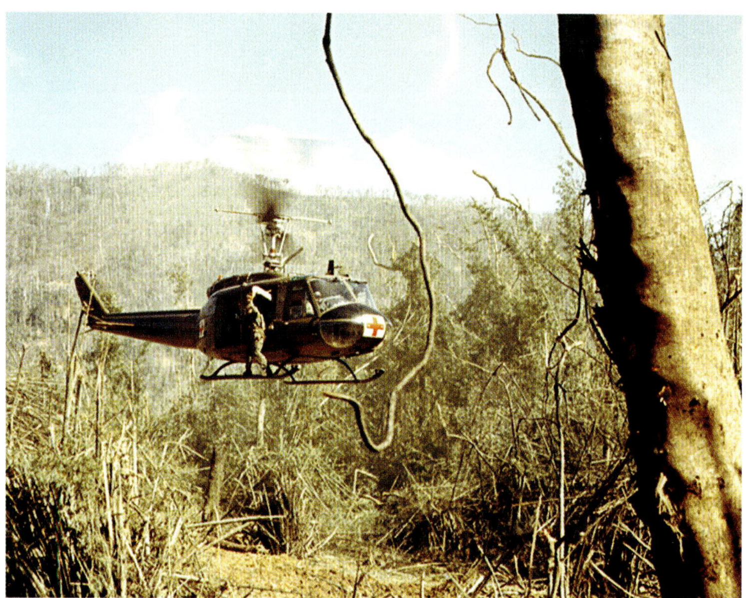

U.S. ARMY, MARINES/A.R.V.N. ATTACKING FORCE

The ten-day battle from May 10 to May 20, 1969, for Hill 937, named "Hamburger Hill" by the men who fought there, was a head-to-head test of will, guts, and technology that gained no lasting victory. The battle to secure Ap Bia Mountain next to the Laotian border was based on faulty intelligence and poor use of previously successful techniques and technology. The 101st Airborne (Airmobile) was helicoptered in to L.Z.s, but new Aerial Rocket Artillery (A.R.A.) Cobra gunships directed fire on American troops due to overloaded controllers. The triple canopy jungle defeated close air support. The assaults climbing narrow trails were stalled. Even distant artillery support bases were attacked. Victory—the summit—was bought with heavy casualties.

Above top: Firing uphill from an improvised trench, an M60 machine-gun crew puts down covering fire for another painstaking advance up Hamburger Hill. The gun crewman has half of a belt fed into the weapon's breech and another two belts are nearby.

Above: With no cleared L.Z. for a landing, a Medevac helicopter hovers over the jungle canopy during the battle and raises a wounded soldier up to the open hatch with a winch arm protruding just below the roof line.

Opposite: From inside the cockpit of a Huey UH-1 Medevac helicopter, the helmeted pilot watches medics and soldiers rush toward him with a wounded man beneath the whirling propeller blades. Frequent "dustoffs" such as this one saved a lot of men's lives.

Following page: At the crest of one of the hill approaches, a Skytrain helicopter brings up another howitzer to add to the firepower provided by the 105mm howitzer already unlimbered.

Dong Ap Bia. When B Company was released from standby status it would be combat-assaulted into L.Z. 2 and then proceed to the southwest to a ridgeline running from Hill 937."

Operation Apache Snow kicked off on May 10, 1969. Its objective was to clear all N.V.A. from this ridge country topped by Hill 937 and cut the supply road from Laos. A flight of 64 Huey helicopters, protected by Cobra gunships, carried the first 400 men. The pilots used rifts and valleys to screen their moves to designated L.Z.s. Awaiting them were N.V.A. in bunkers, deep tunnels, trenches, spider holes, and fortified command posts. The position was not unlike Mount Suribachi on Iwo Jima in World War II.

Air and artillery bombardment went into action before the Huey "slicks" dropped on their L.Z.s. Rockets and machine guns cleared the zones and the troops went in. Beneath the triple canopy jungle men climbed, hauling double rations of ammo. N.V.A. grenades rolled down. Claymore mines spat their shrapnel. N.V.A. snipers targeted officers, noncoms, and medics. Artillery from nearby firebases ripped into the slopes of hill 937 as the men climbed. N.V.A. leaped from concealed spider holes on the flanks. Recoilless rifles slammed their rounds into bunkers. Napalm blossomed orange and black atop the crest. For ten days it was a remorseless, savage battle of climb, advance, and withdraw. Then climb again.

On May 20, surviving American soldiers stood on the churned, blackened, and defoliated summit surrounded by the detritus of battle. A hand-written sign nailed to a charred tree stump announced: "Hamburger Hill." Beneath that another soldier had written, "Was it worth it?"

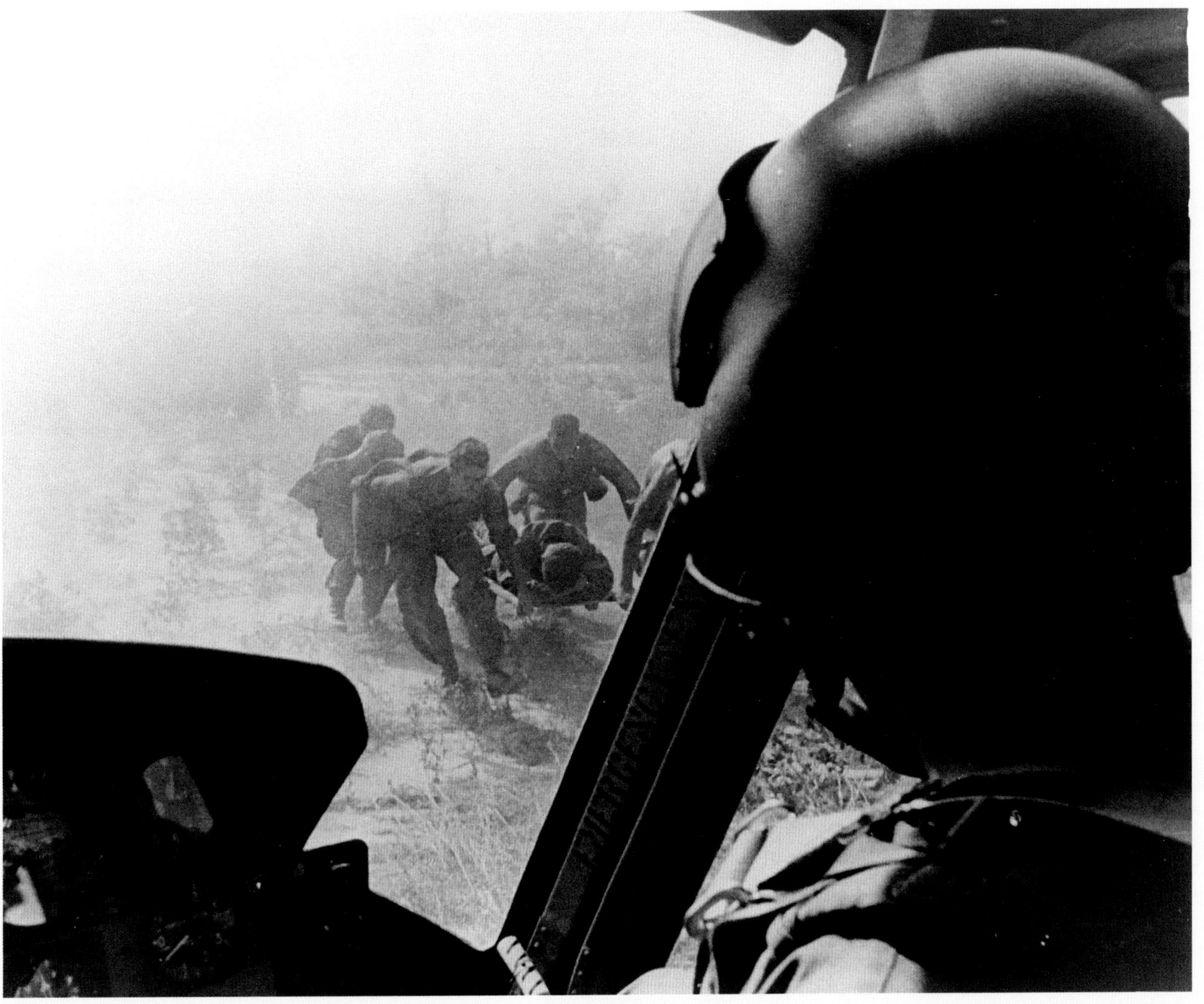

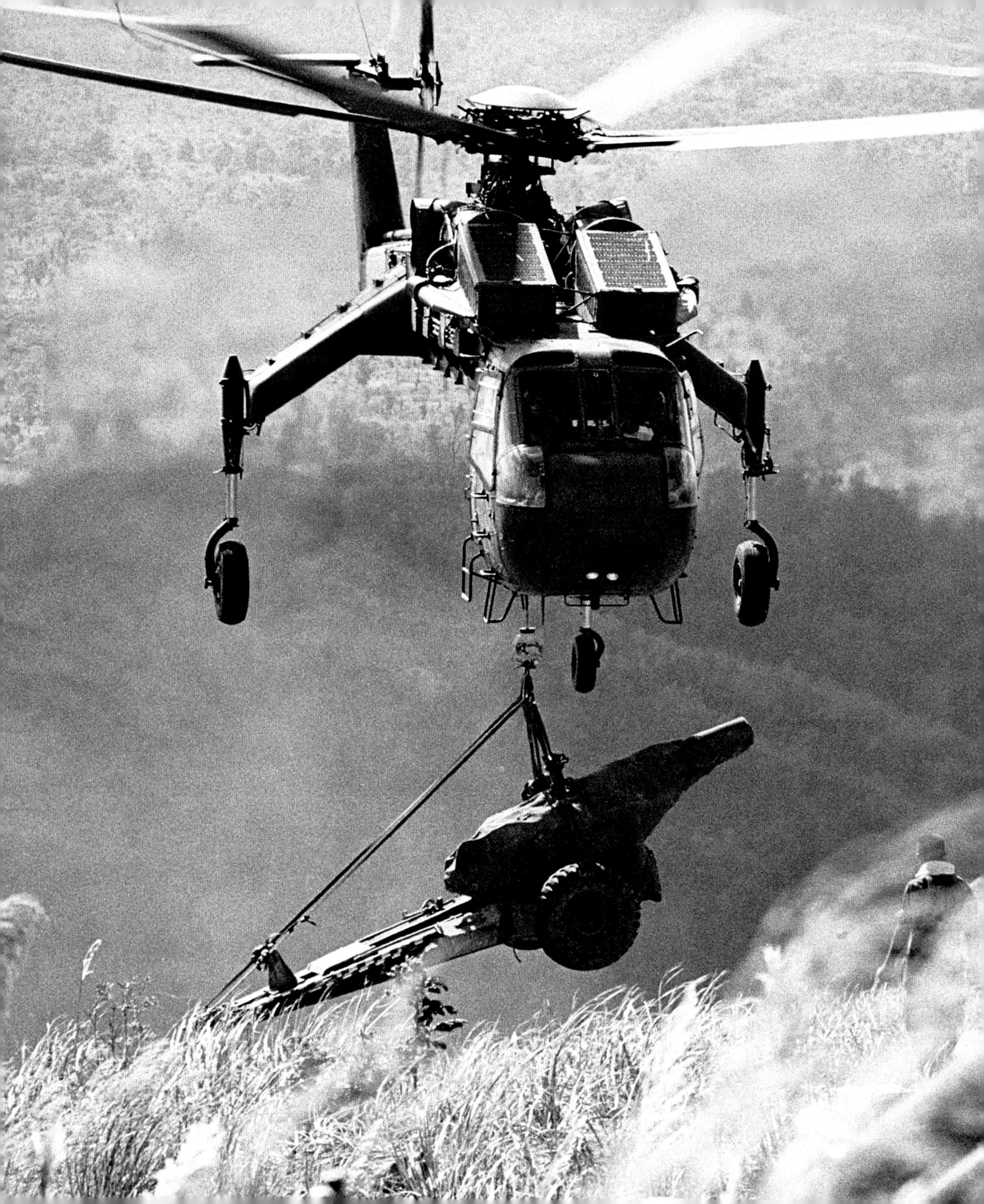

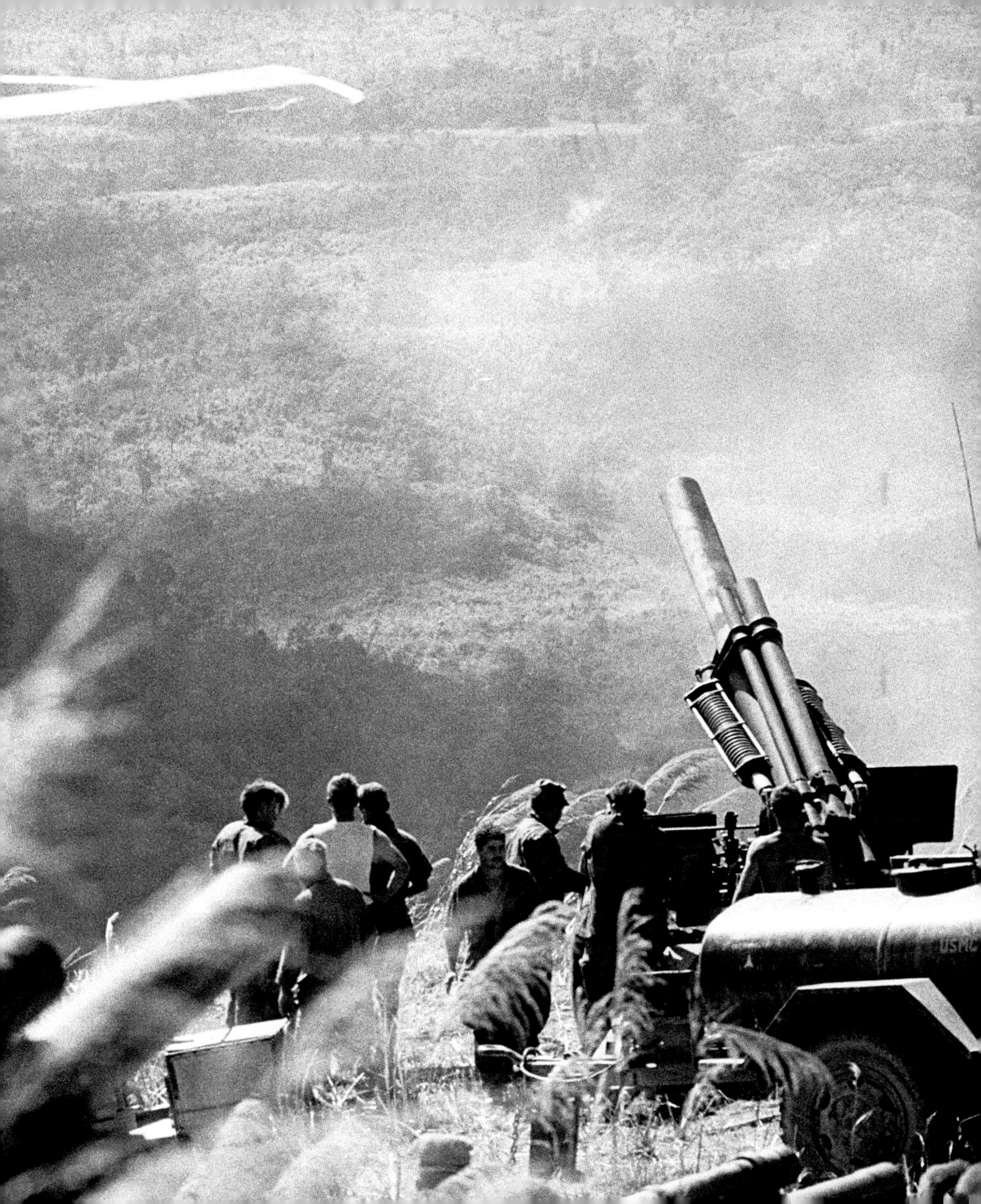
USMC

STRIKE INTO CAMBODIA

PRESIDENT RICHARD NIXON ENTERED OFFICE HAVING GIVEN A PLEDGE TO END THE VIETNAM WAR. BY EARLY 1969, AMERICAN COMBAT DEATHS IN VIETNAM EXCEEDED THE 33,629 MEN KILLED IN THE KOREAN WAR. TELEVISION SHOWED SCENES OF C-130 CARGO PLANES UNLOADING ROW UPON ROW OF AMERICAN DEAD IN ALUMINUM COFFINS AT UNITED STATES AIR BASES, AND RAN STORIES ABOUT THE NEW DRAFT-LOTTERY WHICH DEMORALIZED POTENTIAL DRAFTEES. PRESIDENT NIXON CLAIMED HE HAD A PLAN TO EXTRICATE AMERICAN FORCES WHILE KEEPING THE SOUTH VIETNAM GOVERNMENT STRONG. THIS AT FIRST WAS KNOWN AS THE "NIXON DOCTRINE" AND LATER TRANSFORMED INTO "VIETNAMIZATION."

Together with Secretary of State Henry Kissinger, President Nixon began questioning his commanders. At this time, the N.V.A. and V.C. political leaders in South Vietnam directed their forces to begin a series of raids on American bases in order to kill as many soldiers as possible. Hanoi was aware of the eroded support for the war in the United States. High American "body counts" increased that disillusionment. On February 22 the attacks began, slashing at American and A.R.V.N. forces wherever possible with artillery, infantry, sappers, and hordes of N.V.A. and V.C. All the Communist strikes were blunted or destroyed, but they cost 1,040 American soldiers their lives.

Seeking revenge on Hanoi for violating yet another peace agreement that once again halted U.S. bombing, President Nixon also wanted to give the South Vietnamese Army breathing room while American troops were rotated home. He pushed aside the commanders' answers to his earlier questions and launched attacks of his own.

These attacks were precipitated by Cambodian Prince Norodom Sihanouk's new stand against the Ho Chi Minh Trail supply route and storage bases in his country. With that turnaround, the U.S.A.F. "Operation Menu" went into effect, beginning what became its relentless unloading of thousands

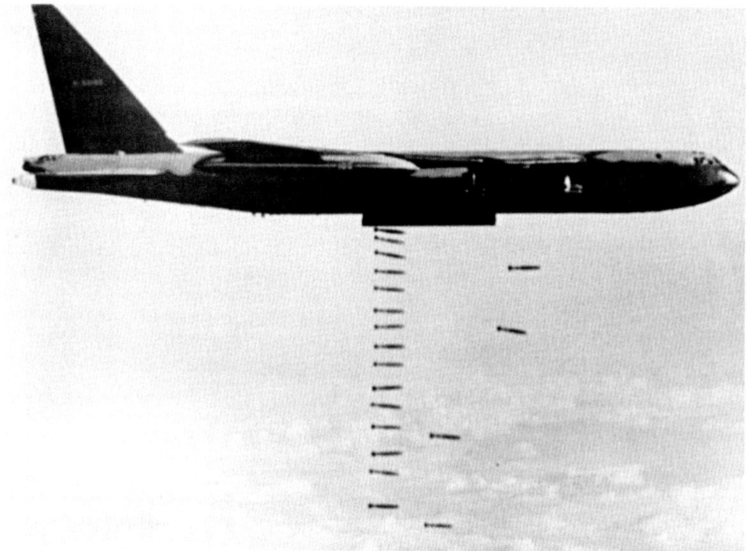

Above: A B-52 Stratofortress unloads its bomb bay over N.V.A. supply routes in Cambodia. The "Big Ugly Fat Fellow" was designed in the 1950s and is still flying today as part of the U.S.A.F. inventory. Bomber wings flew from Andersen Air Force Base in Guam and also from Thailand. President Nixon's "secret" bombing of Cambodia became a lightning rod for the anti-war protesters back in the United States.

Opposite: M41 Walker Bulldog light tanks with 76mm guns accompanied by T-28 Trojan prop trainer aircraft that can carry a small bomb load rush into Cambodia. These planes were replaced later by A-1D Skyraiders and South Vietnam's first jets, the F-5E Freedom Fighter and the A-37 Dragonfly. With these aircraft and tanks it took brave men to attack the N.V.A., who by 1969 were receiving their first T-54 heavy tanks and MiG-21 supersonic fighters.

A.R.V.N. SUPPORT

The U.S. invasion of Cambodia had a number of goals besides countering the N.V.A. attack on the Cambodian government. Since the U.S. pullout from Vietnam was imminent, Cambodia had to be removed as a factor that could harm the South Vietnamese. Aerial bombing, heavy artillery, and airborne raids in their rear shattered the N.V.A. and their headquarters. Also important was a successful operation for the participating A.R.V.N. troops. Their raids on immense supply bases in Cambodia broke the back of the N.V.A. in the South. These successes for the A.R.V.N. raised their morale and supported their independent military operations.

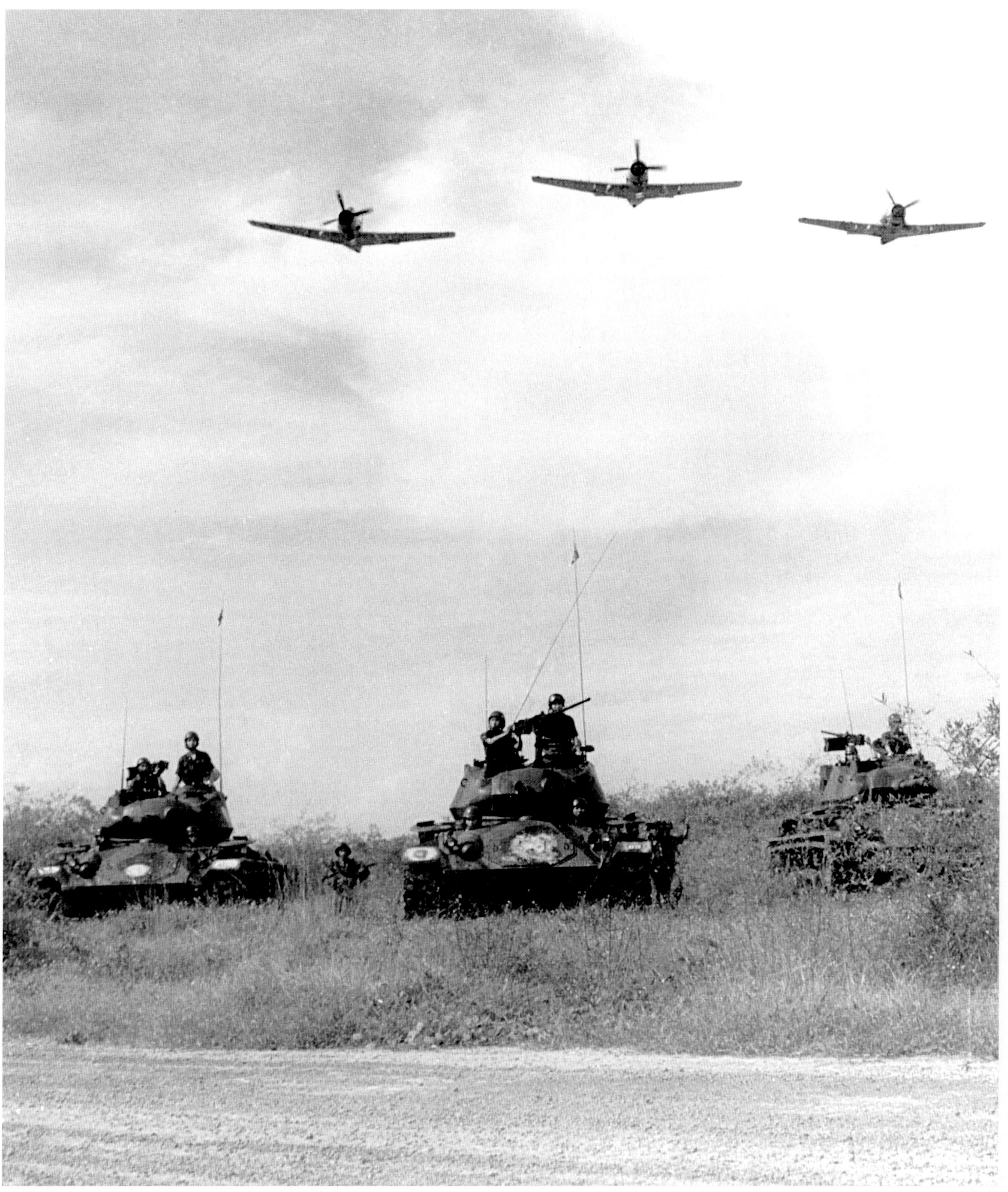

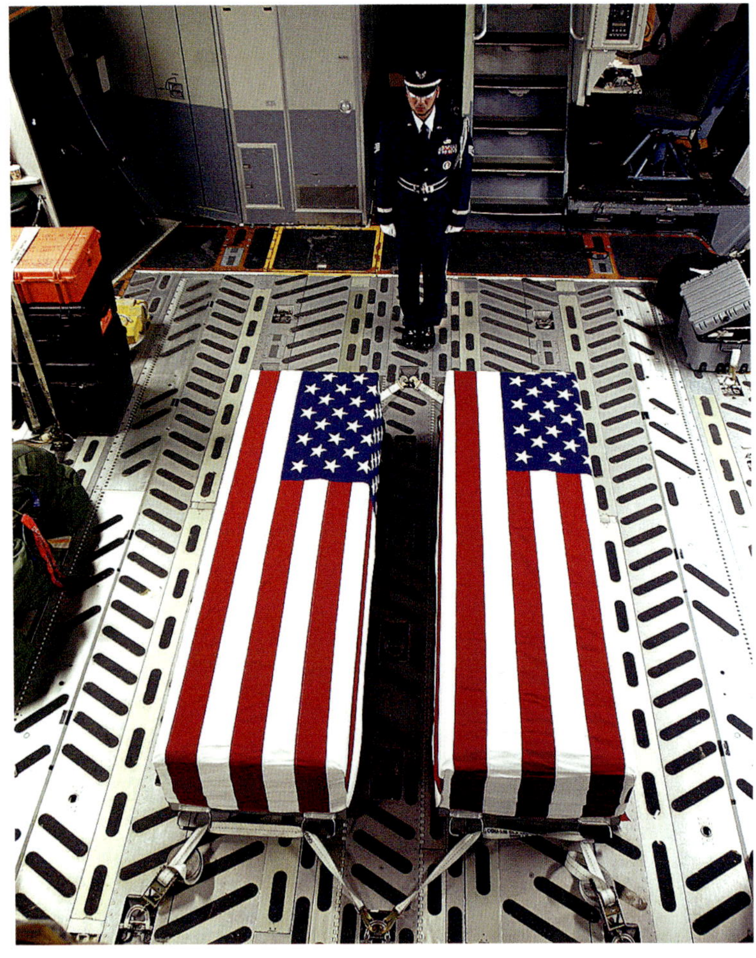

PRESIDENT NIXON'S STRIKE INTO CAMBODIA

The Ho Chi Minh Trail snaking down Cambodian soil along the border of South Vietnam was a constant threat as a jumping-off point for both supplies and N.V.A. troop incursions. After yet another bombing cessation, President Nixon was personally incensed over the N.V.A.'s continued cross-border attacks. The U.S. had pumped considerable aid into Cambodia to maintain its neutrality. With ruler Norodom Sihanouk deposed by West-leaning Prime Minister Lon Nol, the way was open for Nixon to invade Cambodia and end this threat to his "Vietnamization" of the war and withdrawal of U.S. troops.

of tons of bombs on key N.V.A. supply dumps, transfer bases, trail junctures, and attack jump-off points. On March 18, a secret B-52 raid flew along the South Vietnam–Cambodia border. A Cambodian sortie of 12 B-52s broke away from the flight of 36 bombers and dumped their loads specifically in Area 353, ostensibly on top of the N.V.A. Central Headquarters. It was hammered flat and the furious N.V.A. lost their sanctuary.

Nixon and Kissinger authorized a total of 3,630 flights over Cambodia during a 14-month period that ended in April 1970. According to the Pentagon, the planes dropped 2,750,000 tons of bombs, more than was dropped during World War II. The "secret" bombings were ultimately leaked to the public by an article in the *New York Times*. Prince Sihanouk was deposed and Cambodia began its descent toward the brutal Communist Khmer Rouge dictatorship. The bombings and further incursions into Cambodia and Laos translated into even greater dissent and anti-war feeling in the United States and among American Allies.

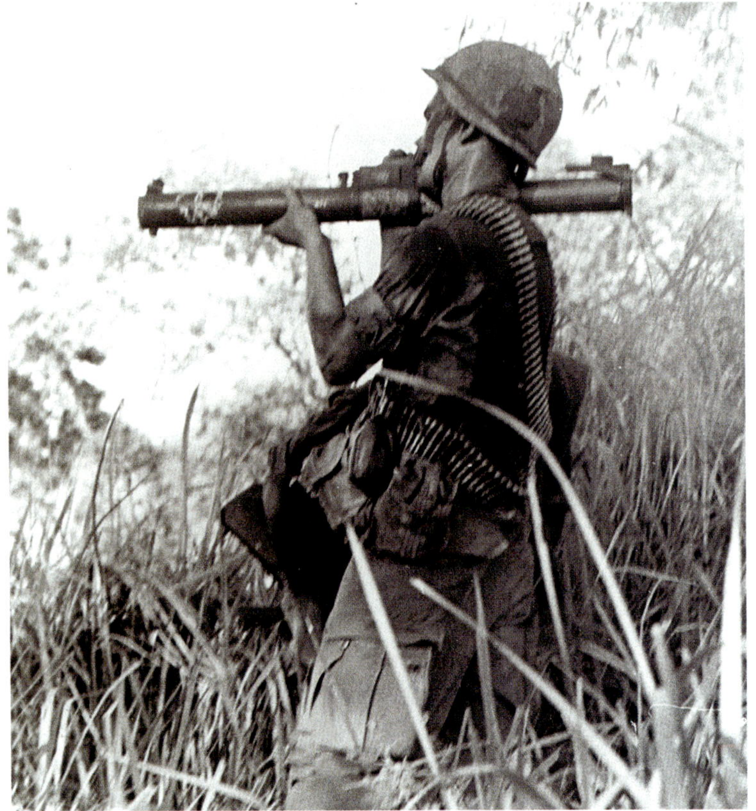

Above: Two aluminum caskets arrive at an American base from Vietnam bearing the remains of two soldiers killed in combat. Rows of these flag-draped caskets arriving back from the war became a symbol for the war protesters, who demonstrated in cities and college campuses across the country until the last troops finally came home.

Left: To remain highly mobile and still carry enough punch to knock out enemy bunkers or light armor such as the Soviet PT-76 tank, U.S., and A.R.V.N. troops carried the L.A.W. This light anti-tank weapon was a self-contained rocket and its launcher. A simple sight folded up atop the tube and once fired, the tube was discarded. The N.V.A. collected the empty tubes and made improvised explosive devices (I.E.D.s).

Opposite above: High over Cambodia, a pair of F-4 Phantom fighter bombers are refueled in the air by a KC-135 Stratotanker. With aerial refueling, Phantoms and Thunderchiefs could remain on station to chase away MiG fighters from the bombers or drop down with bombs for troop support.

Opposite below: The tracked M113 Armored Personnel Carrier (A.P.C.) was armed with a .50 caliber machine gun and could transport a squad of armed soldiers to where they were needed faster than on foot or wheeled trucks over jungle trails. A.R.V.N. troops made use of the A.P.C.s in their interdiction raid on the Ho Chi Minh Trail in Cambodia.

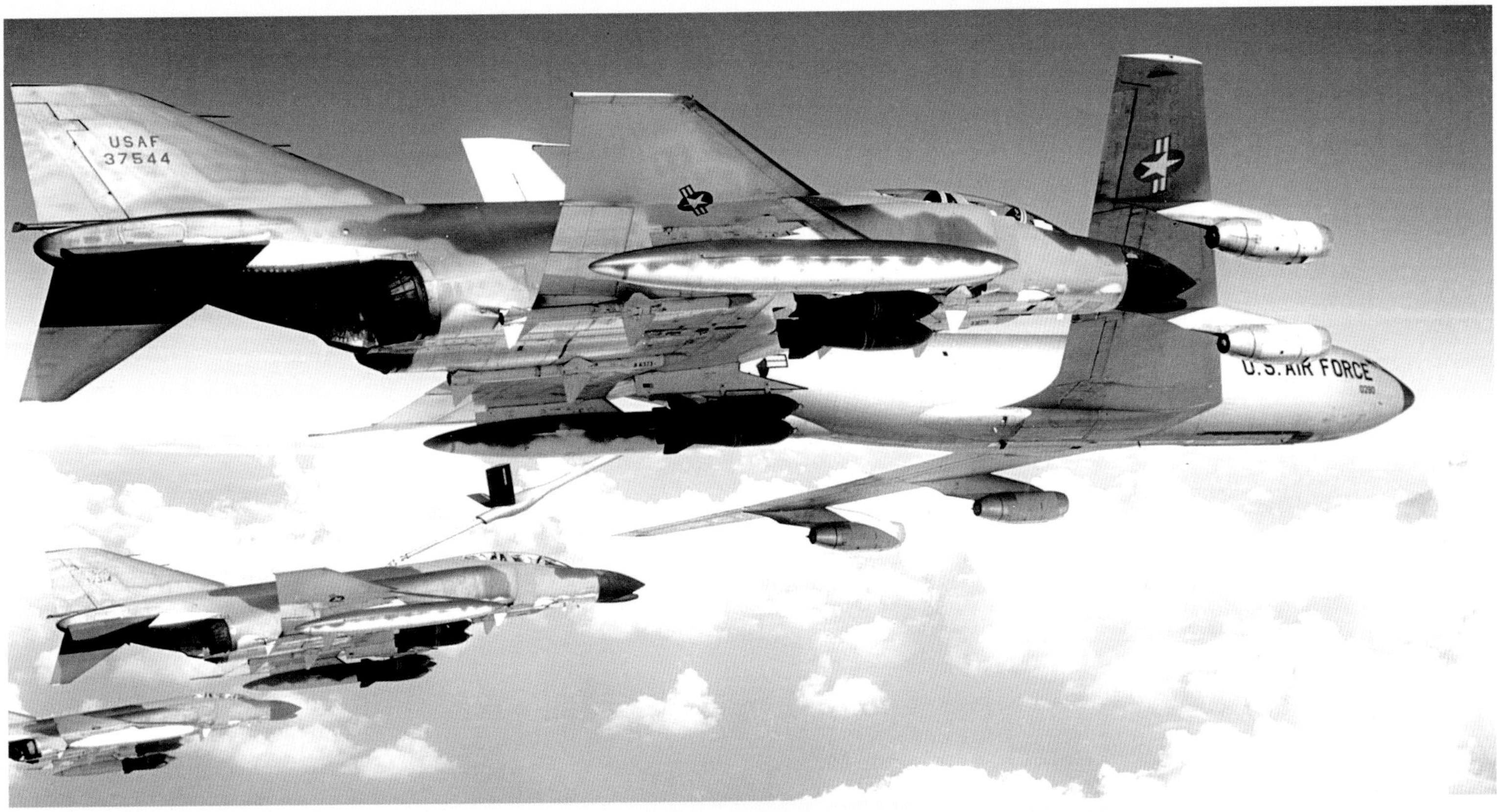
USAF
37544
U.S. AIR FORCE

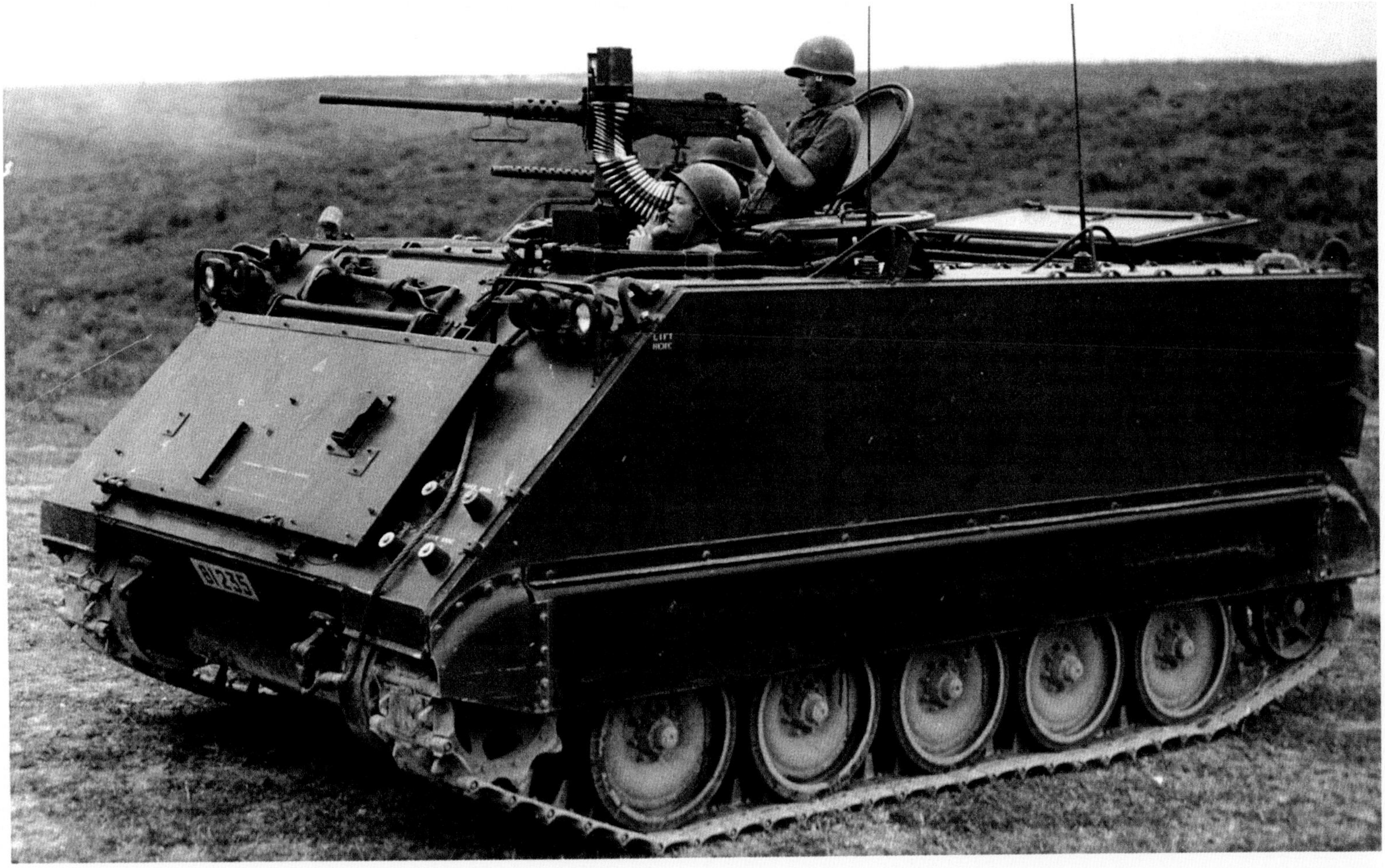
B1235

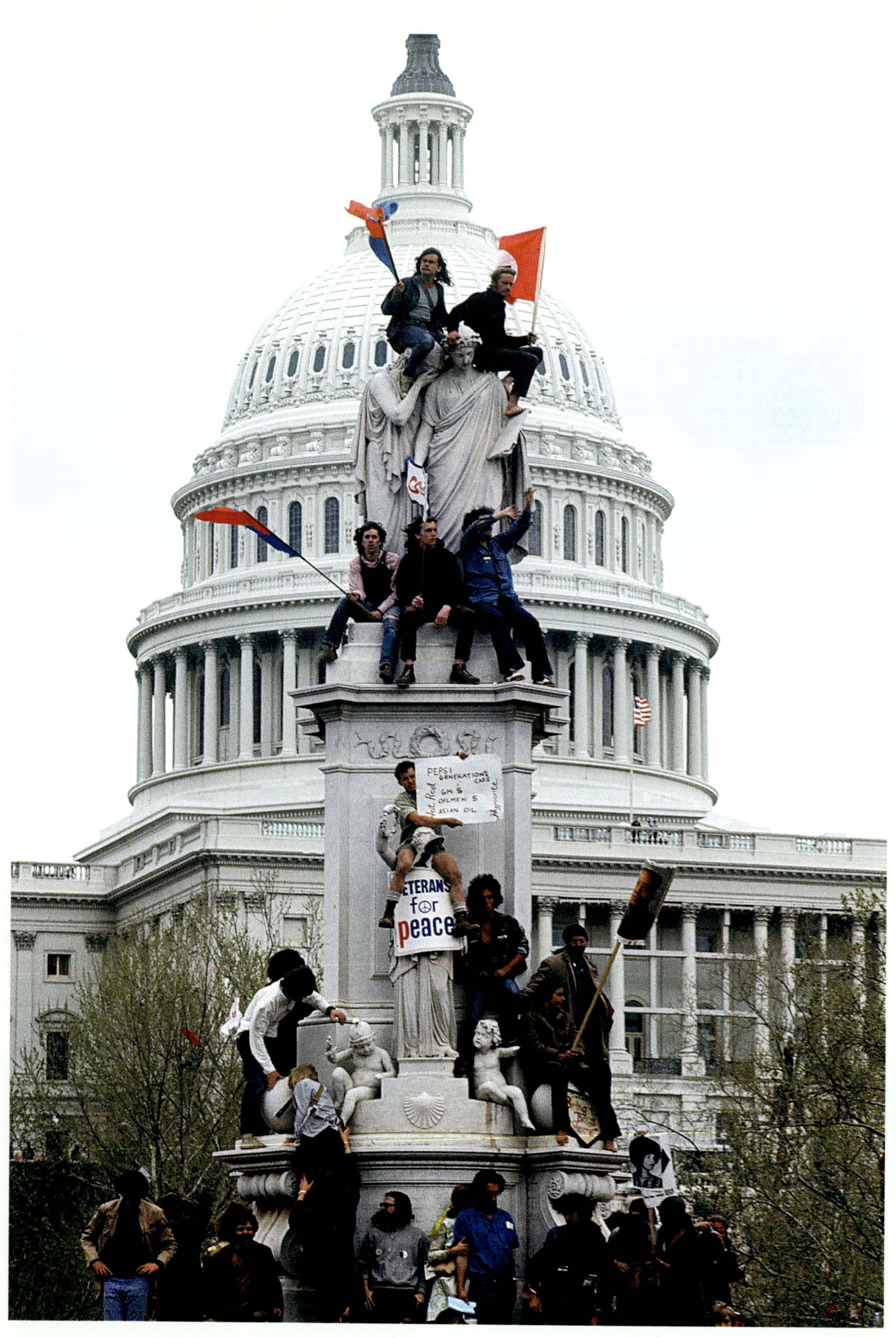
PEPSI GENERATIONS CARS
GM $
OILMEN $
ASIAN OIL
Hot Rod
Hypocrite
ETERANS
for
peace

DECLASSIFIED PER EXECUTIVE ORDER
12356, Section 3.3 873541.
By R.B:/M.I NARA, Date 12-2-93

CONFIDENTIAL

On 12 April E Troop received 7 rounds of 60mm mortars from the north at their NDP at XT 447843 at 0552 hours. There were no casualties.At 1630 hours, E troop had an AA activate resulting in 3 NVA killed, 1 PW wounded and 1 AK-47 captured at XT 472843. F Troop had an AA activate, killing one NVA at XT 415837.On 13 April E troop had an AA activate, killing 1 NVA, 1 SKS and 2 ChiCom grenades at XT 469841 at 0657 hours. At 1210 hours, E Troop received one RPG from the north at XT 473872. F Troop reinforced, along with artillery, Tac AIR, LFT and ARA. There was sporadic contact until 1600 hours resulting in two US wounded and a M551 moderately damaged. There were 31 NVA killed by US forces, 1 POW, 1 60mm mortar, AK-47, 1 RPG-7 launcher and documents captured. At 1715 hours, F Troop hit a 23-lb mine which wounded one US at XT 473832. On 14 April. The F Troop NDP received 20 rounds of 82mm mortars and 3 B40 rockets and small-arms fire at XT 408837 at 0531 hours. There were two US wounded. H Company received small-arms fire at 1606 hours, which broke leaving 2 dead NVA, 2 AK-47?s captured. at XT 474843. At 1807 hours, F Troop while moving to NDP observed and engaged 12 NVA with no results at XT 497820, although 2 bunkers and 1 tunnel were discovered. At 2005 hours, Ft. DEFIANCE received 1 107mm rocket which impacted on a trailer which was destroyed killing one US and wounding 3. At 2027 hours, an RPG hit, causing no damage. On 15 April E Troop conducted maintanance operations at the FOB, checked AA?s and one platoon swept 246 west to 448821. At 1705 hours, XT 471820, they observed 3 NVA, but no results. F Troop continued reconnaissance, and engaged heavy movement at XT 5184, with negative results. Artillery supported. The Troop made its NDP at XT 508847. G Troop found a 23-pound mine at XT 657838 at 1407 hours. H Company continued maintenance at FT. DEFIANCE and closed FSB BURKETT at 2017 hours. 4/919th swept 246 to XT 448821, making their NDP At FSB BURKETT.

On 16 April, E Troop conducted ground reconnissance in box 4584, 4582, 4982, putting out AA?s with NDP at XT 475821. F Troop conducted reconnaisence at FOB and put out 7 AA?s. G Troop found a TM-46 mine at XT 500820. At 1346 hours G Troop found two NVA in graves, killed by AA. They also found one canteen, first aid pack, documents, AK bandoleer, and a ChiCom claymore. HHT, 4/919th and H Company constructed FSB BURKETT. On 17 April, E Troop had AA activate at 1443 hours, killing two NVA at XT 473844. At 1613 hours, E Troop made contact west of DEFIANCE, receiving 3 GPG rounds. They fired, artillery, a LFT and Tac Air supported with no results. At 1713 hours, E Troop spotted one enemy in bunkers and killed him at XT 465838, capturing one AK-47. E Troop made its NDP at XT 475821. With 10 AA?s out. F Troop reconned north of Hill 95 from 495845 to 480842. At 1746 hours G Troop resulted RPG and light machinegun fire from north and southwest of their NDP resulting in two US wounded, 1 NVA POW and 1 NVA killed. One RPG and launcher wer captured. G Troop swept 246 from XT 500820 to FSB Burkett. At 1030 hours, G Troop M551 hit a 23-pound mine while moving to secure downed UH-1H. Also a H Company M48 hit a mine while moving to the Uh-1H at XT 550885.

On 18 April E Troop found a NVA body in a grave, at XT 470821.
They also found 7 60mm mortar rounds, RPG-7 round,. The troop put out 10 AA?s and snipers.

CONFIDENTIAL

DECLASSIFIED PER EXECUTIVE ORDER
12356, Section 3.3 873541.
By R.B:/M.I NARA, Date 12-2-93

CONFIDENTIAL

killing 1 NVA. At 1045H, an M551 hit a 23lb mine at 570843 on the nort side of the road. Atv2154H, 518818, after completing a mad minute, they received AK-47 fire from 300-400m S.
On 19 April at 1800H. F troop sighted 3 NVA in the open 150m W of their NDP. They returned fire. A sweep of the area revealed 1 NVA PW, some documents, and 1 AK-47. At 1850H, the 2/11 C&C ship received 20 rounds of AK-47 fire. At 0745H, on 21 April, G Troop had an AA go off. The sweep revealed 6 NVA KIA, 5 AK-47?s, and documents. At 1254H, 551865, G Troop found 22B 4? by 6? by4? with 1? OHC. And 3 82mm mortar positions. At 1644H, while moving to FOB, they found 1 NVA KBAA 13 hrs ago. At 2149H, 545879, they observed 3 individuals in a bomb crater 150m W. They returned fire with claymores and LFT. HHT, from 0240-0435H, at BURKETT received 10 107mm rockets, 123 rds of 82mm mortars, 20 rds 60mm mortar from the north. They also received moderate s/a and RPG fire. There were 14 US wounded (8 medevaced); 1 M48 lightly damaged, and 1 M113 lightly damaged. Ther3 were 2 NVA KIA. On 22 April E troop at 449821, found 3 NVA bodies from an AA activated the previous night. At 1225H, at 470830, an M551 detonated a mine in old tank bust causing heavy damage. Later at 1300H, while moving to assist, another M551 hit a mine which caused heavy damage. At 1320H, 546886m a G TroopM113A hit 2 23lb mines which wounded one US and heavily damaged the vehicle. At 1330H a G Troop AA detonated killing 2 NVA and capturing 2 AK-47?s. On 24 April at 1635H, 125m NW of BURKETT, they found 4 107mm rockets, 2 flashlights, 6 aiming stakes, 1 hammock, 3 CC grenades, 2 NVA canteens, 5 NVA shovels and a pistol belt.
E Troop NDP was at 580876, F Troop at 518869,and G Troop 537876.

On 25 April, E Troop continued sweep of 246, and F Troop relocated at 536872. They picked up AA?s at Suio Chong Uyen. At 0924H, 545865, an AA was activated within the last 18 hrs. They found 3 sets of field gear, blood spots, and 2 NVA KIA. At 1534H, 522858 and 532854 they found AA?s activated with 1 grave at each location and 2 NVA KBAA. G Troop relocated its FOB at 515863, picked up AA?s on cut N of FSB BURKETT and assumed mission of F Troop S of Suio Chong Yuen. At 1126H, 54876, an M551 hit a TM-46 mine off the shoulder of the road with monor damage. At1136H, 508852, G Troop, while enroute to check AA?s, had an ACAV hit a booby trapped AA which resulted in 3 US KBAA, 1 US WBAA, and 1 KIT CARSON scout WBAA. At 0940H, 553849, H Co found 1 NVA body 4 days old killed by a 50 cal. At 558853, they found commo wire running to all points, 40 small bags of rice, 3 82mm rounds, 3 RPG rds, 1 CC grenade, 1 MG position, 60 shovel handles, 1 BANGALORE TORPEDO, 1 82mm fuse, and 1 35? antenna
used in the last 4 days. On 26 April E troop continued its sweep of ROUTE 246 E to BURKETT. At 0830H, 573878, they found a 23lb mine on the N side of the road. At 0846, 580833, they found a 30lb mine on the S side of the road. Also 150m to the E they found another 30lb mine, both implaced in the last 4 hrs.
F Troop continued GR from 528874 to 505866. G Troop continued GR from 515862 to 542846 to 520820 to 505795. At 1634H H Co found 1 50 cal MG.

DECLASSIFIED PER EXECUTIVE ORDER
12356, Section 3.3 873541.
By R.B:/M.I NARA, Date 12-2-93

On 28 April E Troop continued local patrols N & S of their FOB, checking AA?s. At 1045H, 580843, while checking an AA site, E troop observed 2 NVA 100m away. They fired but the enemy successfully evaded.
F Troop GR?d from FOB to 568873 and at 1025H, 505865, had an AA go off. In the sweep they found HCM sandals, pools of blood, and 2 NVA KBAA. G Troop reconned Hill 95 to check AA?s. On 29 April E troop swept 246 from BURKETT to 551878. They took down AA?s, while at their NDP they received 1 rd of 120mm rocket fire from the S. G Troop, at 1045, 494815, received small arms fire from the S of road by a squad-size force.
At 1805H an AA was set off and the sweep turned up 2 NVA KBAA. On 30 April, E troop moved their NDP to 521899. F Troop secured route to the N. for 2/11 and 3/11 move. They moved their FOB to 512904.
Their NP was at 512904. G Troop secured HHT/2/11 on move to new FSB. At 1247H, 515905, a water trailer detonated a 23-lb mine. During the period, HHT, 4/919th and H Co. performed mostly security missions.
The 4/919th swept route 246 to 244 almost daily, secured by HHT. HHT also secured convoys, and protected the FSB. H Co also served as a RRF for DEFIANCE and BURKETT, performing GR near the base. 4/919th built each base, and was assisted by HHT. They also had the mission of securing and maintaining the erdalator for the squadron.

DECLASSIFIED PER EXECUTIVE ORDER
12356, Section 3.3 873541.
By R.B:/M.I NARA, Date 12-2-93

In April. From 5 April to 11 April there were 18 ground-toair firings, 4 attacks by indirect fire, 11 enemy contacts and 99 mining incidents. The week before there were 5 ground-to-air firings, no attacks by fire, 10 contacts and 51 mining incidents. Analysis of the increased ground-to ?air firings was found to be credited to enemy planning. The enemy has issued armor piercing rounds to be used in AK-47?s for firing at helicopters. The increase occurred when the enemy was preparing for the attack on Ft. Defiance. Since many of the firings occurred when the ships were at high altitude, 2500 to 3000? the enemy may have used them, in part, to divert attention from his other activities. The decrease in mining incidents was the result of two things: one, less Squadron LCC movement, thus lessening the chance for mines, and two, the enemy's preoccupation with preparing the attack. The four attacks by fire were in conjunction with the attack on Ft, Defiance. The first attack's magnitude indicates that it was a pre-ground probe attack. The other three attacks were diversions to allow ground troops and cover disengagement and withdrawal. One significant shift in enemy patterns: the 50th RSG has begun to move through the area west of Defiance. probably caused by the constant interdiction of the east trails by automatic ambushes. Last week the enemy set off 17 AAs, while in this week he set off only 8. This drop was caused by F Troop reconning the Mustang Trail. When troops move west of Hazel the effectiveness of the AA trout lines will increase.

On 7 April G/2/11 established a live ambush with AAs in blocking position. A trip flare went off, and 25 individuals were seen in the kill zone. The NVA fled, leaving 500 lbs of rice, fish, packs, uniforms and medical supplies. It is suspected that the equipment was intended for the 101st Regiment. Since this ambush the enemy has returned to small groups, 4 and 5 men. Overconfidence in the safety of the area and the dire needs of the 101stprobably caused the attempt to move such a large group. The movement was primarily by groups of SR-=1 and 50th RSG, both attempting to get to the 101st south of highway 246 along the Saigon River.

AFTER-ACTION REPORT 1970

This After-Action Report (A.A.R.) details the movements, battles, missions, losses, and victories of U.S. Army Company E and Company G of an unknown but typical infantry battalion in April, 1970. The reports were compiled by company commanders and sent to battalion H.Q.

Opposite: Anti-war protesters gather on a monument near the Capitol Building in Washington, D.C. College students staged sit-downs, hippies camped in public parks, and citizens choked city streets with their marches. Sometimes protesters waved N.V.A. flags, spat on returning American soldiers, and called them "baby-killers." No one had ever seen a war reported on television so vividly with so much emotion.

"VIETNAMIZATION"

AFTER FIVE YEARS OF SLUGGING IT OUT TOE TO TOE, THE UNITED STATES, ITS ALLIES, AND THE NORTH VIETNAMESE ARMY HAD DEVELOPED CONSIDERABLE MUTUAL RESPECT. WHILE THE N.V.A. WAS UNDER STRICT POLITICAL CONTROL BY THE HANOI GOVERNMENT, AND SUPPORTED BY ENTHUSIASTIC PROPAGANDA DIRECTED AT THE NORTH VIETNAMESE PEOPLE , THE AMERICAN, AUSTRALIAN, AND NEW ZEALAND FORCES WERE OVERSEEN BY ELECTED REPRESENTATIVES GUIDED BY THE WILL OF THEIR VOTING PUBLICS. AND THOSE REPRESENTATIVES FELT THE PRESSURE TO END INVOLVEMENT IN THE WAR. AFTER FIVE YEARS IT WAS TIME FOR THE GOVERNMENT OF SOUTH VIETNAM TO TAKE MORE RESPONSIBILITY FOR ITS DEFENSE.

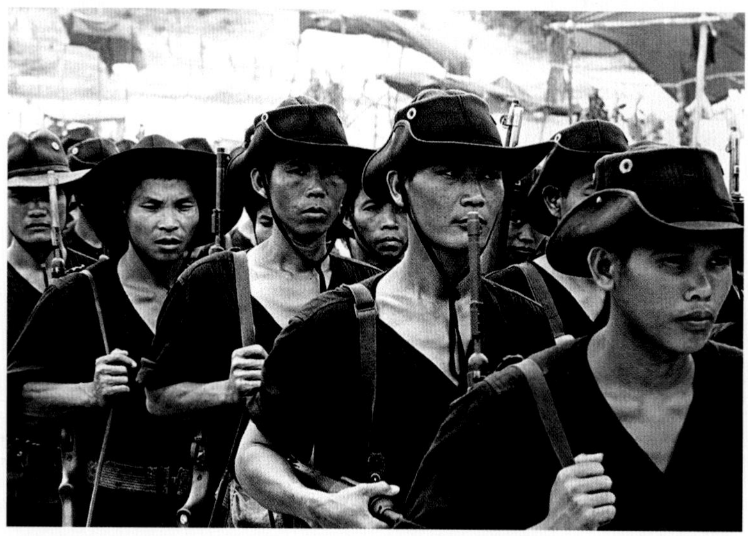

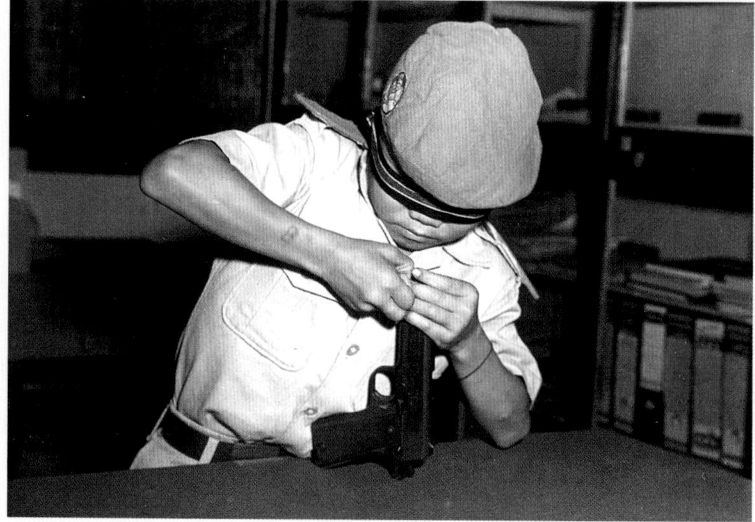

As far back as 1968, the American commanders in Vietnam and the politicians back in Washington had determined that the Republic of Vietnam Armed Forces (R.V.N.A.F.) in the South was a wild card—an unknown quantity. Units such as the A.R.V.N. 1st Division were tough regulars that could be counted on to stand up to a stiff fight, as were A.R.V.N. Rangers and other divisions that had battle experience since the mid-1960s. More recent units, such as the A.R.V.N. 3rd Division, however, had been saddled with half-trained troops and rejects from other elements. Their commanders were often products of the corruption in the South Vietnamese government. Though the R.V.N.A.F. tried to raise its combat standards, instances of entire units of troops, vehicles, and tanks fleeing at the sight of a single N.V.A. T-54 Soviet tank, or abandonment of weapons and artillery positions at first sight of an enemy force, were not uncommon.

A two-phase proposal was put forward by U.S. Secretary of Defense Clark Clifford in April 1968. Phase one provided a considerable upgrade in arms and technology to the R.V.N.A.F. The earliest A.R.V.N. organizations in the early 1960s had been restricted to surplus World War II and Korean War weapons such as the M1 Garand rifle, the M1 carbine, and the Browning

Above left: With many villages and hamlets located in virtually inaccessible jungle and mountainous locations, they had to be defended against Viet Cong raids by their local neighbors. U.S. Special Operations Advisors trained many of these defense cadres. These young villagers are armed with U.S. Army .30 caliber M1 carbines and at least one .45 caliber M3 submachine gun—all from World War II surplus.

Above right: An A.R.V.N. training cadet disassembles and reassembles a Model 1911 U.S. Army semi-automatic pistol while blindfolded. The A.R.V.N. soldiers had good skills and motivation but needed better leadership.

Opposite: A.R.V.N. troops move forward up a hill in pursuit of N.V.A. soldiers. A.R.V.N. soldiers had the patriotic spirit to defend their land, but they lacked training with their new equipment.

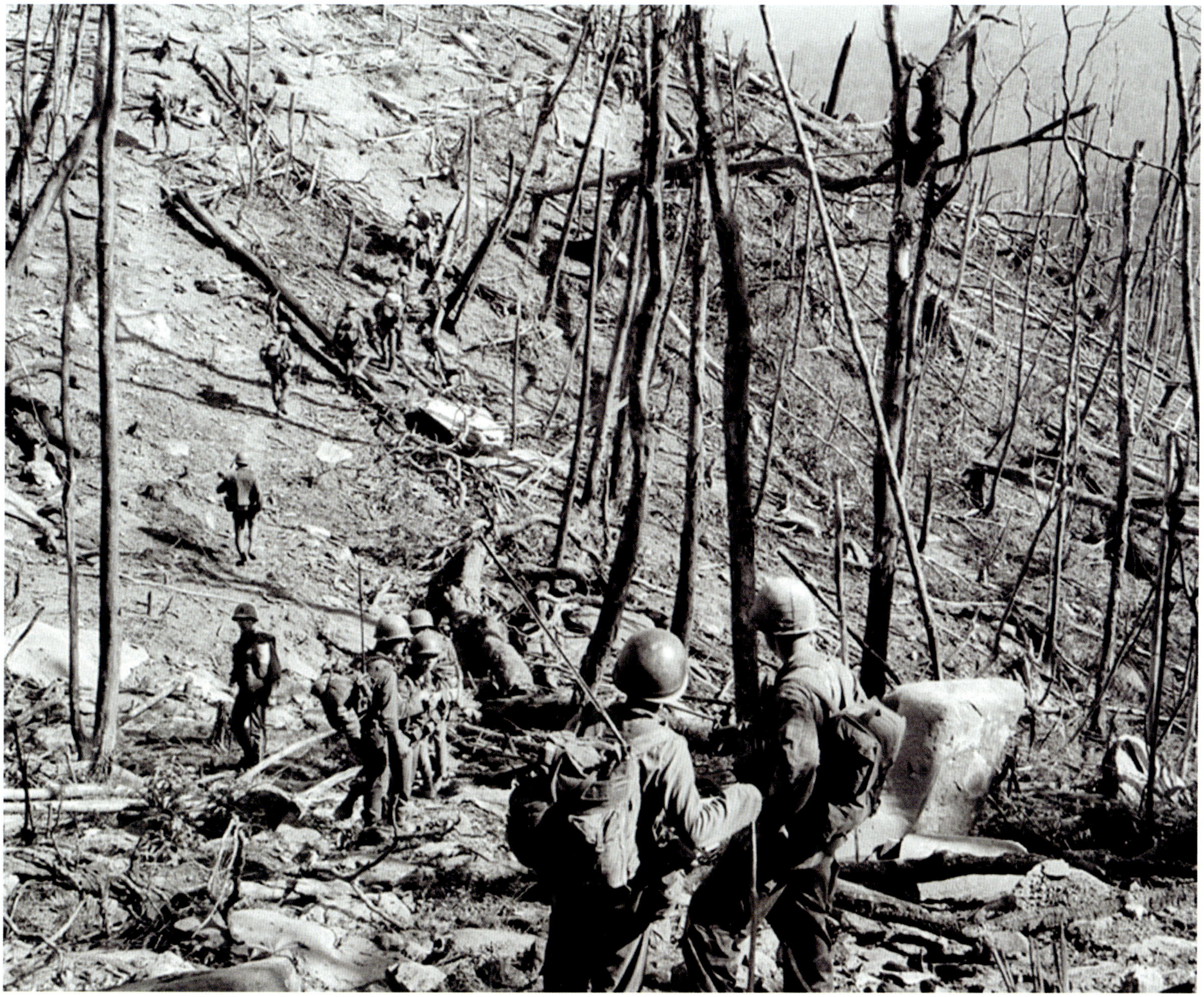

GENERAL CREIGHTON ABRAMS

Born in 1914, General Abrams graduated from West Point in 1936. He distinguished himself as a tank commander under George Patton in World War II. In April 1968, he succeeded General William Westmoreland as commander in Vietnam. He shifted strategy from "search and destroy" to protecting the Vietnamese population. He was the architect of Nixon's invasion of Cambodia in 1970 and Laos in 1971, and was responsible for the upgrading of A.R.V.N. combat capabilities with modern weapons, armor, and organization. Abrams left Vietnam in 1972, once again relieved Westmoreland, this time as Army Chief of Staff, and died in 1974 of lung cancer.

Right: *Time* magazine cover illustration of General Creighton Abrams, who replaced General William Westmoreland as overall commander of forces in Vietnam. By 1970, the "Vietnamization" of the war was fully underway and under Abrams's direction.

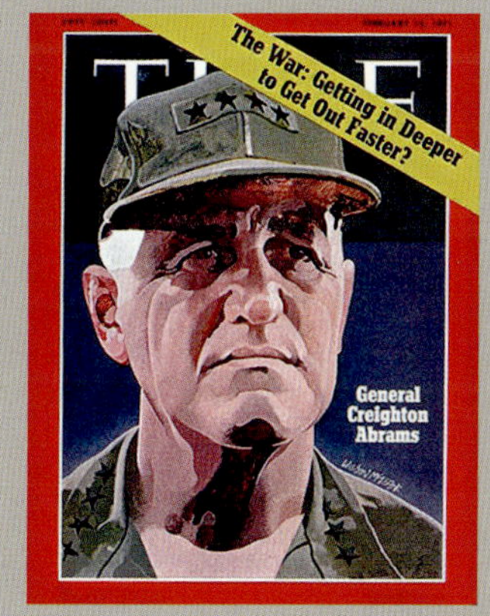

U.S. MORALE AT LOW EBB

American soldiers had been a fighting force in Vietnam since 1965 and morale among the ground forces had slipped to a low point. At home, anti-war protests fueled by the media were calling for an end to U.S. involvement and waving North Vietnam flags. Drug use among the foot soldiers had soared. Being unable to identify the enemy from innocent villagers caused many incidents. As Washington tried to micromanage the targets and politics of the conflict, field officers became more frustrated.

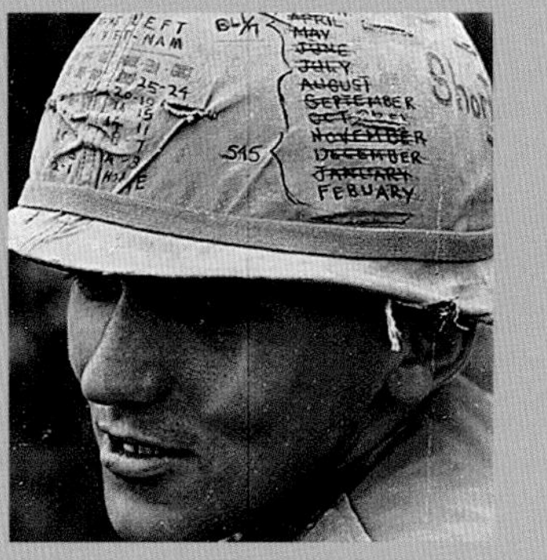

Left: A U.S. soldier has worked out on his helmet cover the time he has remaining in Vietnam before he is rotated home. After eight years of war, morale in the army was at an all-time low. Drug use had increased and nobody wanted to be the last soldier killed before everyone was pulled out.

Below: An A.R.V.N. soldier lays down a barrage of gunfire from his automatic M16 assault rifle. By 1970–72, most A.R.V.N. units had been equipped with modern weapons to replace the World War II equipment they had begun with in the early 1960s.

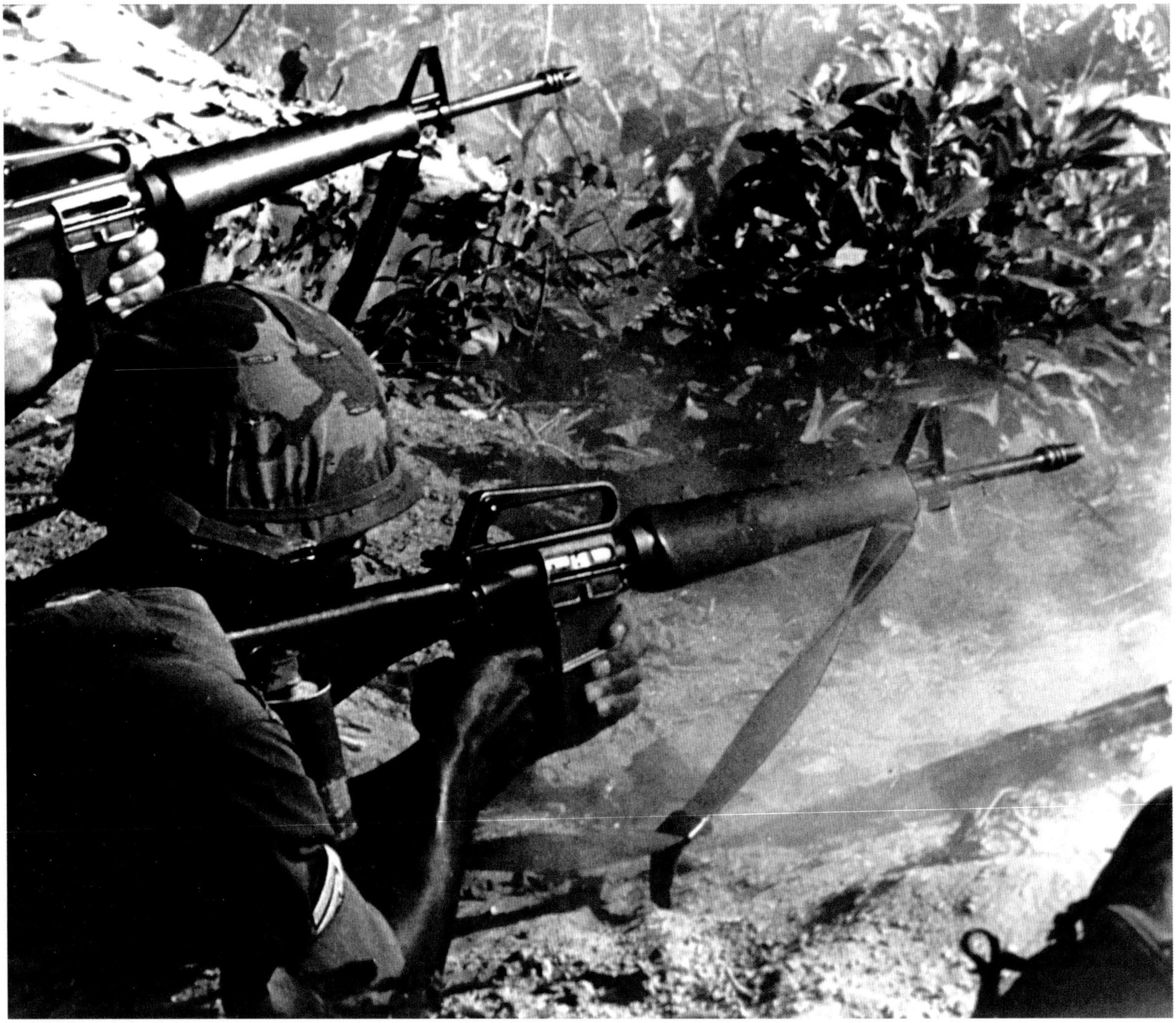

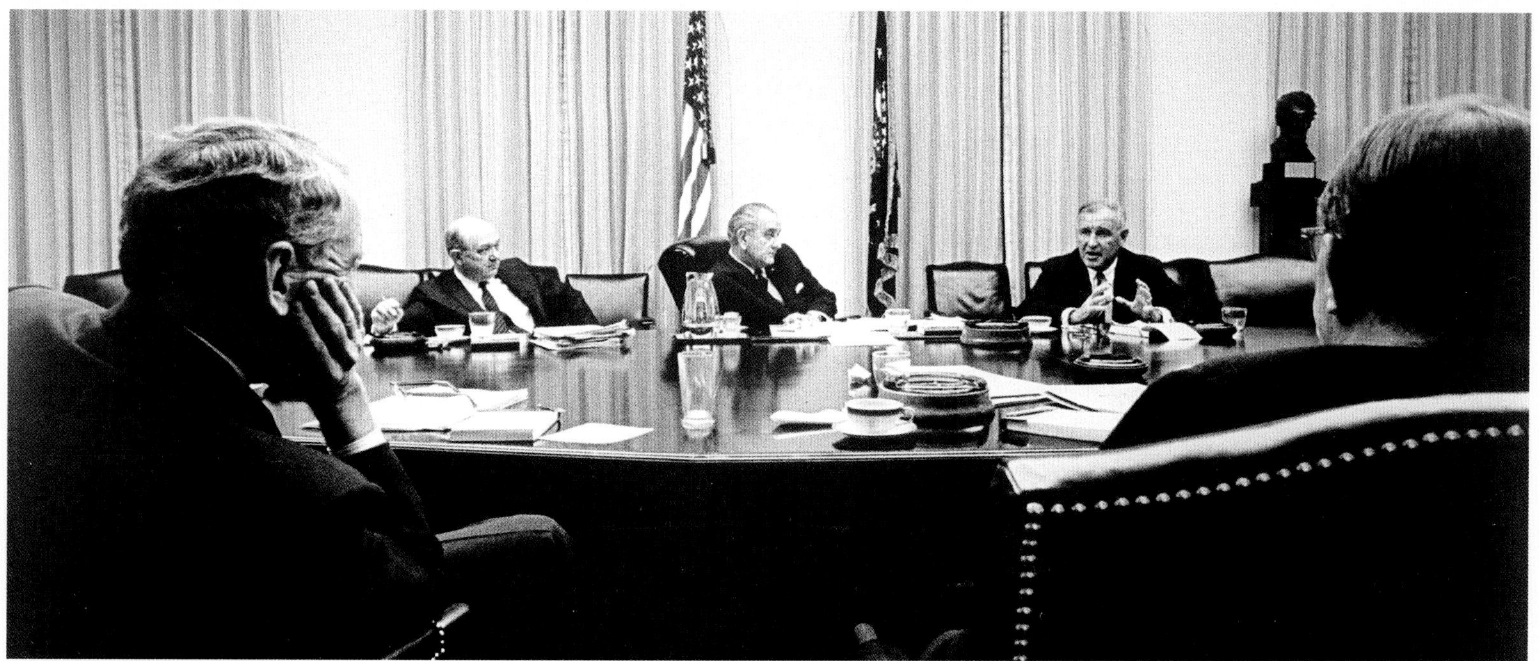

.30 caliber crew-served machine gun. Some forces carried Thompson .45 caliber submachine guns and .45 caliber "grease gun" submachine guns from the same era. As units gained proficiency, new AR-15 rifles were issued—the prototype of the M16. Phase two of the 1968 proposal called for M.A.C.V. training to improve across the board for all R.V.N.A.F. Patrol boats for the Mekong Delta, and aircraft for troop support bombing and armored units were also provided.

The Tet Offensive in 1968 and subsequent search-and-destroy missions had virtually silenced Viet Cong operations in the South. One important factor was the Phung Hoang (Phoenix) Program that encouraged defection. By the end of 1971, some 17,000 V.C. had accepted amnesty. General Creighton Abrams had succeeded General William Westmoreland and continued to prosecute the "insurgency" while battling infiltration of N.V.A. guerrillas from the North. Many A.R.V.N. units had distinguished themselves in these engagements. However, the success of most insurgency combats continued to be measured by "body counts." Since civilians and combatants were often indistinguishable, when the body count exceeded the weapons count, the numbers were suspect.

Between 1970 and 1972 considerable upgrading of the R.V.N.A.F. forces took place. At home in the United States public pressure mounted and President Nixon's administration was under siege. The number of anti-war demonstrators, draft card burners, and those fleeing to Canada to avoid military service was growing.

Above: General Creighton W. Abrams (second from right), U.S. Commander in South Vietnam, discusses the military situation in Vietnam with President Johnson (center) and his advisors at the White House, October 29, 1968.

Right: Marines with V.C. prisoners near Chu Lai ready to transport them to a security compound or turn them into Kit Carson scouts if they accept amnesty under the Phoenix Program.

PHUNG HOANG (PHOENIX) PROGRAM

The Phoenix Program was created to round up or "neutralize" the leaders and cadres of V.C. remaining in South Vietnam following the failed Tet Offensive in 1968. The M.A.C.V.'s C.O.R.D.S. (Civilian Operations and Revolutionary Development Support) program offered safe-conduct to 17,000 surrendering V.C. Besides these, 28,000 were captured and 20,000 killed—the majority in combat and some in targeted assassinations. The North Vietnamese publicly condemned the "assassination squads" in an attempt to score a political victory. They said nothing of the 61,000 civil servants, families, and village officials murdered by the V.C. between 1958 and 1966.

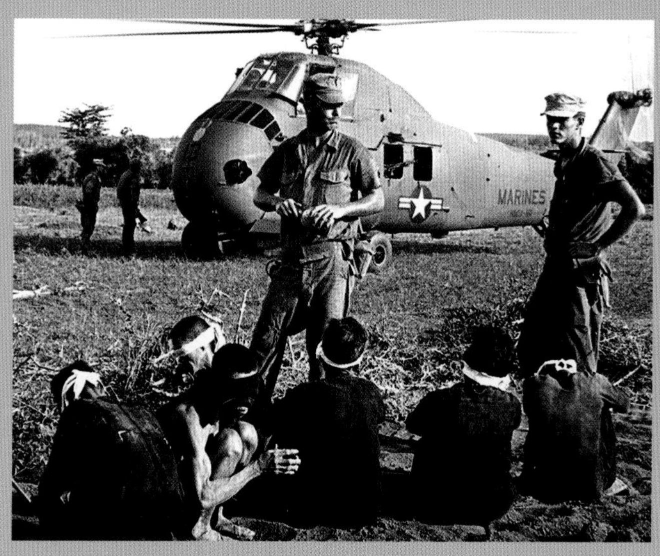

CAMBODIA & LAOS

BY 1970 THE AMERICAN MILITARY FACED A NUMBER OF PROBLEMS. AT HOME THE DRAFT LOTTERY HAD BEGUN. BIRTH DATES WERE INSERTED IN 366 CAPSULES AND DRAWN FROM A GLASS JAR. EACH DATE RECEIVED A DRAFT NUMBER FROM 1 TO 366. LOW NUMBERS WERE DRAFTED, HIGH NUMBERS WERE SPARED. ALSO, COLLEGE DEFERMENTS FOR THE UPPER-MIDDLE-CLASS WORKED AGAINST AFRICAN-AMERICANS AND WORKING-CLASS WHITES. THOUGH AFRICAN-AMERICANS COMPRISED 10.6 PERCENT OF THE MILITARY FORCE, 12.1 PERCENT WERE KILLED IN ACTION BECAUSE THEY MADE UP PROPORTIONATELY MORE OF THE FRONT-LINE INFANTRY UNITS. DRUG PROBLEMS DUE TO LOW MORALE WERE WIDESPREAD AND SOME OFFICER DEATHS WERE THE RESULT OF "FRAGGING"—GRENADES DISCHARGED "ACCIDENTALLY."

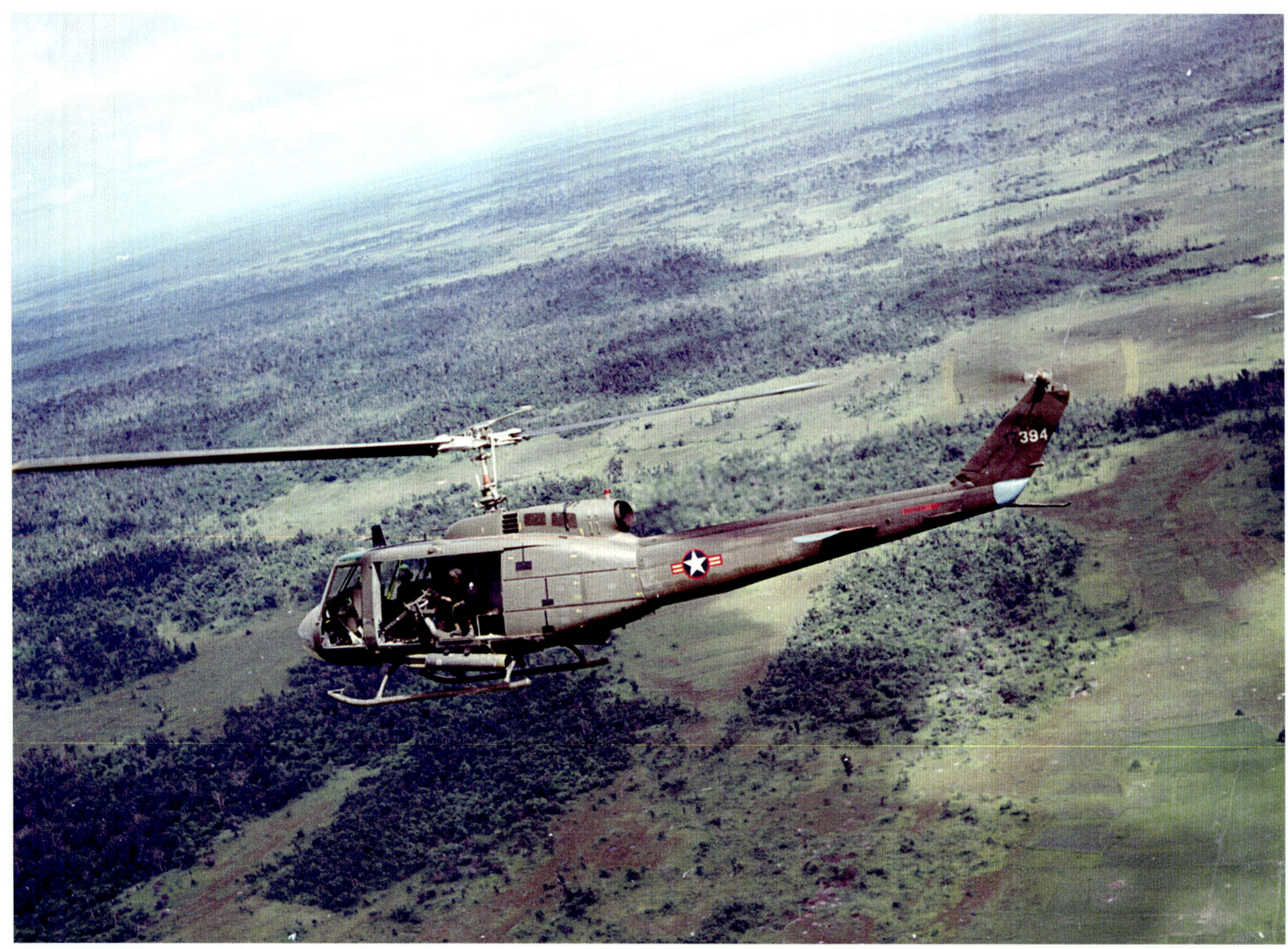

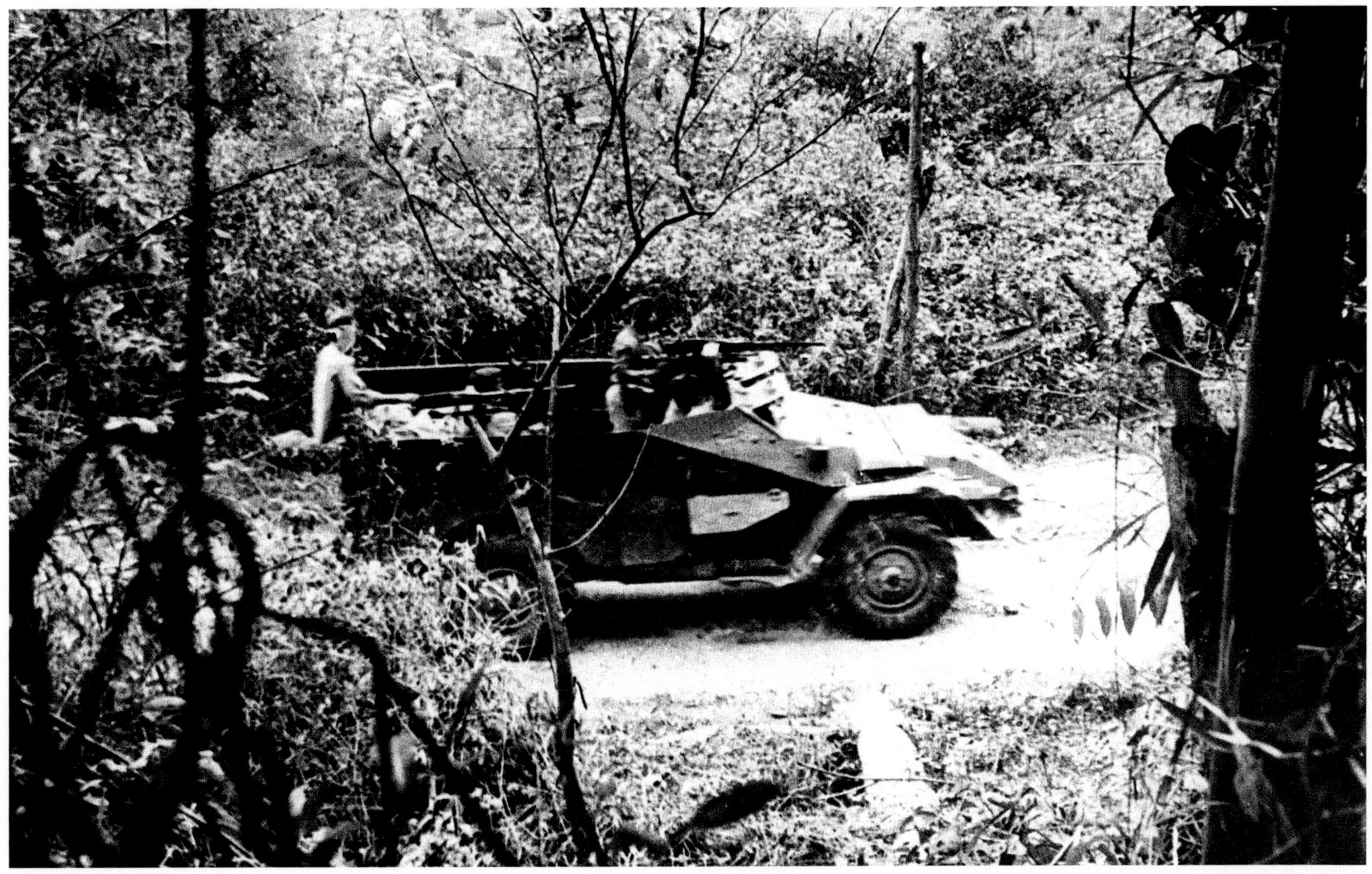

In the war zone, the major threat came from Cambodia. The N.V.A. and V.C. used that country as a staging ground for attacks into South Vietnam. These bases had to be destroyed in order for the South Vietnamese Army to build up its capabilities while the U. S. withdrew its troops. To that end, President Nixon authorized the invasion of Cambodia by American troops on May 1, 1970.

Following the usual preliminary bombardment by B-52 bombers, American troops met with little resistance, scooping up considerable stored supplies until they came upon a huge dump in the area known as the Fish Hook near Snoul. Here they found tons of explosives, small arms, ammunition, a hundred machine guns, and the N.V.A./V.C. Central Office for South Vietnam. Other incursions by U.S. and A.R.V.N. troops had similar if not as spectacular results. By June 29, 1970, all American troops were out of Cambodia and the A.R.V.N. followed in August. President Nixon declared the invasion a great success.

As the fighting in Cambodia ground on, the belief spread among Americans already unsympathetic to the war that the Cambodian invasion was an expansion of the conflict at a time when the Nixon administration spoke of withdrawals. The Vietnamese people as a whole were also tired of war and

ROYAL LAOTIAN ARMY

While the war continued in Vietnam, across the border in Laos, an ongoing civil war simmered between the N.V.A. and N.V.A.-backed Pathet Lao against the U.S.-backed Royal Laotian Army of the legal government. While the issues were strictly Laotian, the prosecution was determined by the see-saw conflict in Vietnam. Early in 1961, the Laotian Air Force flew World War II AT-6 propeller-driven aircraft armed with rockets. Later, 60 T-28D prop jobs were added along with 50 transports and 30 helicopters. Mostly Thai or Air America (C.I.A.) pilots flew them. The army of 60,000 was deemed "overweight in generals and underweight in fighting." When the Americans left Vietnam, the Laotian Army faded away.

Opposite: A South Vietnamese Huey helicopter with a soldier manning its door gun cruises over Cambodian countryside during the invasion of June 1970.

Above: An armored car manned by Laotian soldiers patrols a road during the U.S. and A.R.V.N. invasion of Cambodia to shut down Vietnamese use of roads for supply. Civil wars wracked Laos and Cambodia because of Communist infiltrators and corrupt leaders.

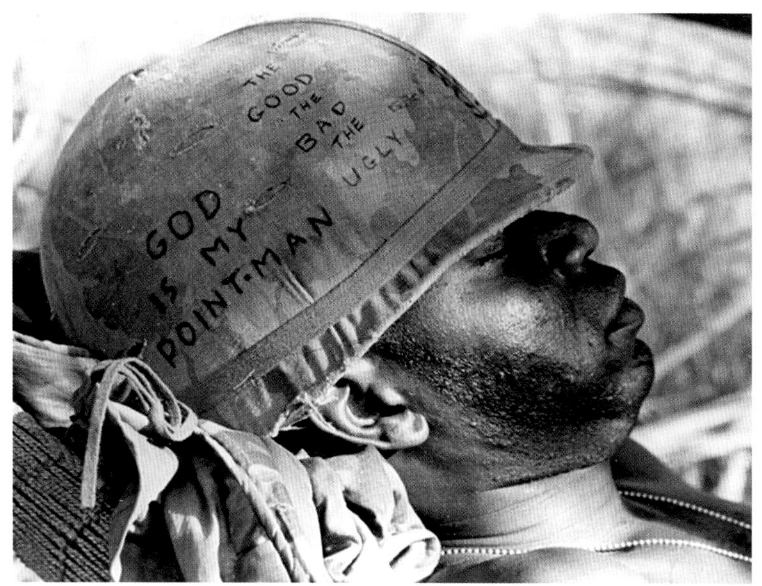

perceived the American effort as only interested in killing Communists—not in helping the Vietnamese win the conflict. One event seemed to confirm that opinion. On June 24, the Gulf of Tonkin Resolution was repealed, meaning the United States was no longer "obligated" to defend South Vietnam. However, they did see their role as to "support" A.R.V.N. operations.

On January 30, 1971, American troops of the 5th Mechanized Division launched an attack to re-establish a firebase at Lang

Left: An American soldier dozes during a patrol halt. His helmet reads, "God is my point man." A point man is a soldier commanded to go ahead of the rest of the unit and scout for possible enemy ambushes, booby traps, or any enemy contact so the unit isn't surprised. As was said in World War II, "There are no atheists in fox holes."

Below: President Richard M. Nixon meets the press to explain his decision to both bomb and invade Cambodia. Though the action was in support of A.R.V.N. troops who were interdicting the Ho Chi Minh Trail and destroying supplies, all the American public saw in the media were B-52 bombers unloading the bombs on Cambodia. Congress later called for impeachment of the President for taking the action.

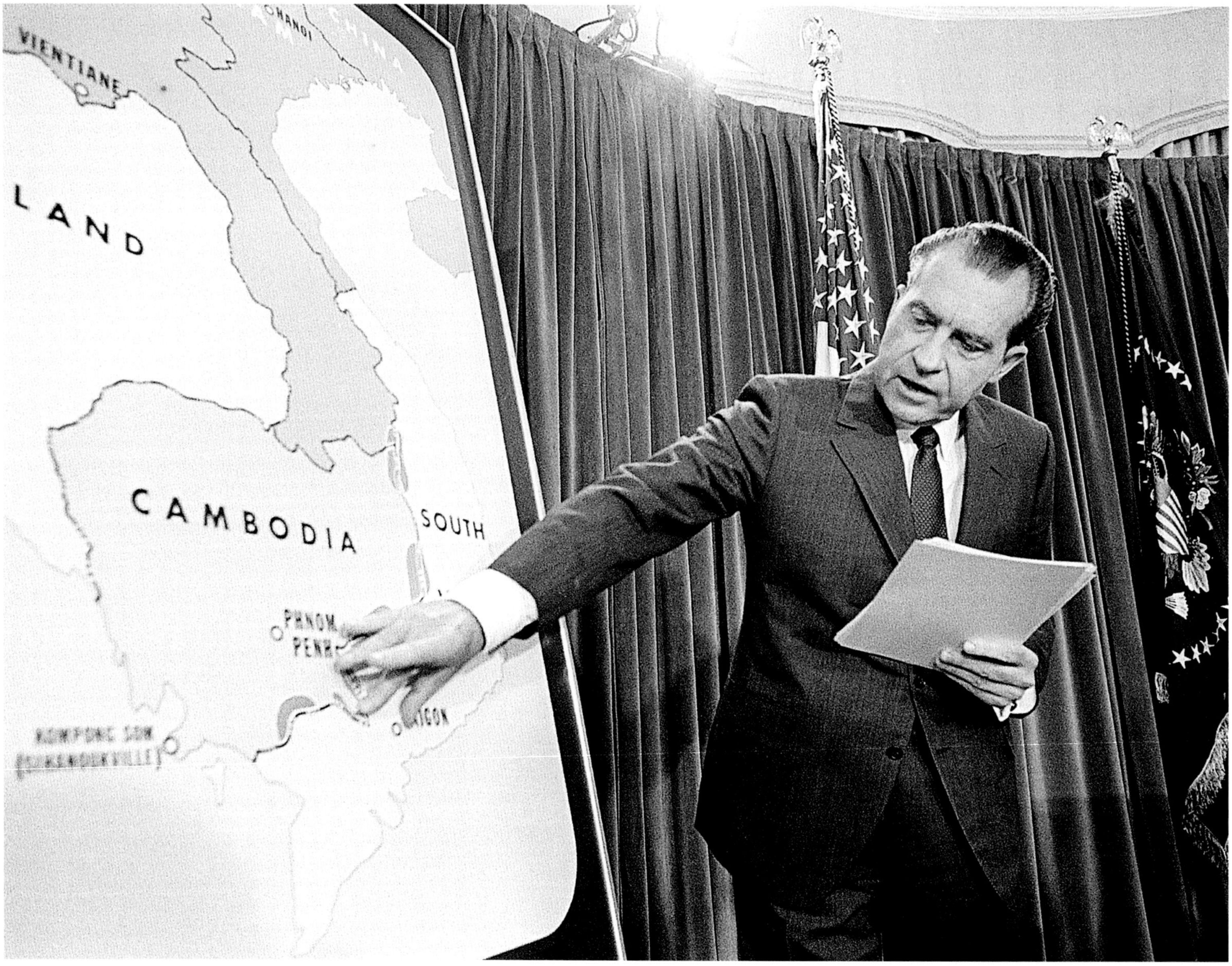

POL POT AND KHMER ROUGE ATROCITIES

In 1962, the short, rotund Pol Pot, leader of the Cambodian Communist Party, angered Prince Norodom Sihanouk and was chased into the jungle. Once there, Pot gathered an army called the "Red Cambodians" or "Khmer Rouge." As this guerrilla civil war raged, from 1969 to 1970, U.S. bombing raids dumped tons of bombs on N.V.A. Cambodian sanctuaries. In the process, they killed 150,000 peasants. Finding the countryside unsafe, hundreds of thousands of peasants moved into the capital, Phnom Penh. That's where Pol Pot found them when he and his teenage Khmer Rouge arrived in April, 1975. He then proceeded to kill everyone with purges and overwork. The "killing fields" became part of Cambodia.

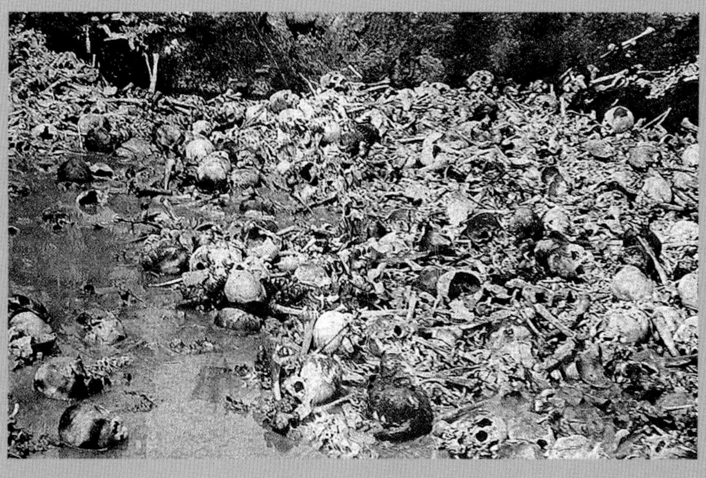

Vei and helped A.R.V.N. troops spearhead a drive into Laos. This limited lunge into a neighboring country fueled more protests from both Moscow and the American Congress. In February, the A.R.V.N., under Lieutenant General Hoang Xuan Lam, began Operation Lan Son 719, bent on repeating the success of the Cambodian invasion.

Once convinced that only the A.R.V.N. were advancing, the N.V.A. released the 70B Corps to attack. On February 15 the A.R.V.N. attack stalled. By March 1 three N.V.A. divisions were hammering the A.R.V.N. American B-52 bombers flattened an area around Tchepone to enable A.R.V.N. helicopters to land and bring out troops. The retreat had become a rout as American helicopter pilots risked their lives to lift overloaded 'copters from hot L.Z.s as panicked A.R.V.N. clamored to escape.

Both Saigon and Hanoi claimed the invasion and its repulse as a victory. The U.S. military was firmly convinced the A.R.V.N. stood no chance without Allied support—support that was on its way out of the country.

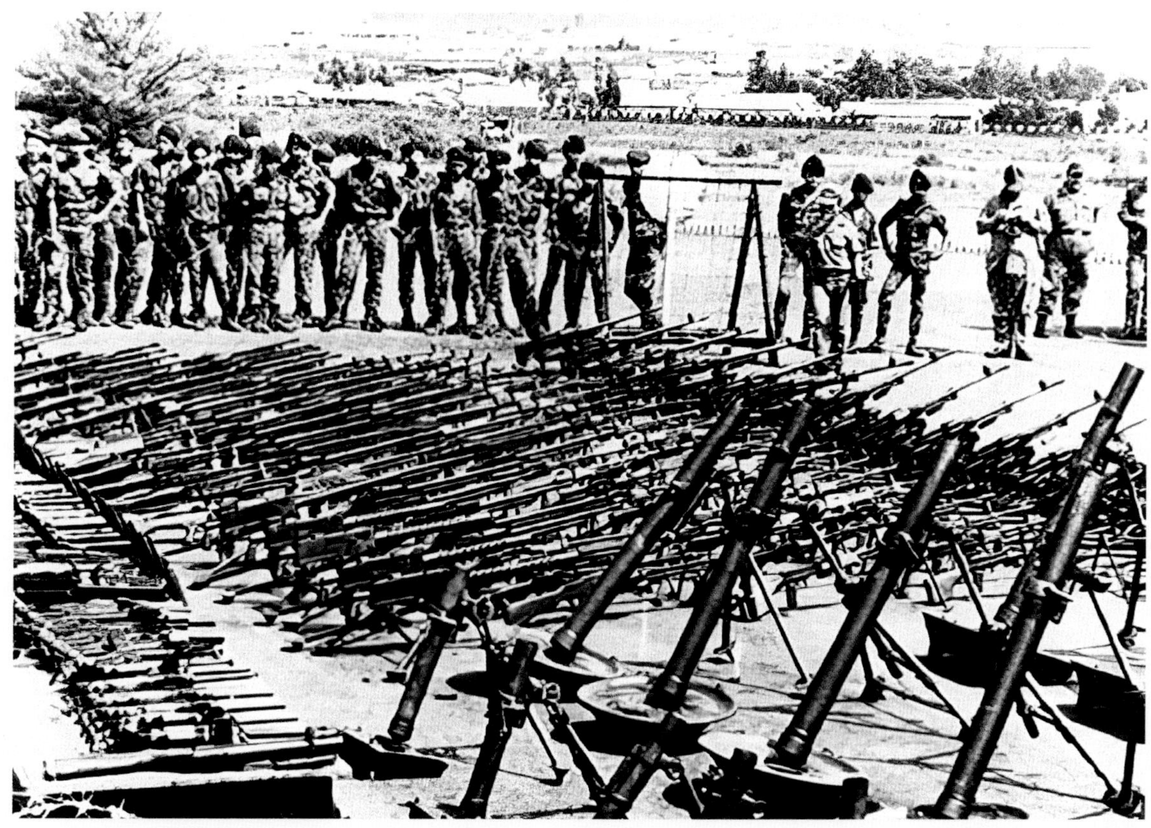

Above: A pile of skulls and bones are all that remain of Cambodian citizens rounded up by the feared Khmer Rouge militias who were busy "ethnic cleansing" their country of Vietnamese who had migrated there over the years during the invasions and revolutions in their own country. Murder and torture centers were established throughout Cambodia, leaving the bodies of victims to fertilize the "killing fields."

Left: A vast number of N.V.A. weapons and supplies were captured by the A.R.V.N. during their incursion into Cambodia and Laos. Here is one stock pile that also contains weapons such as light machine guns, and 60mm and 82mm mortars which have been recaptured from enemy hands.

THE EASTER OFFENSIVE

ON FEBRUARY 21–28, 1972, PRESIDENT RICHARD NIXON VISITED MAO TSE-TUNG IN CHINA TO REESTABLISH DIPLOMATIC RELATIONS. THIS VISIT WORRIED HANOI. GENERAL GIAP DECIDED TO GAMBLE ON THREE SITUATIONS: THE DISAFFECTION WITH THE WAR IN THE U.S., THE ONGOING WITHDRAWAL OF AMERICAN TROOPS, AND THE DEFEAT OF A.R.V.N. FORCES DURING LAM SON 719. HE DECIDED TO ORDER 200,000 TROOPS TO MAKE A THREE-PRONG ATTACK ON QUANG TRI IN THE NORTH OF SOUTH VIETNAM, KONTUM IN THE CENTER AND AN LOC IN THE SOUTH. AS THE ATTACK ON QUANG TRI—NEAR THE DEMILITARIZED ZONE—STEPPED OFF ON APRIL 4, AN ANGRY NIXON WAS QUOTED, "THE BASTARDS HAVE NEVER BEEN BOMBED LIKE THEY'RE GOING TO BE BOMBED THIS TIME."

B-52 strikes began at the D.M.Z. and rolled over targets as far back as 145 miles into North Vietnam. Nine days later N.V.A. divisions attacked An Loc. While the bombs continued to rain down on targets in the North, anti-war demonstrations began in the U.S. and the North Vietnamese returned to the Paris negotiations.

With the bombing support, the A.R.V.N. abandoned Quang Tri to the N.V.A. and fled south. During their retreat, South Vietnamese Army pilots managed to drop napalm on one of their own villages. As this N.V.A Easter Offensive raged on three sides, American troop strength dropped to 69,000. To compensate for this troop withdrawal, President Nixon authorized acceleration in bombing with Operation Linebacker. More flights of B-52s rose from bases in Guam and Thailand to hit targets in the north.

Surface-to-air missile sites were targeted by U.S.A.F. F-105 Wild Weasel hunter-killer teams, and F-111 fighter-bombers bombed N.V.A. MiG-21 fighter bases. The B-52s had electronic protection systems against the homing S.A.M.s, but the systems only worked as long as the three-cell flights flew in close formation. If one plane broke away, the protection envelope disappeared. As harbors, roads, bridges, and supply facilities went up in flames, B-52s were being hit with greater frequency. The mining of Haiphong harbor brought international condemnation to the U.S.

Gradually, however, the bombing throttled North Vietnam's ability to supply its troops and the A.R.V.N. retook Quang Tri while other N.V.A. attacks stalled. Soon, high- and low-level American bombing and long-range naval gunfire aided the A.R.V.N. advancing everywhere. By October 22, Linebacker ended after dropping 125,000 tons of bombs in 40,000 sorties. General Vo Nguyen Giap, the hero of Dien Bien Phu in 1954, was

N.V.A. ANTI-AIRCRAFT WEAPONS

Without an effective air force to achieve battlefield superiority, good defensive fire was needed to have some kind of parity. The N.V.A. had three effective anti-aircraft weapons. The Soviet DShK 12.7mm machine gun offered a mechanical computer aiming device that was effective on ground attack aircraft. The crew-served Soviet 37mm anti-aircraft gun, when used in massed firing set-ups, had a high success rate with well-trained crews. The prime weapon was the Soviet SA-2 S.A.M. The missiles were guided to their targets by dual-radar tracking systems and had an effective record against both jet fighter-bombers and high-altitude B-52s.

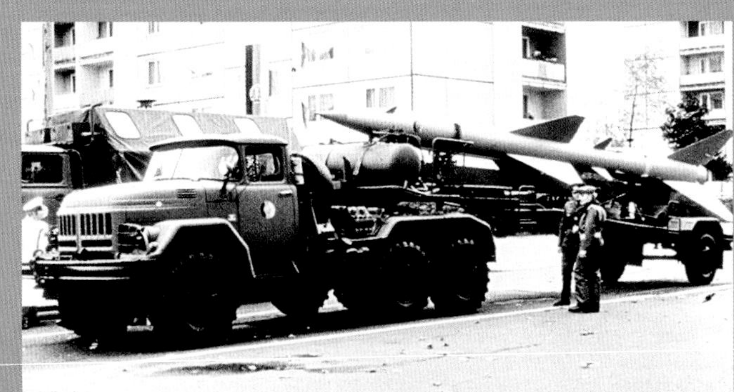

Above: A Soviet S.A.M. on its mobile transporter is on its way to a launch site in or near Hanoi to counter American bombers and fighter-bombers. This surface-to-air missile was guided by as many as two radar units, but could be defeated with electronic signals emitted by the B-52s and by rapidly executed maneuvers by the fighters.

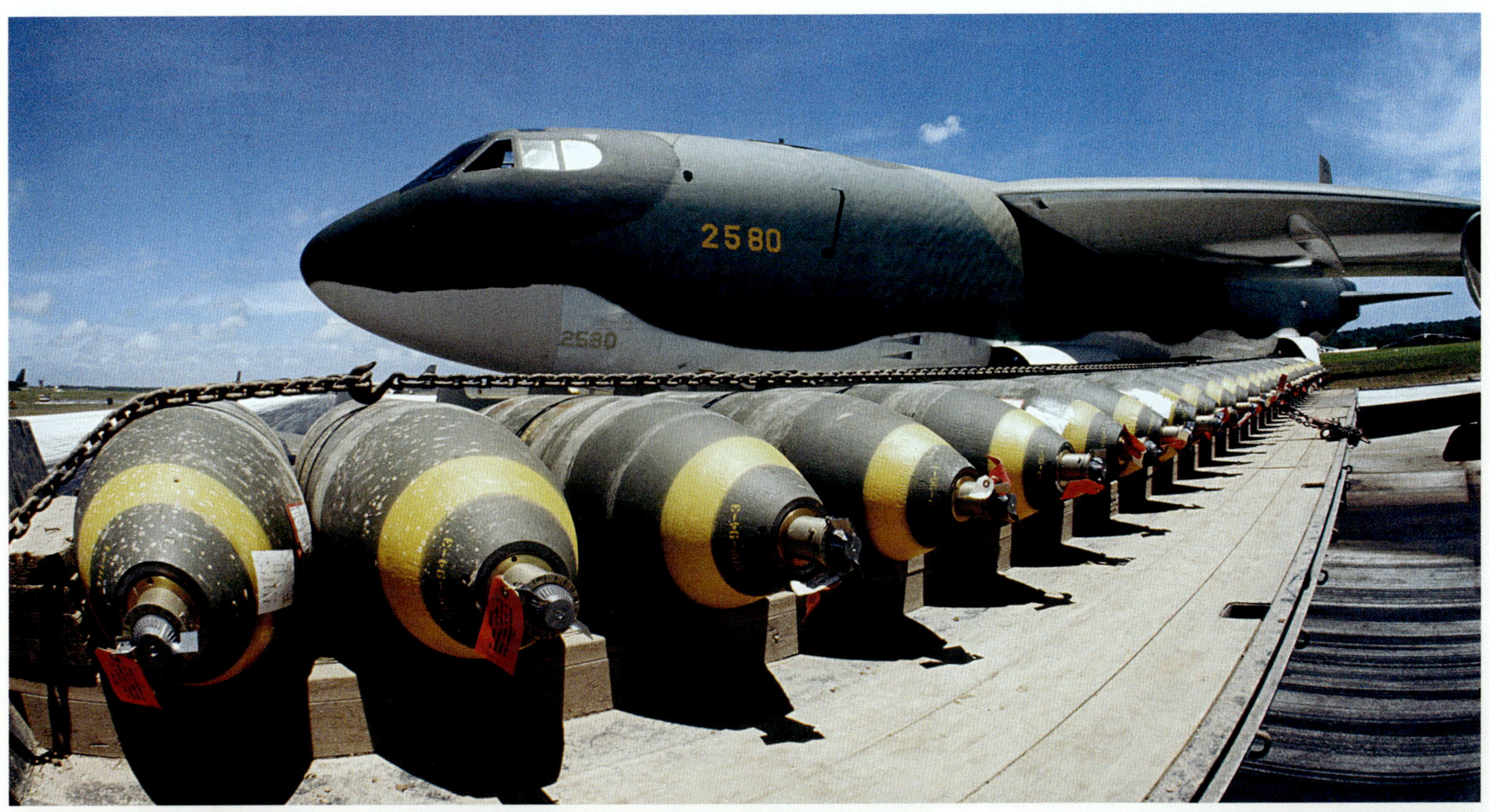

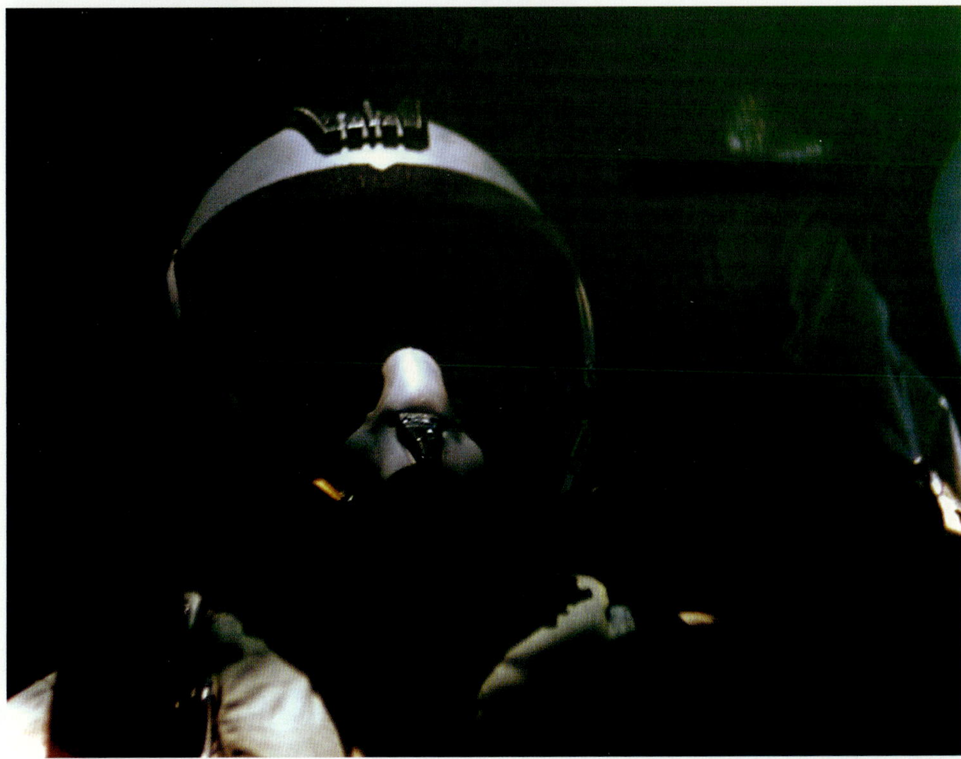

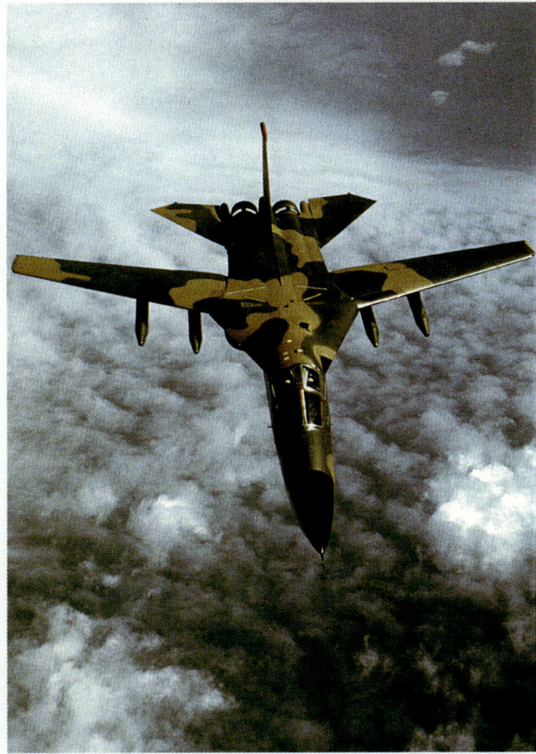

Above top: During the day, a B-52 Stratofortress awaits its cargo of 84 iron bombs on the tarmac at Andersen Air Force Base in the U.S. Territory of Guam. Designed to carry nuclear weapons, the B-52 had a maximum capacity of 60,000 pounds of ordnance between its bomb bay and hard points under its wings.

Above left: Photo of an air crewman aboard a B-52 bomber, illuminated only by minimal cockpit lighting as he watches his duty station instruments during the long flight from the U.S. base in Thailand to the target near Hanoi, North Vietnam in 1972.

Above right: An F-111 "swing-wing" fighter with wings fully extended for low and slow flight. After considerable teething problems, the F-111 emerged as a first-class fighter-bomber that kept many MiG squadrons pinned to their airfields by low-level raids during high-level horizontal bombing runs by the B-52s. They also knocked out many N.V.A. S.A.M. sites.

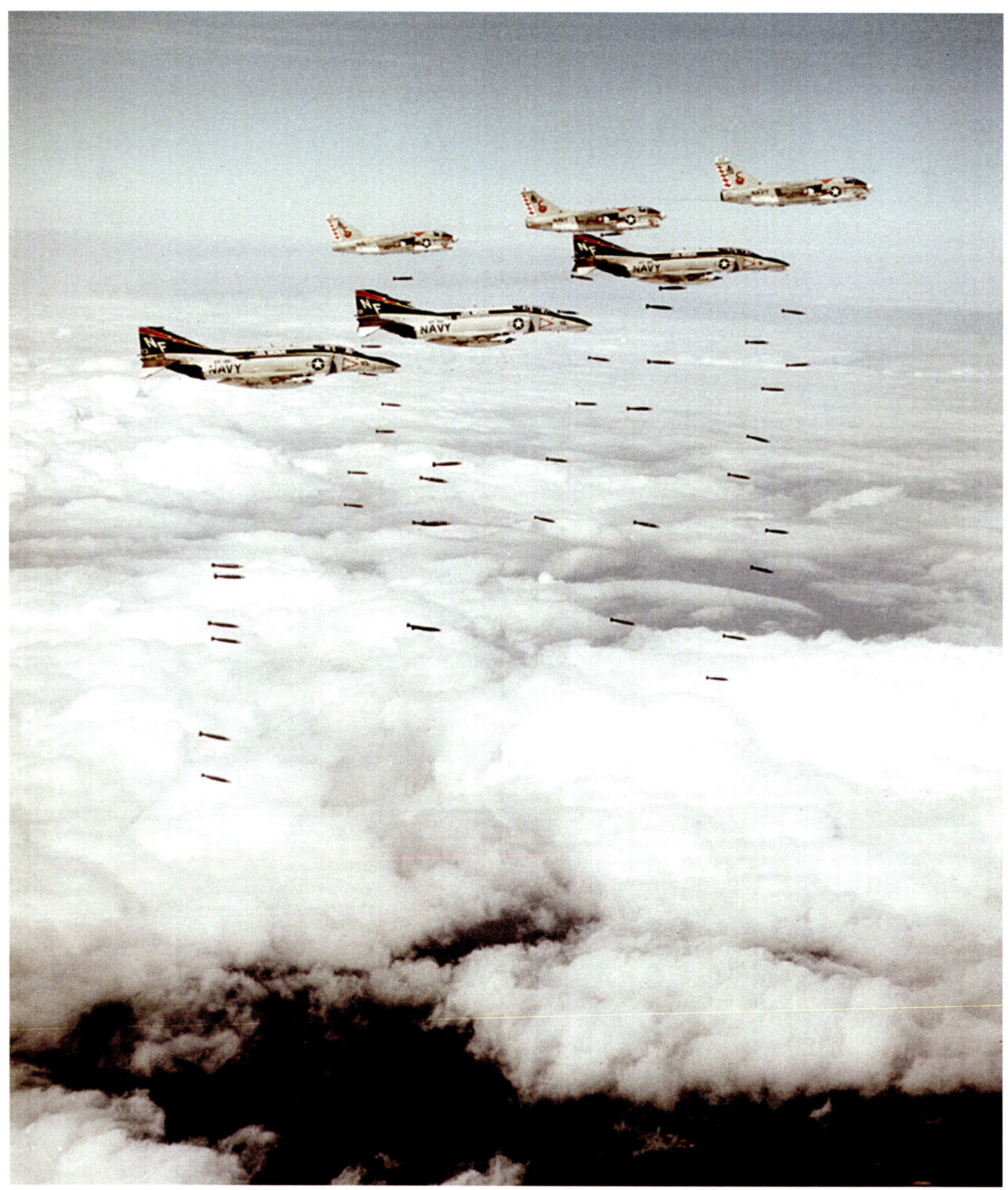
NF
NAVY
NF
NAVY
NF
NAVY

ousted from command as the Easter Offensive ended in failure with 40,000 dead N.V.A.

But soon diplomacy also failed, and by November 30 all American troops had been withdrawn from Vietnam except for 16,000 advisers to aid the A.R.V.N. Once again, North Vietnam balked at the negotiations and on December 18, Linebacker II began an 11-day nightmare of day-and-night bombing—adding Hanoi and Haiphong to the target list—that cost 15 of approximately 220 B-52 bombers, shot down by S.A.M.s. After a 36-hour Christmas Eve cease-fire, Nixon and Kissinger sent an ultimatum and North Vietnam agreed to return to negotiations. On December 29, Linebacker II ended.

MiG-21 FIGHTER

Some North Vietnamese pilots preferred flying the more agile MiG-17 to the less forgiving MiG-21. The MiG-21 was a supersonic, delta-wing, missile and gun dogfighter that arrived in the late 1960s. Its speed and gun armament forced U.S. planes to install guns on their missile-only Phantom F-4 fighters. The MiGs had success against less-maneuverable F-105 Thunderchiefs and subsonic planes in aerial combat, but had to be tricked or coaxed by numbers into fights with Phantoms. Only one B-52 was shot down by a MiG-21 over Hanoi by V.P.A.F. pilot Pham Tuán on December 26, 1972. U.S.A.F. F-4 and A-4D fighters downed 68 MiG-21s.

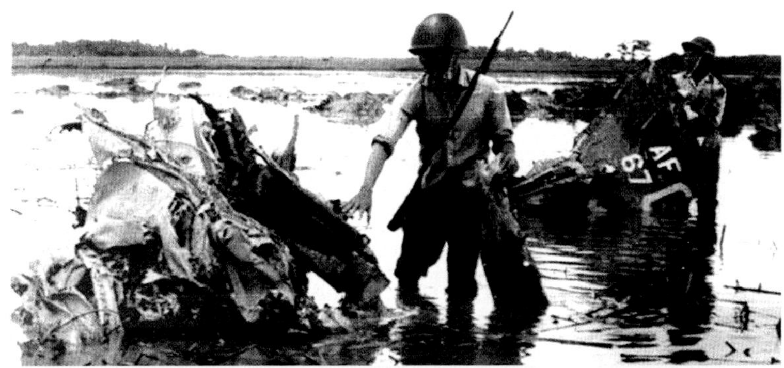

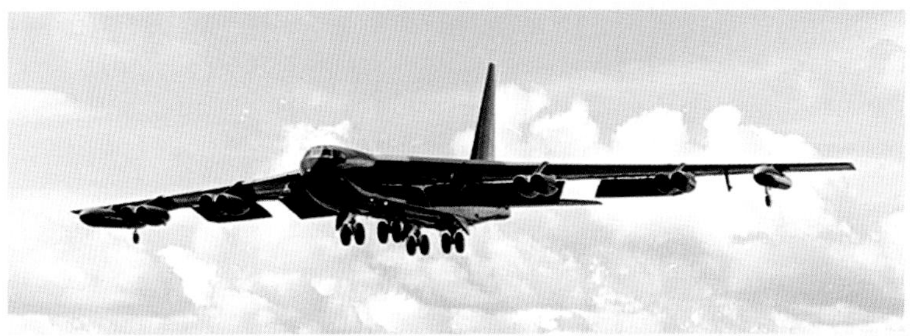

Opposite: A flight of F-4 Phantom fighter-bombers unload their cargos over strategic targets in North Vietnam during the Linebacker missions that countered the N.V.A. Easter Offensive attacking targets in the South.

Above left: A helmeted N.V.A. looks over the wreckage of an F-111 fighter-bomber brought down either by a S.A.M. or by one of the hundreds of anti-aircraft sites that ringed Hanoi. Many American pilots parachuted into captivity until after the war ended. Their treatment sometimes included torture and beatings by soldiers and civilians.

Above right: A B-52 bomber returns to its Guam base with wheels and flaps down. The round-trip to Vietnam took hours and during the Linebacker raids, pilot and crew fatigue was considerable. S.A.M.s could only be electronically defeated if the B-52s held tight formations over their target.

Below: Families and children run in a panic down a South Vietnamese road. The young girl received severe burns after A.R.V.N. pilots accidentally dropped napalm on her village.

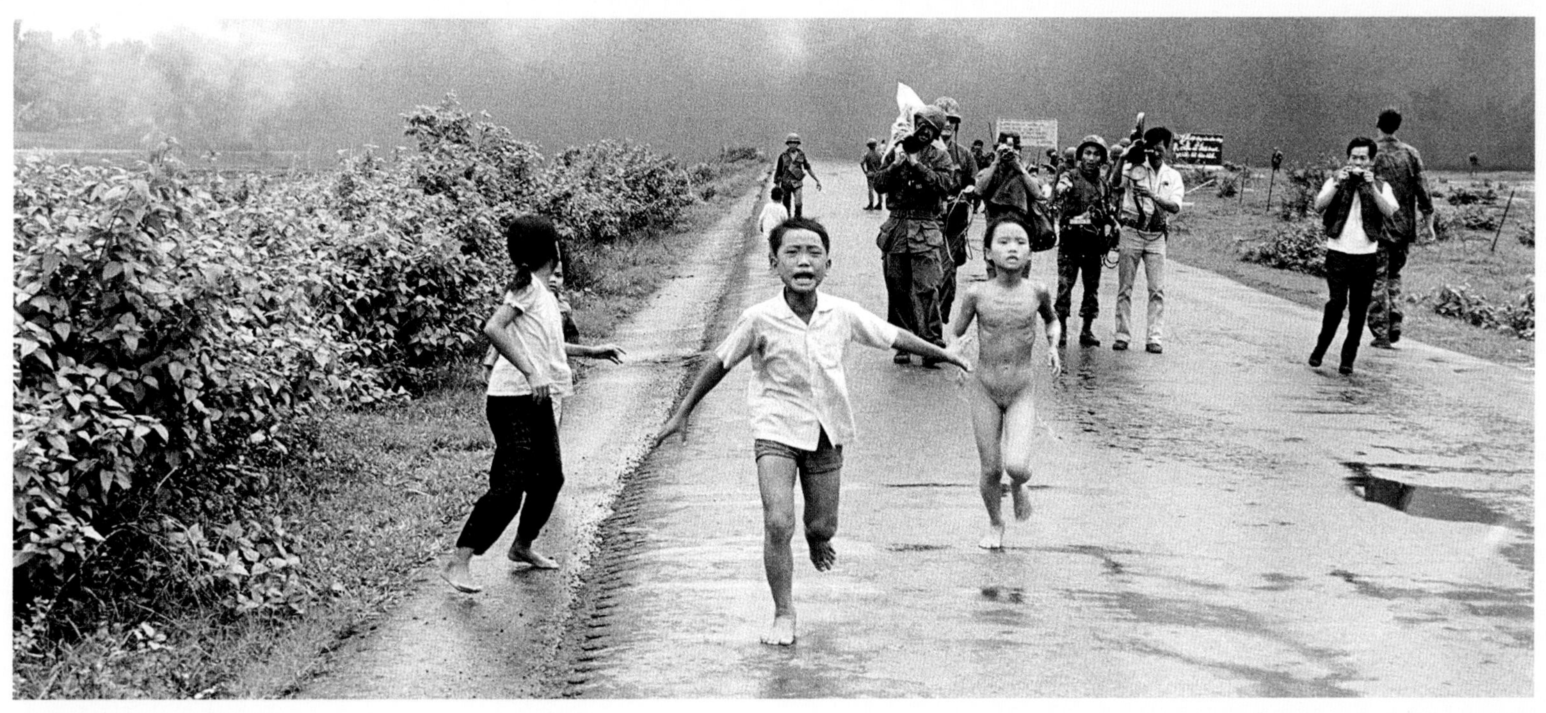

THE U.S. DEPARTS

ON JANUARY 27, 1973, THE UNITED STATES AND NORTH VIETNAM SIGNED THE PARIS PEACE ACCORDS, BRINGING WHAT PRESIDENT NIXON CALLED "PEACE WITH HONOR." THE U.S. AGREED TO WITHDRAW ALL PERSONNEL WITHIN 60 DAYS AND THE NORTH VIETNAMESE AGREED TO RETURN ALL AMERICAN P.O.W.S. NORTH VIETNAMESE SOLDIERS, NUMBERING SOME 150,000, WERE ALLOWED TO REMAIN IN THE SOUTH, AS TWO GOVERNMENTS—ONE LED BY VIET CONG, THE OTHER BY PRESIDENT THIEU—CLAIMED CONTROL OVER THE COUNTRY. EXCEPT FOR EMBASSY STAFF, THE LAST AMERICAN SOLDIERS DEPARTED BY MARCH 29. IN APRIL, PRESIDENT NIXON BROUGHT PRESIDENT THIEU TO SAN CLEMENTE, NIXON'S CALIFORNIA HOME, AND RENEWED AN EARLIER SECRET PROMISE THAT THE U.S. WOULD "RESPOND MILITARILY" IF NORTH VIETNAM VIOLATED THE PEACE AGREEMENT. AT THE END OF THAT MONTH, HOWEVER, THE WATERGATE SCANDAL HAD CAUSED THE RESIGNATIONS OF NIXON AIDES H.R. HALDEMAN AND JOHN EHRLICHMAN, AND NIXON'S PRIORITIES SHIFTED TO SELF-PRESERVATION.

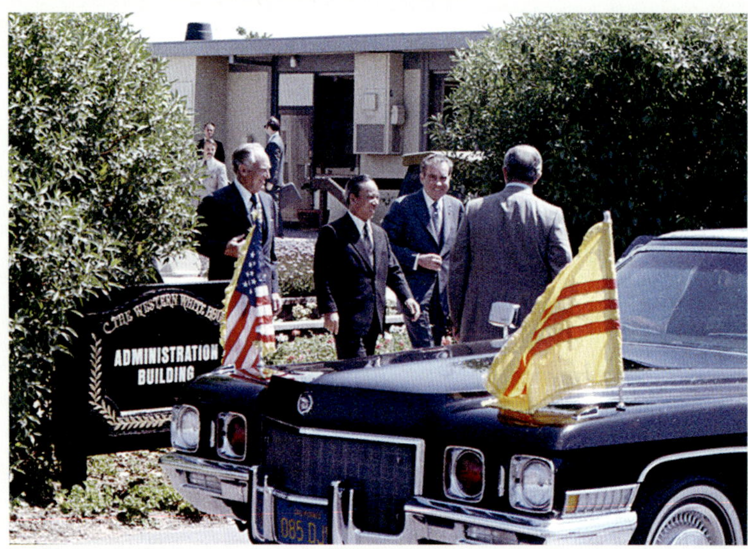

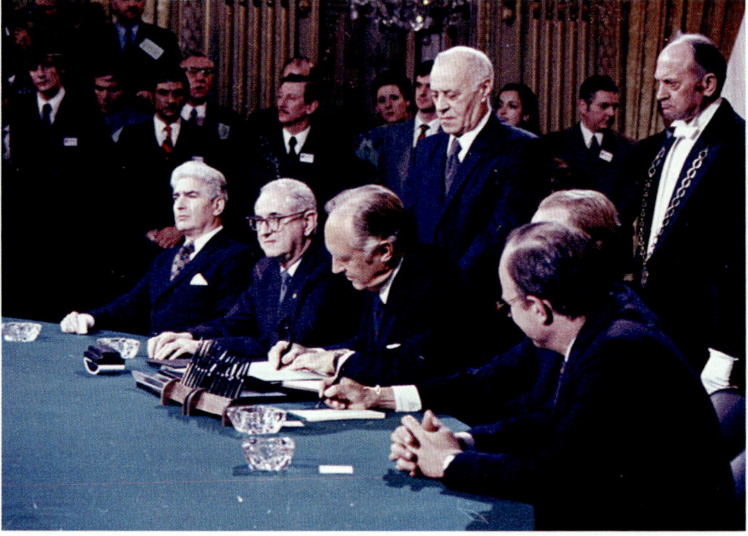

The longest war in American history had lasted 15 years, and ended in defeat. Two million Americans served in Vietnam. Of the 500,000 who saw combat, 47,244 had been killed. The seriously wounded numbered 153,329 military personnel, and there were 10,446 non-combat deaths. By the end of 1973, over 2,400 P.O.W.s/Missing in Action (M.I.A.s) were unaccounted for.

The Case-Church Amendment, which was passed by Congress on June 19, 1973, forbade any U.S. involvement in south-east Asia as of August 15. With that vote, North Vietnam no longer had to fear U.S. bombing or any other American military responses to their actions.

Above left: President Richard M. Nixon invited South Vietnam President Thieu to the president's San Clemente, California, residence to assure Thieu that the United States would do everything within its power to prevent a Communist takeover in the South. President Nixon was facing impeachment charges for the Watergate political scandal at that time and resigned later in 1974.

Above right: The Paris Peace Accords were signed in 1973 by the governments of North Vietnam (D.R.V.), South Vietnam, and the United States, as well as the Provisional Revolutionary Government (P.R.G.) that represented South Vietnamese revolutionaries. The intent was to establish peace in Vietnam and an end to the Vietnam War. The accords ended direct U.S. military involvement and temporarily ended the war.

Opposite: A former prisoner of war runs to meet his family after a long absence. Once the repatriation papers were signed, regular "Hanoi Taxis" (United States Air Force Transport planes) made runs to American bases where the P.O.W.s could eat, shower, and get new clothes. Then it was a long hop to the nearest Air Force base for reuniting with families.

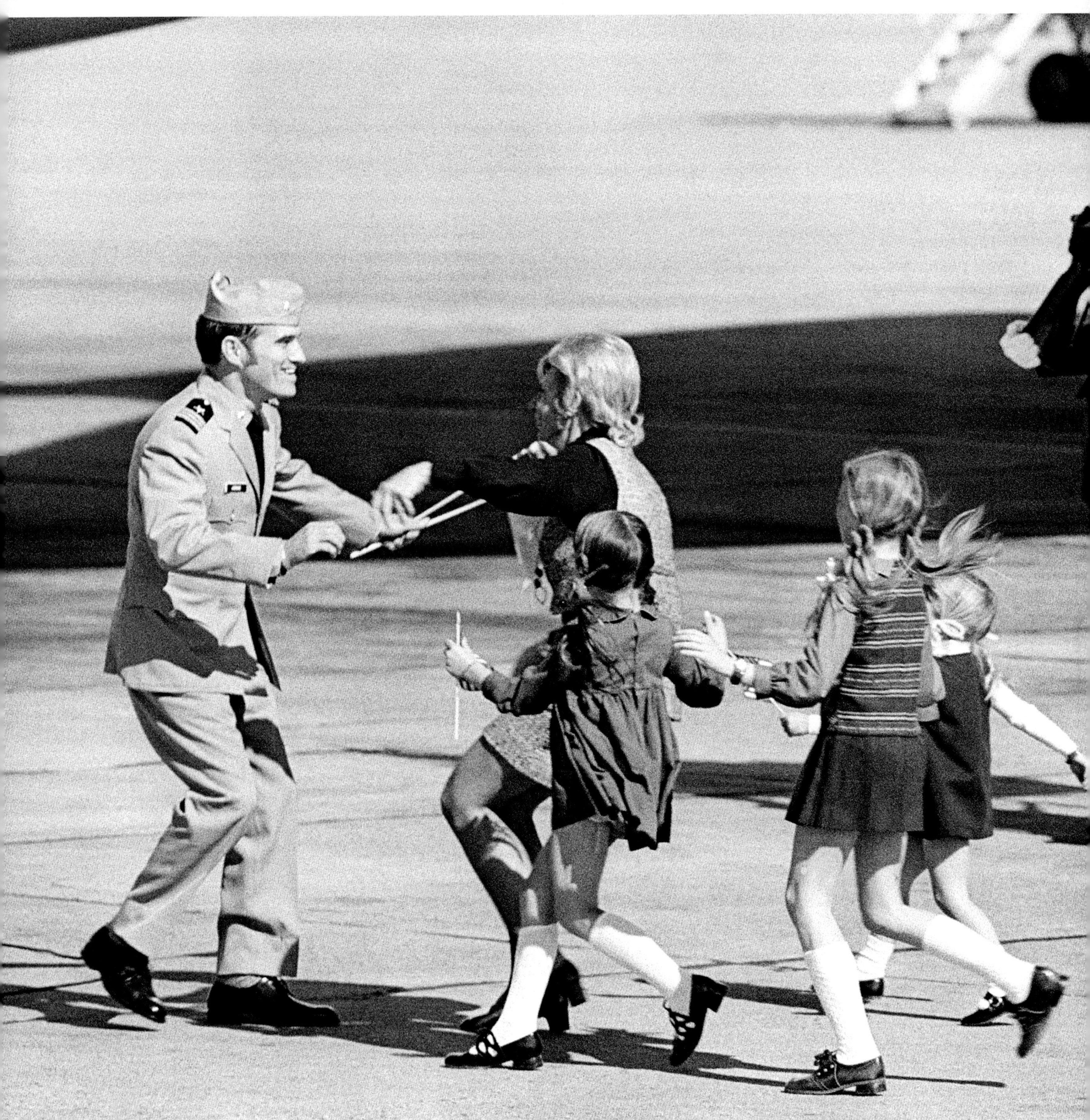

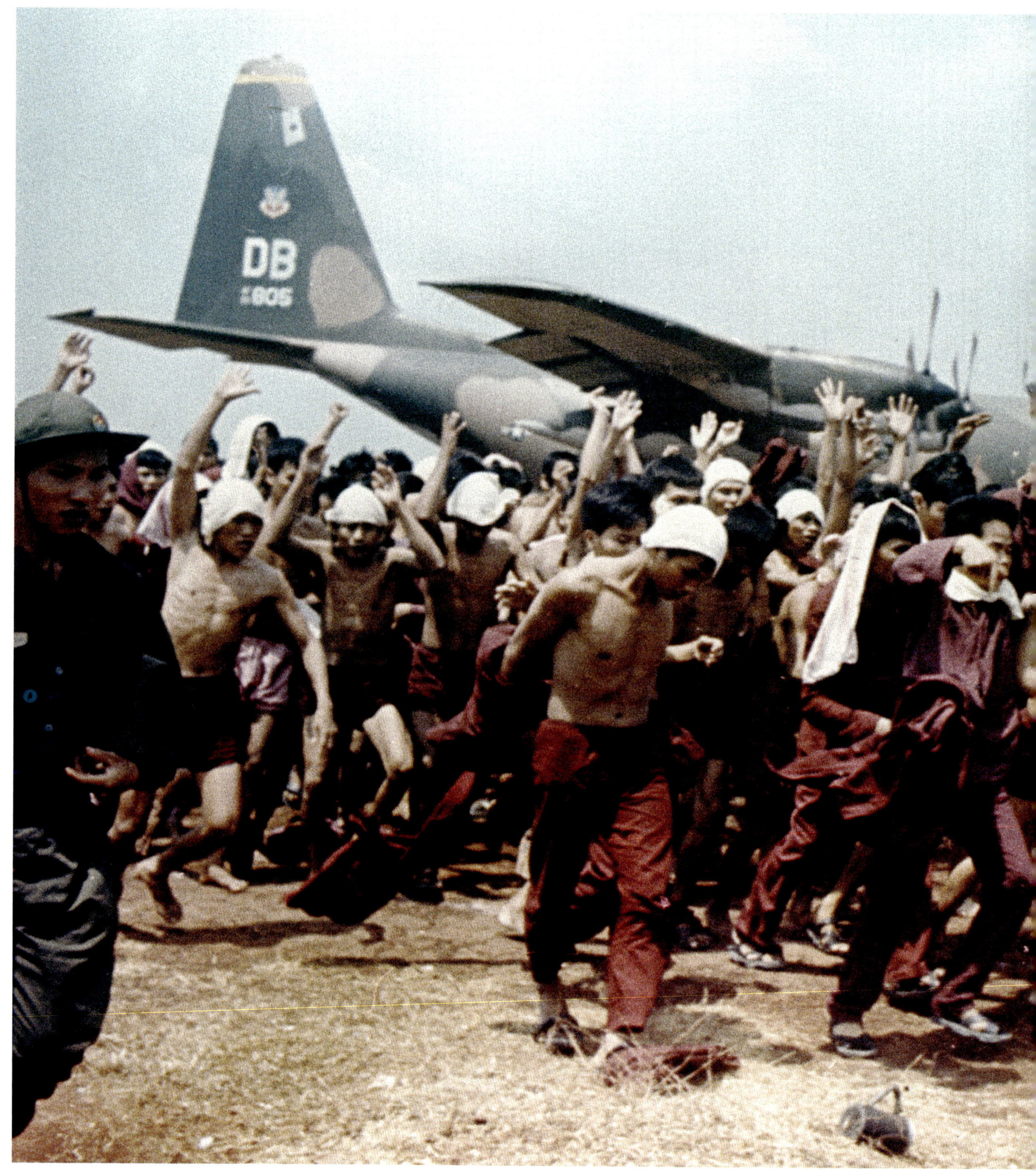
DB
805

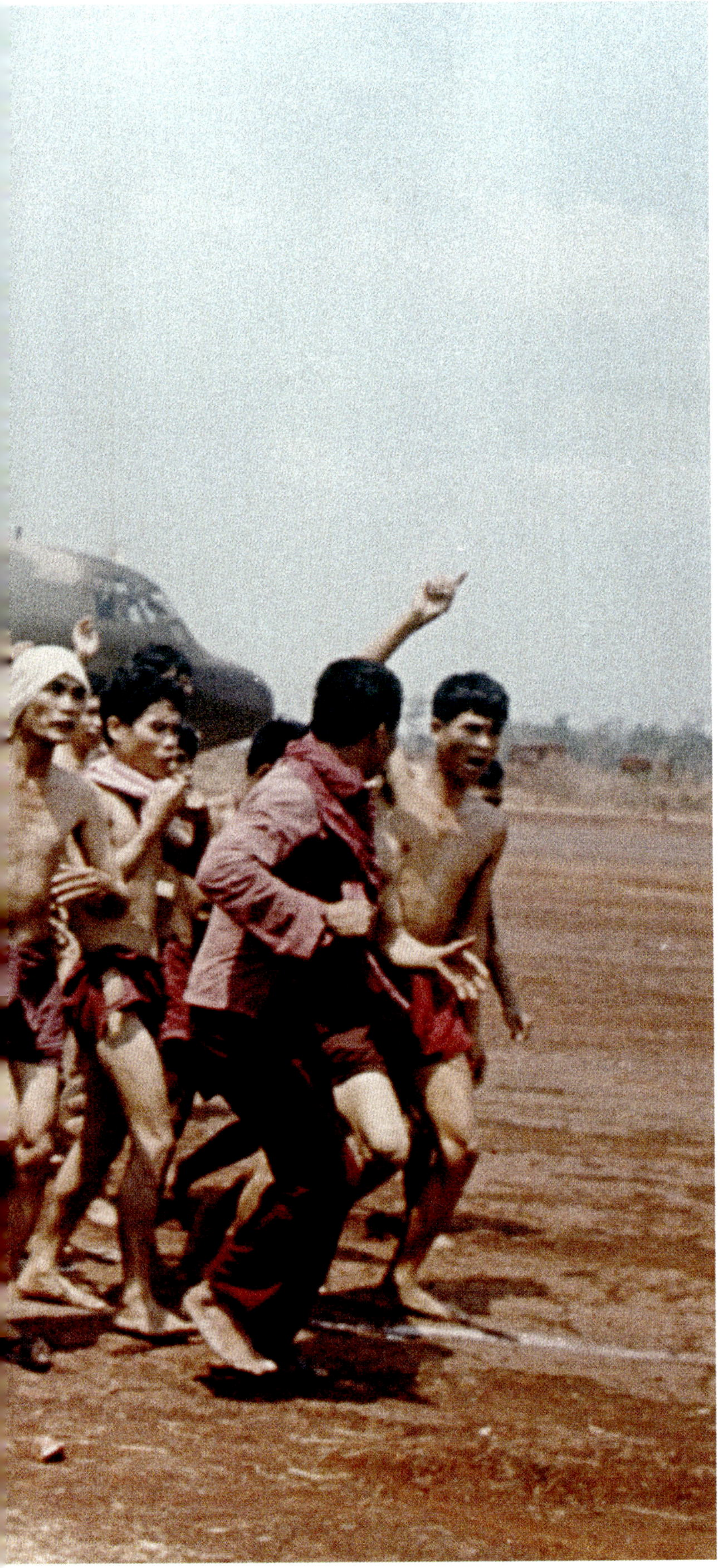

U.S.A.F. AIRCRAFT WITHDRAWAL

By 1973, the United States' involvement in Vietnam had virtually come to an end. Political solutions and deals were happening in Washington and Hanoi. The bombing in the North was over. B-52 fleets were rotating out of Thailand and Guam, fighters and fighter-bombers staged out of Vietnamese air bases, and at sea, the Crusaders, A-4Ds, and F-4 Phantoms were moved below decks to make room for evacuation helicopters that were making round trips with V.I.P. refugees as the N.V.A. drive headed south in 1974.

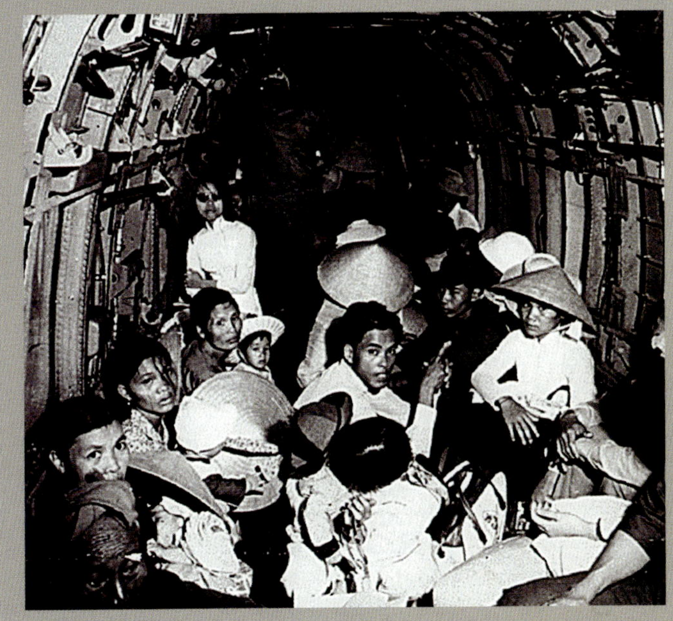

Above: South Vietnamese refugees crowded into a Chinook helicopter heading for a U.S. aircraft carrier. They could bring only what they could carry and needed a pass to show they had worked for U.S. or South Vietnam in some capacity which had endangered their lives.

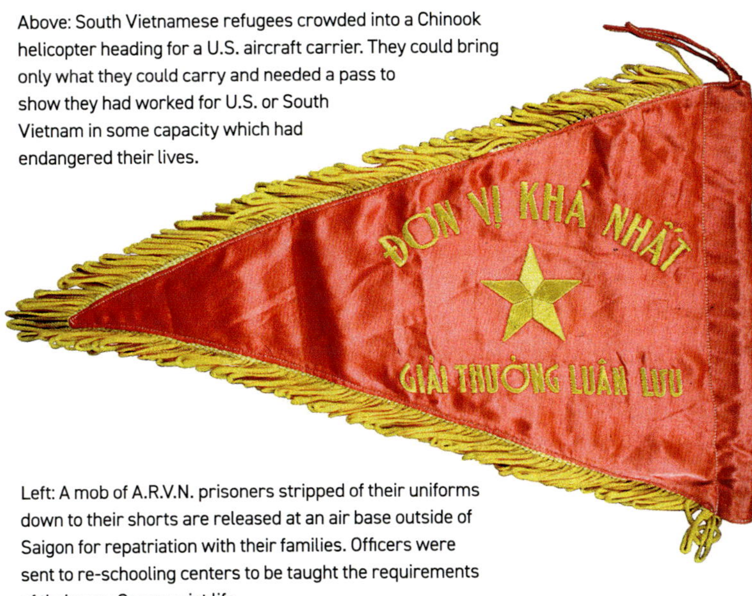

Left: A mob of A.R.V.N. prisoners stripped of their uniforms down to their shorts are released at an air base outside of Saigon for repatriation with their families. Officers were sent to re-schooling centers to be taught the requirements of their new Communist life.

Above: An N.V.A. battle flag "emulation" pennant.

After paying the South Vietnamese $2.8 billion in aid, Congress continued to dismantle the structure of presidential war powers. Hearings about Nixon's 3,500 "secret" bombings of Cambodia brought on the first call for the President's impeachment. In October, Vice President Spiro Agnew was convicted of bribery and replaced with Representative Gerald R. Ford. Interest in Vietnam's problems continued to dwindle even after the N.V.A. destroyed large fuel tanks holding 18 million gallons near Saigon. Freed from American interdiction raids, N.V.A. supply dumps and troop reserves throughout the South swelled to capacity. The A.R.V.N. were stretched dangerously thin and had prepared few fallback positions in case of invasion. The Americans had always come to their rescue. But Congress had begun drawing up articles of impeachment against President Nixon for his obstruction of justice in the Watergate scandal. On August 9, 1974, President Thieu was stunned when his only apparent American ally resigned the presidency and was replaced by Ford.

Shackled by Congress, Ford could only use threats of diplomatic sanctions after a North Vietnamese offensive in the province of Phuoc Long on December 13, 1974. Two divisions, including tanks and artillery, struck A.R.V.N. positions only 80 miles from Saigon. The South Vietnamese rushed Ranger battalions with air support into the fight. The Rangers were overwhelmed, and 20 R.V.N.A.F. aircraft were shot down by SA-7 missiles. With Phuoc Long province in their hands, North Vietnamese leaders scheduled a meeting in Hanoi for December 18, 1974, to discuss their final offensive against the South.

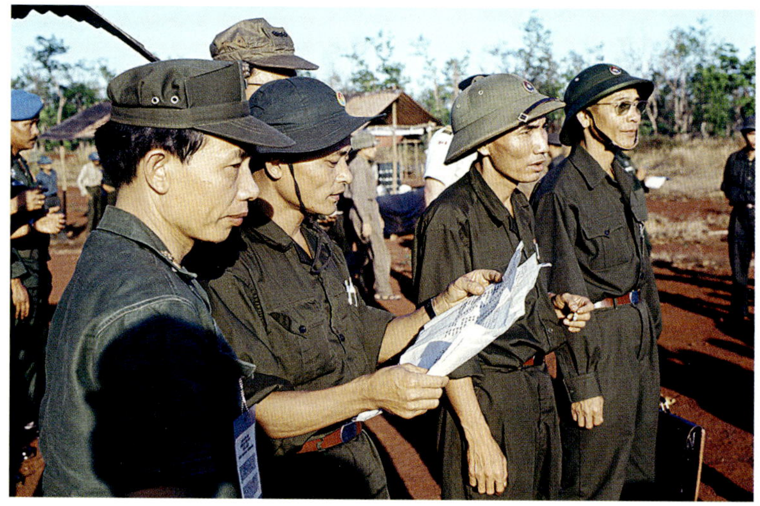

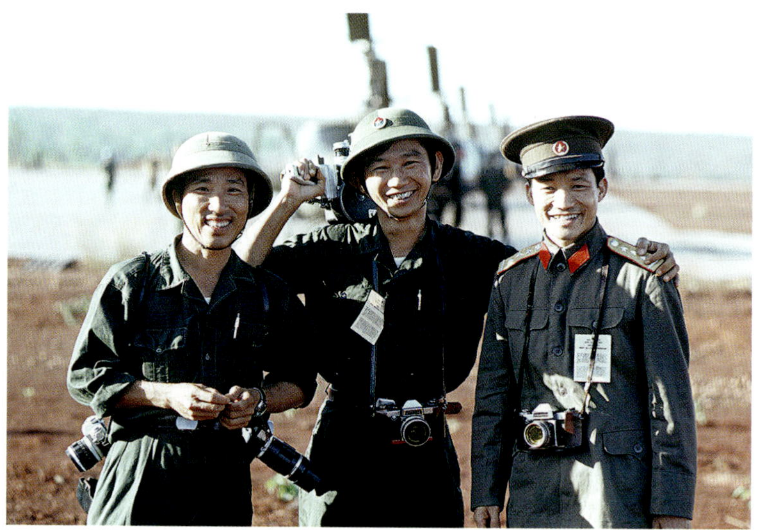

Top: An N.V.A. delegation of officers consult their lists before American P.O.W.s are escorted into U.S. custody in downtown Saigon after it had fallen. The P.O.W.s had been given civilian clothes for the exchange.

Middle: Just like tourists anywhere, three N.V.A. photographers pose for a photograph at the prisoner exchange event in Saigon (now Ho Chi Minh City) by one of their number.

Below: Cargo-carrying Chinook helicopters were used only for humanitarian relief as war ended. Food, supplies, and evacuating refugees were their primary tasks.

A.R.V.N. AND R.S.V.A.F. SUPPORT REMAINING

Air bases throughout South Vietnam were now home to the remaining Huey helicopters, Caribou transport planes, and T-28 propeller-driven ground attack planes of the Airborne A.R.V.N., as well as some small A-37 Dragonfly jets for ground troop support. In the field, the A.R.V.N. could count on their remaining M48 tanks and M113 armored personnel carriers, but with the aid money from the U.S. gone, along with spare parts, maintenance was impossible. Artillery ammunition was restricted in many cases to only a few rounds per gun and transportation of guns to distant firebases was impossible without the big U.S. Chinook helicopters—which were now restricted to carrying humanitarian supplies and lifting out refugees as directed by the Paris Peace Treaty rules.

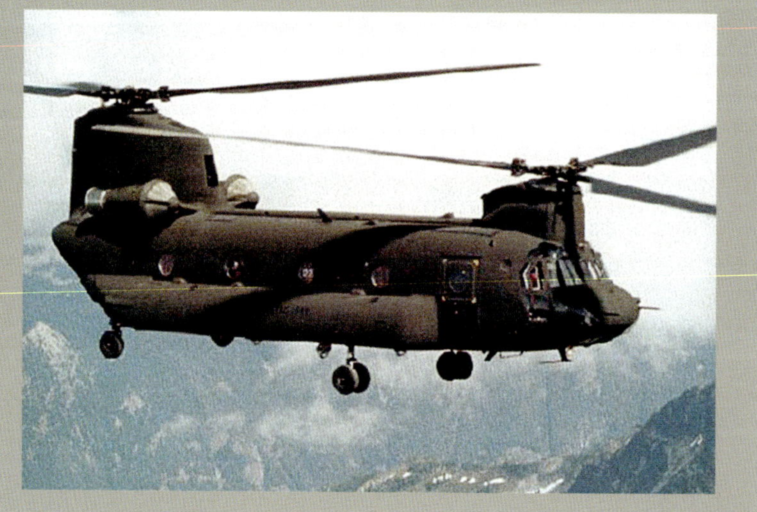

THE WHITE HOUSE

WASHINGTON

August 9, 1974

Dear Mr. Secretary:

I hereby resign the Office of President of the United States.

Sincerely,

Richard Nixon

11.35 AM

HK

The Honorable Henry A. Kissinger
The Secretary of State
Washington, D.C. 20520

NIXON RESIGNATION

One single sheet of paper was all that was needed to complete Richard M. Nixon's resignation from the presidency to avoid impeachment on August 9, 1974. Secretary of State Henry Kissinger initialed the document and it was passed on to Congress.

N.V.A. DRIVE INTO VIETNAM

WITH A GUTTURAL RUMBLE THE MODEL V-54 12-CYLINDER WATER-COOLED DIESEL ENGINE OF THE LEAD T-54 TANK FROM KHARKOV DIESEL FACTORY NO. 75 COUGHED TO LIFE. ONE BY ONE THE OTHER TANKS AT THE EDGE OF THE WOODS STARTED THEIR ENGINES. WITH A PONDEROUS CLANKING, THE ARMORED REGIMENT STARTED TOWARD BAN ME THUOT, A KEY POSITION FOR THE A.R.V.N. IN CENTRAL VIETNAM, SOME DISTANCE BEHIND THE MAIN COMBAT ZONE ALONG THE BORDER WITH CAMBODIA TO THE WEST. THERE THEY MET A.R.V.N. TROOPS PUTTING UP RESISTANCE, AN INEFFECTIVE L.A.W. ROCKET CAROMED OFF 200MM OF FRONTAL TURRET ARMOR. MACHINE-GUN BULLETS RATTLED WITH NO MORE EFFECT THAN A HANDFUL OF GRAVEL. THE SQUADRON OF TANKS PAUSED, TURRETS ADJUSTED, AND A VOLLEY OF FIRE RIPPLED DOWN THE LINE OF 100MM-RIFLED GUNS. THE DEFENDERS BROKE AND RAN. SOME SHED THEIR UNIFORMS FOR CIVILIAN SHIRTS AND PANTS. OTHERS JUST RAN. OFTEN, THE WAY WAS LED BY THE OFFICERS.

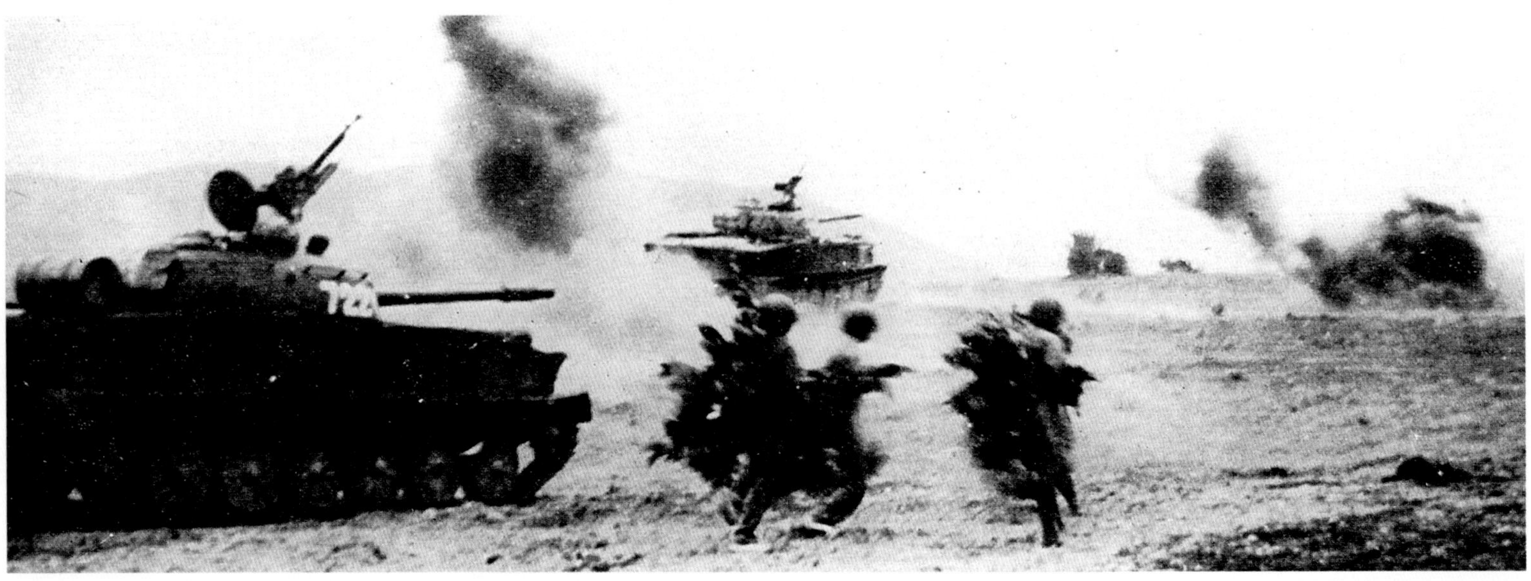

On March 10, 1975, the 316th and 320th N.V.A. divisions overran Ban Me Thuot. The men ran to rescue their families who were staying nearby—a typical concern that caused many units to bolt.

The Ho Chi Minh Offensive had begun on March 1, with N.V.A. troops attacking further north at Kontum and Pleiku. With Ban Me Thuot now in Communist hands, President Nguyen Van Thieu of South Vietnam ordered the northern region to be abandoned to the enemy. The A.R.V.N. with their dependents—60,000 in all—streamed down Route 7B toward Tuy Hoa on the coast. The dilapidated bridges and ruined surface made the road a bad choice. Forty thousand never made it to Tuy Hoa. Most who did surrendered or perished there when the Communists arrived. Only 700 of 7,000 A.R.V.N. Rangers survived. This kind of slaughter became the rule as A.R.V.N. broke under poor leadership and rumors of deals with the Communists to hand over the northern provinces without a fight. But on occasion, as with the N.V.A. attack on

Above: T-54 tanks and N.V.A. soldiers in full field packs attack across an open plain, driving the A.R.V.N. forces south toward Saigon. Without U.S. air and artillery support, A.R.V.N. troops often deserted and fled with their families.

Opposite: N.V.A. uniformed troops, part of a heavy-weapons squad, manhandle a Czech T-21 82mm recoilless anti-tank gun, its mounting hardware, and H.E. rockets down a narrow jungle trail.

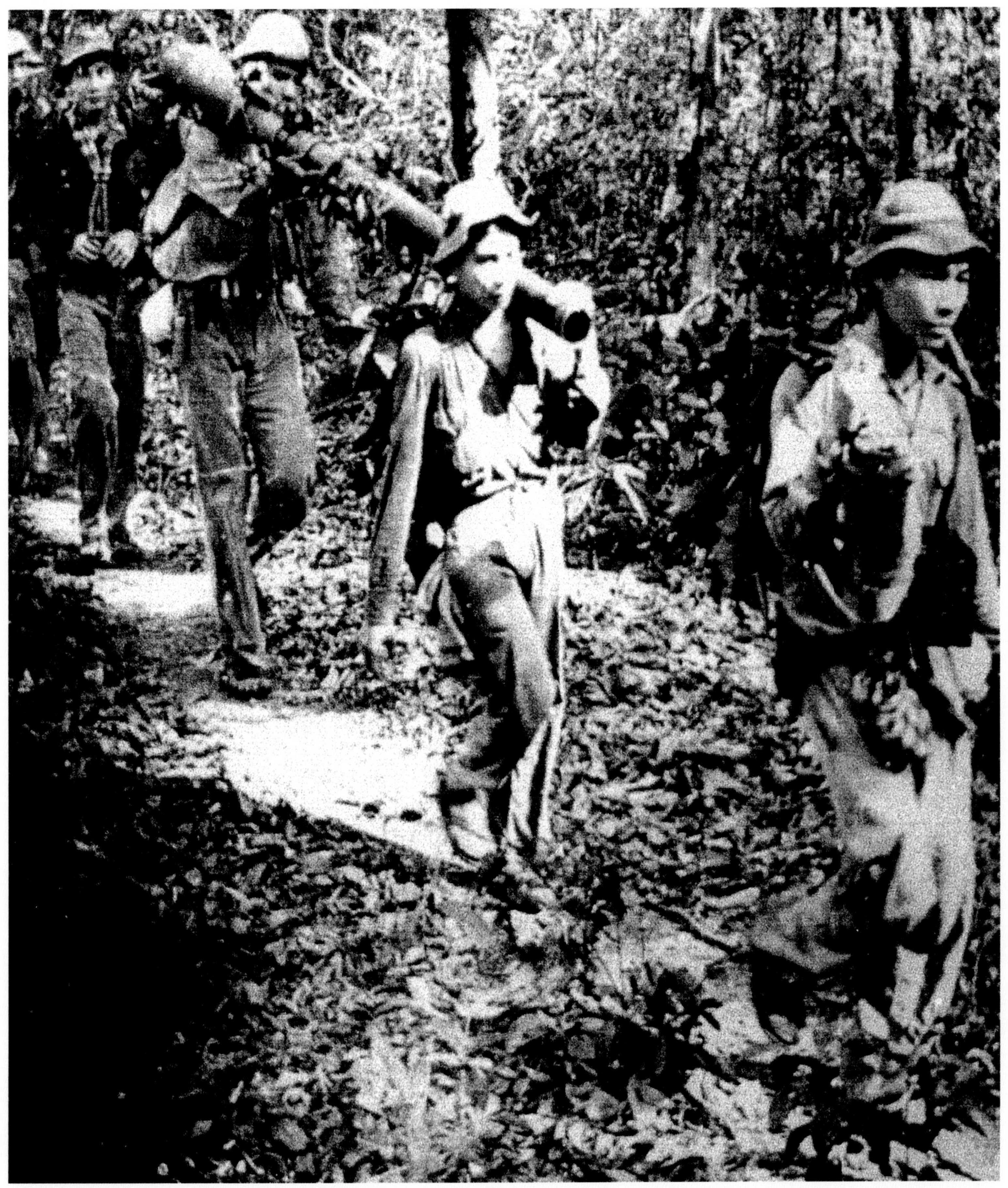

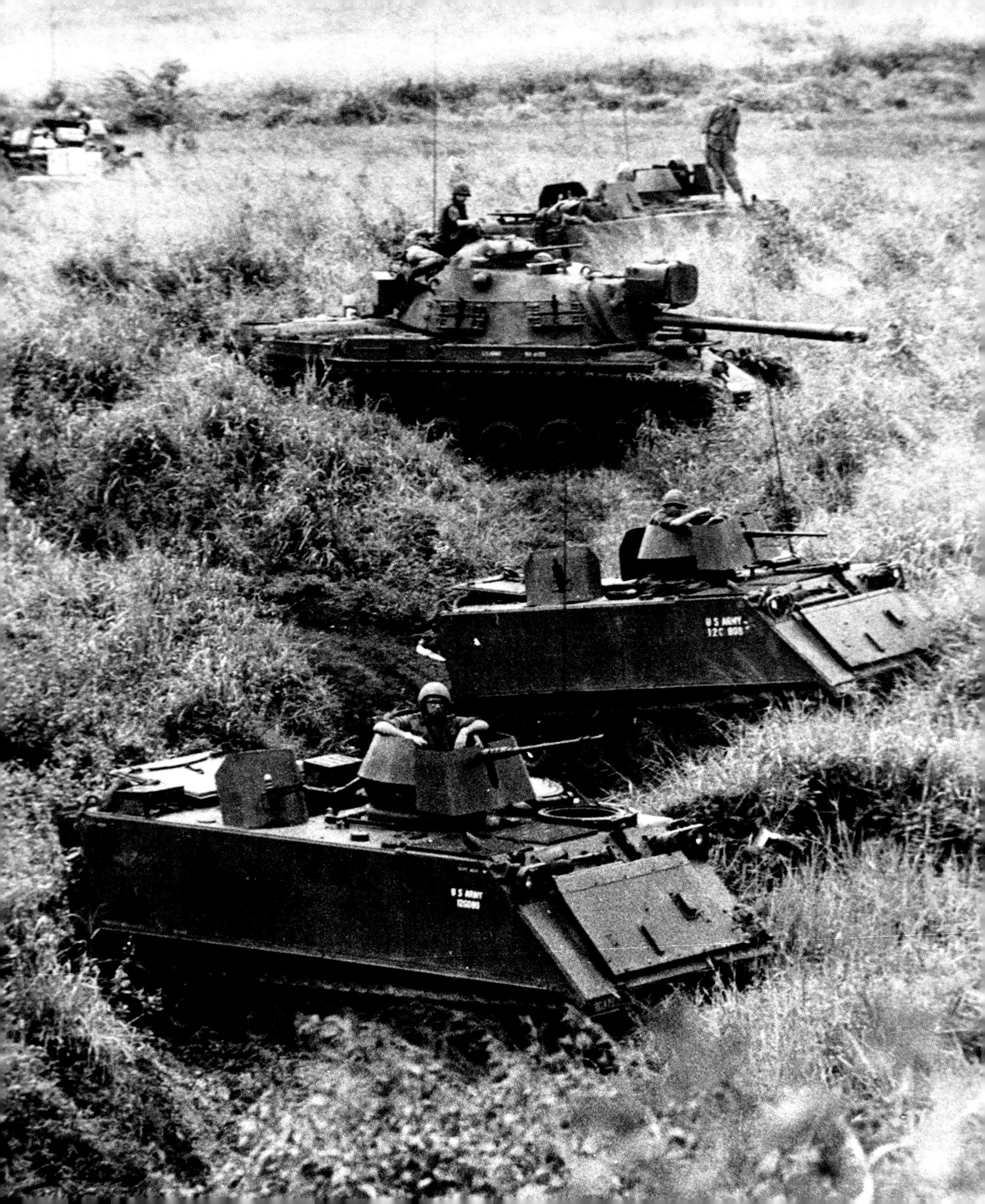
U S ARMY
U S ARMY

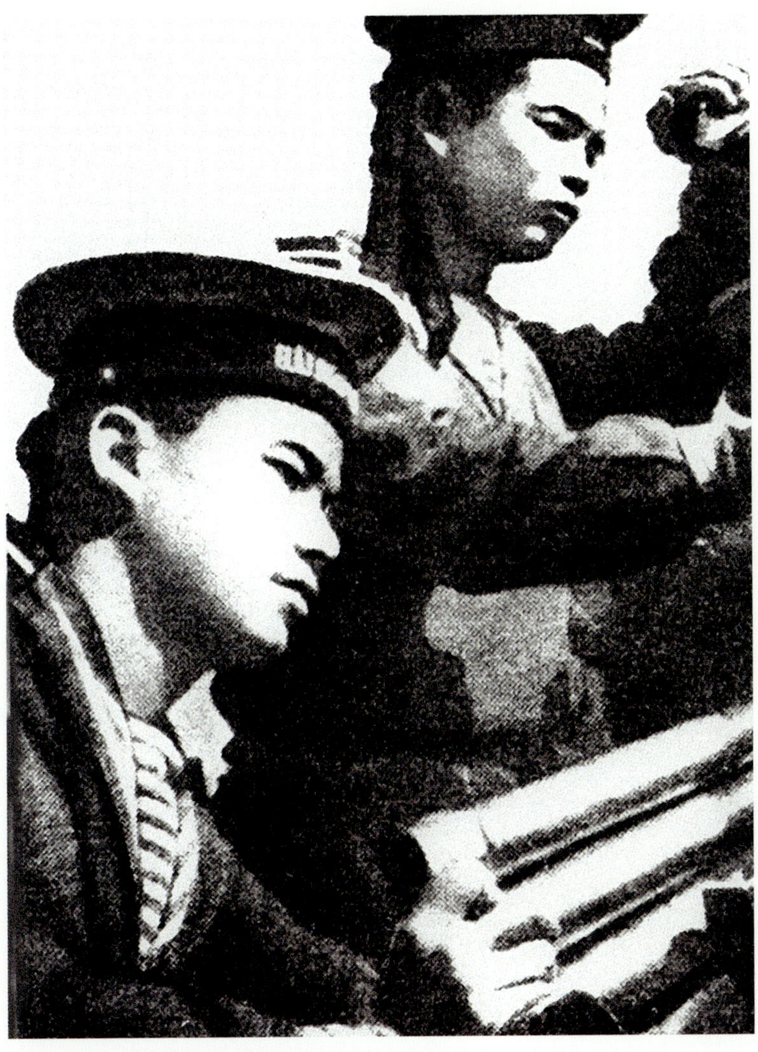

DAISY CUTTER BOMB

As the South Vietnamese retreated from the advancing N.V.A., they called upon the most destructive piece of non-nuclear ordnance left behind by the U.S. The general purpose (G.P.) bombs used most often in Vietnam were the Mark 80 series weighing 250–2,000 pounds. Trumping those weapons was the "Daisy Cutter" weighing 15,000 pounds. The bomb is named for the probe that extended from its nose which, upon contact with anything, triggered the explosion that scoured the surface of the ground in a 600-yard-diameter circle from point of impact. The bombs were dropped by parachute from the rear of a C-130 cargo plane.

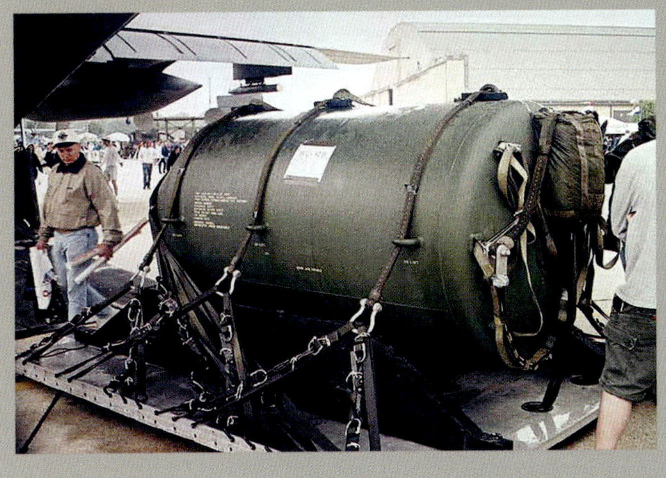

Opposite: An A.R.V.N. M48 tank and two later-model M113 armored personnel carriers wait in a defilade for the advancing N.V.A. The newer A.P.C.s had an armor-protected "pulpit" for their .50 caliber machine gun and an added 40mm grenade launcher with a frontal shield.

Above: Two N.V.A. Navy ratings load and point a 40mm rapid-fire cannon on their P-6 patrol boat as the Danang beaches and South Vietnamese coastal facilities come under attack.

Above right: A "Daisy Cutter" bomb sits strapped to its loading skid before being hoisted into a C-130 transport plane to be dropped on concentrations of N.V.A. troops and armor.

Right: Heavily loaded N.V.A. troops follow a T-54 tank across a field. The T-54's 100mm gun and armor were a match for the U.S. M48 used by the opposing A.R.V.N. forces.

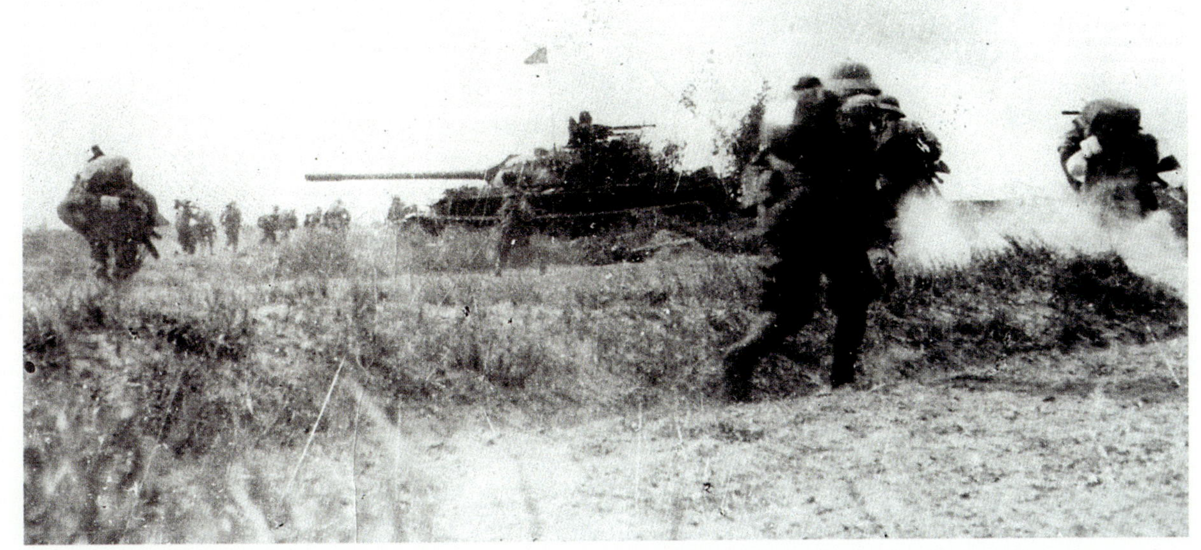

Hue, the South Vietnamese Marines dug in, held, and cost the Communists dearly at Phu Bai just south of the Old City.

On March 25, Hue was evacuated by sea as discipline dissolved. Most refugees and troops fled toward Danang, swelling the city to over one million displaced Vietnamese. The A.R.V.N. 3rd Division and two Marine brigades were ready to defend it as the N.V.A. closed in. Then, Saigon ordered the troops still under any form of command to board ships for the capital. About half the division and 4,000 troops from a mix of units escaped before the N.V.A. entered Danang and began rounding up A.R.V.N. armed deserters and political refugees.

Outgunned and seemingly without a government prepared to fight, A.R.V.N. troops were driven from hastily prepared positions as the tide flowed south. A.R.V.N. Air Force units used the C-130 transports to carry 17-foot-long, 15,000-pound "daisy cutter" bombs that were rolled out from open cargo ramps to fall with devastating effect on massed Communist troops. Everything within a 600-yard circle was killed. But even these desperate measures could not stop N.V.A. advances.

The South Vietnamese were abandoning territory to N.V.A. tanks and troops. This loss of connection with the land and their families—in many cases retreating with them—affected their loyalty to a military establishment where senior officers deserted and commandeered aircraft to fly to Saigon. Still, well-trained A.R.V.N. bravely held back the Communists for weeks in some locations until outflanked and out of supplies.

President Thieu, in ordering mass retreats with no prepared fallback positions, doomed his armed forces to confusion and chaos. A corruption-riddled officer corps did the rest.

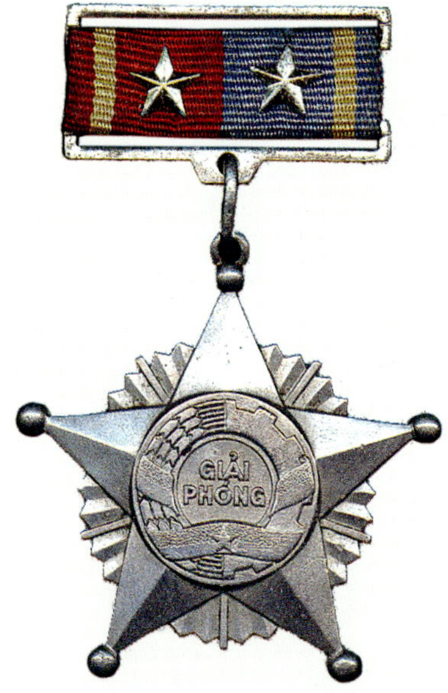

Left: Early N.V.A. medal for bravery in combat, stamped in steel with two previous award stars.

Below: A Chinese model T-59 tank that was developed from the virtually identical Soviet T-54 poses outside the factory. A simple, basic tank, it squandered no luxuries on the crew such as extracting fumes from the gun's open breech and engine exhaust.

Opposite: Platoons of N.V.A. soldiers with rifles slung make their way across one of the frequent jungle ravines trusting their safety to a rope and cut-wood bridge.

CHINESE/SOVIET T-54 TANK

The N.V.A. attacked into South Vietnam behind squadrons of T-54 main battle tanks (the Chinese version was the T-59). The T-54 is the most produced tank in history, with some 95,000 clanking about in Europe and the Middle East. Built between 1947 and 1962, the T-54 required several modifications and gun upgrades until it was comparable to N.A.T.O. designs. Its 100mm rifled gun was supported by a 12.7mm anti-aircraft machine gun on the turret, and a pair of 7.62mm guns. With 120mm of overall armor plate and 200mm turret frontal armor, it had adequate protection. Poor fume extraction and cramped crew quarters caused considerable fatigue among the four crew members.

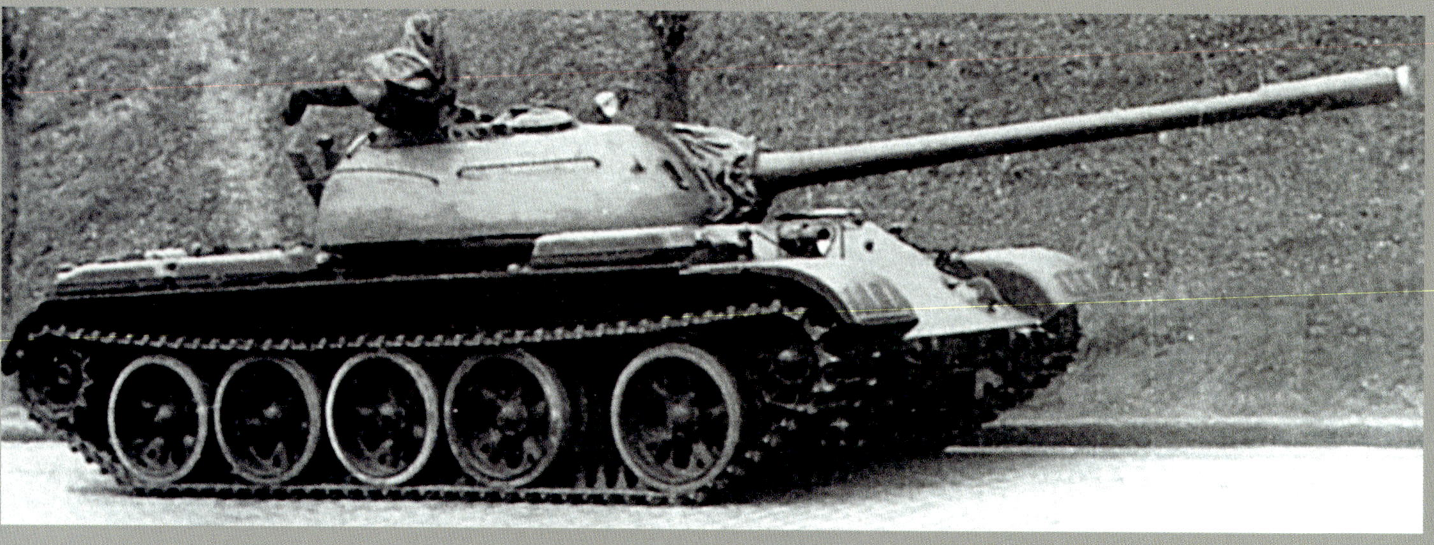

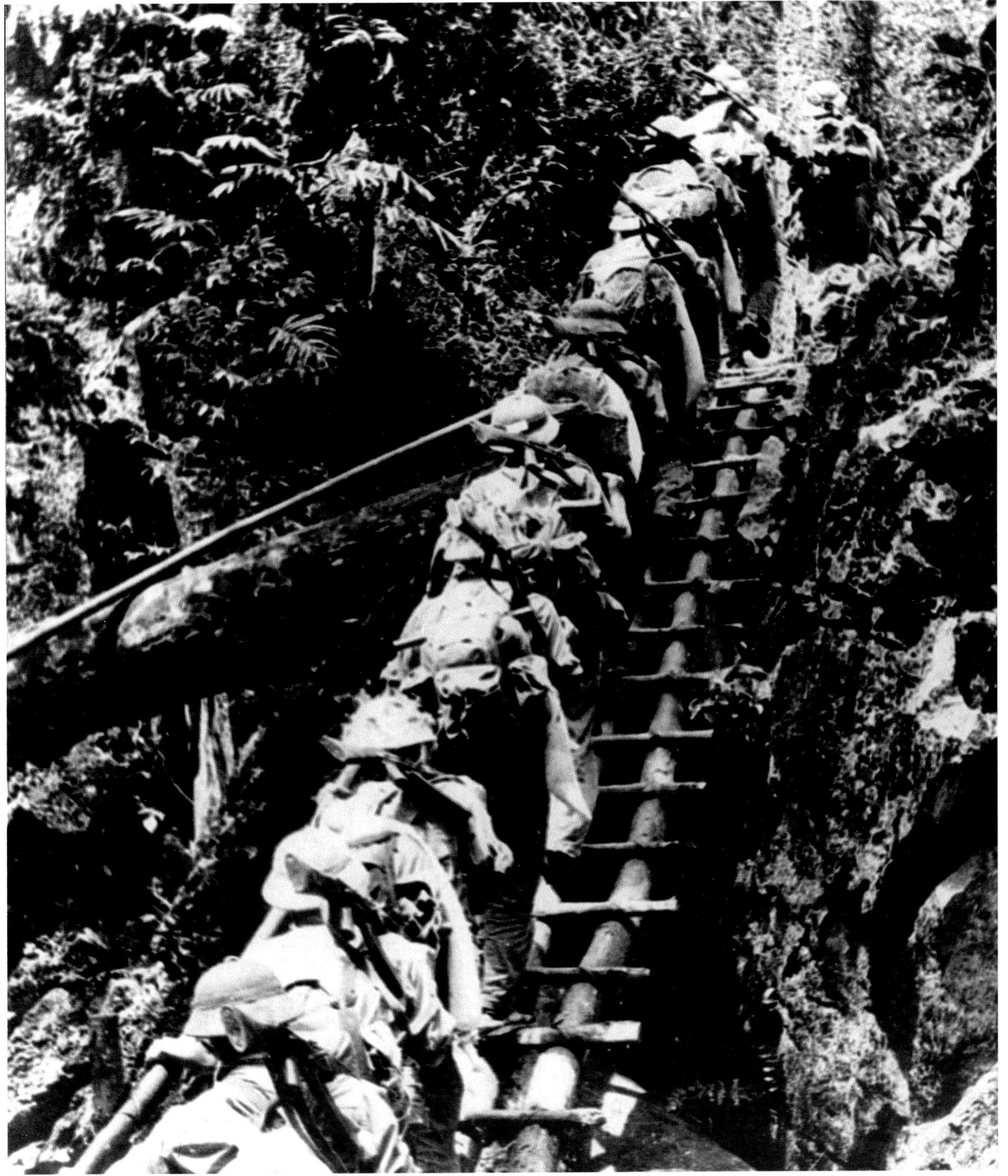

SAIGON FALLS

THE WAR WOUND DOWN QUICKLY IN THE FIRST WEEKS OF APRIL. ON APRIL 9, N.V.A. FORCES WERE ONLY 38 MILES FROM SAIGON WHEN THEY ENCOUNTERED SUDDEN AND STIFF RESISTANCE BY THE A.R.V.N. 18TH DIVISION. THE VAUNTED "HO CHI MINH CAMPAIGN" GROUND TO A HALT FOR TWO WEEKS AND LOST 5,000 CASUALTIES BEFORE THE SOUTH VIETNAMESE WERE FORCED TO GIVE GROUND.

With no hope for negotiation with the Communists, President Thieu received American Ambassador Graham Martin on April 20, searching for some way the Americans could save the day. Martin explained how the American Navy anchored offshore was there only as an evacuation force. No B-52s would flatten the N.V.A. this time. South Vietnam was alone.

On the next day, President Thieu broadcast a speech to the South Vietnamese people. He tearfully railed against his former ally: "The United States has not respected its promises. It is inhumane. It is untrustworthy. It is irresponsible." He lashed out at the Paris Peace Accords and the architect of the Pyrrhic "peace with honor," Henry Kissinger. After rambling on for 90 minutes, he was led away and bundled off by the C.I.A. to Taiwan and exile.

On April 23, Saigon was jammed with terrified refugees as 100,000 N.V.A. soldiers advanced on the city gates. Even though 30,000 armed A.R.V.N. troops were also in the city, they had no leaders, nor was there a coherent defense plan. The N.V.A. dropped rockets where civilians congregated in the downtown, creating waves of chaotic panic. To try and quell the disaster, General Duong Van "Big" Minh was asked by the National

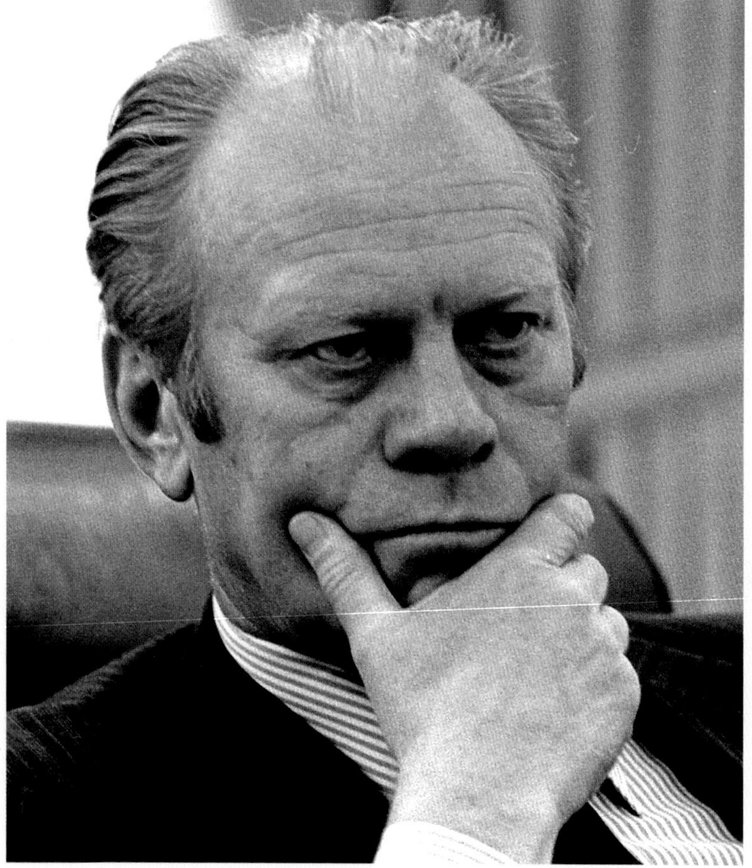

Left and below: Two film frames of President Gerald Ford—the fifth American president to be involved in the Vietnam War—and his Secretary of State Henry Kissinger, held over from the Nixon administration, who finally severed all ties with South Vietnam in 1975.

Opposite above: South Vietnamese line up outside the United States Embassy to apply for visas and seek space aboard evacuation aircraft and ships leaving Vietnam as the North Vietnamese approach Saigon.

Opposite below: South Vietnamese civilian evacuees rush the lowered ramp of an HH-3 helicopter for the flight out of Saigon. Government employees and former A.R.V.N. officers feared being captured by the N.V.A., who had been ruthless with the U.S. and western allies. More than 36,000 civilians had been murdered by the N.V.A. during the war.

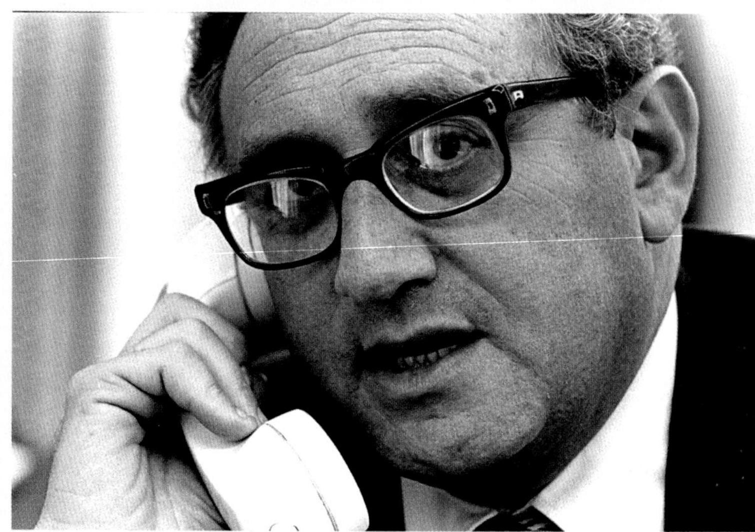

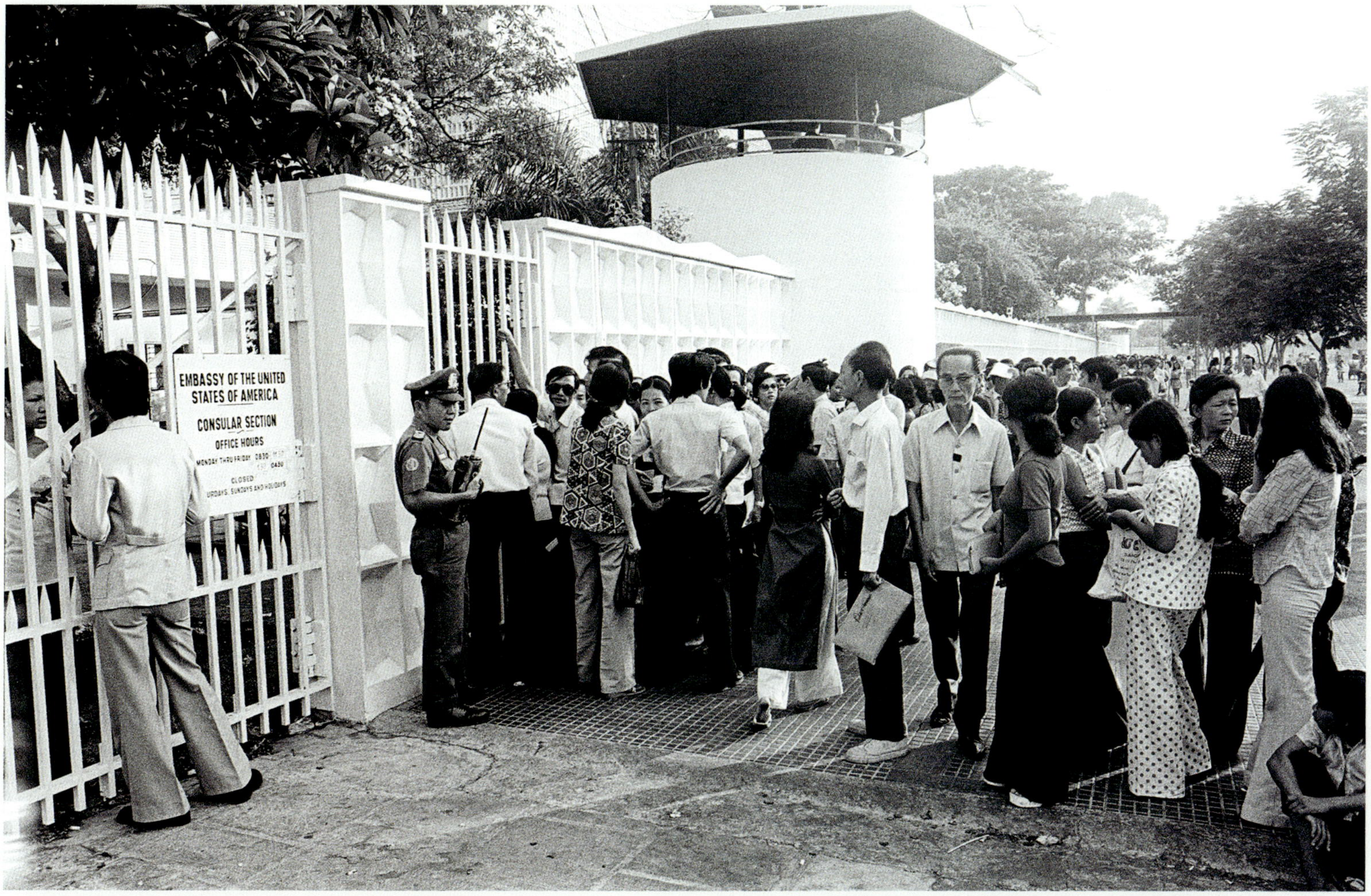

THE LAST U.S. EVACUATION

On April 29, Washington decided to evacuate the last of the Americans in the U.S. Embassy along with V.I.P. South Vietnamese, clerical staff, etc. who feared being left behind. Huey and CH-33 helicopters had set up a rotating shuttle to the U.S. carrier fleet offshore. About 70 Vietnamese could fit in each load and only 40 Americans due to their larger size. For a day and a night the evacuation went on until, with 420 people left, a miscommunication caused the trips to be halted except for U.S. personnel. Sick at heart, those Americans boarded the last helicopter, leaving behind many friends, the last victims of the fog of war.

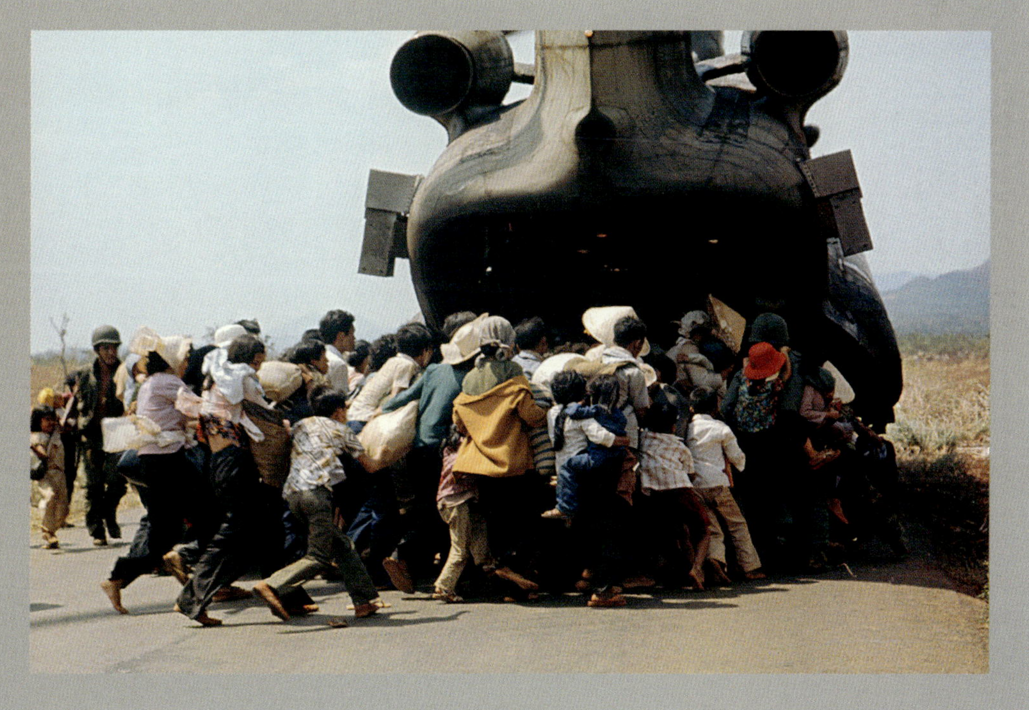

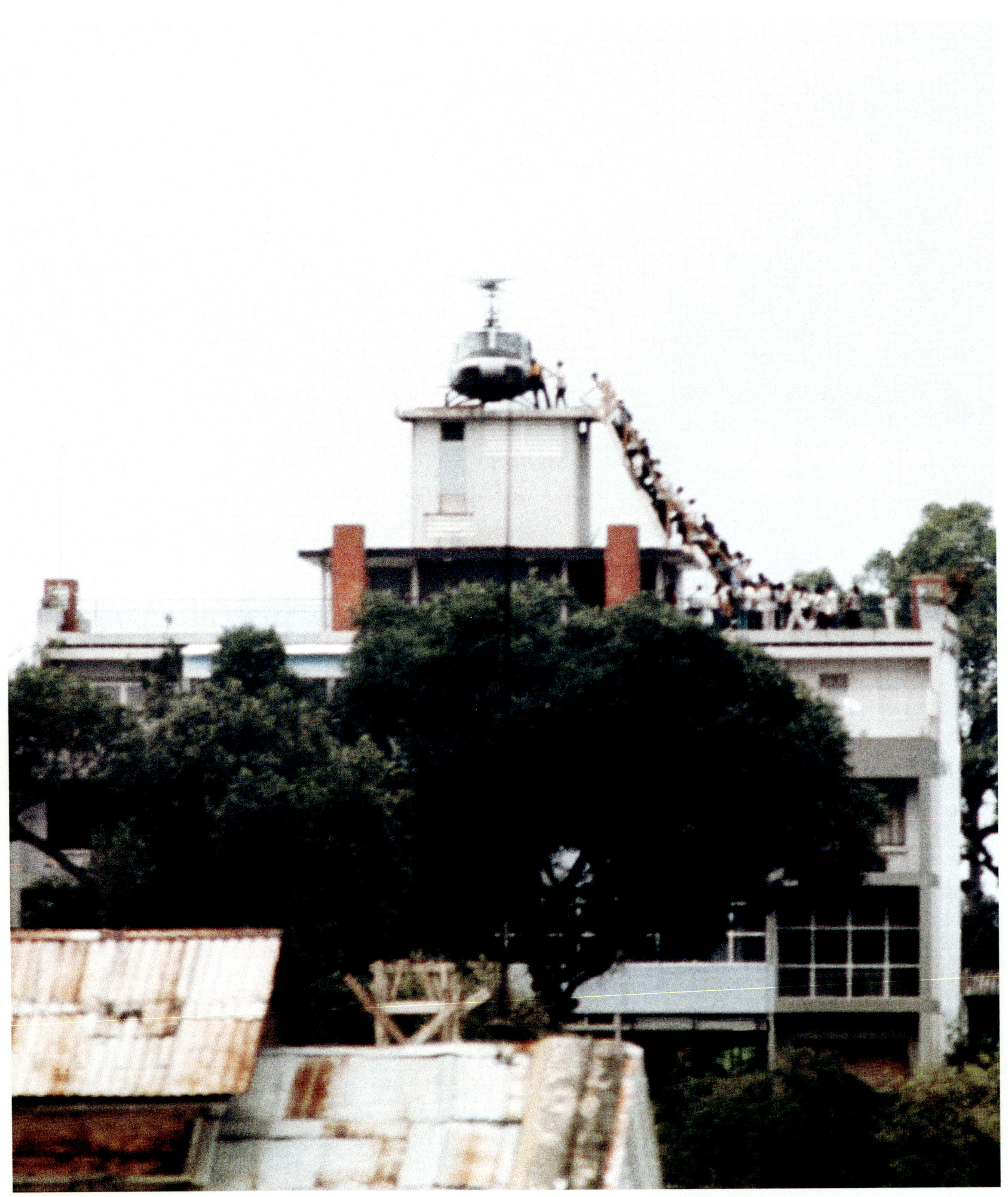

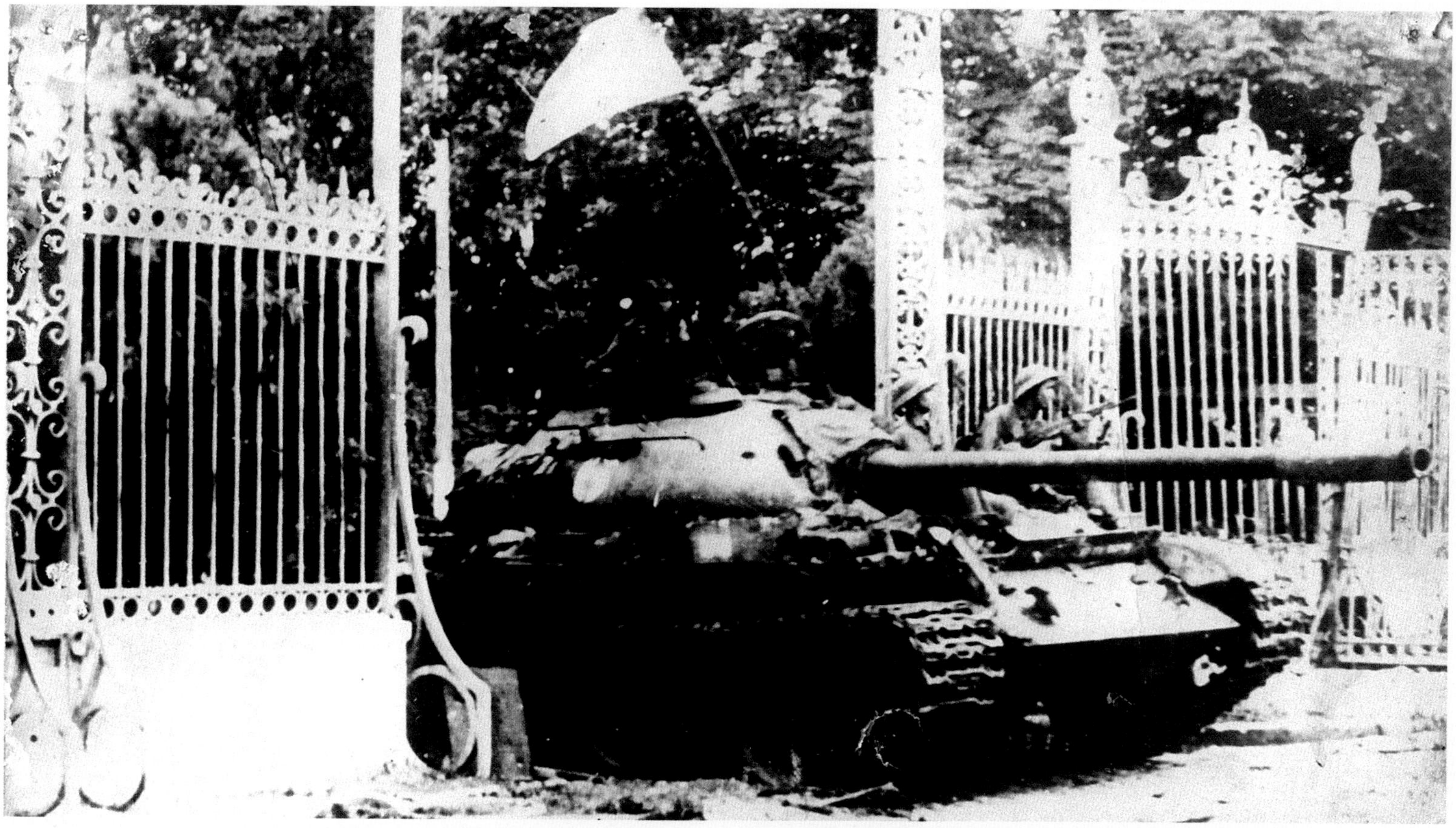

Assembly to assume the presidency and he called for a cease-fire. The North Vietnamese ignored this self-proclaimed "neutralist."

The final act began when the song "White Christmas" was heard from radios around Saigon. At the American embassy and Tan Son Nhut Air Base, that song initiated Operation Frequent Wind—the evacuation of all Americans from the Saigon area. The N.V.A. had already shelled the air base killing two marines. Helicopters began loading American staff and their dependents. Waiting offshore were American aircraft carriers, their decks cleared for the fleeing civilians and military personnel.

At the American Embassy, Marines guarded the gates as frantic South Vietnamese stormed the enclosure to get aboard Huey helicopters lifting off from the rooftop. Like ants, the swarm of frightened people climbed walls and gates, and up stairs to gain the roof. Some individuals who had worked closely with the Americans had passes to escape. Seeing them boarding enraged the crowds. Many without passes tried to fight their way aboard the helicopters. Out to sea, once the $250,000 helicopters were unloaded, they were quickly pushed over the side into the South China Sea to make room for the next flight.

Ten Marines from the American Embassy were the last to leave at 8:35 on April 30, 1975, as North Vietnamese troops and T-54 tanks advanced virtually unopposed into Saigon. President Minh looked out from the windows of the Presidential Palace as the tanks rumbled across the lawn and into the courtyard, the red and blue Viet Cong flag fluttering from their whip antennae. He broadcast the order for A.R.V.N. soldiers to put down their arms. The war was over.

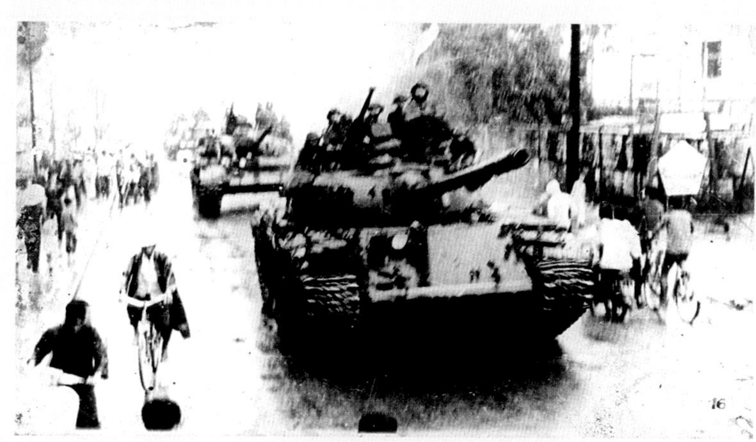

Opposite: South Vietnamese and American civilians climb precarious ladders on a rooftop half a mile from the American Embassy to a waiting helicopter. A rotating helicopter service flew from American aircraft carriers to and from Saigon during the evacuation. Helicopters were later pushed into the sea when the decks became too crowded.

Above top: An N.V.A. Soviet T-54 tank crushes the front gate as it rolls into the grounds of the Presidential Palace in Saigon. The army followed close behind.

Above: A column of N.V.A. (P.A.V.N.) T-54 tanks rolls through the streets of Saigon while civilians try to continue their daily lives as yet another regime comes to power in their country.

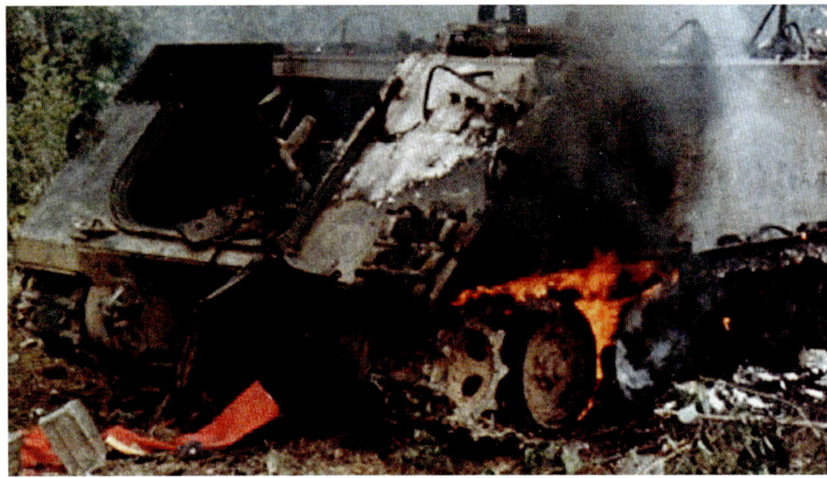

Left: A.R.V.N. M113 A.P.C. gutted by fire crackles alongside the road to Saigon. The remains of the A.R.V.N. fighting retreat.

Below: Ships of the American fleet on station off the coast of Vietnam were destinations for fleeing civilians in any kind of boat that would float. Here, a small child is hoisted across to the waiting arms of two American sailors. Whole families were rescued from many leaking boats.

Opposite: N.V.A. (P.A.V.N.) regulars in full uniform for the cameras crowd together as they follow their tanks to the South Vietnam Presidential Palace in the distance, as Saigon falls.

VIETNAMESE BOAT PEOPLE FLEE IN SMALL BOATS

Anticipating what happened following the North Vietnamese take-over (executions, torture, and wholesale revenge killings) many South Vietnamese used the last of their money to purchase small fishing and coaster boats and trusted their lives to the open sea. Over-crowded and crammed with children and extended families, they were at the mercy of Malaysian pirates, weather, and collision with large ships at night. Many antique motors died, leaving the boats adrift. Fortunately, the U.S. Navy and many other private vessels took these refugees aboard for resettlement in a growing number of camps.

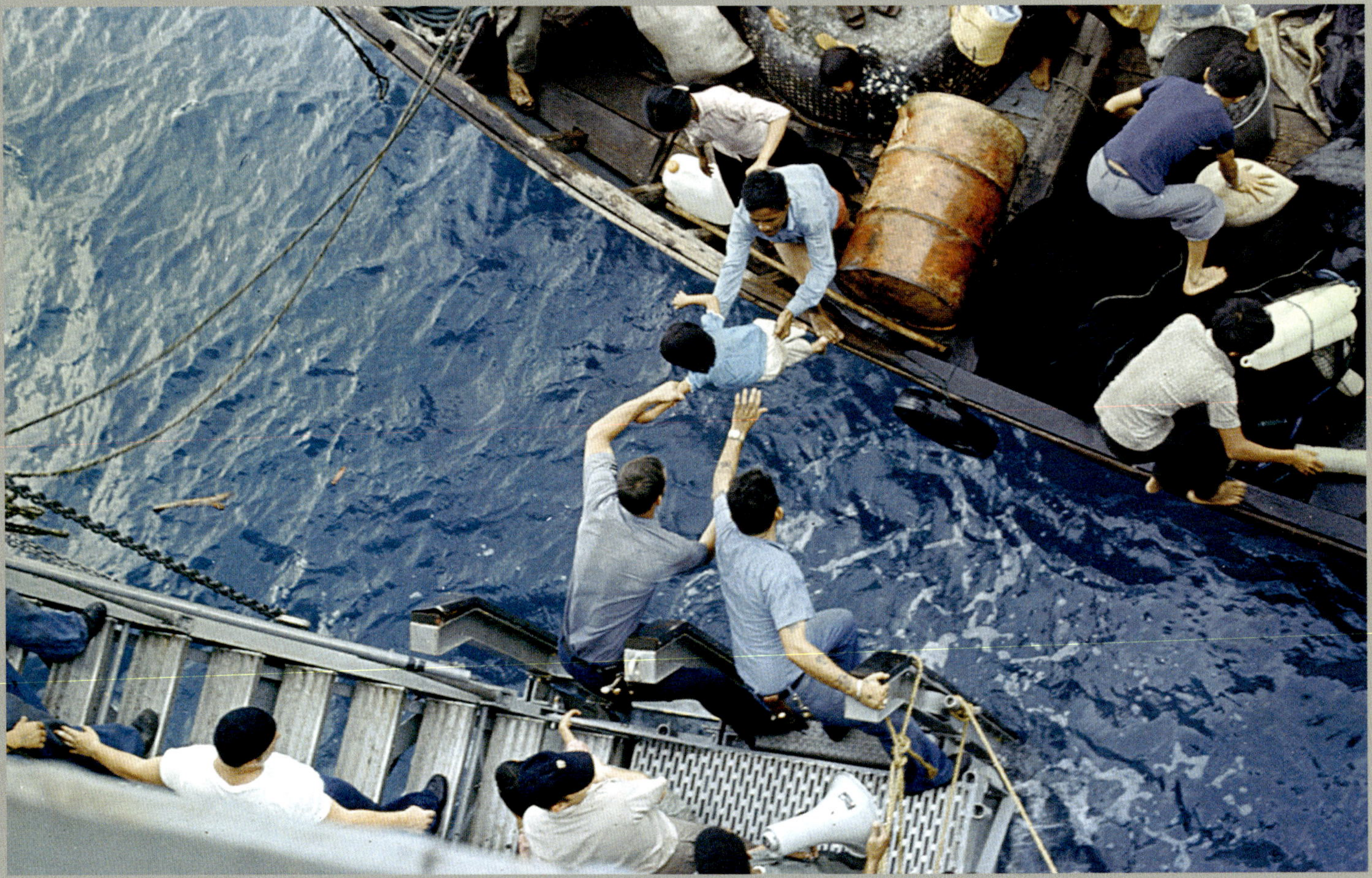

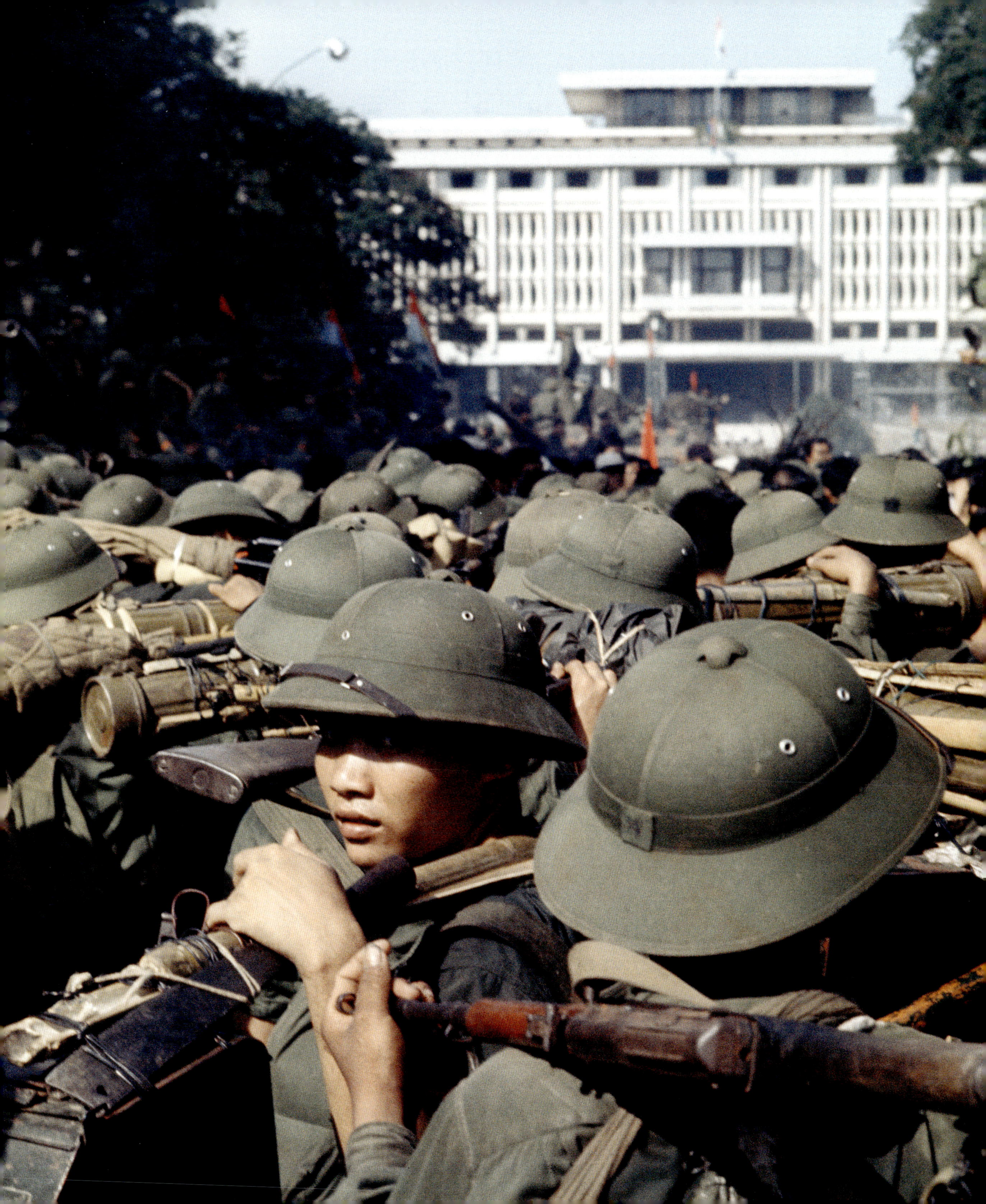

AFTERMATH

IF THE COMMUNIST GOVERNMENT IN HANOI BELIEVED THE UNIFICATION OF NORTH AND SOUTH VIETNAM WOULD RESULT IN A PEACEFUL REBUILDING OF THEIR COUNTRY, THEY WERE WRONG. THE PEOPLE'S ARMY OF VIETNAM (P.A.V.N.)—FORMERLY THE N.V.A.—FOUND THEMSELVES CALLED OUT TO FIGHT RAIDS FROM PERSISTENT INSURGENCIES OPPOSED TO COMMUNIST RULE. THE MONTAGNARD TRIBES OF THE CENTRAL HIGHLANDS AND RELIGIOUS GROUPS SUCH AS THE CAO DAI AND HOA HAO JOINED IN RESISTANCE WITH A MIXED ASSORTMENT OF ANTI-COMMUNISTS WHO FOUGHT UNDER THE BANNER OF CHU QUOC MEANING "NATIONAL SALVATION." AMONG THESE DISSIDENTS WERE THE NATIONALIST ORGANIZATIONS: DAI VIET AND VIET NAM QUOC DAN DANG—ARMED AND MADE UP IN PART OF TRAINED FORMER A.R.V.N. SOLDIERS.

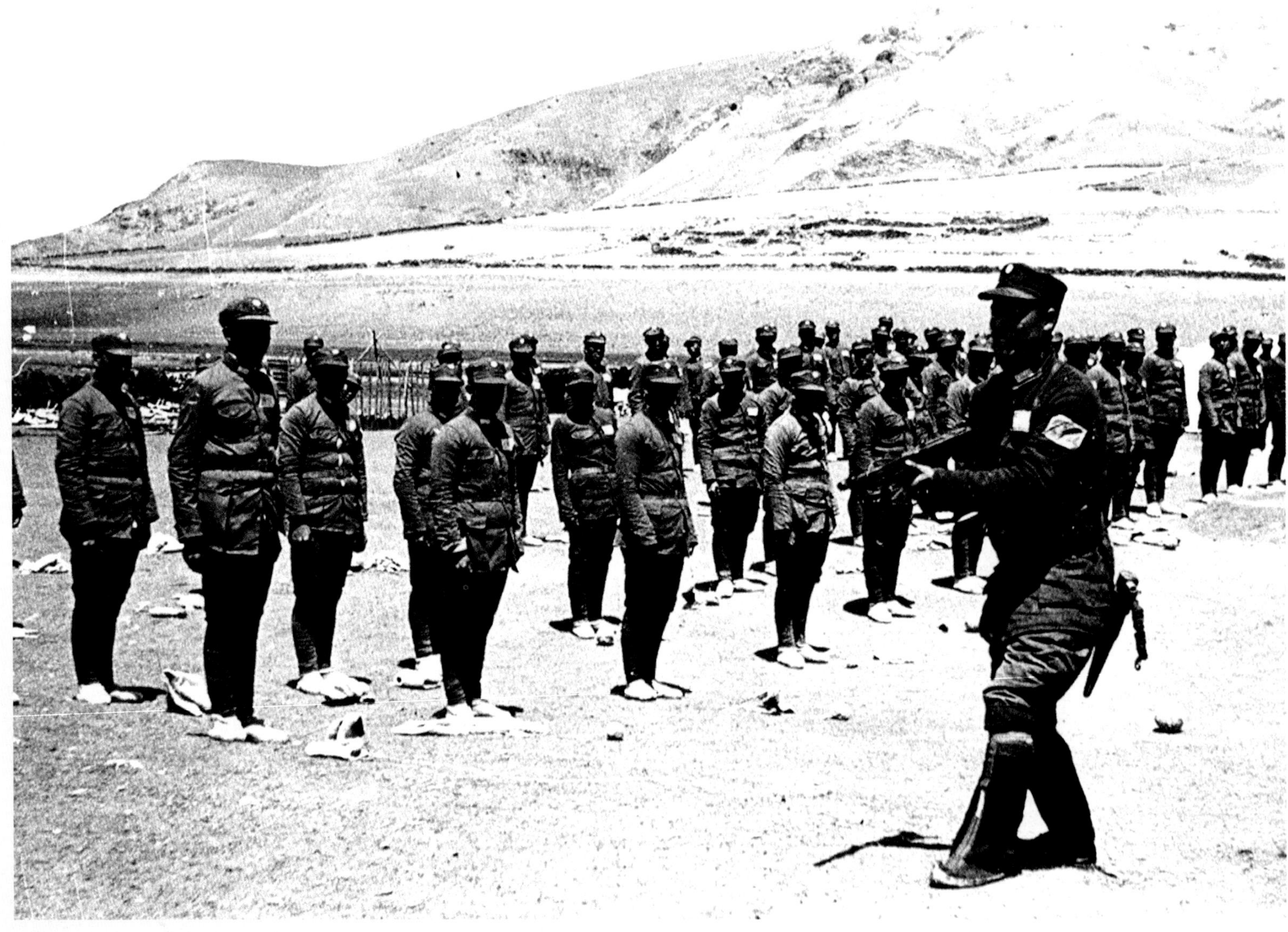

At the same time, across the Laotian border, the Hmong Rebellion against the Communist Pathet Lao was an ongoing nuisance. The ethnic Hmong—formerly armed and supported by the United States in the Laotian Civil War—were also attacked by P.A.V.N. troops to bolster the Communist Laotian government. But it was the conflict with Cambodia that kept Hanoi on an almost constant and economy-crippling war footing from 1977 to 1991.

The combatants in the Cambodian-Vietnamese War, the Khmer Rouge and the Vietnamese Communists, were allies when they had fought the American-backed regimes in Saigon and Phnom Penh. Cambodians and Vietnamese were traditional enemies, but the Communist groups set their differences aside until the war ended. Following the victory of the Khmer Rouge in Cambodia, ethnic Vietnamese residents were persecuted and many were killed, along with anyone else whose social background was deemed to be a threat to the new regime. In 1978, to counter the slaughter, the P.A.V.N. surged across the Cambodian border, captured Phnom Penh, and established a new Cambodian government that in turn began fighting a

Opposite: Chinese Communist troops are trained by an officer—wielding an old Thompson submachine gun—in the use of captured weapons. The Chinese Army sent troops boiling down into Vietnam in 1979 to chastise the country after its attack on Cambodia. The P.A.V.N. sent the Chinese back across their border in embarrassing retreat.

Bottom left: A Soviet-designed, Chinese copy of a T-59 tank named the T-54 stands in Ho Chi Minh City as a memorial to the troops that arrived in Saigon in 1975. The city has numerous memorials to remember what they call "The American War."

Below: A Khmer Rouge drowning torture tub discovered at a Khmer prison for Vietnamese nationals and ethnic Vietnamese persecuted by the Khmer regime under Pol Pot. The ending of the Vietnamese War sent N.V.A. into Cambodia to attack their former Khmer allies.

Bottom right: A Vietnamese woman has her baby torn from her to be killed while she is beaten. Over a million Vietnamese living in Cambodia were murdered by Khmer Rouge troops. Elaborate torture and ethnic cleansing prisons slaughtered men, women, and children daily, dumping the bodies in the fields. The Cambodian-Vietnamese War lasted until 1991. This invasion angered Cambodia's ally, China.

CHINESE ATTACK TO AVENGE CAMBODIA IN 1979

Attacking along almost the entire Sino-Vietnamese border at dawn on February 17, 1979, the Chinese People's Liberation Army brought the weight of their military might. T-54 tanks rumbled across the frontier followed by waves of infantry and preceded by a barrage of artillery. Overhead, Chinese MiGs flashed firing rockets and cannon in close troop support. The horde of soldiers and crush of ordnance soon outran their supply lines and slowed as P.A.V.N. forces dug in and countered the invasion with hard-learned skills. Both sides claimed a victory. The only real loser was the Soviet Union, which failed to come to the aid of its Vietnamese "ally" during the 29-day event and lost considerable credibility.

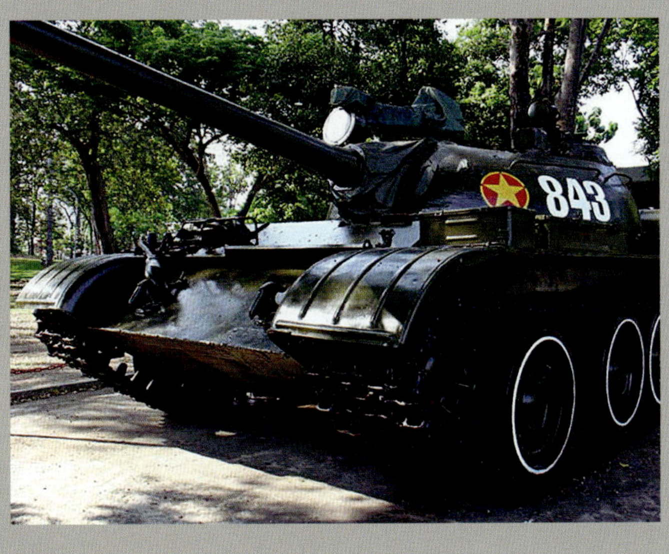

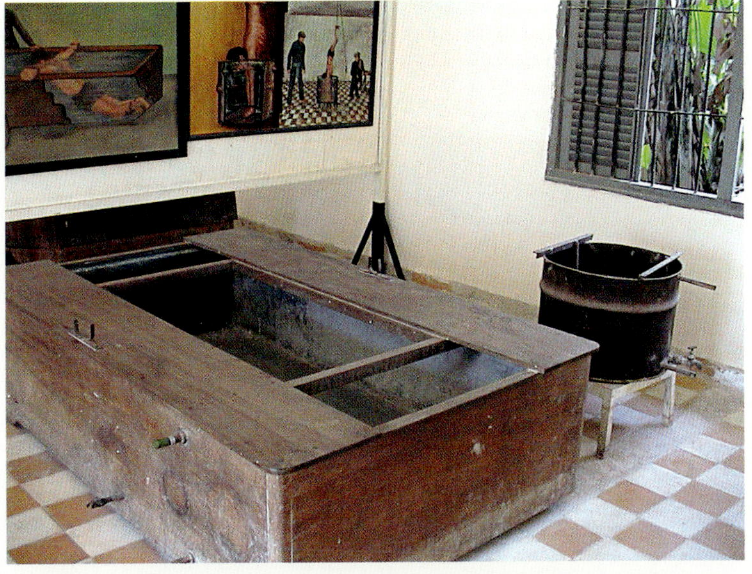

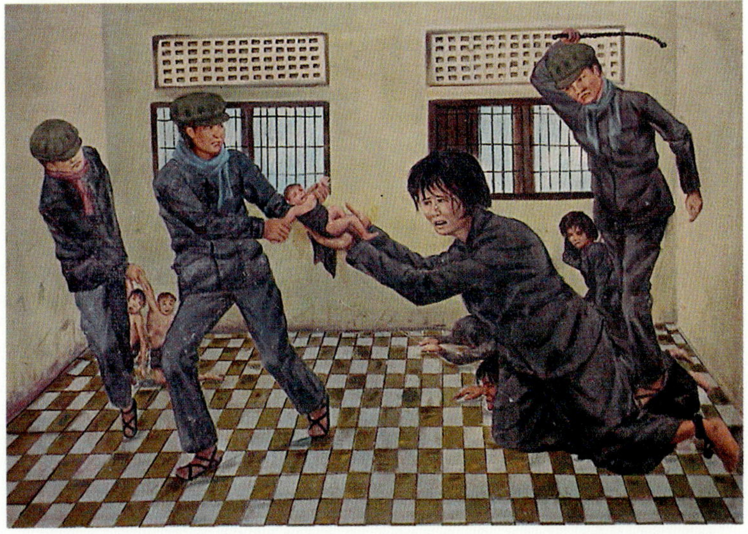

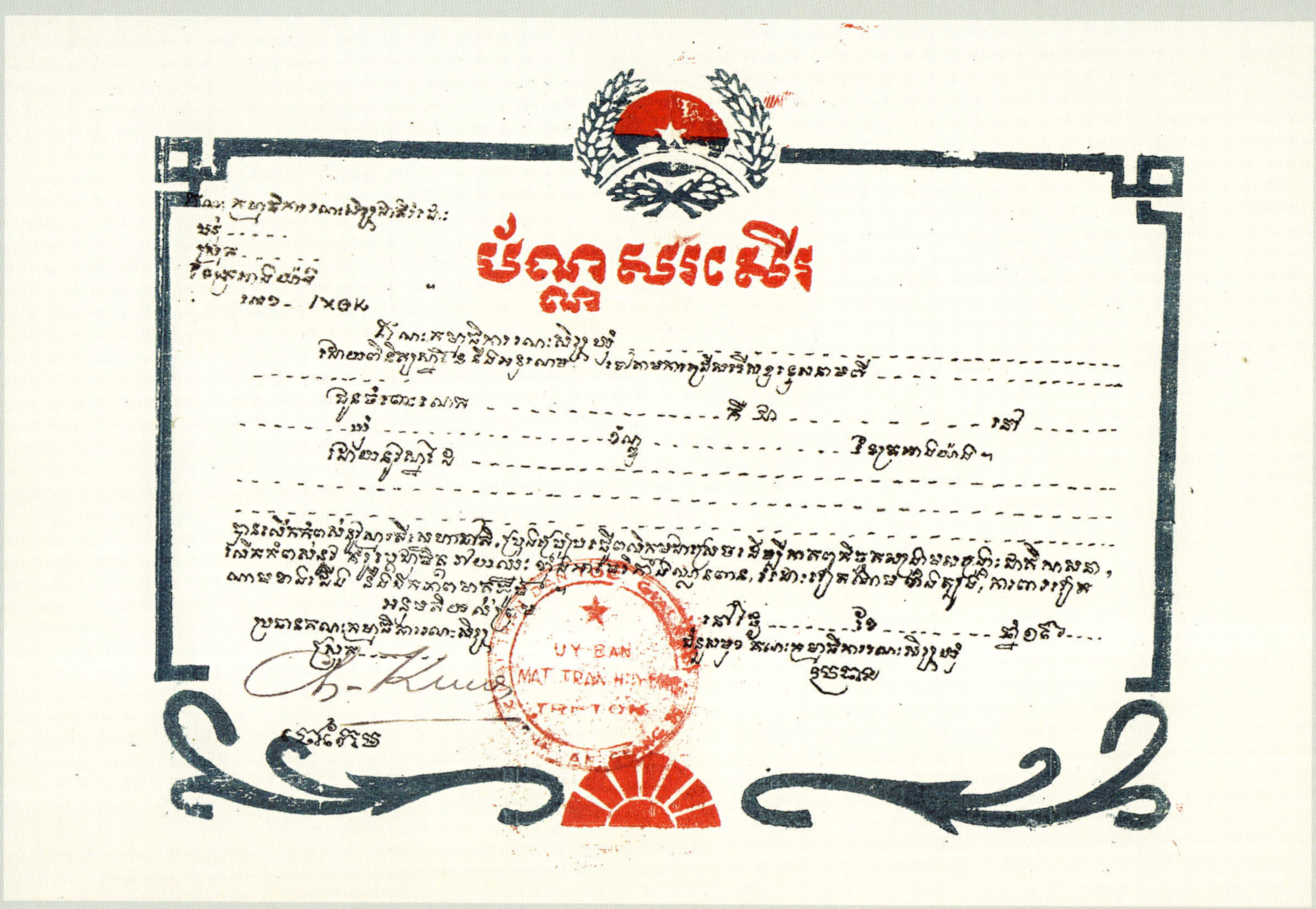

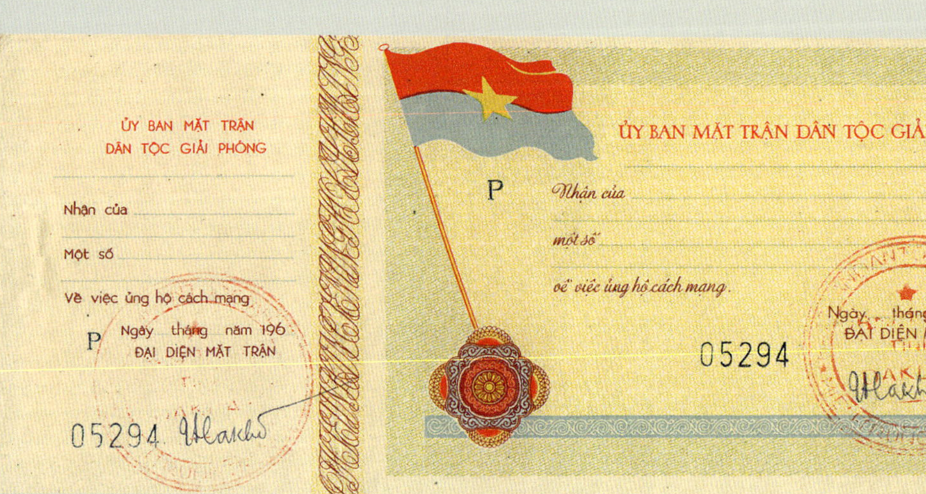

ỦY BAN MẶT TRẬN DÂN TỘC GIẢI PHÓNG

Nhận của

Một số

Về việc ủng hộ cách mạng

P Ngày tháng năm 196

ĐẠI DIỆN MẶT TRẬN

05294

ỦY BAN MẶT TRẬN DÂN TỘC GIẢI PHÓNG

P

Nhận của

một số

về việc ủng hộ cách mạng

Ngày tháng năm 196

ĐẠI DIỆN MẶT TRẬN

05294

KHMER V.C. AWARD

This Viet Cong award certificate is written in the Khmer language. During the war, the V.C. and Khmer Rouge troops fought side by side for Communism, but at its end the Khmer began the "ethnic cleansing" of Vietnamese who had fled to Cambodia.

For translation, see page 156.

N.L.F. CONTRIBUTION TO THE REVOLUTION RECEIPT

This was issued for a wide variety of general merchandise to make the peasant farmers feel somewhat less ripped off by the V.C. in the hope of engendering continued support for their efforts.

For translation, see page 156.

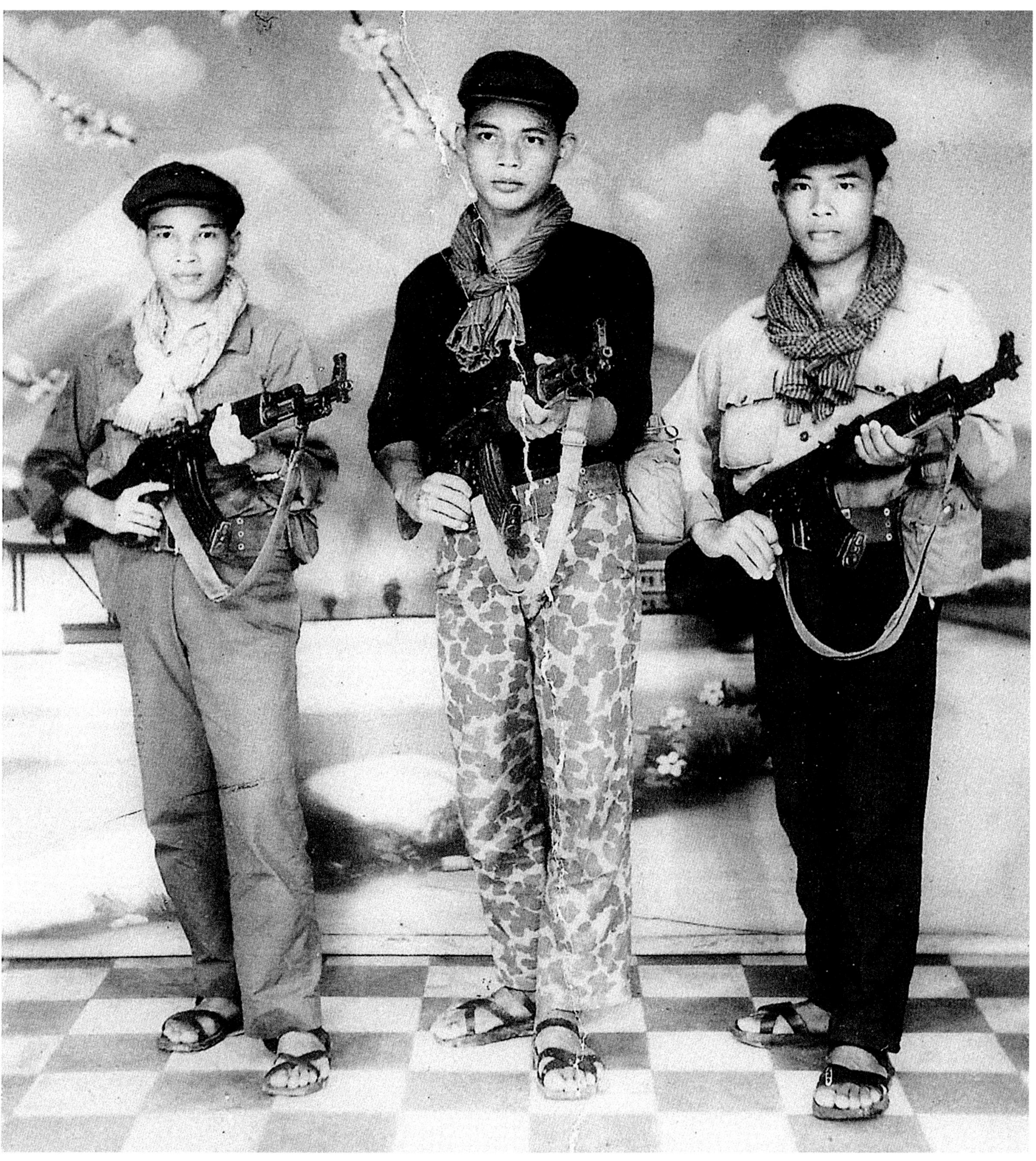

Above: Three Viet Cong youths wearing their checkered neck scarves and heavily armed with weapons—probably supplied by the photographer—want their participation in the "American War" recorded for posterity.

war against the Khmer Rouge and its leader, Pol Pot, who was responsible for a million deaths. The war lasted until most of the Khmer Rouge gave up the struggle in 1996.

This invasion angered Cambodia's ally, China, as the vicious circle of Communist bloc politics wreaked its ill effects. China was at odds with the Soviet Union, which had been Hanoi's strongest supporter. On February 17, 1979, China launched a "punitive attack" on Vietnam, boiling down from the north with 100,000 troops to destroy Cao Bang and Lang Son. The Vietnamese, fighting on familiar terrain, halted the attack and in a series of battles exacted 30,000 Chinese dead. Beijing was horrified that their army was devastated by this little country and called off the invasion, claiming that they had taught the wayward Vietnam "a lesson."

Emboldened by their success, Vietnam continued raids into China from a base on Mount Laoshan. The war ultimately degenerated into a relatively harmless exchange of artillery rounds over many years. Meanwhile, ethnic Chinese who had settled in Vietnam were hounded and persecuted by the government in Hanoi.

Today, the government of Vietnam has finally achieved the degree of peace to implement programs of infrastructure improvement and to develop trade agreements. Relations with the United States have warmed, and Vietnam War veterans are welcomed as tourists to revisit the cities and battlefields. These visits allow many former soldiers to come to grips with post-war traumas that crippled them emotionally. Deep resentments still reside with many who were badly treated when they returned home. Only in the 1990s did the Vietnamese recognize their own "Heroic Mothers" who lost sons and husbands in the war. Warriors from both sides who have now grown gray are learning to put the war behind them and enjoy the respect that is their due.

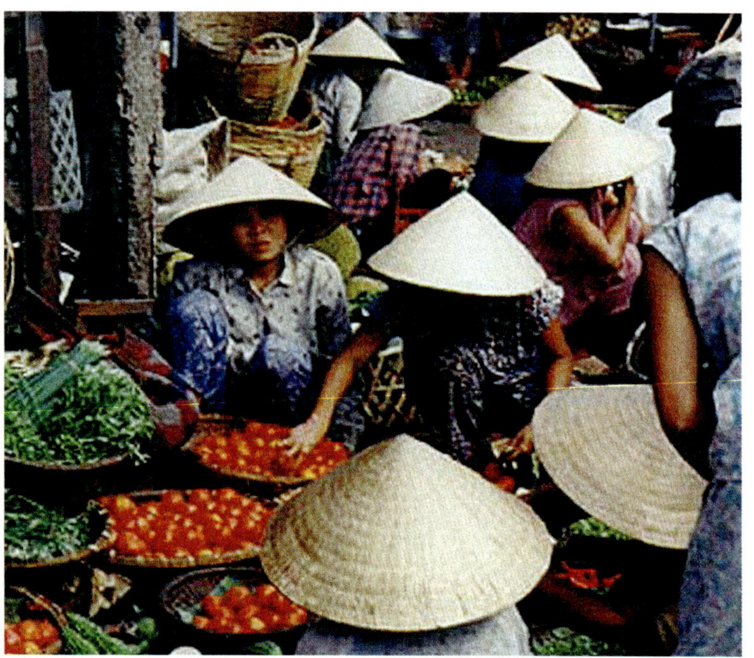

H.C.M.C. WAR MEMORIALS AND MUSEUMS

Today, the former Saigon is Ho Chi Minh City, named for "Uncle Ho" who died in 1969, never seeing his dream of a unified Vietnam. Tourists wander streets and markets where grenades and gunfire once crashed. Formerly the scene of prisoner exchanges and presenting medals to heroes of the P.A.V.N., downtown suffers from scooter traffic jams. Government buildings are now museums and propped-up Allied aircraft—shot down or recovered from captured airfields—decorate the airport grounds. For a small fee, a tourist can even tour the caverns of the tunnels at Cu Chi. American Vietnam veterans make up a large portion of those tourists.

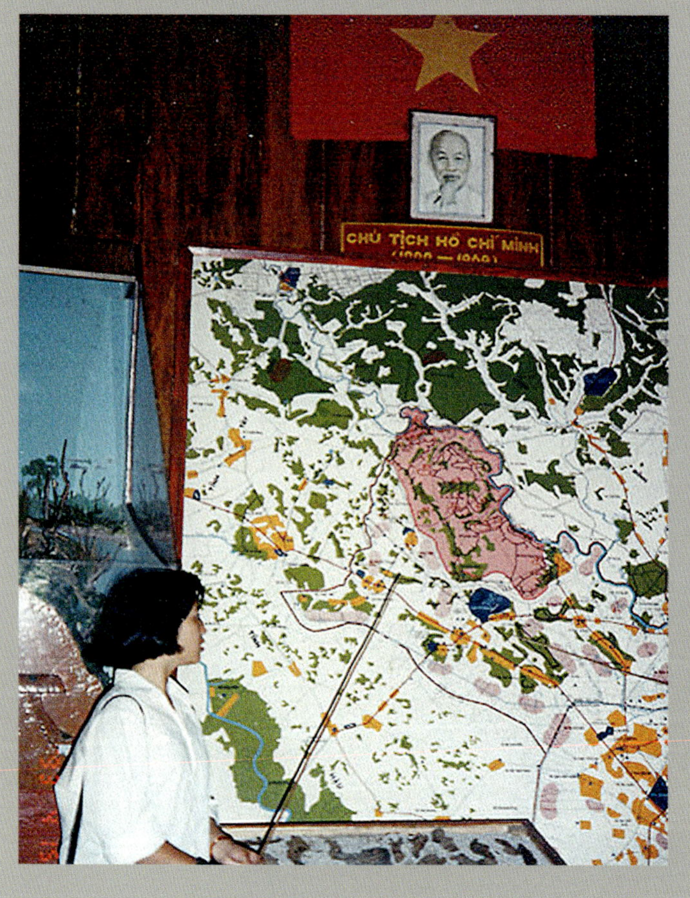

Left: A busy market in today's downtown Ho Chi Minh City (formerly Saigon) is typical of the entrepreneurship allowed by the present government. American corporations have poured vast sums of money into Vietnam's industrial complex, and political relations with Vietnam today are cautiously cordial.

Above: A guide uses a large illustration to show tourists the complex tunnel system used by the Viet Cong during the war. Ho Chi Minh City has many museums and memorials to the conflict.

Opposite above: After a long delay, mothers of N.V.A. soldiers receive awards for their sons' sacrifice in combat from P.A.V.N. officers in a Ho Chi Minh City ceremony.

Opposite below: The Vietnam Veterans Memorial in Washington, D.C. All the names of military personnel who died in the war are engraved in the wall's surface. The memorial has had more than 25 million visitors since its dedication in November, 1982.

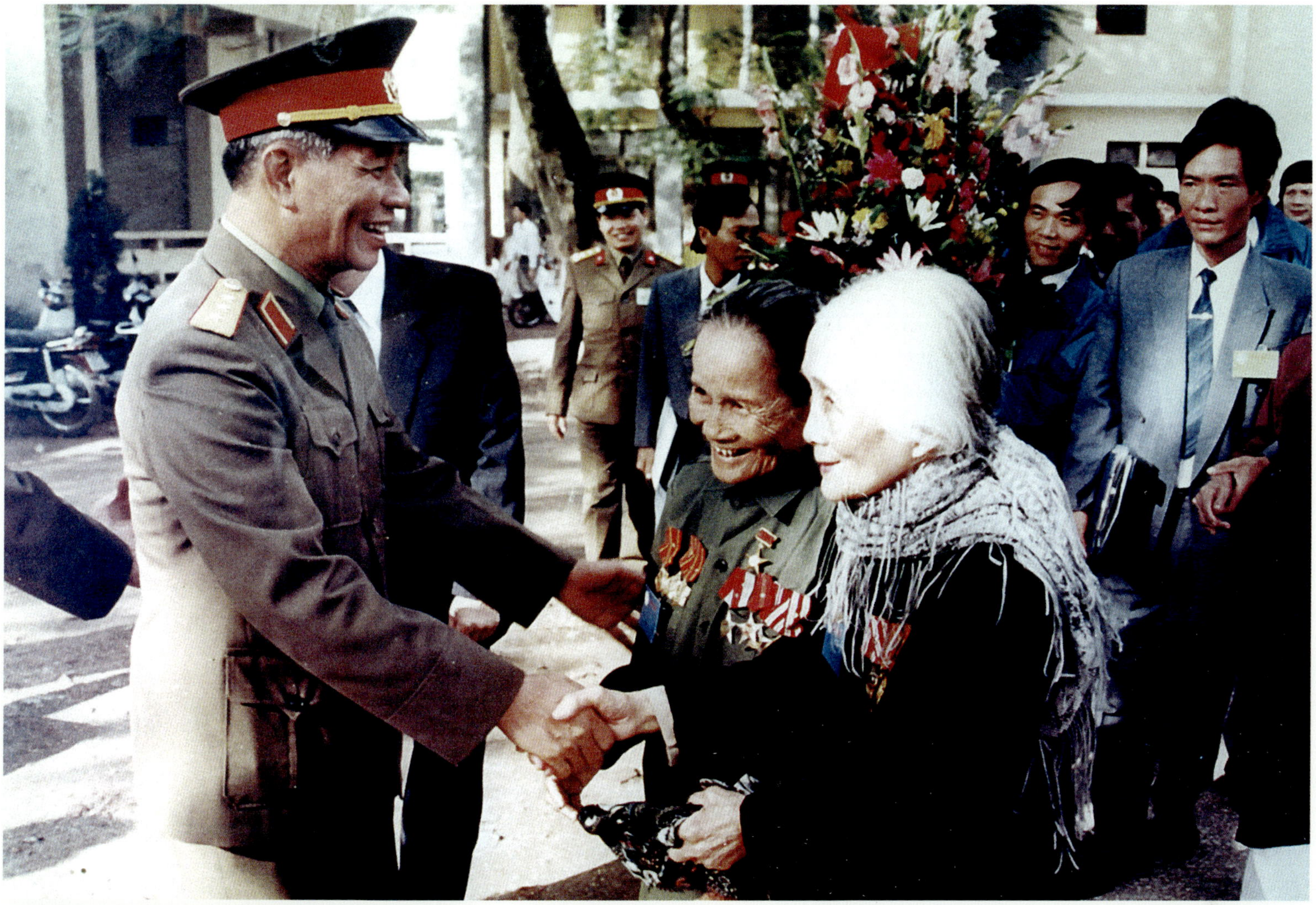

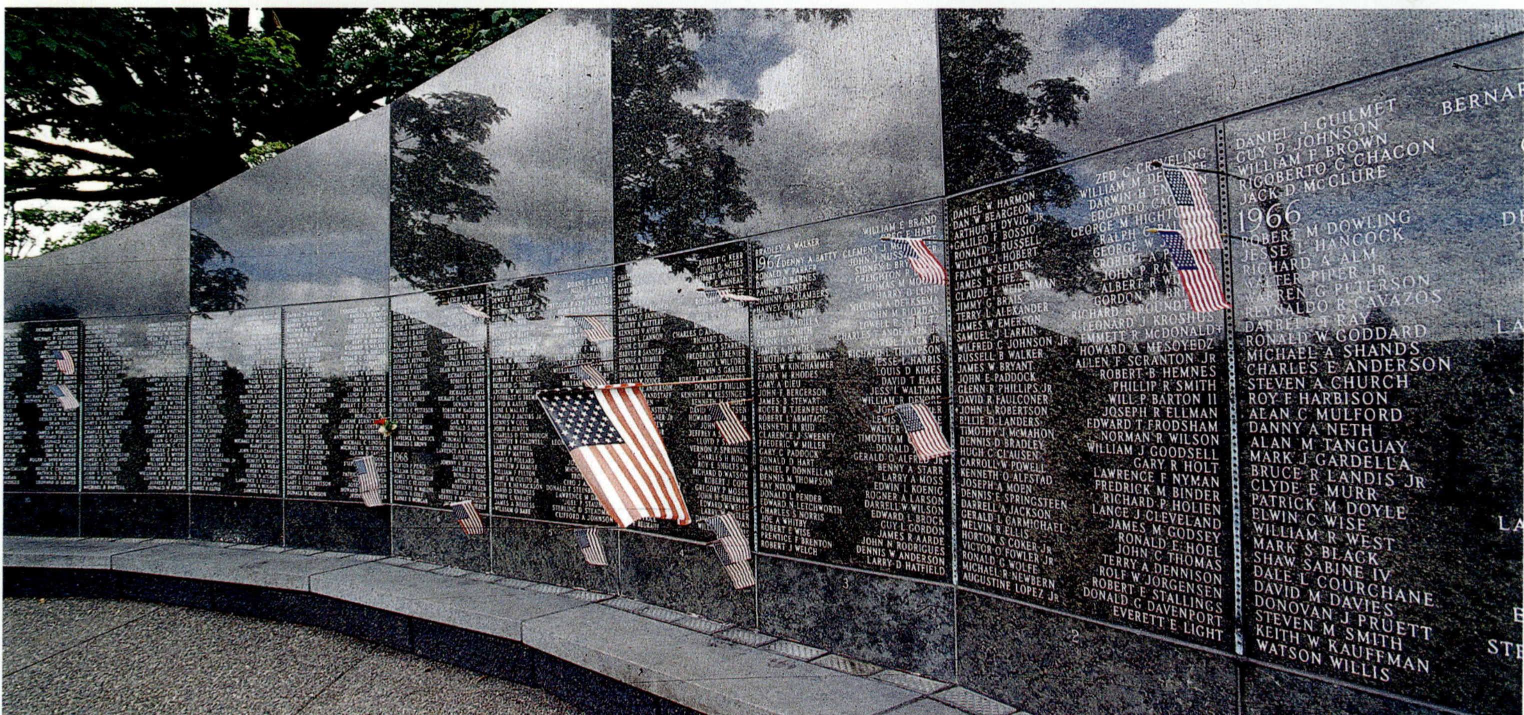
DANIEL J GUILMET
GUY D JOHNSON
WILLIAM F BROWN
RIGOBERTO C CHACON
JACK D McCLURE
1966
ROBERT M DOWLING
JESSE L HANCOCK
RICHARD A ALM
WALTER PIPER JR
WARREN G PETERSON
REYNALDO R CAVAZOS
RONALD W GODDARD
MICHAEL A SHANDS
CHARLES E ANDERSON
STEVEN A CHURCH
ROY F HARBISON
ALAN C MULFORD
DANNY A NETH
ALAN M TANGUAY
MARK J GARDELLA
BRUCE R LANDIS JR
CLYDE E MURR
PATRICK M DOYLE
ELWIN C WISE
WILLIAM R WEST
MARK S BLACK
SHAW SABINE IV
DALE L COURCHANE
DAVID M DAVIES
DONOVAN J PRUETT
STEVEN M SMITH
KEITH W KAUFFMAN
WATSON WILLIS

TRANSLATIONS

DOCUMENT ON PAGE 25
P.A.V.N. Letter of Appreciation

DEMOCRATIC REPUBLIC OF VIETNAM
Independence – Freedom – Happiness

THE EXECUTIVE COMMITTEE OF THE WOMEN'S ASSOCIATION OF VINH PHU PROVINCE
AWARDS
LETTER OF APPRECIATION

Nguyen Thi Hang
(who is in charge of) Women's work in Co Khi secondary school of the farm who achieved the title of "Three Responsibilities" in 6 years (1965–1970)
Letter of Appreciation No... Day..15...month...9...year 1972

ON BEHALF OF THE EXECUTIVE COMMITTEE
OF THE WA OF VINH PHU PROVINCE
Chairwoman
(signed and sealed)
DANG THI HONG NHUNG

DOCUMENT ON PAGE 50, TOP
U.S. Army calling card

Death is awaiting Viet Cong soldiers. Surrender or die!

DOCUMENT ON PAGE 72, RIGHT
Vanguard Youth ID for Chau Quoc Tuan

(Front)
VIETNAM'S YOUTH UNION
HO CHI MINH CITY
(photo)
Signature of member

SOCIALIST REPUBLIC OF VIETNAM
Independence – Freedom – Happiness
MEMBERSHIP CARD No: 0076/THV
Full Name: Chau Quoc Tuan Age: 25
Occupation: Worker
Address: 87, Ward An Binh Dong
Being a member of the Vietnam's Youth Union
Chapter: Ward 14, District ....
Day.. 12 month.. 03 year 1979
On behalf of the Committee of the Vietnam's Youth Union
[signed and sealed]
NGUYEN THANH TONG

(Back)
Transfer of activities of the Union

ACTIVITIES AND MEMBERSHIP FEE
Month.. Month.. Month.. Month.. Month.. Month..
Month.. Month.. Month.. Month.. Month.. Month..

This card is used for activities within the Union

DOCUMENT ON PAGE 73
Van Nghe Quan Zo Army booklet

(Page 1)
OUR ARMY
ARE LOYAL TO THE PARTY, FILIAL TO THE PEOPLE, READY TO FIGHT AND DIE FOR THE INDEPENDENCE AND FREEDOM OF THE COUNTRY, FOR SOCIALISM, FULFIL ANY TASKS, OVERCOME ANY DIFFICULTY, DEFEAT ANY ENEMY
President
HO CHI MINH

(Pages 2 and 3)
IN COMMEMORATION OF THE 50TH ANNIVERSARY OF THE FORMATION OF THE VIETNAM COMMUNIST PARTY

RESOLUTION
OF THE FOURTH CONGRESS OF THE PARTY
(Excerpt)
– To have a thorough grasp of proletarian dictatorship, to promote the right to collective ownership of working people, to undertake concurrently three revolutions: the revolution of production relationships, the revolution of science-technology and the revolution of ideology and culture, of which the revolution of science-technology plays the key role; to step up socialist industrialization as the central task of the entire transitional period to socialism; to build up the system of socialist collective ownership, to develop the socialist large scale production, to develop a new culture, to develop the new socialist person; to eliminate the people-exploiting-people system, to eliminate poverty and backwardness; to keep heightening vigilance, to strengthen our defence regularly, to maintain political security and social order; to construct successfully a peaceful, independent, united and socialist Nation of Vietnam; to contribute actively to the fight of people in the world for peace, national independence, democracy and socialism
– To be loyal to Marxism-Leninism, our Party incessantly educates the Party's members and our people to absorb the pure revolutionary aspirations of President Ho, to continue holding aloft the flag of national independence and socialism, to combine smoothly true patriotism and proletariat internationalism, to fight against all trends of opportunism and all manifestations of bourgeois and small bourgeois nationalism, to uphold independence and autonomy, to exercise the best efforts to fulfill the duties to the nation and to discharge the international obligations to people of other countries.

(Page 4)

11 Monday	25	
12 Tuesday	26	
13 Wednesday		27
14 Thursday	28	
15 Friday	29	
16 Saturday 1st lunar month of Canh Than Year (full)		
17 SUNDAY	2	

(Page 5)

STRONG WILL
HIGH QUALITY
GOOD SOLIDARITY
STRICT DISCIPLINE
DETERMINED TO FIGHT
DETERMINED TO WIN

(Page 6)

Doan Thuong	141 km	Lang Thip	228 km
Van Phu	149 –	Bao Ha	237 –
Yen Bai	154 –	Thai Van	248 –
Co Phac	166 –	Cau Nho	
Ngoi Hop	177 –	(station)	255 –
Mau A		187 – Pho Lu	
262 –			
Mau Dong	195 –	Lang (station)	271 –
Trai Hut	203 –	Thai Nien	278 –
Lam Giang	211 –	Lang Giang	284 –
Mo Da		215 – Pho Moi	293 –
Lang Khay	219 –	Lao Cai	295 –

LANG GIANG – PO HAN: 5 km
DOMESTIC LONG DISTANCE RAIL AND COACH WAYS

Hanoi – Cao Bang 281 km
Hanoi – Lai Chau 509 km
Hanoi – Nghia Lo 239 km

DOCUMENT ON PAGE 72, LEFT
V.C. Order of Soldier of Liberation Award

(Front)
NATIONAL FRONT FOR THE LIBERATION
OF SOUTH VIETNAM
No. 267

CERTIFICATE OF ORDER AWARD
Comrade: Luong Van Long
Date of birth:______________
Place of birth: ______________Dinh Tuong
Has been awarded with an: Order of Soldier of Liberation
Day 11th month October year 1972

(Back)

Order	Decision – decree No.	Day, month, year	Certification
Soldier of Liberation grade three	433/42	11 October 1972	Has been awarded

NOTE: This certificate must be carefully maintained – When the letter (of appreciation) or order is awarded, this certificate must be stamped and written with the following wording: The letter or order has been awarded.

DOCUMENT ON PAGE 152, TOP
A Khmer National Liberation Front Committee Award

National Liberation Front Committee
Commune: ....
District:..................................
Province: Ang Yang
No. 1X0K

LETTER OF COMMENDATION
The Front Committee of ....commune;
Pursuant to achievements and in accordance with the selection of appointment from ....;
It is hereby awarded to Mr. ......who is ......In .... commune, ... district, Ang Yang province;
For his achievements in ....
And for achieveing a record of promoting a spirit of patriotism, being prepared to make sacrifices in service of the cause of the war, to rescue the nation and religion, to promote an example of commitment, to defeat the land invasion by American enemy forces, to liberate Southern Vietnam, to protect Northern Vietnam and for the sake of National Unity.

Approval comments................................., 196...
Chairperson of the Front Committee of .... District
pp Commune Committee Front
(Signature and stamp)
Chairperson

DOCUMENT ON PAGE 152, BOTTOM
N.L.F. Contribution to the Revolution Receipt

NATIONAL FRONT FOR THE
LIBERATION COMMITTEE
Received from:______________________
The amount of_______________________
For support of the revolution
Date month year 196

REPRESENTATIVE OF THE FRONT

05294 (signed and sealed)

NATIONAL FRONT FOR THE LIBERATION COMMITTEE

Received from:________________________________
The amount of________________________________

For support of the revolution
Date month year 196
REPRESENTATIVE OF THE FRONT
05294 (signed and sealed)

FURTHER INFORMATION

BOOKS

Bush, Peter, *Vietnam Generation*, Volume 4, Number 3-4, Summer-Fall, 1992.
Carhart, Tom, *Battles and Campaigns in Vietnam 1954–1984*, Crown Publishers, NY, 1984
Committee on Foreign Relations, *C.I.A./D.o.D. Phoenix Program: Targeting non-combatants (civilians) Also: Exit strategy, rigged elections, puppet government, CIS: 71 S381-2 SuDoc: Y 4.F 76/2:V 67/17 Vietnam:* Policy and Prospects, 1970, Hearings before the Committee on Foreign Relations, United States Senate, Ninety-first Congress, Second Session.
Duiker, William J., *Ho Chi Minh, Hyperion*, New York, 2000
Emering, Edward J., Vietnam interviews, 1990
Emering, Edward J., *Weapons and Field Gear of the North Vietnamese and Viet Cong*, Schiffer Books, Atglen, PA, 1998
Galbraith, James K., "Exit Strategy: In 1963, JFK ordered a complete withdrawal from Vietnam," Boston Review, October/November, 2003
Gilmore D.L., & D. M. Giangreco, *Eyewitness Viet Nam*, Sterling Publishing Co., NY., 2006
Gravel, Mike, *The Pentagon Papers: The Defense Department History of United States Decisionmaking on Vietnam.* Senator Gravel edition, 5 vols. Boston: Beacon Press, 1971.
Halbfinger, David M., and Steven A. Homes, *Military Mirrors Working Class America*, New York Times, March 30, 2003
Hersh, Seymore M., *The Price of Power, Kissinger in the Nixon Whitehouse*, Summit Books, 1983
Ho Chi Minh, *Selected Works*, Hanoi, 1960-1962
Lodge, Henry Cabot, For the President from AMB Lodge (Saigon 2399), January 5, 1966 (declassified), Lyndon B. Johnson Library and Museum, Austin, Tex.
Mangold, Tom and John Penycate, *The Tunnels of Cu Chi*, Random House, New York, 1985
McGeehee, Ralph, *CIA and Operation Phoenix in Vietnam* – compilation of U.S. Army statistics, 1996.
Moore (ret.), Lt. Gen. Harold G., and Joseph L. Galloway, *We Were Soldiers Once... and Young*, Random House, New York, 1992
McNab, Chris, *Modern Military Uniforms*, Chartwell Books, Inc., New Jersey, 2000
Simpson, Howard R., *Dien Bien Phu*, Brassey's Inc., Washington, 1994
Stanton, Shelby, *U.S. Army Uniforms of the Vietnam War*, Stackpole Books, Harrisburg, PA, 1992
Starry, General Donn A., *Mounted Combat in Vietnam*, Department of the Army, Washington, D.C., 1998
Summers Jr., Colonel Harry G. (ret), Last Days in Vietnam, U.S. Army War College/U.S. Army military Institute's Senior Officer Oral History Program, *Eyewitness Vietnam*, Sterling, NY, 2006
LaFantasie Glenn W., (editor), *Foreign Relations of the United States, 1961-1963*, Volume VI, Kennedy-Khrushchev Exchanges, Bureau of Public Affairs, Office of the Historian, Washington D.C., 1996
Welsh, Douglas, *The Complete Military History of the Vietnam War*, Brompton Books, Greenwich, CT, 1990

FILMS

The Battle for Dien Bien Phu, (video), Best Film & Video Corp., New York, 1999
Norman Films, "Battlefield Diaries", *Tank Battle Vietnam*, The Military Channel

WEBSITES

http://www.afa.org/home. Air Force Magazine June 1999 Vol. 82, No.6

http://www.diggerhistory.info/pages-air-support/vietnam/rolling_thunder.htm

http://www.FAS.org

http://www.globalsecurity.org/military/

http://www.history.navy.mil/docs/vietnam/tonkin-2.htm#maddox002. United States Navy, Naval Historical Center, Washington Navy Yard, DC, USS Maddox "Report of Action, Gulf of Tonkin, 2 August 1964" dated 24 Aug.

http://www.historycentral.com/vietnam/

http://www.historyinfilm.com. Lt. General E. M. Flanagan, Jr., USA (Ret), The Rakkasan – The Combat History of the 187th Airborne Infantry.

http://www.historynet.com. Brent Swager, Rescue at LZ Albany.

http://www.historynet.com. Colonel Harry G. Summers, Jr., U.S. Army (ret.), Battle for Hamburger Hill During the Vietnam War.

http://www.historyplace.com

http://www.militaryfactory.com

http://www.militaryhistoryonline.com Wild Weasels- Daredevils of the Skies, Mike Nastasy

INDEX

Page numbers in *italics* indicate illustrations. Page numbers in **bold** refer to chapters, and include both text and photos.

ACKNOWLEDGEMENTS

Providing the content for *Vietnam: The Unwinnable War* has been a truly international effort and has enriched our lives in the process. Many people went out of their way to help us collect facts and images related to this horrific conflict. Dennis Giangreco, our expert editor and co-author with Donald L. Gilmore of *Eyewitness Vietnam* [Sterling Publishing Co.] besides keeping our facts accurate, made photos available to us from his collection. Ed Emering, author of *Weapons and Field Gear of the North Vietnamese Army and Viet Cong* [Schiffer] and webmaster of www.TheMedalHound.com (http://www.themedalhound.com/) gave us a rare look at the battlefield culture, medals, flags, and images of the Viet Minh, N.V.A., and V.C. from his incredible collection.

Brett Emblin and Simon Shaw in the U.K. contributed photographs of memorabilia and field hardware from their website, www.VietnamGear.com (http://www.vietnamgear.com/), a well-researched historical resource that features an extensive photo gallery, a comprehensive timeline plus details and information on uniforms and hundreds of items of equipment from the war. Wally Beddoe from Trumbull, Connecticut, has an uncanny knack for finding public domain, high-resolution military images on the web and graciously shared his skill with us. Lucien Schranz, 17, an apprentice Food Technologist in Zurich, Switzerland, used his photographic ability with a Canon 300D to provide many aircraft images shot in postwar North Vietnam. From Sweden, Peter Liander, another aircraft photographer, also added images to our project.

From Russia with photos came Maxim Popenker. A small arms historian, author of several books and maintainer of the Modern Firearms and Ammunition website (http://www.world.guns.ru/), Max contributed to our Chinese, and former Soviet Union weapons images as well as some American pieces from his St. Petersburg collection. Many agencies and archives sent us photos, maps, and posters from their vaults. Jim Parker of Double Delta, a research company in College Park, Maryland, was a valuable and patient resource, digging through the National Archives photo files for us.

Tammy Kelly helped us with photos from the Harry S. Truman Presidential Museum and Library and Nancy E. Mirshah was our courteous archives specialist at the Gerald R. Ford Presidential Library and Museum. John Wilson retrieved critical photos from the Lyndon Baines Johnson Library and Museum. We thank the archives that provided high-resolution photos as public domain web downloads including: the Department of Defense, U.S. Army Center for Military History, U.S. Air Force Media Center, and the Naval Historical Foundation Photographic Service.

Finally, the commercial agencies, Corbis and Nick Crawford with Lila Dlaboha at The Granger Collection provided specific images available nowhere else. We also want to thank the authors who are cited in the Further Information section for their scholarship that provided us so many resources.

Gerry and Janet Souter
Arlington Heights, Illinois, USA

CREDITS

The publishers would like to thank the following sources for their kind permission to reproduce the pictures in this book.

Abbreviations: t = top, c = centre, l = left, r = right & b = below

Dennis Giangreco Collection: 52r; /**Edward J. Emering Collection:** 2, 10l, 10r, 11t, 12r, 24, 22t, 23, 26, 47t, 56br, 68, 69t, 69bl, 69br, 70-71, 72, 86, 127t, 138, 139, 141tl, 141b, 147t, 147b, 152t, 152b, 155t; /**Federation for American Scientists (F.A.S.), Military Network:** 142b; /**Gerald R. Ford Presidential Museum and Library:** 144l; /**Gerry Souter Collection:** 99b; / Getty Images: Bettmann 131b, 147; /CORBIS: 87t, 132l, 133, 144r, 145b; /© Jacques Pavlovsky/Sygma/CORBIS/Sygma 149; /**Granger Collection, The:** 6 bl, 7, 13, 14, 15, 16, 20c, 35b, 40t, 107t, 118, 126b, 128, 134-135, 135, 142t; / **Gruntsmilitary.com:** 62br; /**Harry S. Truman Library 8**, 17l, 17r; /**Jonah Blank, Tuol Sleng Prison in Phnom Penh, Cambodia:** 151cr; /**Lyndon Baines Johnson Library and Museum:** 123t; /**M. Kunstlers:** 61b; /**Maxim Propeker Collection:** 51l, 59, 65bl, 109br; /**Moremilitaria.com:** 21t, 81br; /**National Archives and Records Administration Archive:** 34, 54, 55br, 56c, 57, 74, 76b, 85, 83l, 84t, 84b, 87b, 90b, 91, 95cl, 110t, 117b, 119, 122t, 123b, 127b, 130, 145t, 150, 153; /**Naval Historical Center:** 55tl; /**Art Collection Branch**: 108l ; /Private Collection 12l, 19b; /Richard M. Nixon Library and Birthplace: 137; /**Time, Inc:** 121bl; /**U.S. Army Center for Military History:** 4, 9b, 27, 51br, 63tl, 63r, 65 tl, 79b, 89, 90t, 95b, 100b, 105tr, 102, 105tl, 106, 110b, 116b, 120l,, 121t, 125, 131tl, 135br, 136c, 155b; / U.S. Engineers: 101; /**U.S. Army Tank-automotive and Armaments Command (T.A.C.O.M.), Rock Island:** 136b; /**U.S. Department of Defense:** 9tl, 9tr, 16 b, 18, 19tr, 19cr, 20 b, 21b, 22b, 28, 29, 30r, 31, 32t, 32b, 42, 45l, 44, 45bl, 45br, 46, 47b, 48, 49t, 49b, 50b, 51tr, 52l, 55tr, 53, 56bl, 58-59, 60tl, 60b, 60r, 61t, , 64b, 63b, 65tr, 76t, 77, 78, 80, 83r, 83tr, 94b, 96r, 98, 99t, 103b, 104, 107b, 108r, 109t, 112-113, 120r, 122b, 126t; /**U.S. Naval Historical Center:** 11br, 36, 37t, 37b, 38, 40b, 40t, 40b, 148b; /**United States Air Force (U.S.A.F.) Media Center: 43,** 45tr, 88, 92l, 92r, 93, 94t, 95t, 95cr, 97, 105t, 111, 114, 115, 116t, 117t, 124, 129,t, 129bl, 129br, 131cr, 141tr, 143; /**United States Information Agency (U.S.I.A):** 75, 79t, 148t; /**Vann Nath:** 151br; /**Vietnamgear.com Collection: 25, 33, 50t,** 50bl, 65tc, 66-67, 73, 96l, 103t; /**Vietnam Photo Service:** 151bl, 154l, 154r; / **Vietnam Tourism:** 100tr; /**Virtual Vietnam Archive, Texas Tech, Lubbock, Texas:** 82; /**www.usmcvta.org/contributionsothers/fox2-5hue: 81t**

Every effort has been made to acknowledge correctly and contact the source and/or copyright holder of each picture and Carlton Books Limited apologises for any unintentional errors or omissions which will be corrected in future editions of this book.